French Masculinities

French Masculinities

History, Culture and Politics

Edited by

Christopher E. Forth and Bertrand Taithe

First published 2007 by
PALGRAVE MACMILLAN
Houndmills, Basingstoke, Hampshire RG21 6XS and
175 Fifth Avenue, New York, N.Y. 10010
Companies and representatives throughout the world

PALGRAVE MACMILLAN is the global academic imprint of the Palgrave Macmillan division of St. Martin's Press, LLC and of Palgrave Macmillan Ltd. Macmillan® is a registered trademark in the United States, United Kingdom and other countries. Palgrave is a registered trademark in the European Union and other countries.

ISBN-13: 978-0-230-00661-4   hardback
ISBN-10: 0-230-00661-2   hardback

This book is printed on paper suitable for recycling and made from fully managed and sustained forest sources. Logging, pulping and manufacturing processes are expected to conform to the environmental regulations of the country of origin.

A catalogue record for this book is available from the British Library.

Library of Congress Cataloging-in-Publication Data

French masculinities: history, culture, and politics / edited by Christopher E. Forth and Bertrand Taithe.
        p. cm.
    Includes bibliographical references and index.
    ISBN-13: 978-0-230-00661-4 (cloth)
    ISBN-10: 0-230-00661-2 (cloth)
    1. Masculinity–France. 2. Men–France. I. Forth, Christopher E. II. Taithe, Bertrand.

HQ1090.7.F8F74 2007
305.310944–dc22

                                                                2007060002

10   9   8   7   6   5   4   3   2   1
16   15   14   13   12   11   10   09   08   07

Printed and bound in Great Britain by
Antony Rowe Ltd, Chippenham and Eastbourne

Contents

List of Figures

vii

Acknowledgments

This collection would not have been possible without the helpful suggestions of a number of supportive colleagues: Guy Austin, Carolyn Dean, Rachel Fuchs, Alec Hargreaves, Cheryl Koos, Mark Micale, and Joan Tumblety.

Notes on Contributors

Robert Aldrich is a Professor of European History at the University of Sydney. He is the author of several works on the French in the South Pacific, *Greater France: a History of French Overseas Expansion, Colonialism and Homosexuality*, and *Vestiges of the Overseas Empire in France: Monuments, Museums and Colonial Memories*.

Jean-Pierre Boulé is a Professor of Contemporary French Studies at Nottingham Trent University, where he specializes in twentieth-century French literature and culture with specific reference to Hervé Guibert and Jean-Paul Sartre, as well as AIDS writing in France. His latest book is *Sartre, Self-formation and Masculinities* (2005).

Christopher E. Forth is a Reader in History at the Australian National University, where he specializes in the cultural history of gender, sexuality, and the body. The author of *Zarathustra in Paris: the Nietzsche Vogue in France, 1891–1918* (2001) and *The Dreyfus Affair and the Crisis of French Manhood* (2004), he is co-editor of *Cultures of the Abdomen: Diet, Digestion, and Fat in the Western World* (2005) and *Body Parts: Critical Explorations in Corporeality* (2005). He is currently completing a book entitled *Civilization and its Malcontents: Masculinity and the Body in the Modern West*.

Claire Gorrara is a Reader in French Studies in the School of European Studies, Cardiff University, UK. She has published extensively on representations of the Second World War in French literature and culture. Her research interests have shifted in recent years towards post-war French crime fiction. She is the author of *The Roman Noir in Post-war French Culture: Dark Fictions* (2003) and is currently editing a collection of essays on French crime fiction traditions.

Michael J. Hughes is an Assistant Professor of Modern European History at Iona College. He specializes in the history of revolutionary and Napoleonic France, and the military history of modern and early modern Europe. He is particularly interested in the relationship between war, military institutions, culture, and gender. His scholarly work has been published in the *International Bibliography of Military History*, and accepted for publication in the *Consortium on Revolutionary Europe, Selected Papers*. He is currently preparing his doctoral dissertation, '"*Vive la République! Vive l'Empereur!*": Military Culture and Motivation in the Armies of Napoleon, 1803–1808,' for publication.

Robert A. Nye is the Thomas Hart and Mary Jones Horning Professor of Humanities and Professor of History at Oregon State University. Among his major publications are *Masculinity and Male Codes of Honor in Modern France*

(1993) and *Crime, Madness and Politics in Modern France* (1984). He has also edited *Sexuality*, a reader published by Oxford University Press in 1999.

Martin O'Shaughnessy is a Reader in Film at Nottingham Trent University. He has written widely on French film, engaging with areas such as masculinity, stardom, genre, and colonialism. He is the author of *Jean Renoir* (2000) and co-editor of *Cinéma et engagement* (2005). He is currently completing a manuscript on the return of commitment to contemporary French cinema.

Miranda Pollard is an Associate Professor of History and Women's Studies at the University of Georgia, Athens. Apart from her book, *Reign of Virtue: Mobilizing Gender in Vichy France, 1940–1944* (1998), she has also published articles on women and Vichy France. She is currently working on a book on history and film, which explores the politics of nostalgia and narrative pleasure with regard to ten French films documenting the twentieth century. Her next book project will be on the city of Nice, from the 1930s to the 1950s, focusing on work and leisure in this unique urban space.

Sean Quinlan is an Assistant Professor of History at the University of Idaho. He was a Mellon fellow at UCLA and a Fulbright IIE scholar in Paris. His scholarly work has appeared in *Social History, Eighteenth-century Studies, History Workshop,* and *French History*. His book, *The Morbid Social Body: Sexuality, Social Reform, and Health Politics in France, ca. 1750–1850*, will be published in 2007.

André Rauch is a Professor of History at the Université Marc Bloch de Strasbourg. He is the author of *Le Premier sexe: Mutations et crise de l'identité masculine* (2000), *Vacances en France de 1830 à nos jours* (2001), and *L'Identité masculine à l'ombre des femmes: De la Grande Guerre à la Gay Pride* (2004).

Michael Sibalis is an Associate Professor of History at Wilfrid Laurier University, Canada. The author of several articles and book chapters on homosexuality in France, Sibalis is co-editor of *Homosexuality in French History and Culture* (2001) and is currently working on a history of male homosexuality in Paris since 1700 as well as a study of the political police of Napoleonic France, 1799–1815.

Judith Surkis is an Assistant Professor of History and of History and Literature at Harvard University, where she teaches courses in modern European cultural and intellectual history, with an emphasis on France, and the history of gender and sexuality. She has written on the place of masculinity in the work of Georges Bataille and michel Foucault, and is the author of *Sexing the Citizen: Masculinity and Morality in France, 1870–1920* (2006).

Bertrand Taithe is a Professor of Cultural History at the University of Manchester. He has published extensively on nineteenth-century French history (*Defeated Flesh*, 1999; *Citizenship and Wars*, 2001), in the history of ideas (*Benjamin's Arcades*, 2006) and the cultural history of war (edited collections include *Propaganda*, 1999, and *War*, 1998). He has edited three volumes and three special issues of journals. He is the main editor of *European Review of History/Revue Européenne d'Histoire* (Routledge). He teaches the history of the body and leads the Cultural History MA at the University of Manchester, where he is a director of the Cultural Theory Institute and a member of the Gender and Sexuality Research Centre.

Anne C. Vila is an Associate Professor in the Department of French and Italian at the University of Wisconsin-Madison. She is the author of *Enlightenment and Pathology: Sensibility in the Literature and Medicine of Eighteenth-century France* (1998). She is currently completing a book entitled *Thinking Bodies: Literature, Medicine, and the Cult of the Intellectual in France, 1700–1840*.

Introduction: French Manhood in the Modern World

Christopher E. Forth and Bertrand Taithe

Do we need another book on masculinities, this time on France? What light can a consideration of French masculinities shed on our understanding of gender, societies, and nations? Nation-based studies of masculinity have the unique benefit of articulating elements of national identity that are often seen as self-evident. The nation, it has often been remarked, is a profoundly Janus-faced entity. A product of the developmental and forward-looking outlook of the eighteenth and nineteenth centuries, it keeps its gaze fixed upon its myth-ical past and the kinds of men and women who supposedly thrived there. Viewed in terms of bodies, moralities and activities, nationalist ideologies often seek a continuity between the virtues of the past, the realities of the present and the challenges of the future. It is also widely known that the techniques for integrating people into this 'imagined community' have differed for men and women. 'Women are typically constructed as the symbolic bearers of the nation,' notes Anne McClintock, 'but are denied any direct relation to national agency.' This temporal tension is a deeply gendered one, with women usually situated on the side of atavistic elements of the nation. Even when they become engaged with modern developments, women continued to be associated with what McClintock calls the nation's 'conservative principle of continuity.'[1]

McClintock rightly shows that women participate in nation-building in important ways; yet, a look at the corporeal requirements for nationalism suggests that men have not always been securely located on the side of what she calls the 'forward-thrusting, potent and historic' elements of national progress. Given the importance of military prowess to many nationalist rep-resentations of masculinity, in order to be effective agents of the nation men have been repeatedly implored to draw upon bodily habits and experiences more closely associated with images of the idealized past than with the 'soft' conditions of modern society. When combined with the representational work of creating a national culture based on collective symbols, images and texts, military training, compulsory sport and physical fitness have been integral to the processes of masculinization that are the historical concomitant of nation-building. They are methods of making up people who would both

1

embody and serve the interests of the state. The well-trained male body is thus an example of what Ana María Alonso describes as 'the fusion of the ideological and the sensory, the bodily and the normative, the emotional and the instrumental, the organic and the social, accomplished by these tropes and particularly evident in strategies of substantialization by which the obligatory is converted into the desirable.'[2] By laying down these state-sponsored demands for able-bodied manhood, the militarization of citizenship since the eighteenth century placed demands upon men's bodies in times of peace as well as war. In order to be proper soldier-citizens, men had to retain this mixed identity in peacetime as well. As the urgency of this military-national project increased towards the end of the nineteenth century, so too did the practical difficulties of living up to this almost impossible ideal.

The historiography of masculinity thus has closer connections to the history of a nation and to the writing of that history than any other form of gender studies. In many ways, since Leopold von Ranke at least, national and international histories have been written as the competitive struggle of one gendered model against another.[3] The ideas of national efficiency and competitiveness have saturated any descriptions of nations and the perceived strengths and weaknesses of nations often revolve around the presumed qualities of their men, and thus include an often neglected transnational dimension. French masculinities are often perceived in this way, at least in anglophone countries. For instance, an ordinary Google® internet search for the phrase 'French military victories' yields many web pages; yet, a right-wing American organization managed to corrupt the search engine, so that a click of the 'I'm Feeling Lucky' button produces no results whatsoever. Rather the surfer is asked: 'Did you mean: <u>French military *defeats*</u>?'[4] As the war in Iraq polarized public opinion, it also emphasized the association of national greatness with idealized military manhood and success in war for a large part of the Anglo-American public. In this context a partisan reading of French military history emphasized the long sequence of major defeats from the Seven Years War to the war of Algerian independence. This pessimistic reading of their own history had also been a central feature of French perspectives on their success in military and colonial ventures.

Over the years this somber backwards gaze has given rise to anxieties and questions about the state of French manhood. Yet it is striking that, aside from a few notable exceptions, the country of Simone de Beauvoir has largely ignored the singular history of its male gender roles, even after the rise of masculinity studies in other countries. That men, as well as women, are not born but made (and even unmade) should have been apparent after the humiliation of the French defeat and occupation.[5] Contemporary examples of a renewed interest in the history of masculinity, such as André Rauch's broad histories of French masculinity, have started to consider more extensively one of the key themes of this book: the relationship between gender roles, individual agency and national identity.[6] To the extent that masculinities are invested with social significance, they lie poised between the personal and the public, and the national and transnational. Inspired and challenged by British and German modes of being men, the French state and society have pursued contradictory paths of emulation and repulsion in relation to foreign gender models.

This book seeks to bring a fresh and comprehensive insight to the evolution and changes in masculinity in France. By building upon Robert Nye's highly influential work in this area, it seeks to develop some of its more salient conclusions by examining the changing discourses and practices of French masculinities from the *Ancien Régime* through the nineteenth and twentieth centuries to the recent disturbances in the *banlieue*.[7] It will reinforce the importance of masculinities for representations of the nation by showcasing some of the scholarship that is being conducted in this area as well as pointing to areas where more work is needed.

* * *

That masculinities are socially constructed is now a truism of gender scholarship. But just how new is this idea? The history of gender in the modern West shows a tacit acceptance that masculinities, in addition to being shaped by a variety of social, cultural and psychological factors, also require effort and regular maintenance. Angus McLaren is just one historian among many when he observes that, in the nineteenth century, a 'male had to "prove" repeatedly at work and at play that he was a "man".'[8] This implicit understanding that manhood is an act of *becoming* rather than *being* has also had its theorists. Indeed, Freud had stressed the competitive and violent work on oneself and on homosocial groups that reacted against, while nevertheless mimicking, idealized patriarchal role models.[9] Moreover, five years before Simone de Beauvoir famously claimed that 'One is not born, but rather becomes a woman,' the critical theorists Max Horkheimer and Theodor Adorno asserted, in a similarly philosophical vein, that 'Men had to do fearful things to themselves before the self, the identical, purposive, and virile nature of man, was formed, and something of that recurs in every childhood.'[10]

From a literal interpretation of patriarchy to a more abstract one, much of *The Second Sex* describes the illusory and contradictory ideals that society encourages men to accept, especially in regard to women, whose presence and compliance has so long been demanded as a means of complementing and thus completing them. Nevertheless, in de Beauvoir's book as in much second-wave feminism, the category of 'men' is often accepted as a more or less monolithic group that collectively benefits from the subjection of women. Of course there is much evidence to support this view, especially when one considers that most males benefit from what Bob Connell refers to as the 'patriarchal dividend' that comes from being a man in an androcentric world, regardless of one's personal views on women and gender equality.[11] Yet patriarchy cannot be easily equated with the spectrum of masculinities that are possible at any given time. Pierre Bourdieu's account of the naturalized construction of male domination reveals a symbolic work carried out through 'a profound and durable transformation of bodies (and minds), that is to say, in and through a work of practical construction that imposes a *differentiated definition* of the legitimate uses of the body, especially sexual uses, that tend to exclude from the universe of the thinkable and doable all that marks one as belonging to the other gender.'[12]

What is less clear in Bourdieu's analysis is the practical impossibility of approximating this condition, or the ways in which, under certain conditions, flouting these rules can also affirm masculinity. In this sense the essential issues attached to the practice of masculinity relate to individual qualities and changing attributes: age, class, ethnicity, wealth play a crucial part in the performance of masculinity. Some handicaps can be temporarily overcome, yet a man who remained a bachelor, a *vieux garçon*, the old man, the invalid, the disabled, even war veterans, may see their performance impaired and their status diminished.[13] As a lived experience, then, masculinity is always subject to scrutiny, lapses, and failed performances, and is thus forever in a contested state. Masculinity is a *becoming* that does not have the luxury of coming to rest in *being*. The defense of one's masculinity and its corollary concept of honor was an investment one could not always afford. This is perhaps why, despite second-wave feminism's successes in opening up our definitions of womanhood, the perception that masculinity is really the most unstable gender seems to persist. As the sociologists Georges Fauconnet and Nadine Lefaucheur observe in their analysis of French manhood in the 1970s: 'One says to a woman: *remain* feminine, keep your femininity. One does not say to a man: remain virile, but *be* a man. Become it. Prove it. Femininity is a natural state to preserve. Virility, on the contrary, is never acquired, never assured. One must ceaselessly display it.'[14] This need to reiterate endlessly a norm that can only be grasped momentarily, if at all, attests to the always unstable nature of masculinity, which Judith Surkis describes as a contingent norm 'constituted by ever-present possibilities of abnormal deviation.'[15]

French masculinities in context

Historians of gender rightly point out the significance of discourse in the formation of gendered identities and practices, often insisting on the importance of key concepts at specific times. Yet 'masculinity,' which in American English only came into general usage around 1900, denotes a surprisingly complex array of qualities that arguably reflect ongoing disagreements about the defining characteristics of what a man ought to be. While certain masculine attributes may become 'hegemonic' in relation to the practical or imagined requirements of this or that group at any given time, they are also comprised of elements that, to borrow the terms of Raymond Williams, are residual and tied to earlier ideals, as well as traits that are emergent and oriented towards future social formations. However oppositional a residual element may be in relation to the dominant culture, Williams explains, 'some part of it, some version of it – and especially if the residue is from some major area of the past – will in most cases have had to be incorporated if the effective dominant culture is to make sense in these areas.'[16]

The history of masculinities in the modern world reflects this unstable coexistence of dominant, residual and emergent images of the ideal man. As a glance at German dictionaries of the eighteenth century reveals, the physically robust warrior is the residual masculine element par excellence. For much of the century, the adjective *männlich* (manly) was defined in robustly corporeal terms, and illustrated with adjectives like brave, strong, forceful, valiant, resolute and unyielding. By the 1780s these martial and physical ideals were complemented by more 'civic' qualities such as learnedness, seriousness, wisdom and gravity, thus perhaps reflecting the impact of the Enlightenment on central European gender ideals.[17] By the turn of the nineteenth century, the qualities implied by *männlich* ranged from the aggressive and martial to the civic and moral, even if it was unclear whether men needed to possess all these qualities at the same time. This instability was also true of the nineteenth-century notion of manliness in Britain, which, as John Tosh explains, connoted energy, will, directness and courage, as well as 'bodily associations which were less universally acclaimed', among which he counts physical robustness, self-defense and readiness for combat. As Tosh rightly observes, 'manliness' also had much to do with participation in what were called 'manly exercises' (such as cricket, fox-hunting and rowing) as well as physical bearing and sexual potency. It could even imply engagement in strenuous physical activities such as boxing and dueling, which, while most often practiced by proletarians and aristocrats respectively, were also described as 'manly' activities.[18] It is evident that many of these qualities would go on to form central elements of 'masculinity' around 1900. Though Gail Bederman rightly suggests that this was partly a reaction against earlier ideals of the gentleman, a new focus on 'aggressiveness, physical force and male sexuality' arguably tapped into qualities that were present, if much less prominent, in the notion of manliness itself.[19]

If the French too knew about *masculinité*, it was partly because they had invented the term. In 1762 the fourth edition of the *Dictionnaire de l'Académie française* recorded *masculinité* as referring broadly to 'the character, the quality of the male.'[20] Yet when French speakers refer to the spectrum of personal qualities and physical traits that English speakers might describe as 'manly' or 'masculine,' they are more likely to employ terms like *virile* and *virilité*.[21] Published in 1690, Furetière's *Dictionnaire universel* reflects images of manhood that would recur, with some modifications, throughout the modern era. Furetière's definition of the virile male was biologically mature (*l'âge virile* was said to occur between the ages of thirty and forty-five), energetic, strong, virtuous, confident and courageous. According to the differential logic that structures gender binaries, that which is *virile* is 'opposed to the flowery and the effeminate [*à fleuri, à efféminé*].'[22] This qualification is important for the anxiety it evokes about the state of French manhood around the time of the court society. According to Furetière, the verb *efféminer* denoted taking on 'the qualities and weaknesses of a woman' and was illustrated with observations that spoke directly to contemporary concerns about an emerging commercial society: 'luxury *effeminates* peoples.' Thus, at the end of the seventeenth century, *un efféminé* referred to 'a soft, voluptuous man who has become like a woman',[23] at least partly due to his immersion in a culture of abundance, ease and appearances.

'Effeminacy' was perhaps the most widespread anxiety of the eighteenth century, at least among elites. For those wishing to celebrate the distinctiveness of their own national culture, France itself came to embody Western civilization's putative concern with mere appearances and the 'insincere' concealment of impulses. Hence, the value that was often placed on 'plain-speaking' English gentlemen as opposed to the more elegant *honnête homme*. In the German states this trend was furthered mainly by the politically powerless middle classes, who, when carving out a distinct identity for themselves, emphatically rejected what they saw as the 'French' superficiality of the nobility for the purportedly deeper and more virtuous educational ideal of *Kultur*.[24] In *Observations on the Feeling of the Sublime and the Beautiful* (1764), Immanuel Kant connected French national character squarely with the beautiful and the feminine. In France, Kant claimed, 'woman gives the tone to all companies and all society,' and the individual French male displays 'a predominant feeling for the morally beautiful. He is gracious, courteous, and complaisant,' all qualities that were in Kant's work encoded as 'feminine' (and thus the opposite of the 'masculine' sublime). At best these national character traits made French men pleasing and sociable companions; at worst, they rendered them a 'frivolous' people who lacked the putatively nobler and sublime qualities of the Germans and English.[25]

It is perhaps unsurprising that, in Britain and Germany, the manly ideal would evolve into more overtly physical forms earlier than in other countries, with German gymnastics and English team sports gaining a strong foothold in educational practice during the first half of the nineteenth century. The French elites of the Old Regime were aware of these transnational stereotypes about French over-refinement, as Anne Vila shows in her chapter. They sought to negotiate the 'civilized' need to preserve politeness and refinement with a social system founded on the willingness and ability to serve in warfare. This delicate balance between libertinage, valor and *honnêteté* was forever unstable and subject to corruption, vulgarization and demotion. Ultimately refocusing on Enlightenment notions of civilization, French masculinity of the Enlightenment was able to promote its elite values throughout Europe, but could not fully overcome its inner contradictions.

Whatever stereotypes the English or Germans might spin about the shortcomings of French manhood, no 'civilized' country was spared the stigmatizing label of 'effeminacy', which was hurled back and forth across the Western world during the 1700s. Attempts to remasculinize commercial societies in the face of 'feminine' over-refinement, luxury, and corruption were manifest across Europe during the eighteenth century, affecting movements in painting, sculpture and music as well as social and political theory. This was true in France as well, where political and social reformers condemned the Old Regime as exercising a feminizing influence on the body politic.[26] If, as Jean-Jacques Rousseau had alleged, aristocratic women threatened to turn men into women through the teaching of refined manners, then the revolution logically represented a remasculinization of French manhood.[27] Revolutionaries turned to classical images for their depiction of how the ideal male should look and act. Jacques-Louis David's paintings just before the revolution often represented men as muscular, upright, and heroic. Free of any softness or sentiment, their muscularity attested to lives of action and war. The apparently impermeable nature of these bodies was 'proven' through their ability stoically to endure pain and punishment, precisely what the previous French elites had been thought incapable of doing.[28] As Sean Quinlan confirms in the second chapter of this book, the revolution changed ideas both about masculinity and male sociability itself. Not only did it create new forms of physical beauty, public virtue, political activism, domesticity, and fraternity, but the revolutionaries tried to create a distinctly male utopian space that fostered deep, almost primitive, fraternal bonds among men. In this homosocial space, French men would be free from paternal power, class distinctions, consumer trappings, or corrupting female influences.

The renewed virility that the revolution was said to inspire may have seemed ample proof that France was no longer an 'effeminate' nation softened by luxurious refinement. As André Rauch rightly suggests, by extending the right to bear arms in the *levée en masse*, the revolution profoundly altered the masculine condition in France: what had been the prerogative of a few men had now become the duty of all.[29] Viewed in theoretical terms, one might view this as a psychosomatic integration of males into the body politic as the citizenry became masculinized for the first time. This represented a transfer of virility from the body of the king to the bodies of French men generally. 'The body is no longer leased to the state,' Norman Bryson suggests, 'it *is* the state; the state emerges as a new kind of biopolitical entity, and by virtue of gender the male body belongs to the state, as state property . . . the state is no longer figured in the king, but in the male body itself, and the body's destiny for glory or defeat is that of the nation as a whole.'[30] As Michael Hughes points out in Chapter 3, the military meaning of such impressive bodies if anything increased with the ascendance of Napoleon and his empire. The forms of sociability as well as the effects of such training for the embodiment of the nation would be profound, both in material bodies and in their representations.

Regardless of these strident images of martial manhood, the bourgeois society of the post-Waterloo era was not quite the virile paradise imagined by some revolutionaries. As Jan Goldstein has recently shown, the bourgeois male self of the early nineteenth century, at least as it was conceptualized in Victor Cousin's influential 'spiritualist' philosophy, was a deliberate contrast to the more corporeal exemplars of manhood that circulated during the revolutionary and Napoleonic eras. Calculating and rational, the male self was presented as a mind whose body was largely excluded, as was any anatomical basis, for asserting the exclusively bourgeois or male nature of this kind of person.[31] Yet the would-be hegemony of this bourgeois stereotype needs to be contextualized, as Bertrand Taithe does in Chapter 4. Despite bourgeois attempts to locate hegemonic manhood in rational and economic practices, the virility of most French men remained grounded in locally-based sociocultural realities. Outside metropolitan bourgeois circles, male identities retained decidedly provincial and local connotations that undermined attempts to generalize about the French man's body, even in relation to competing European masculine types. Even the bourgeois male did not escape scrutiny during this period. Despite calls to 'civilize' the habits of rural and proletarian men, within the bourgeoisie itself movements were afoot to rescue the overly cerebral and sedentary male from potentially emasculating physical and mental ailments. As Christopher Forth demonstrates in the following chapter, eighteenth-century tensions between warrior and 'civilized' ideals persisted during the nineteenth century, and came to a head around 1900, when middle-class men were implored to adopt more 'primitive' corporeal habits in order to preserve their virility and the strength of the nation. In the absence of men capable of doing this, many recommended, like General Charles Mangin, that the 'black strength' of West African soldiers be conscripted in order to replace and inspire the flagging virility of white males.[32]

In the years leading up to the Great War, which some claimed pitted a barbaric German *Kultur* against Gallic *civilisation*, achieving a balance between refinement and savagery was seen as a way of preserving both Frenchness and manhood. The post-war period not only witnessed widespread disillusionment with the warrior ideal, but was marked as well by renewed attempts to maximize the quantity and quality of the racial stock of the nation. In Chapter 6, Judith Surkis shows how, in the 1920s, hygiene reformers and social critics warned of the potential dangers of venereal disease to the future health of a nation that was now viewed as dangerously open to 'enemies' both within and without. With the opening of metropolitan borders, the image of alien, albeit often subjected, colonial identities threatened racial and sexual purity, thus constructing imperial subjects and immigrant workers as predatory forces of contamination. Yet the vulnerability of metropolitan manhood was in some respects compensated by tales of the superior virility of French men in the colonies. As Robert Aldrich shows in Chapter 7, the colonial man was endowed with all the attributes of a physically robust and energetic masculinity which were tested, sometimes to the point of destruction, in the vast territories and alien cultures of the colonial empire. Here, too, a hard life removed from bourgeois habits and comforts seemed to promote France's *mission civilisatrice* without compromising the *virilité* of its emissaries.

Images of French imperial superiority were troubled by the defeat of June 1940, and the years following the Second World War brought further humiliations in several bloody wars of independence. In some respects warrior masculinity was not too hard to overcome anyway: since the end of the First World War, many returning veterans evinced contempt for the dehumanizing nature of war and thus destabilized the link between manhood and the military. This 'unmanning of the warrior' was a dominant motif in films, novels, and popular songs right up to 1939–40. The 1940 defeat and occupation at the hands of Germany humiliated French men in the very activities that anchored male identity: work, warfare, and the protection of women and children. While women and children figured prominently among those sent to concentration camps, millions of French men had been taken to Germany either as prisoners of war or as part of the conscripted labor forces. Many of those who remained in France were left working directly or indirectly for the Germans without any autonomous forms of identity or expression (for example, trade unions). The eventual collapse of the Vichy regime sent this reconstruction into crisis as well. The fact that women often become more active in the economy as well as in the resistance movement represented further proof that French manhood was in disarray.[33] That the 1940 defeat shattered images of French warrior manhood is the focus of Miranda Pollard's chapter. In the context of this unraveling of traditional French manhood, divided now between competing centers such as Paris, London, and Vichy itself, Pollard shows how this 'crisis' opened spaces for the performance of 'female masculinity' as well.

From such disarray, as Michael Kelly rightly observes, after the liberation 'masculine identity was one of the devastated reaches of French life that had to be reconstructed.'[34] As Claire Gorrara explains in Chapter 9, the influx of American culture during the post-war years played a key role in this reconstruction. In the *roman noir*, a literary genre that drew upon American crime fiction, French authors like Léo Malet and André Héléna reworked the terms of this overseas style to present a critique of French gender and society. The tough guy heroes of the *roman noir*, symbolically emasculated and powerless in spite of their violence, convey deep anxieties about the defeat of the occupation and the receding role of aggressive manhood in the post-war era. This confirms Robin Buss's suggestion that 'fictional characters who adopt Hollywood styles and Americanized language, far from demonstrating their subjection to a foreign culture, assert their freedom from the constraints of French society, from the norms of their native language, from class and background. They extend the possibilities of what it means to be "French".'[35]

The tough guys of the *roman noir* also provide a fictional and cinematic counterpoint to the kind of men who seemed to thrive during *les trentes glorieuses*. The economic boom of the 1950s produced a male elite of technocrats, *les jeunes cadres*, who spent considerable leisure time engaged in a narcissistic cult of comfort and appearances that negated traditional notions of active and virile manhood. 'In fact,' Kristen Ross observes, 'the qualities required of the new middle-class businessman – a certain amorphous adaptability bordering on passivity, serviceability, a pleasant nature, and being on the whole devoid of singularity – amounted to a distinct loss in virility.' This point was made in a number of novels of the period, notably Christiane Rochefort's *Les Stances à Sophie* (1963), where the working-class Céline, having become disillusioned with her marriage to the technocrat Philippe, has an affair with an Italian peasant. This satisfying experience leads her to conclude that: 'virility seems to recede as urbanization rises.'[36] This suggestion that manhood and modernity were in a state of tension not only mirrored anxieties about white-collar manhood in other countries, but helped to idealize the virility of African men who, according to Frantz Fanon, represent in the white imagination 'the sexual instinct (in its raw state).'[37] In some cases, it was claimed, the presumed effeminacy of these male elites could slip into outright perversion as sexologists contended that the 'more or less morbid intellectualism' of this lifestyle was a *cause* of the homosexuality they claimed was rife within this professional class.[38] As Michael Sibalis shows in Chapter 10, the French homosexual came to be associated with effeminacy to the point of making both categories interchangeable in public perception. Far from being a novelty of the post-war years, this association rested on long-established cultural associations between modernity and effeminacy, and encouraged many gay men to seek more 'macho' forms of manhood that rejected any whiff of effeminacy.

Chapter 11 probes the tensions between 'macho' and 'effeminate' male styles in the cinema of this period. Among the many possible sites of cultural production, Martin O'Shaughnessy argues, French post-war cinema provided opportunities for a compromise between old and new styles of manhood. The body and face of the young actor, Alain Delon, were closely associated with the consumerism of this period. As Ginette Vincendeau notes, Delon's characters 'desire commodities (money, cars, parties, women), while he himself metonymically signifies them.'[39] Nevertheless the values that Delon seemed to embody were often countered by those expressed by Jean-Paul Belmondo, a less handsome and more rugged (even comical) action hero who represented a far less polished image of French manhood.[40]

Such fantasies of power belie continuing anxieties about male sexual inadequacies, not least due to recurring fears about impotence. One French study faithfully recited the litany of factors that connected male weakness to the dysgenic influences of modern society: 'Deprived of its *élan vital* by debilitating conditions of life, comfortable habits, the slackening of bodily functions, and an excess of often adulterated food, the body gives precedence to a cerebrality that is pushed beyond its breaking point . . . Among men this ceaseless, overexcited use of intellect leads to the exhaustion of the vital forces.'[41] The same point was made two years later in the *Dictionnaire de la virilité*, an A-to-Z of modern impotence which offered what it called a 'map of exhausted France.' Here too male sexual impotence was cast as a primarily urban phenomenon connected to the 'breathless rhythm of civilization,' the stresses of modern life and the hygienic problems of the bourgeois profes-sions.[42] Beyond physiological causes, history itself could conspire to the undermining of virility, as Chapter 12 shows. As Jean-Pierre Boulé points out in his analysis of the novelist Serge Doubrovsky, the shadow of the war and the victimization of Jewish people became interiorized in some instances to constitute a causal route for impotence and sexual angst.

Following 1968 and the growth of a consumer society based on formal equality between the sexes, modes of masculinity have become even less easy for men to decipher. The sustained economic crisis of the last thirty years and evolutions in gender roles were sometimes explained as an effect of what Norbert Elias called the 'civilizing process.' In a 1993 special issue of *Esprit* devoted to changing gender relations in France, Claude Fischler associated the civilizing process with what he diagnosed as a 'féminisation des moeurs' where ideas and practices 'traditionally considered specifically feminine are increas-ingly adopted by the other sex,' a development he saw as especially marked in the areas of consumption, appearances and the body.[43] Commissioned by the popular women's magazine, *Elle*, in 2002 the Centre de Communication Avancée conducted a survey of forty-eight men between the ages of twenty and fifty-five on their views of masculinity and women. Discovering a great 'malaise' among respondents, who reported considerable hostility towards feminism, *Elle* invited opinions from musicians, novelists, psychologists and philosophers to flesh out these dismal findings. Popular singer Patrick Bruel observed that contemporary women expect men to be able to do it all, even if to do so requires contradictory demands: 'The man should at once forget the threadbare values of machismo to cast himself in the values of femininity, or at least sometimes seem to cast himself in them . . . But, once he has inte-grated those values, the woman will reproach him for his lack of virility.' Bruel also cited reproductive technologies as posing perhaps the greatest threat to manhood, not least because they could displace men even from their role in propagating the species. 'Take cloning,' Bruel explained: 'it's terrifying to think that women could go beyond men one day. Over the very long term, there might no longer be any men on the planet.' Bruel claimed that this was an unconscious fear that haunts most men. 'Their panic, today, is about being eliminated.'[44] In that context, perhaps it is not so surprising that the singer would release a compilation of nostalgic interwar love songs evoking tradi-tional gender roles.

The 'malaise' of contemporary (white) French men has been exacerbated in recent years by mounting ethnic and social tensions. In 2005, tens of thousands of Parisian high school students peacefully protesting government educa-tional reforms were attacked by bands of black and Arab youths totaling around 1000, many of whom claimed to enjoy beating up 'little whites' who cannot fight and who 'look like victims.'[45] The 'France d'en bas,' the sub-urban housing developments on the edges of large cities (*les banlieues*), have presented sites where Islam, as Christine Castelain-Meunier suggests, offered a form of 'rescue' for the crises faced by modern men.[46] As André Rauch argues in Chapter 13, the *banlieue* violence of the last twenty years, associated with a fundamentalist revival, does not necessarily reflect a 'crisis' of masculinity, but rather the territorial expression of traditional modes of masculinity drawing equally upon immigrant culture and French patriarchy for its forms of expression. In a society confronted with the challenges posed by its revolutionary past, the multicultural blossoming of its post-colonial population and the threat of divisive forms of masculinity, fractured responses to virile performance are neither new nor completely original. As the chapters in this book show, these recurring tensions make the exploration of the history of masculinity a highly topical and important matter.

Ironically, though, as Robert Nye explains in the afterword to this volume, the unstable nature of masculinity is more obvious to academics than to French people themselves. Strong associations between anatomy and the expression of physical power and strength remain dominant among men and women. While this perspective is largely shared throughout Europe and the West more generally, France presents the singular example of a nation facing a measurable decline in fertility and waning international status. In that close association of almost imperceptible trends, where causal links are unclear at best, the history of French masculinities presents traits that, if not unique, are at least uniquely salient.

Notes

1. Anne McClintock, ' "No Longer in a Future Heaven": Nationalism, Gender, and Race,' in *Becoming National: a Reader*, eds Geoff Eley and Ronald Grigor Suny (New York: Oxford University Press, 1996), p. 261.
2. Ana María Alonso, 'The Politics of Space, Time and Substance: State Formation, Nationalism, and Ethnicity,' *Annual Review of Anthropology*, 23 (1994): 386.
3. Roger Cooter and Steve Sturdy, 'Science, Scientific Management and the Transformation of Medicine in Britain, c.1870–1950,' *History of Science*, 36 (114) (December 1998): 421–66.
4. http://www.albinoblacksheep.com/text/victories.html (last consulted 11 September 2006). This trick has become the subject of considerable critical attention; in spite of its notoriety, it remains the only active link on Google's 'I'm Feeling Lucky' function. See http://www.answers.com/topic/french-military-victories and http://sethf.com/infothought/blog/archives/000268.html (last consulted 17 September 2006).
5. Robert A. Nye, *Masculinity and Male Codes of Honor in Modern France* (New York: Oxford University Press, 1993).
6. André Rauch, *Le premier sexe: mutations et crise de l'identité masculine* (Paris: Hachette Littératures, 2000); *L'identité masculine à l'ombre des femmes: de la Grande Guerre à la Gay Pride* (Paris: Hachette Littératures, 2004).

7. McClintock, ' "No Longer",' p. 263.
8. Angus McLaren, *The Trials of Masculinity: Policing Sexual Boundaries, 1870–1930* (Chicago: University of Chicago Press, 1997), pp. 33–4.
9. See Sigmund Freud, *Totem and Taboo* (New York: W.W. Norton, 1989), p. 180.
10. Simone de Beauvoir, *The Second Sex*, trans. H.M. Parshley (1949; New York: Vintage, 1989), p. 267; Max Horkheimer and Theodor W. Adorno, *Dialectic of Enlightenment*, trans John Cumming (1944; New York: Continuum, 1989), p. 33.
11. R.W. Connell, *Masculinities* (Sydney: Allen & Unwin, 1995), p. 79.
12. Pierre Bourdieu, *La domination masculine* (Paris: Seuil, 1998), p. 29.
13. Sophie Delaporte, *Gueules cassées de la Grande Guerre* (Paris: Agnès Viénot Éditions, 2004); David T. Mitchell and Sharon L. Snyder, *Narrative Prosthesis: Disability and Dependencies of Discourse* (Ann Arbor, MI: University of Michigan Press, 2000).
14. Georges Fauconnet and Nadine Lefaucheur, *Le fabrication des mâles* (Paris: Éditions du Seuil, 1975), p. 34.
15. Judith Surkis, *Sexing the Citizen: Morality and Masculinity in France, 1870–1920* (Ithaca, NY: Cornell University Press, 2006), p. 12.
16. Raymond Williams, 'Base and Superstructure in Marxist Cultural Theory,' *New Left Review*, 82 (November–December 1973): 10–11. Many thanks to David Buchbinder for drawing this to our attention.
17. Matthew Head, ' "Like Beauty Spots on the Face of a Man": Gender in 18th-century North-German Discourse on Genre,' *Journal of Musicology*, 12 (3) (Summer 1995): 148.
18. John Tosh, *A Man's Place: Masculinity and the Middle-class Home in Victorian England* (New Haven: Yale University Press, 1999), pp. 111–12.
19. Gail Bederman, *Manliness and Civilization: a Cultural History of Grender and Race in the United States, 1880–1917* (Chicago: University of Chicago Press, 1995), p. 97.
20. Académie française, 'MASCULINITÉ,' *Dictionnaire de l'Académie française* (fourth edition: Paris: La veuve de B. Brunet, impr. de l'Académie française, 1762), II: p. 102.
21. Historically, the *masculine* has more often referred to matters of language and classification. Drawing upon antecedents from Old French, in his *Dictionnaire universel* (1690) Antoine Furetière linked the *masculin* broadly to sexual difference in the animal world, as well as to grammar. The masculine is 'the most noble of the genders of words. One calls the *masculine* gender that which belongs to the male or to something which is analogous to it, to that which is strongest.' Antoine Furetière, 'MASCULIN,' *Dictionnaire universel* (La Haye: Arnout & Reinier Leers, 1690), 2: n.p. In Old French '*masculine*' referred mainly to genealogy (*en ligne masculine*) or grammar, and to some extent it has retained this denotation to the present. Frederic Godefroy, *Dictionnaire de l'ancienne langue française* (Paris: F. Vieweg, 1888), 5: p. 193.
22. Furetière, 'VIRIL, ILE,' 'VIRILITE,' *Dictionnaire universel*, 3: n.p.
23. Antoine Furetière, 'EFFEMINER,' 'EFFEMINE,' *Dictionnaire universel*, 1: n.p.
24. Norbert Elias, *The Civilizing Process*, trans. Edmund Jephcott (Oxford: Blackwell, 1994), p. 22.
25. Immanuel Kant, *Observations on the Feeling of the Sublime and the Beautiful*, trans. John T. Goldthwait (1764; Berkeley: University of California Press, 1960), pp. 101–3.
26. Madelyn Gutwirth, *Twilight of the Goddesses: Women and Representation in the French Revolutionary Era* (New Brunswick, NJ: Rutgers University Press, 1992), pp. 3–22.
27. Joan B. Landes, *Women and the Public Sphere in the Age of the French Revolution* (Ithaca, NY: Cornell University Press, 1988).

28. Dorinda Outram, *The Body and the French Revolution: Sex, Class and Political Culture* (New Haven: Yale University Press, 1989), pp. 86–8.
29. Rauch, *Le premier sexe*, p. 48.
30. Norman Bryson, 'Géricault and "Masculinity," ' in *Visual Culture: Images and Interpretation*, eds Norman Bryson, Michael Ann Holly and Keith Moxley (Hanover, NH: Wesleyan University Press, 1994), p. 147.
31. Jan Goldstein, *The Post-revolutionary Self: Politics and Psyche in France, 1750–1850* (Cambridge, MA: Harvard University Press, 2005), pp. 174, 202, 205–6, 231, 235.
32. Éric Deroo and Antoine Champeaux, *La Force noire: gloire et infortune d'une légende coloniale* (Paris: Tallandier, 2006).
33. Michael Kelly, *The Cultural and Intellectual Rebuilding of France after the Second World War* (New York: Palgrave, 2004), p. 118.
34. Kelly, *Cultural and Intellectual Rebuilding*, p. 118.
35. Robin Buss, *French Film Noir* (London: Marion Boyars, 1994), pp. 123–4.
36. Kristin Ross, *Fast Cars, Clean Bodies: Decolonization and the Reordering of French Culture* (Cambridge, MA: The MIT Press, 1996), pp. 61, 175.
37. Frantz Fanon, *Black Skin, White Masks*, trans. Charles Lam Markmann (1952; St Albans, UK: Paladin, 1970), pp. 117, 125.
38. Antony Copley, *Sexual Moralities in France, 1780–1980* (London: Routledge, 1989), p. 217.
39. Ginette Vincendeau, *Stars and Stardom in French Cinema* (New York: Continuum, 2000), p. 175; see also Graeme Hayes, 'Framing the Wolf: the Spectacular Masculinity of Alain Delon,' in *The Trouble with Men: Masculinities in European and Hollywood Cinema*, eds Phil Powrie, Ann Davies and Bruce Babington (London: Wallflower Press, 2004), pp. 42–53.
40. Martin O'Shaughnessy, 'Le surhomme à bout de souffle: le Belmondo des années 1974–1985,' *Cinémaction* (2004): 107–15.
41. Marcel Rouet, *Virilité et puissance sexuelle* (Paris: Productions de Paris, 1971), pp. 9–10.
42. Paul Vincent, *Dictionnaire de la virilité* (Paris: Maloine S.A. Editeur, 1973), pp. 9–10, 84, 289–90.
43. Claude Fischler, 'Une "féminisation" des moeurs?' *Esprit*, 196 (November 1993): 10.
44. Quoted in 'États généraux de l'homme: ce qu'ils ont à nous dire,' *Elle* (10 March 2003): 78–112.
45. Olivier Guitta, 'Mugged by *la Réalité*,' *The Weekly Standard*, 10 (28) (11 April 2005).
46. Christine Castelain-Meunier, *Les hommes aujourd'hui: virilité et identité* (Paris: Acropole, 1988), p. 73.

1
Elite Masculinities in Eighteenth-century France

Anne C. Vila

Foppish, fatuous, mincing, effeminate – such was the eighteenth-century French aristocrat as portrayed by playwrights and caricaturists across the English Channel (Figure 1.1).[1] Manliness is, admittedly, not the first idea that leaps to mind when one thinks about the social elite of late *Ancien Régime* France: the period that fell between the age of the Sun King and the revolution more typically conjures up ritualized codes of *politesse*, a mode of socializing dominated by frivolity and erotic dalliance, and a penchant for tears in which men were just as likely to indulge as were women. What styles of masculinity, we might well ask, could or did coexist with those behaviors? Clearly, the answer cannot be found by viewing eighteenth-century France through the distorting lens of a rival national culture, particularly not one that, like eighteenth-century England, fashioned its models of 'proper' masculine identity first by emulating and then by denigrating French moral codes and social practices.[2] Rather, we must scrutinize those codes and practices themselves – a line of inquiry that leads us well away from the notion popular among some English gentlemen that their French counterparts were unmanned, either because they spent too much time making small talk with salon ladies, or because they practiced the seductive art of pleasing others in the name of *honnêteté*, or quite simply because they were too vain.

This chapter will explore what, exactly, being a man entailed for those who belonged to the upper echelons of eighteenth-century French society, especially those who read and absorbed the ideas issuing forth from the period's social essayists and literary authors. Reaching back to the absolutist reign of Louis XIV, it will retrace the evolving meanings of the *honnête homme*, that estimable but not entirely unambiguous figure who set the tone for appropriate male comportment until the end of the *Ancien Régime*. Seen from a French perspective, *honnêteté* was, indeed, an ideology in need of renewal; but it was not, in and of itself, viewed as emasculating. Quite the contrary: male members of France's social and cultural elite perceived the ideals related to *honnêteté* as the ultimate means of distinguishing themselves, both as men, proper, and as uniquely French. The same quest for distinction also drove

Le Francois a Londres.
The FRENCHMAN in LONDON.

Figure 1.1   'The Frenchman in London' (1770) © The Trustees of the British Museum

the development of various personae that came to compete with the *honnête homme* as models of elite masculinity: the *petit-maître*, an impudently swaggering figure created during the Fronde (the aristocratic rebellion against royal authority during the minority of Louis XIV), who went on to become a stock figure on the stage and in narrative prose; the *libertin*, who deployed the gallant language and manners of the *honnête homme*, but for distinctly uncivic purposes; the Rousseauian 'natural' man, who eschewed the artifice of polite society in favor of liberty and ethical transparency; the family man, a deep-feeling, inward-turning *homme de bien* promoted both by sentimental authors and by populationists; the *philosophe*, a new brand of intellectual who fitted smoothly into polite society yet also kept his distance from it; and the military hero, who, after being eclipsed by both the polite courtier and the *philosophe*, re-emerged at mid-century as an exemplar of patriotism and distinctly French greatness.

Frenchness, *honnêteté* and masculinity

Although French proponents of Enlightenment often appealed to timeless universal values such as reason, tolerance and virtue, the period's literary writers and moralists focused just as intently on the traits that (in their eyes) set the French apart from other nations, usually for the better. Voltaire, for example, declared in *Le Siècle de Louis XIV* (1751) that the French of his day were naturally superior in the realm of sociability, thanks both to the glorious example that had been set by the court of Versailles and to the innate refinement of the French language: 'The social spirit [*l'esprit de société*] is the natural endowment of the French: it is a merit and a pleasure of which other peoples have felt the need. Of all languages, French is the one that expresses with the greatest facility, clarity, and delicateness all the objects of conversation for well-bred people [*honnêtes gens*], and in this it contributes throughout Europe to one of the greatest enjoyments in life.'[3] It would be erroneous to characterize Voltaire as chauvinistically pro-French or even pro-contemporary: he pronounced the French to be less advanced than other European peoples in certain areas (such as 'healthy' philosophy, for which he singled out the English), and he viewed his own era as less impressive in its literary and artistic productions than the reign of Louis XIV. At the same time, however, Voltaire believed that sociability, along with clarity and 'delicateness' of expression, belonged to a set of general civilized ideals that were better realized in modern-day France than anywhere else.[4] Moreover, even while acknowledging, as in *L'Ingénu* (1767), that the nation had its fair share of fickle or roguish types, he stressed that it also abounded in 'wise, upstanding [*honnêtes*], and enlightened souls' – a designation he applied both to the men who had written the nation's laws, and to the *homme de bien* who dutifully respected them.[5]

In some instances, the claims made for French superiority were overtly facetious, as when Rica, one of the fictional Persian travelers of Montesquieu's *Lettres persanes* (1721), observed: 'They say that man is a sociable animal. On those grounds, it seems to me that a Frenchman is more of a man than any other: he is Man par excellence, for he seems to be made uniquely for society.'[6] Yet even as Montesquieu mocked French presumptions to have reached one of the summits of human achievement by maintaining a social pace that (as Rica described it) was so frenetic as to approach the superhuman, he also voiced the widespread natural-philosophical belief in the benefits which France derived from its exceptionally temperate climate. Moderation in climate, Montesquieu argued in *De l'Esprit des lois* (1748), fostered moderation in mores and politics as well; and those circumstances had collaborated to make Frenchmen gracious husbands, gallant lovers and passionate seekers of glory, whether on the battlefield or in a field of intellectual endeavor.[7] In the same semi-deterministic vein, Montesquieu maintained that a monarchic system like that of France 'naturalized' politeness in its royal court, cultivated 'a delicacy of taste in all things' and made honor the driving principle of its subjects' every thought and sentiment (*L'Esprit des lois*, 263). All of those elements were, he asserted, evident in the type of education received by elite French males, which aimed to produce 'what we call an *honnête homme*, who has all the qualities and all the virtues required in this government' (264).

A degree of ambivalence lurked beneath those remarks: although Montesquieu often employed the term *honnête homme* to praise men whom he admired for their discretion, integrity, love of country, and disinterested generosity toward others, he did not approve of what passed for *honnête* in his day.[8] Rather, like his moralist predecessors, he emphasized the role of envy and pride in making the nobility polite and took pains to distinguish between the true versus the false *honnête homme*, emphasizing that the designation should not be applied to those who only act the part. Moreover, ever attuned to the darker motives that sometimes fuel action in the political realm, Montesquieu pointedly criticized the French monarchy for excluding the low-born but meritorious *honnête homme* from service to the state, and he fretted that the laws of honor were sometimes as 'fantastical' and capricious in France as in an Oriental harem (*L'Esprit des lois*, 256, 264). French noblemen, as he saw them, often focused more on garnering preferences and distinctions than on serving the country. In short, although honor and virtue were equally important to Montesquieu's conception of genuine *honnêteté* and to his model of a just society, he did not see them as well integrated in his own: despite its salutary balance between the Crown and the nobility, the French political system only occasionally, and only inadvertently, produced citizens worthy of the title *honnêtes gens*.[9]

Montesquieu's mixed perspective illustrates two aspects of the period's larger debate over *honnêteté* and *politesse*, qualities identified by Peter France as 'essential values for the educated men and women of seventeenth- and eighteenth-century France and Britain.'[10] The first was a growing concern over the apparent gap between *honnêteté* and honor: despite their semantic kinship, the two were frequently seen as having parted company in actual social practice.[11] The second was an effort, evident throughout the literature, pedagogical works, moral essays, and courtesy books of the eighteenth century, to redefine the system of social distinction that had originally given birth and shape to *honnêteté*. That campaign did not strip *honnêteté* of its elite connotations; rather, it shifted the foundations of the social distinction enjoyed by the *honnête homme* with the aim of setting them on firmer moral ground and updating them for the contemporary socio-political context.

Beginning with Norbert Elias, historians have underscored that *honnêteté* was the invention of a specific cultural phenomenon: the rise of a permanent court society, which, by the end of the sixteenth century, had codified a brand of courtly worldliness in which 'new signs of social excellence – wit, grace, conversational skill' predominated over older terms of noble self-definition, such as chivalric bravery, dueling and gallantry.[12] From its inception, the *honnête homme* was a recognized social type, a person of noble birth who reinforced his high standing by emulating the refined vocabulary and comportment illustrated in civility manuals like Nicholas Faret's *L'honeste homme, ou l'art de plaire à la cour* (1630). At the same time, the *honnête homme* embodied an ethical ideal of polished personal demeanor, deferential attention to others, fluid grace in social interactions, and flawless self-control. *Honnêteté*, in this sense, signified the studied but natural-seeming internalization of the rules for 'civilized' behavior, a principle central not only to the chevalier Antoine Gombauld de Méré's paradigmatic model of the perfectly self-contained, ever-pleasing *mondain*, but also to René Descartes's philosophical method for rightly directing one's reason.[13] As Ian MacLean has observed, 'In France, this ideal is given a national, almost Parisian character, as it is associated with the *honnête liberté* of French society, which French commentators on the life and customs of other European nations, especially Spain and Italy, find lacking outside the frontiers of their own country.'[14]

Women were, without question, major agents in the growth and popularization of the ethos of *honnêteté*: prominent Parisian ladies like Mme de Rambouillet and Madeleine de Scudéry exemplified the virtues of refined civility and polite conversation in the salons they famously hosted (some also took up the pen to write voluminous works on love, language, philosophy, and proper social comportment).[15] Ultimately, however, the achievement of *honnêteté* as a secular ideal was a masculine affair: the social role of the *honnête femme* was considerably more passive than that of the *honnête homme*, and the meaning of *honnête* when applied to women was restricted mostly to Christian virtues such as chastity, piety, and humility. Clear-cut distinctions were drawn between what *honnêteté* signified for each sex, right down to the manner in which each should speak in polite conversation; and although literary authors from Molière to Marivaux often used female characters to unmask a deficiency of *honnêteté* on the part of another, it was almost invariably their male characters who committed the most serious infractions against the ideal.

Such infractions were uppermost in the minds of many writers who discussed *honnêteté* from the end of the seventeenth century on. However much theoreticians of *honnêteté* praised it as the highest form of civic-minded altruism, the period's social critics suspected it of masking a deep egotism. The moralist La Bruyère, for example, saw the *honnête homme* as poised halfway between the moral extremes of social skillfulness (*habileté*) and genuine goodness; and La Rochefoucauld drew only a thin distinction between the true versus the false *honnête homme*, implying that the former was better than the latter only because he was perfectly aware of his own corruption and confessed it to those around him.[16] It was, in part, the almost machinelike mastery over the passions promoted by *honnêteté* that opened up the breach between the ideal and the reality of the *honnête homme*; yet the multiplicity of ways in which men could embody the property also played an important part.

Molière's somber comedy *Le Misanthrope* (1666) illustrates the range of masculine self-constructions which *honnêteté* made possible as both an ideal and a counter-ideal. In the rigid view of Alceste, the misanthrope of the play's title, being *honnête* means the very opposite of honest: it signifies a fawning, exaggerated politeness that leaves no room for distinguishing between the true *honnête homme* and the fatuous cad.[17] Alceste's solution – loudly proclaimed in arguments with everyone, including his oddly chosen love interest, the elegant and coquettish Célimène – is to fashion himself as a lonely but virtuous sage, bravely bucking the trend by following a philosophy of strict, unvarnished sincerity. Serving as foils to Alceste are the marquis Clitandre and Acaste, a pair of pompous aristocrats who count themselves among Célimène's suitors more for the pleasure of gossiping with her than out of heartfelt passion, and who, through their showy self-presentation, demonstrate the highly stylized aesthetic that underpinned *honnêteté* as a social practice. And then there is Philinte, Alceste's peacemaking friend, whose every word and action exemplifies the lucidity, discretion, and self-sacrificing generosity of the perfect French nobleman (as some defined him). None of these male characters are truly heroic or sympathetic: Philinte, although clearly meant to serve as the voice of reason, seems overly concerned with assuaging the prickly egos of other persons of quality; whereas Alceste, however admirable in his moral purity, sometimes comes across as egotistical and ridiculous. *Le Misanthrope* is, of course, a satire; but it nonetheless provides one of the period's most incisive commentaries on the moral and psychological risks incurred for those who embraced a system of social values that emphasized 'polite' conversation and pleasing external demeanor over genuine sentiment and well-placed esteem. Ultimately, the play's moral is perplexing: Molière aimed not simply to expose the fundamental dishonesty implicit to *honnêteté* as practiced by urbane Parisian aristocrats, but also to show that no escape from that dishonesty was possible, short of renouncing the 'world' altogether.

Some eighteenth-century authors, notably Rousseau, declared themselves happy to accept that extreme option: they did not reject politeness and *honnêteté* altogether, but they did undertake to redefine them in terms that made few if any compromises with the worldly social ethic. Others took inspiration from Molière's cynical marquis, creating aristocratic male characters who, whether fashionable social butterflies or libertine *roués*, cultivated style over substance, played with the limits of propriety, and took full advantage of the privileges of their caste. The largest number of Enlightenment-era writers, however, followed the moderate path sketched by Molière's Philinte and sought to salvage the ideal of *honnêteté* by rectifying it from within – or at least, by developing guidelines to allow the virtuous man to participate in polite society, despite its follies and contradictions, without compromising his principles.

'Bad boys' of the eighteenth century: the *petit-maître* and the *libertin*

If any anxiety haunted the self-perception of eighteenth-century French noblemen, its object was probably not so much the 'political emasculation by courtesy' which their caste had suffered under the reign of Louis XIV, as the trivialization of honor and *honnêteté* at the hands of contemporary nobles and non-nobles alike.[18] As the anonymous author of the *Encyclopédie* article 'Honnête' put it, a 'profanation' was committed every time that the name *honnête* was 'given to the manners and attentions of a polite man' rather than being reserved for the truly noble soul who 'respects order and virtue' and sacrifices his own penchants, tastes, and interests to those of his friends and family.[19] Such a semantic abuse, this author opined, went hand in hand with the advancing corruption of French society – a development that could be stopped only by those who knew how to recognize and avoid the 'factitious and frivolous *honnête*' that often masqueraded as the genuine article.

Avoiding the factitious and frivolous was a project pursued both by the *philosophes* (whom I shall consider shortly) and by many who belonged to the ranks of the old, military-minded aristocracy. In the latter group, proud gentlemen like Henri de Boulainvilliers and the chevalier d'Arc took up the pen to warn that noble male identity was being compromised by numerous forces, including the lure of luxury and material splendor, the vogue of 'useless' pastimes (such as learning, in the eyes of the pre-Rousseauian Boulainvilliers), and the rise of the *noblesse commerçante*.[20] These writers clearly pined for the return of traditional, dignified affirmations of noble nature. Others, however, embraced artifice and triviality with zeal: encouraged, no doubt, by the loosening of French politics and mores that followed the death of Louis XIV in 1715, they reveled in the freedom to display themselves via morally meaningless expressions of superiority, such as ostentatious dress, haughty manners, or (in a more extreme variant) outrageous sexual conduct.

Both of the major 'bad boy' figures of eighteenth-century France, the *petit-maître* and the *libertin galant*, blossomed during the eight-year regency of Philippe d'Orléans, a period infamous for its dissolution and brazenly impolite male behavior.[21] In 1715, the pious clique that had dominated the royal court during the waning years of the Sun King was replaced by an interim ruler with a reputation for immorality, debauchery and impiety (Philippe d'Orléans was even accused of committing incest with his daughter and trying to poison his wife).[22] According to some contemporary observers, the scandalous example set by the regent and his roués triggered a revolution throughout the realm, prompting many French – the men in particular – to dispense with decency and pursue their desires with audacity and impetuousness.[23] The regency was indeed, revolutionary, in that it saw the rise of an Epicurean personal philosophy that made private pleasure-seeking paramount.[24] It was not, however, uniquely responsible for the creation of the era's best-known models of disreputable male conduct. Rather, both the *petit-maître* and the *libertin* initially appeared as political or ideological figures in the seventeenth century and became increasingly sexualized in the next.

Although it dates back to the Renaissance, the term *petit-maître* was popularized as part of the 'explosion of discourtesy' that erupted during the Fronde: it designated the proud, pugnacious, intemperate young seigneurs who belonged to the circle of the Prince of Condé and assisted him in his various failed efforts to seize control of the realm with his own army (1649–53).[25] As Fréderic Deloffre notes, Condé's *petits-maîtres* were seen as *petits* only in comparison to le Grand Condé, a larger-than-life general famous for his wealth, power, and military successes.[26] In the minds of most period observers, the glory that *petits-maîtres* achieved on the battlefield compensated for their bravura, their showy clothes and attitude and their dissolute way of life. Over the next hundred years, however, an extraordinary mutation occurred in the image of this persona: the *petit-maître* transformed in the French cultural psyche from a daring military type to an insufferably affected and flamboyant young nobleman. By the time the term *petit-maître* was defined for the *Encyclopédie* (1765), the figure was widely seen as a ridiculous social butterfly, a type of 'youth intoxicated with self-love, conceited in their speech, affected in their manners, and meticulous in their dress. Someone has defined the *petit-maître* as a light insect that shines in its ephemeral attire, flitting about and shaking its powdery wings . . . Our *petits maîtres*, as M. de Voltaire says, are the most ridiculous species that proudly crawls on the surface of the earth.'[27]

Despite – or perhaps, because of – the disapproval with which the *petit-maître* came to be viewed, the figure enjoyed a spectacular career both on the stage and in prose fiction written for and about the worldly social set. Approximately sixty plays were produced between 1685 and 1770 that feature a *petit-maître* (at least one set in London, to magnify the figure's vanity and impertinence[28]). Novelists such as Claude-Prosper Jolyot de Crébillon found fame writing the fictional adventures of superficial, narcissistic noblemen who considered themselves irresistible to the fair sex but tended to treat women with barely concealed contempt. With this incarnation of the *petit-maître*, the earnest, respectful gallantry of the classical period gave way to a far more cynical ethos, in which relations between the sexes were stripped of all correlation with honor, virtue and love seemed like empty myths, and love-making became the lubricious pastime of the jaded, idle rich.[29] Thus, along with brashness and vanity, the *petit-maître* of the 1730s to the 1750s bore promiscuity as a signature trait. That promiscuity was, however, undercut by a nagging inability to achieve full satisfaction from an attempted sexual conquest: the *petit-maître*, as French novelists portrayed him, was plagued by impotence in the clinch.[30]

In that sense, the *petit-maître* could be characterized as a poor cousin to the period's more successful roué, the male libertine, a figure who inspired a huge body of writings ranging from scandalous memoirs such as *La Véritable vie privée du maréchal de Richelieu* (1725) and Casanova's *Histoire de ma vie* (1791–98) to more overtly fictional works like Laclos' *Les Liaisons dangereuses* (1782) and the novels of the Marquis de Sade. Tied, like the *petit-maître*, to an earlier ideology of resistance to social norms, the libertine evolved along different tracks.[31] One of the more curious aspects of the libertine is the degree to which he was integrated into proper society, often at the very highest levels, even as he flouted propriety. A striking example is the maréchal-duc de Richelieu, also known as Louis François Armand de Vignerot du Plessis (1696–1788), who crossed several boundaries at once: he was both an accomplished military hero and a brilliant courtier who exerted great influence on Louis XV; he had a prodigious number of male lovers as well as mistresses – particularly, as he recounted, during the period in which he served as ambassador in Venice (1715–25); and although he barely knew how to spell, he was unanimously elected to the Académie Française in 1720.[32] In the first two of those accomplishments, one could compare Richelieu to the famously crossdressing chevalier d'Eon, who managed to balance two models of masculinity: that of the suave, polite, foppishly dressed French diplomat, and that of the military warrior, ever ready to defend his honor by dueling.[33]

In many ways, eighteenth-century *libertinage* was constructed both to exploit and to explode myths, from the myth of male virility that became popular during the regency to the ethos of *honnêteté* that had long defined the social identity of the elite French male. Although libertinage clearly placed a premium on sexual prowess – proven, oftentimes, through extraordinary exploits involving multiple partners and multiple rounds of energetic lovemaking – it also celebrated both the caprices of the imagination and the erotic capacities of discursive exchange.[34] At the same time, the *libertin* exerted just as strict a command over his social persona as did the *honnête homme*: characters such as Versac of Crébillon's *Egarements du coeur et de l'esprit* (1736–37) and Valmont of *Les Liaisons dangereuses* are, as Elena Russo points out, outwardly *honnête* in that they are consummate smooth talkers, effortlessly impertinent but also 'coolly likeable and always pleasing' – displaying sociable (or sociable-seeming) qualities that make them all the more dangerous to their female victims.[35] Thus, even though *libertinage* often sounded like an aspiration to individual freedom and happiness, it placed considerable constraints on affirmations of private selfhood: the code of behavior it imposed, even for the conduct of the libertine imagination, was so regimented as to seem military – or, as Roland

Barthes has proposed, Jesuit.[36] Moreover, the personal philosophy it entailed was less self-affirming than society- and sentiment-denying (take, for example, the sad fate of Valmont at the end of Laclos' novel). In sum, the connection between the *libertin galant* and the *honnête homme* was rife with paradoxes: the libertine's language and comportment were deeply indebted to *honnêteté*, but his view of the self in relation to society was so misanthropic as to be antithetical both to that ethos and to the moral code of the Enlightenment – a code that continued to ascribe transcendent value to the community of *honnêtes gens*, while introducing different principles for defining that community.

'Enlightened' masculinities: the 'natural' man, the family man, the *philosophe*, and the 'new' French military hero

Although commonly called the 'Age of Reason', the eighteenth century was just as much an age of uncertainty and soul-searching, regarding everything from the operations of the mind to the foundations of human society. Thanks, in part, to that soul-searching, this era ushered in changes that deeply affected the ways in which elite masculinity was lived and represented. One important development was the forging of new norms of sociability and new models of the public, both tied to the growth of the salon and the Republic of Letters as eminent cultural spaces that were separate (if not altogether freed) from the royal court.[37] Another was the lively political debate over the very idea of social distinction, which produced new criteria for judging a man's merit that were widely disseminated by moralists and reflected in the culture of power that framed the monarchy's operations.[38] Yet another development was the rising respectability of merchants and other non-nobles, social personae that, although frequently ridiculed in the previous century, received a place of honor in eighteenth-century French literature (most particularly the theatrical genre known as the *drame*).[39] However, some of the major forces that reshaped masculine identity were those most directly indebted to some aspect of the old ideal of *honnêteté*: the eighteenth-century 'cult' of sensibility; the renewed valorization of the 'natural' as a moral and aesthetic principle; the ideological promotion of fatherhood (which, for a time at least, redeemed the public image of Louis XVI, widely rumored to be impotent[40]); the dramatically improved social stature of male intellectuals; and the changing contours of French patriotism and French national identity.

As the Enlightenment movement gained influence, so, too, did the effort to remake the *honnête homme* into a useful, universally estimable figure. This entailed adjusting the concept of *honnêteté* to fit values such as sincerity, civic sentiment and good taste.[41] The art of pleasing shifted to an art of feeling: what proved a man *honnête* in this cultural climate was his capacity to experience and express compassion for the needy or afflicted – even to the point of shedding a manly tear or two, thus signaling his membership in the community of humane, sensitive souls.[42] In some authors, like Rousseau, promoting authentic feeling went hand in hand with lamenting what they perceived as the inauthentic and over-refined condition of civilized society.[43] However, these authors did not portray contemporary French society and its 'soft,' frivolous, artificial denizens as hopelessly corrupt: even those given to primitivist reveries saw something redeeming and remediable in the French, if only they could retrieve their essential nature, improve their education system, and rediscover simple principles like respect for themselves and for others.[44] Even Rousseau held out hope for improvement: although he deliberately excluded Parisians from his models for wholesome living in works like *La Nouvelle Héloïse* (1758) and *L'Emile* (1762), he did not reject the ethos of politeness and *honnêteté* outright. Rather, like his friend Duclos, he equated true politeness with humanity and benevolence, and fused the image of the *honnête homme* with that of the good citizen.[45] Rousseau's ideal of masculinity was likewise a fusion, a curious blend of three male types: the patriotic soldier – modeled, in his imagination, on the battle-toughened warriors of ancient Sparta; the fatherly *philosophe* (like the character Wolmar of *La Nouvelle Héloïse*), who was endowed with profound insight into human nature and selflessly devoted to his community; and the earnest man of feeling, the type with which the acutely sensitive Rousseau identified the most fully.

According to some cultural historians, the true heir to the classical *honnête homme* was the eighteenth-century *philosophe*, a new-style intellectual portrayed by its champions as the personification of an enlightened but still polite sociability.[46] As depicted by authors such as Voltaire and Diderot, the *philosophe* was, indeed, an *honnête homme* for the new generation: equally comfortable in the salon and in the library, he was a virtuous, tolerant, compassionate man who eschewed metaphysical speculation in favor of useful knowledge.[47] He was also an exemplary patriot, so committed to the cause of improving humanity and the size of the nation that, like Dorval in Diderot's drama *Le Fils naturel* (1757), he did not shrink from his procreative and familial duties.[48] As a member of the broader category known as *gens de lettres*, the *philosophe* was, of course, most directly connected to activities such as study and writing, both of which acquired almost glamorous connotations in the eighteenth century despite growing medical warnings about the dangerous health effects of 'overstudy.' Study was also invested with broad edifying qualities: the famous eighteenth-century pedagogue Charles Rollin argued that the systematic use of great examples taken from the pages of Greek and Roman literature was one of the best means to instill virtue and civic sentiment – not simply in the sons of the aristocracy, but in the French people as a whole.[49] In other words, education, properly conjoined with wholesome social commerce, took on the formative function previously assigned to *honnêteté*, but on a much larger public scale.

Those who wrote for and about the eighteenth-century Republic of Letters played an active role both in reconfiguring the notion of aristocracy to include prominent writers (whatever their social origins), and in expanding the concept of 'fields of honor' to include intellectual and literary production as well as military achievement.[50] The eulogistic and biographical literature that proliferated in this period created a veritable cult around meritorious men from both realms, using the ancient Greco-Roman idea of a canon of 'great men' as a frame for celebrating notable French lives from the contemporary era.[51] As David A. Bell has noted, 'greatness' in this context was an almost exclusively male attribute: a woman could be *célèbre* or *illustre*, but she couldn't be *grande* in the sense of possessing the attributes which the architects of this cult identified as hallmarks of proper citizenship: namely, 'independence, steadfastness, virtue defined as a solemn dedication to the common good, immunity to the seductions of luxury, lucre, and sensual pleasure.'[52] Taking their cue from sentimentalist models of male heroism, writers who strove to raise a given scholar or soldier to the ranks of the great typically located their subject's admirable qualities in his everyday life: a 'great' man was exemplary not so much for his brilliance on the battlefield or in the academy, as for the caring and devotion he expressed for his fellow human beings.

A certain notion of French-ness was also central to this cult: although those who identified strongly with the Enlightenment movement often proclaimed themselves to be cosmopolitans, patriotism was very much on the minds of French intellectuals (along with everyone else). This was particularly true after 1754, when English troops shocked the French nation by allowing Senecan Indians to execute and scalp the French officer Joseph Coulon de Jumonville (and several of his men) during what would be the opening skirmish of the Seven Years' War. Responding to this atrocity, French writers disseminated an image of the English as 'barbarians' – a label that (to quote Bell once more) simultaneously 'de-Europeanized' the English and 'helped to place France itself at the symbolic center of Europe,' here construed as the locus of true politeness, sociability, and respect for the law. Thanks to the pattern that was set in the 1750s, the French began to see themselves as 'a new Rome, the open and welcoming center of a universal civilization'[53] and they increasingly saw that universal civilization as led by all of those exemplary French males who, with their pens or with their swords, proved themselves to be the true benefactors of humanity.

Notes

1. 'The Frenchman in London' is also reproduced in Amelia F. Rauser, 'The Butcher-kissing Duchess of Devonshire: between Caricature and Allegory in 1784,' *Eighteenth-century Studies*, 36(1) (Fall 2002): 23–46.
2. See Michèle Cohen, *Fashioning Masculinity: National Identity and Language in the Eighteenth Century* (London and New York: Routledge, 1996).
3. Voltaire (François-Marie Arouet), *Le Siècle de Louis XIV*, in *Oeuvres historiques* (Paris: Gallimard, 1957), pp. 1017–18. All translations are my own.

4. Voltaire was more optimistic about the consequences of civilization than some of his contemporaries. On the terms and ideas involved in that debate, see Jean Starobinski, 'Le Mot "civilisation",' in *Le Remède dans le mal: Critique et légitimation de l'artifice à l'âge des Lumières* (Paris: Gallimard, 1989), pp. 11–59.
5. Voltaire, *L'Ingenu*, in *Romans et contes* (Paris: Garnier Flammarion, 1966), p. 340.
6. Charles-Louis de Secondat de Montesquieu, *Les Lettres Persanes*, in Montesquieu, *Oeuvres complètes* (Paris: Gallimard 1949), vol. 1, p. 261 (letter 87).
7. Montesquieu presented his views on climate in Part 3, Book 14 of *De l'Esprit des lois*, in *Oeuvres complètes*, vol. 2, pp. 474–89. On climate theory in Montesquieu and other authors, see Eric Gidal, 'Civic Melancholy: English Gloom and French Enlightenment,' *Eighteenth-century Studies*, 37(1) (2003): 23–45. Montesquieu's jaundiced but affectionate view on marriage in France is reflected in letter 55 of *Les Lettres persanes* (pp. 211–12); letter 90 (pp. 265–6) illustrates his opinions on the French nation's 'general passion for glory' and the point of honor.
8. The *honnête homme*'s qualities of discretion and patriotism are underscored in letter 127 of *Les Lettres Persanes* (pp. 319–20) and in various other letters in Montesquieu's correspondence. He objected to the application of the term to Mark Anthony in *Les Considérations sur les causes de la grandeur des Romains* (1748), in Montesquieu, *Oeuvres complètes*, vol. 2, p. 137.
9. See Jay Smith's discussion of Montesquieu in *Nobility Reimagined: the Patriotic Nation in Eighteenth-century France* (Ithaca, NY: Cornell University Press, 2005), pp. 69–78.
10. Peter France, *Politeness and its Discontents: Problems in French Classical Culture* (Cambridge: Cambridge University Press, 1992), p. 4.
11. See Robert Nye's discussion of *honnêteté* and remarks on the 'remarkable polysemy inherent in *honneur*' in *Masculinity and Male Codes of Honor in Modern France* (Berkeley: University of California Press, 1993), pp. 16–17 and 21–22.
12. Smith, *Nobility Reimagined*, p. 34. The classic study of the rise of court society is Norbert Elias, *The Civilizing Process*, vol. 3, *The Court Society*, trans. Edmund Jephcott (New York: Pantheon, 1983). See also Robert Muchembled, *L'invention de l'homme moderne: Sensibilités, moeurs et comportements collectifs sous l'Ancien Régime* (Paris: Fayard, 1988); Emmanuel Bury, *Littérature et politesse: L'invention de l'honnête homme, 1580–1750* (Paris: Presses Universitaires de France, 1996).
13. Méré's writings on topics like *honnêteté*, conversation and wit are considered key sources for the theory and aesthetics of the *honnête homme*. On Méré, see Domna Stanton, *The Aristocrat as Art: a Study of the Honnête Homme and the Dandy in Seventeenth- and Nineteenth-century French Literature* (New York: Columbia University Press, 1980), *passim*; Bury, *Littérature et politesse*, esp. pp. 179–82 and 190–5; and Maurice Magendie, *La politesse mondaine et les théories de l'honnêteté, en France au XVIIe siècle, de 1600 à 1660* (1925; Geneva: Slatkine Reprints, 1970). On the relation between *honnêteté* and Cartesian philosophy, see Peter Dear, 'A Mechanical Microcosm: Bodily Passions, Good Manners, and Cartesian Mechanism,' in *Science Incarnate: Historical Embodiments of Natural Knowledge*, eds Christopher Lawrence and Steven Shapin (Chicago: University of Chicago Press, 1998), pp. 51–82.
14. Ian MacLean, *Woman Triumphant: Feminism in French Literature, 1610–1672* (Oxford: Clarendon Press, 1977), p. 124.
15. On seventeenth-century *salonnières*, see MacLean, *Woman Triumphant*, pp. 119–54; Erica Harth, *Cartesian Women: Versions and Subversions of Rational Discourse in the Old Regime* (Ithaca, NY: Cornell, 1992), and Myriam Maistre, *Les précieuses: Naissance des femmes de lettres en France au XVIIe siècle* (Paris: Champion, 1999).

16. La Bruyère, *Les Caractères, ou les moeurs de ce siècle* (9th edition, 1696; Paris: Union Générale d'Éditions, 1980), p. 264; La Rochefoucauld, *Maximes* (1665; Paris: Garnier, 1967), p. 214.
17. Molière, *Le Misanthrope*, Act I, Scene 1, lines 41 to 56 (Paris: Classiques Larousse, 1971), p. 27.
18. Orest Ranum coins the colorful expression 'emasculation by courtesy' in 'Courtesy, Absolutism, and the French State,' *Journal of Modern History*, 52 (1980): 426–51, 449.
19. 'HONNÊTE' (probably written by the Chevalier de Jaucourt), in Denis Diderot and Jean d'Alembert (eds), *Encyclopédie, ou Dictionnaire raisonné des sciences, des arts et des métiers* (Paris, 1751–65; New York: Pergamon Press, 1969), vol. 8, pp. 286–7.
20. See Henri de Boulainvillier, *Essais sur la Noblesse de France* (1732), discussed in Smith, *Nobility Reimagined*, pp. 37–41; and Philippe Auguste de Sainte-Foy, chevalier d'Arc, *La Noblesse militaire, opposée à la noblesse commerçante* (1756), a reply to Gabriel-François Coyer's *La noblesse commerçante* (1756). On the Coyer-d'Arc debate, see Pierre Serna, 'Le Noble,' in *L'Homme des Lumières*, ed. Michel Vovelle (Paris: Editions du Seuil, 1996), pp. 39–93, 66–75.
21. Mme de Lambert blamed men for the collective decline in French mores during her lifetime: see her *Réflexions nouvelles sur les femmes* (1729), discussed in Philip Stewart, *Le masque et la parole: Le langage d'amour au XVIIIe siècle* (Librairie José Corti, 1973), pp. 21–2.
22. See Jay Caplan, *In the King's Wake: Post-absolutist Culture in France* (Chicago: University of Chicago Press, 1999), pp. 44, 50–1. The French public was equally fascinated by the active sex life of Louis XV: see Robert Darnton, 'Mademoiselle Bonafon and the Private Life of Louis XV: Communication Circuits in Eighteenth-century France,' *Representations*, 87 (2004): 102–24; and Jean-Pierre Guicciardi, trans. Michael Murray, 'Between the Licit and the Illicit: the Sexuality of the King,' *Eighteenth-century Life*, 9(3) (1985): 88–97.
23. Both the duc de Saint-Simon (eminent courtier to Louis XIV) and the poet/eulogist Antoine Thomas made such remarks; see Stewart, *Le masque et la parole*, p. 14.
24. Through the failed experiment in monetary speculation known as the System of Law, the regency also introduced an unprecedented degree of economic instability in France, not unrelated to the vogue of pleasure-seeking; see Thomas M. Kavanagh, *Esthetics of the Moment: Literature and Art in the French Enlightenment* (Philadelphia: University of Pennsylvania Press, 1996), pp. 14–16.
25. I borrow the term 'explosion of discourtesy' from Peter France, *Politeness and its Discontents: Problems in French Classical Culture* (Cambridge: Cambridge University Press, 1992), p. 63.
26. Frédéric Deloffre provides a richly detailed summary of the semantic history of the term *petit-maître*, along with an analysis of the figure's theatrical career, in his introduction to Marivaux's play *Le Petit-Maître corrigé* (1734; Geneva: Droz, 1955), pp. 6–140. See also Pierre Saint-Amand, 'Le Triomphe des Beaux: petits-maîtres et jolis hommes au dix-huitième siècle,' *Esprit créateur*, 43(3) (Fall 2003): 37–44.
27. 'PETIT-MAÎTRE,' in Diderot and d'Alembert (eds), *Encyclopédie*, 12: p. 465.
28. Bernard Dort provides the count of sixty such plays, including Louis de Boissy, *Le Français à Londres* (1727), in Marivaux, *Théâtre complet* (Paris: editions du Seuil, 1964), p. 388.
29. Charles-Pinot Duclos lamented these developments in *Mémoires pour servir à l'histoire des moeurs du dix-huitième siècle* (1751), discussed in Stewart, *Le masque et la parole*, pp. 14–16.

30. Both Stewart and Yves Citton note that impotence is practically an obsession in Crébillon's works; see Stewart, *Le masque et la parole*, pp. 56–8 and Citton, *Impuissances: Défaillances masculines et pouvoir politique de Montaigne à Stendhal* ([France]: Aubier, 1994), pp. 227–300.
31. On libertinage in the eighteenth century, see Claude Reichler, *L'Age libertin* (Paris: Editions de Minuit, 1987). On earlier forms of this doctrine, see René Pintard, *Le libertinage érudit dans la première moitié du XVIIe siècle* (Paris: Boivin, 1943).
32. See Jacques Levron, *Le maréchal de Richelieu, un libertin fastueux* (Paris: Perrin, 1971).
33. Anna Clark, 'The Chevalier d'Eon and Wilkes: Masculinity and Politics in the Eighteenth Century,' *Eighteenth-century Studies*, 32(1) (1998): 19–48.
34. See Michel Delon, *Le Savoir-vivre libertin* (Paris: Hachette, 2000) and *Libertinage and Modernity*, ed. Catherine Cusset, *Yale French Studies*, 94 (1998).
35. Elena Russo, 'Sociability, Cartesianism, and Nostalgia in Libertine Discourse,' *Eighteenth-century Studies*, 30(4) (1997): 383–400, 384.
36. See Joan DeJean, *Literary Fortifications: Rousseau, Laclos, Sade* (Princeton, NJ: Princeton University Press, 1984) and Roland Barthes, *Sade, Fourier, Loyola* (Paris: Éditions du Seuil, 1971).
37. See Dena Goodman, *The Republic of Letters: a Cultural History of the French Enlightement* (Ithaca, NY: Cornell University Press, 1994); Daniel Gordon, *Citizens without Sovereignty: Equality and Sociability in French Thought, 1670–1789* (Princeton, NJ: Princeton University Press, 1994); and Antoine Lilti, *Le monde des salons: Sociabilité et mondanité à Paris au XVIII siècle* (Paris: Fayard, 2005).
38. See Jay Smith, *The Culture of Merit: Nobility, Royal Service, and the Making of Absolute Monarchy in France, 1600–1789* (Ann Arbor, MI: University of Michigan Press, 1996).
39. As Sarah Maza underscores, the name *bourgeois* was applied to such plays mostly after the eighteenth century; *The Myth of the French Bourgeoisie: an Essay on the Social Imaginary, 1750–1850* (Cambridge, MA: Harvard University Press, 2003), p. 62. The most successful *drame*, Michel Sedaine's *Le philosophe sans le savoir* (1765), makes its businessman hero, Monsieur Vanderk, the ultimate embodiment of *honnêteté* (Vanderk is, admittedly, born a nobleman).
40. See the chapter 'The Defeat of the Body of the King: Essay on the Impotence of Louis XVI,' in Antoine de Baecque, *The Body Politic: Corporeal Metaphor in Revolutionary France, 1770–1800*, trans. Charlotte Mandell (Stanford: Stanford University Press, 1997), pp. 29–75. On the eighteenth-century cult of paternity, see Jean-Claude Bonnet, 'De la famille à la patrie,' in Jean Delumeau and Daniel Roche (eds), *Histoire des pères et de la paternité* (Paris: Larousse, 2000), pp. 245–67.
41. Rémy G. Saisselin argues that the eighteenth-century notion of taste involved many of the attributes of *honnêteté* in the preceding century; see 'De l'honnête homme au dandy,' in *L'honnête homme et le dandy*, ed. Alain Montandon (Tübingen: Gunter Narr Verlag, 1993), pp. 9–17.
42. On solemn, 'manly' crying, see Jay Caplan, *Framed Narratives: Diderot's Genealogy of the Beholder* (Minneapolis: University of Minnesota Press, 1985), pp. 10–12 and 23–9; and Anne Vincent-Buffault, *Histoire des larmes, XVIIIe-XIXe siècles* (Paris: Rivages, 1986), chapter 5. On manly feeling in the British context, see Philip Carter, *Men and the Emergence of Polite Society, Britain 1660–1800* (Harlow and New York: Longman, 2001), chapter 3.
43. See particularly Rousseau's *Discours sur les sciences et les arts* (1749).
44. See, for example, Zilia's observations on the 'Peruvian' attributes of certain French men, in *Lettres d'une Péruvienne* (1747).

45. Duclos, *Considerations sur les moeurs de ce siecle* (Amsterdam, 1751), p. 65. Rousseau cited this definition of *honnêteté* in *L'Emile*.

46. Emmanuel Bury, for example, characterizes the ideal of *philosophe* as a purified version of the *honnête homme*; *Littérature et politesse*, p. 202.

47. The most celebrated portrait of the 'enlightened' *philosophe*, smoothly integrated into worldly society, is that sketched in the *Encyclopédie* article 'Philosophe'; 'Philosophe,' in Diderot and d'Alembert (eds), *Encyclopédie*, 12: pp. 509–11.

48. By the 1770s, the image of the sociable, fatherly man of letters was so widespread as to inspire a poetry competition at the Académie Française; see Éric Walter, 'Le complexe d'Abélard ou le célibat des gens de lettres,' in *Dix-huitième siècle*, 12 (1980): 127–52.

49. Rollin, *Traité des études*, or *De la manière d'enseigner et d'étudier les belles lettres par rapport à l'esprit et au coeur* (1730); discussed in Bury, *Littérature et politesse*, p. 227 and in Smith, *Nobility Reimagined*, p. 87.

50. On Voltaire's aspiration to a 'noblesse de plume,' see Jay Caplan, *In the King's Wake*, pp. 41–9. On the effort to endow the literary field with honorable traits, see Gregory S. Brown, *A Field of Honor: Writers, Court Culture and Public Theater in French Literary Life from Racine to the Revolution* (New York: Columbia University Press, 2002).

51. See David A. Bell, 'National Memory and the Canon of Great Frenchmen,' chapter 4 in *The Cult of the Nation in France: Inventing Nationalism, 1680–1800* (Cambridge, MA: Harvard University Press, 2001), pp. 107–39. On the glorification and self-glorification of thinkers in eighteenth-century France, see also Jean-Claude Bonnet, *Naissance du Panthéon: Essai sur le culte des grands hommes* (Paris: Fayard, 1998) and Dinah Ribard, *Raconter, vivre, penser: histoire des philosophes, 1650–1766* (Paris: Vrin, 2003).

52. Bell, *Cult of the Nation*, pp. 126–7.

53. Bell, 'English Barbarians, French Martyrs,' in *Cult of the Nation*, pp. 78–106, quoted passages at 94–5.

2
Men without Women? Ideal Masculinity and Male Sociability in the French Revolution, 1789–99

Sean M. Quinlan

The French Revolution holds a central place in the making of modern masculinity. It conjures images that are both sublime and stirring – heroic martyrs, patriotic workers, and new citizen-soldiers – as well as the ideas that motivated them – liberty, equality, fraternity, and patriotism. For significant reasons, recent scholarship has framed the revolution's impact upon masculinity in more negative terms. In the crucible of war and terror, revolutionaries created violent and exclusionary models of manhood, fusing male identity with nationalist, militarist and racist sentiments. At the same time, the revolution consolidated bourgeois ideas about male respectability and honor, especially with regards to individualism, merit, and property. In this process, men defeated feminist challenges and consolidated their dominion over public life, monopolizing citizenship rights, political power, and professional advantages – as seen with the closing of women's political clubs in October 1793 and the restrictive Civil Code in 1804 (which denied women active citizenship). To justify this power, men then created biological models that naturalized male authority and separate spheres.[1] In so doing, revolutionary men turned bourgeois values into universal norms, and established new sexual standards in the new democratic-industrial age. Accordingly, the French Revolution produced what R.W. Connell calls 'hegemonic masculinity' – that is, the conditions that perpetuate any system of patriarchy.[2]

While true in broad terms, this narrative often overlooks another aspect of the French Revolution: namely, that many men and women experienced the revolution in terms of personal emancipation and political empowerment. In overturning traditional power and authority, the revolution allowed ordinary people, from a variety of social and political backgrounds, to challenge inequalities based upon social status, privilege, sexuality, religious belief, and race. The revolution enabled these people to dream about new political and social possibilities and gave them the opportunity to turn these dreams into reality. Not surprisingly, revolutionaries seized this explosive moment and set about changing sexual attitudes and experiences. Rarely have politics and sexuality been so fused, and masculinity was central to this experience. In the spring of

1789, the political deputies at the Estates-General attacked the principles of patriarchal authority – seen as arbitrary and tyrannical government – and caused revolutionaries to ask what it meant to be a man and what this ideal man should act like in the public and private world. In place of monarchical patriarchy, revolutionaries advocated fraternity – that is, an egalitarian relation between all men – and tried to legislate it by limiting paternal authority, granting divorce and egalitarian inheritance, recognizing bastardy, and decriminalizing sodomy. At the same time, revolutionaries linked masculinity with mass politics: either they used male ideals to advance political agendas, or they sought, in sincere but sometimes horrible ways, to achieve a deeper fraternal union. Revolutionaries thus promoted masculine ideals to unite a divided nation and escape the class and gender divisions that drove the revolution itself. Their failure potentially explains the revolution's misogyny and explosive violence.

In this chapter, I argue that the French Revolution produced multiple, competing experiences of masculinity, and that these experiences were the product of struggle and contestation. Each stage of the revolution – constitutional monarchy, popular democracy, bourgeois republic, military dictatorship – created its distinctive political culture, which in turn shaped the culture and practice of masculinity. In 1789, revolutionaries believed that French society had been reborn: men and women were swept away by brotherly love and sought out new associational bonds to substantiate these feelings. After 1792, foreign war and socioeconomic collapse transformed these earlier experiences and created new radical understandings of masculinity, especially within political clubs and the popular movement. Emphasizing political unity and violence, these beliefs permeated political associations and official pageantry, finding expression in public festivals and patriotic art. After the Reign of Terror, many men rejected collective activism and instead turned to associational life, both in and out of the family, seeking fraternal bonds in small communities such as urban gangs, artists' studios, and dissection laboratories. These experiences shifted elite mentalities, as prominent intellectuals saw sex and violence as deep-seated elements of human nature.

Throughout all this, masculinity unfolded on two levels – symbolic and behavioral – and the tensions between the two gave revolutionary masculinity its particular energy and violence. On the symbolic level, revolutionaries tried to redefine ideal manhood and establish what cultural anthropologists call 'the sacred'. According to Clifford Geertz, human societies are regulated by 'master fictions' which gravitate toward a political center, a center that orders the political universe and consequently assumes a sacred status.[3] In France, under the Old Regime, this sacred center was filled by the king, who ruled by divine right as father of the people. All this changed in 1789: when revolutionaries asserted the principle of popular sovereignty against royal absolutism, they overturned the traditional symbols of male authority, and the execution of the king in 1793 completed this process.[4] Consequently, revolutionaries struggled to create new masculine ideals to reconstruct this sacred center and reorder revolutionary society – thereby mobilizing political energies.[5]

On the behavioral level, the revolution transformed masculinity in more affective ways: it put men into dialogue with other men (and women) and fundamentally altered self-understanding and behavior. Without doubt, the revolution unleashed powerful libidinal charges – 'seismic affective energy,' to use Lynn Hunt and Margaret Jacob's phrase – that exploded in public and private life.[6] Men and women rubbed shoulders in this new public arena and debated fundamental questions about citizenship, duties, rights, equality, fraternity, patriotism, and nationhood. These new forms of sociability included popular activism, political clubs, sectional meetings, revolutionary spectacles, and, most importantly, military service. In these interactions – whether voluntary or mandated – revolutionaries saw male relations in more egalitarian terms, governed by the ideals of 'liberty, equality, and fraternity.' Strikingly, they then translated these public experiences into the intimate realms of private life, fusing them in the new experience of revolutionary fraternity.

* * *

The particular dynamism of revolutionary masculinity stemmed from two longstanding concerns: the first about fatherhood and paternal authority; the second about sexual decline and degeneracy. These concerns first developed in the early eighteenth century, and were linked to the protracted crisis in royal authority that followed the death of Louis XIV. Critics attacked absolutist policies and sought new ways to substantiate sociopolitical authority, especially patriarchy. In this process, they reconsidered ideal manhood and what it meant – in the words of a later revolutionary – to be a 'good son, good husband, and good father.'[7] Whereas the Sun King had defined masculinity through ostentation and martial prowess, a new generation saw manhood in more classical or humanist terms, emphasizing instead stoic discipline and control.[8] By the 1750s, according to Lynn Hunt, contemporaries had begun to question patriarchal authority on a variety of cultural fronts, a trend that emerged most clearly in the eighteenth-century novel. In the style and taste of the period, contemporaries reconsidered fatherhood both as a vocation and as a source of social authority.[9]

The second concern over masculinity involved powerful fears over sexual degeneracy and depopulation, and here ideas of masculinity took a more violent form. In the mid-eighteenth century, moral crusaders claimed that fashionable society had been corrupted by luxury, libertinism, and disorderly women, and they urged men to reform manners and morals in order to put a halt to decadence and decline.[10] These concerns possibly reflected a feeling of social and political castration: moral critics charged that personal character, not privilege or heredity, determined social status. In response, moral critics countered with new masculine ideals that moved beyond the aristocratic ideal of the *honnête homme*, combining domestic sentiment, religious homilies and classical ideals.[11] In alternating ways, the new man was to be virile but virtuous, passionate but self-controlled, loving but firm, sensible but full of sense. Some prominent figures, such as J.-J. Rousseau and J.-L. David, even imagined a utopian space free of all feminine trappings of manners and refinement.[12] These ideas were internalized, either consciously or unconsciously, by a generation of men who made the French Revolution.

The revolution allowed men to put these values into practice. In the early months of 1789, many revolutionaries believed that this new man had regenerated himself from the decayed body politic. In political writings, revolutionaries described this event as sudden and spontaneous; like a religious conversion, body and soul were reborn and rendered pure and whole again.[13] For revolutionaries, this rebirth was both affective and corporeal: it was affective in that regeneration liberated men from tyranny and prejudice and let them see their fellow man with fraternal love; but it was also corporeal, in that the male body regained the beautiful qualities associated with classical freedom.

On the affective level, men (and women) were overcome by fraternal feeling – regardless of rank, religion, or race – and they tried to substantiate these fraternal feelings in associative rituals. This powerful 'emotional charge' – the phrase is Mona Ozouf's – emerges in the great federative festivals in 1789 and 1790, where legislators and priests preached fraternal love in civic and religious sermons, and iconography celebrated female allegories, birds, hearts, children, kisses, and flowers.[14] These large-scale events were duplicated at the local level, in which villages and communes created public rituals to overcome regional boundaries and rivalries. Men and women gathered together, danced, sang patriotic songs, and planted liberty trees. For participants, these improvised rituals could overcome social conflict, allowing the individual citizen to merge into a universal brotherhood.[15]

On the corporeal level, revolutionaries believed that liberty had struck men like a lightning bolt, transforming their decayed and effeminate bodies into beautiful and desirable figures. In this sense, politics could achieve aesthetic ideals about the male body. For example, these beliefs were captured in J.-L. Pérée's engraving, *L'homme régénéré* (1795). Like an unbound Prometheus, the regenerated man sprang from the wreckage of despotism and superstition, his head thrown back in the ecstasy of the political moment. Galvanized by revolutionary energy, the new Adam constituted a paragon of sensual but imposing beauty, complete with amplified muscles and orthopedic posture (Figure 2.1).

These ideas about affective and corporeal rebirth were combined in J.-L. David's incomplete *Tennis Court Oath* (1790–92), which used neoclassical rhetoric to show the passionate fraternity experienced at the birth of a new nation (Figure 2.2).[16] When taking their oath, the deputies united in the bonds of fraternity, becoming one and indivisible – out of many, came the one – and they literally incarnated a new body politic. To achieve this effect, David

Figure 2.1   J.-L. Pérée, *L'homme régénéré* (1795) (Bibliothèque Nationale de France)

36

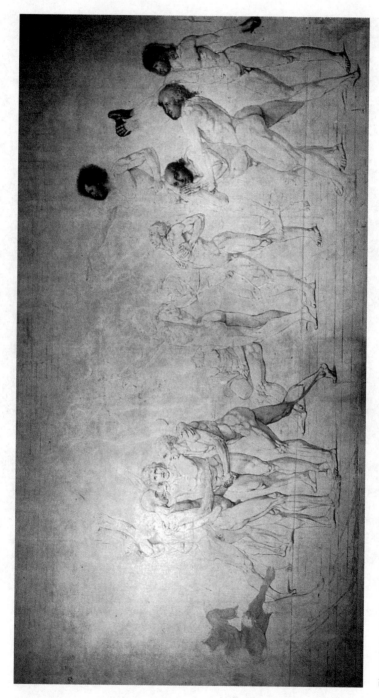

Figure 2.2 Jacques-Louis David, *Tennis Court Oath* (Versailles)

used a pedimental design (as found on ancient monuments) and reiterated this scheme in the construction and placement of the delegates' bodies. From head to torso, the figures form individual pyramids that merge into a larger structure; the astronomer J.-S. Bailly, who administered the oath, appears at the apex like the vigilant eye found in Masonic iconography.[17] As individual men, they have regained a primitive beauty formerly enjoyed by the free citizens of Greece and Rome. A new republic of muscles replaces the nervous degeneracy of the Old Regime.[18]

At the same time, David transfigured the neoclassical aesthetic. As Antoine de Baecque has shown, however, David's *Tennis Court Oath* juxtaposed traditional images of neoclassical control with new forms of emotional intensity, showing how ideal beauty inhered in real flesh-and-blood bodies: here, the real met the ideal and they became one in the revolutionary present.[19] In this manner, David showed both a moment of national unity and an archetypal masculinity, as the delegates discovered joyous fraternal bonds. His image was 'homosocial' – to borrow Eve Kosofsky Sedgwick's phrase[20] – because it privileged the horizontal bonds 'between men' and the pleasures that these same-sex bonds engendered.

However, David's vision of fraternal union wasn't entirely hegemonic. In his original sepia drawings, he showed women in ways that departed from earlier images like *Oath of the Horatii* and *Brutus*.[21] Although he did not put woman on the tennis court itself, he did portray them as engaged spectators who formed a legislative gallery. According to Warren Roberts, women witnessed this event in the public arena itself as 'part of the patriotic impulse felt by men and women alike.'[22] This is an important point, suggesting that David and his patrons accepted some public role, however limited, for women. His image recorded the new political sociability experienced by men and women at the early stages of the revolution as they worked out new political associations in social exchanges such as the festivals of federation. Whereas some revolutionaries saw manhood in aggressive and exclusionary ways – and David's *Tennis Court Oath* records these underlying beliefs – it coexisted with new forms of political sociability that were less structured by gendered dichotomies and exclusions.

* * *

Though revolutionaries, in the summer of 1790, believed that they had inaugurated a new era of brotherly love, revolutionary consensus rapidly fell apart. Between 1791 and 1792, a number of events divided the nation and radicalized popular politics, causing the constitutional monarchy to collapse: the king's aborted flight to Varennes, the Champs de Mars massacre, new political clubs such as the Jacobins and Cordeliers, and, above all, the declaration of war in April 1792.[23] At the same time, revolutionaries altered daily life by instituting civil marriages, divorce, paper currency, a secular calendar, new weights and measures, and even civic religion.[24] In this chaotic environment, revolutionaries asserted more radical ideas about masculinity, making it part of mass politics. These ideas unfolded in the military, political clubs, popular activism, official pageantry and, above all, in the new cult of revolutionary heroes.

By far the most important development was the war. Starting in 1792, France began almost a quarter century of unremitting warfare, and this experience transformed collective mentalities. Warfare brought together unprecedented numbers of young men from different regional, linguistic, and kinship backgrounds and exposed them to the new world of mass politics. Public officials used the army to instill revolutionary ideas among conscripts – ranging from festivals to parades and newspapers – and they disciplined peasant bodies and morality through rigorous drilling, warning against public lewdness, drunkenness, prostitution, and venereal disease. Nevertheless, this process was neither easy nor welcomed, as Alan Forrest's work on conscription and desertion has demonstrated.[25]

The war propagated two powerful ideas: patriotic sacrifice as the ultimate sign of manhood and the battlefield as the quintessential testing-ground of masculinity.[26] For men, military service became one of the highest vocations, displacing even family and religious calling. In theory, it treated all men as equal, and encouraged all soldiers, whether common conscripts or officers, to treat each other as fraternal members of the same nation.[27] In turn, the army spread masculine ideals among the civilian population. Soldiers participated in new republican baptisms, civil marriages, and *décadi* celebrations, in which authorities distributed alms to poor families. Military parades celebrated martial heroism and victories, and the government built monuments and orchestrated civic masses to commemorate the war dead.[28]

Propaganda art visualized slogans such as 'courage and liberty' or 'win or die for the country.' For example, Bizard's *Dévouement à la patrie d'un homme qu'on vient d'amputer d'un bras* (n.d.) showed how a soldier used patriotic devotion to overcome the pain of an amputation. With the severed limb lying on a kitchen table, the soldier turned towards the tricolor flag, while a woman, child, and others watched with admiration and horror. The painting affirmed that loss of life and limb was an appropriate sacrifice and that patriotism could animate men to do superhuman acts.

Political clubs, which proliferated in 1790–91, also helped mold male identities, especially among the middling orders – in Edmund Burke's words, that propertied group comprising 'the moneyed men, merchants, principal tradesmen, and men of letters.'[29] In these clubs, men experimented with new masculine ideas in actual social exchanges. Whereas clubs drew upon older forms of male sociability – Masonic lodges, academies, religious confraternities, guilds, and so on – the revolution channeled them into the explosive matrix of mass politics.

The most important club was the Jacobins, a nationwide network of about half a million men. According to Patrice Higonnet, the Jacobins fused ideas of passionate friendship and fraternal sacrifice, and tried to live them out by adopting an austere, almost puritanical lifestyle.[30] Rejecting luxury and libertinism, they wanted to reconcile true needs and interests in a modern world that preyed upon vile desires and caprices.[31] Robespierre himself discussed these weaknesses in his notorious speech on the 'Principles of Political Morality,' asking how republicans could transcend modern decadence and regain their primitive virtue. For some revolutionary men, Jacobinism allowed them to overcome the degrading and effeminate qualities of modern life.

However, clubs also put men into contact with women activists. As Dominique Godineau has shown, women contributed to the Jacobin and Cordelier clubs by giving speeches, voting by acclamation and taking oaths. Elsewhere, men encountered women as political equals: there were about thirty clubs exclusively for women, as well as sexually mixed societies (called 'hermaphroditic societies'), which counted for between 19.3 and 38.7 per cent of all Paris club members. In urban areas where women held independent trades, men even had to swear they accepted women members before they joined.[32] These data suggest that revolutionary men wanted to create new political associations with women, or were at least willing to share political space with them. As men, they believed in the revolution's ideas about human rights and egalitarianism, and saw women as partners, not as political or social threats – though misogynistic views ultimately prevailed when the government outlawed women's clubs in October 1793.[33]

The urban popular movement – the sans-culottes – offered a radically different vision of masculinity. In Albert Soboul's classic study, the sans-culottes were 'a coalition of small employers and journeymen' who were 'hostile to the interests of commercial capital'[34] – though recent historiography suggests that the movement was led by a few thousand propertied militants who pulled political strings in sectional life and then used their economic power to mobilize the labor force in times of political crisis.[35] Though socioeconomic concerns unified the sans-culottes, another factor may have been gender. Like the Jacobins, the sans-culottes sought new forms of male sociability, but the circumstances were different. In 1791, the Le Chapelier law overturned trade guilds and cast working people into the new world of the indivisible republic. As William H. Sewell has shown, the sans-culottes took republican rhetoric seriously and introduced these beliefs into quotidian experience.[36] In this process, they fused republican and popular ideals of masculinity and challenged Jacobin ideas of middle-class male virtue.

In their gender politics, the sans-culottes drew deeply from urban popular culture.[37] A real man, they argued, embodied several qualities: he worked with his hands, he loved his family, and he defended his nation. He provided the basic necessities for his wife and children and protected them, as fiercely as he could, from want and danger – and from political enemies as well.[38] His family shared these sentiments and loved him for his sacrifice. As the radical journalist Hébert wrote in his *Père Duchesne*, the 'bon sans-culotte' came home from work every evening, where his wife embraced him and his children gathered around. Lacking airs, the sans-culottes rejected upper-class morality as hypocritical, and wanted to recognize common-law unions and non-naturalized children. At the same time, they believed that fatherless households posed an acute economic and moral problem, and demanded public services for families whose men had sacrificed life, limb, and labor for the nation.[39]

The sans-culottes used style to substantiate these beliefs. More than any other political group, they measured personal worth by outside appearances, believing that fashion and gesture signified political allegiance and moral character itself.[40] The sans-culotte costume alone – the phrygian hat, striped pants, wooden clogs and weapons – distinguished their virile patriotism from 'effeminate' counter-revolutionaries.[41] Like the Jacobins, the sans-culottes acted out these masculine ideals in political associations. In sectional meetings, they appeared in full regalia and carried weapons. Leaders and members read patriotic speeches; the groups sang patriotic songs; and they swore oaths to live as free men or die fighting.[42]

In this popular idea of the nation, universal brotherhood was key. When appropriating the ideas of fraternity, however, the sans-culottes made it more insistent and violent. Brotherhood, they said, was a feeling experienced between equal persons who exercised political activism and vigilance.[43] As Soboul points out, there was something sacred or even 'mystical' about this idea of fraternity. It involved corresponding with other activists and fraternizing together (especially to combat moderates in sectional meetings); and the sans-culottes sealed these exchanges with fraternal embraces and collective oath-taking (an activity in which women also participated).[44]

In all this, the sans-culottes waged a culture war. For them, manhood was rooted in a moral vision of society. A man was independent and community minded – simultaneously good father and a good citizen – and he existed in a society of small property owners who were relatively equal in rights and status and who shared the same moral values. However, for the sans-culottes, being a man also meant being a political agent. By their family values and patriotism, they had earned active citizenship and could live out these male fantasies in political life.

* * *

In order to control revolutionary events, Jacobin leaders appropriated male ideals and behavior that had emerged from the more spontaneous collective experiences of 1789 and 1790. These efforts accompanied the mass cultural mobilization of the Reign of Terror.[45] At this time, revolutionaries wanted to enforce political conformity by creating a compelling male 'ego ideal' with which ordinary men could identify and aspire.

The efforts appeared in educational policies, official festivals, rhetoric, iconography and insignia. Here, ideal manhood assumed its most disturbing guises, drawing upon images of heroic sacrifice, redemption through violence, and purification by blood. The most powerful mass images date from the Festival of Unity and Indivisibility held in Paris (10 August 1793). Scripted by David,

Chénier, and Gossec, this festival was supposed to inspire popular support just as the foreign war and the Vendéan revolt escalated. The festival highlighted images of male heroism and rebirth: there was, for example, an enormous 'fountain of regeneration', where elderly men drank water that squirted from a statue's breasts (Figure 2.3), and a colossus of the people trampling the hydra of federalism. Revolutionaries were so moved that they proposed to erect a permanent colossus on the Pont-Neuf. This figure of Hercules quickly displaced earlier allegories of liberty and fraternity (usually symbolized by a woman) and became the republic's avatar – a virile 'emblem of the people.'[46]

Radical masculinity found its strongest expression in the national cult of revolutionary heroes. At state funerals and in pantheonization rites, revolutionaries made a gallery of modern-day 'grands hommes' who had honored their nation.[47] This process began in 1792 when the Convention transformed the Sainte-Geneviève church into the Panthéon.[48] By autumn 1793, Montagnards had further democratized these ideas, saying that ordinary men could assume a heroic level – 'to die for the country is to acquire immortality'[49] – and celebrated them with a new patriotic art. Three of these assassinated martyrs were commemorated by J.-L. David – the regicide deputy Lepeletier, the journalist J.-P. Marat, and a young volunteer named Bara – but revolutionaries treated other figures with similar pageantry, notably Lazowski, Chalier, Beauvais, Gasparin, Mirabeau, Hoche, and Joubert.[50]

Heavily orchestrated, these commemorations combined different media in graphic and shocking ways. Throughout, the male body occupied center stage. The martyrs were often disfigured (for example, Chalier had been repeatedly bludgeoned by a guillotine blade). Public officials relayed these stories in schools, committees, and clubs through texts and images, even publishing autopsy reports of heroes who had died from 'physical exhaustion' while struggling for the republic. Public officials hoped these graphic reports would elicit popular outrage against anti-republican forces.[51]

Authorities displayed the martyrs in macabre ways. At Lepeletier's and Marat's funerals, David used their wounded bodies as props alongside other theatrical pieces (though Marat was so decomposed that David couldn't keep him in the bathtub in which Charlotte Corday had stabbed him). This spectacle then became an industry: revolutionaries put the ashes in urns, commissioned official paintings, and mass-produced busts and images (there were over a hundred different images of Marat alone). Personal objects were venerated (such as Marat's bathtub and night-dress) and their 'orphaned' children were adopted by the Convention (as with Lepeletier's daughter).[52]

Wounded veterans also became popular spectacles. These living heroes were welcomed at sectional meetings, political clubs, and, above all, public ceremonies, where they showed their wounds to an admiring public. Between 1792 and 1794, over 100 wounded veterans presented their bodies to the National Assembly and inspired a sentimental outpouring.[53] A number of cases were compiled by Léonard Bourdon de La Crosnière and A.-C. Thibaudeau and

42

La Fontaine de la Régénération.

Sur les Debris de la Bastille, le 10 Août 1793.

Paris chez l'Editeur, rue Honoré N.º 1097. Section Butte des Moulins.

Figure 2.3 Charles Monnet, *La Fontaine de la Régénération, sur les dévris de la Bastille, le 10 août, 1973* (Bibliothèque Nationale de France)

published by the Committee of Public Instruction as *Recueil des actions héroïques et civiques des républicains français* – a new book of secular martyrs for a new revolutionary age.[54] Their bodies provided moral or patriotic allegories, giving palpable evidence of revolutionary sacrifice.

* * *

The Thermidorean and Directorial republics (1794–99), which followed the fall of the Robespierrists, again transformed masculinity. Traumatized by terror and civil war, the propertied classes steered between radicalism and reaction in the hope of consolidating the hard-won principles of 1789. Consequently, they broke with Jacobin spectacle, forced conviviality, and doctrinal devotion, turning instead towards the family and voluntary associations.[55] This shift towards private life split in two conflicting directions: the first towards an official rhetoric of family values; the second towards sensualism and sartorial excess. Both changed masculinity in important ways.

In terms of official morality, the propertied classes blamed the terror and civil war on the uncontrolled emotion sparked by individual emancipation. To maintain the social order, they argued that society needed strong domestic laws so families could control personal behavior before it exploded in public life.[56] Prominent intellectuals, such as the Idéologues and neo-Kantians, joined this effort, preaching male control and moderation.[57] Mistrusting human nature, they divided private and public life into gendered spheres of behavior: man was a rational, public actor – sober, moderate, and self-controlled – while women remained in the domestic sphere because nature had marked them for marriage and motherhood.[58] Crucially, men were not defined by austere virtue and patriotic devotion; rather, reason and family prevailed. As the Constitution of the Year III reminded: 'No one is a good citizen if he isn't a good son, a good father, a good brother, a good friend, and a good husband.'[59]

However, official morality contrasted with the anarchic cultural life of the Directory. Reacting against Jacobin puritanism, social elites indulged in hedonistic pursuits, flocking to new salons and fashionable cliques. Men and women now turned their bodies into sites for self-expression, not collective indoctrination. These practices included shocking modes that imitated the look of guillotined victims, the alleged victims' balls attended only by people whose relatives had died on the guillotine, and sartorial dress that highlighted sex and figure.[60] However, this dandyism undermined the official rhetoric of family values, and shaped masculine ideas and behavior in unsettling and unexpected ways.

In this cultural context, when everything seemed up for grabs, men sought out smaller, more intimate associations. On the one hand, former radicals missed the spectacle and intensity of Jacobin masculinity and hoped to recreate these experiences in the private sphere; on the other hand, alienated men sought out fraternal associations, outside the family and state, to escape revolutionary chaos and anomie. A striking example of this new male sensibility, from a counter-revolutionary perspective, were the flamboyant muscadin gangs, the so-called 'gilded youth' of the Thermidorean period. According to François Gendron, these youth gangs became the shock troops of the Thermidorean reaction. Thermidorean political leaders first used them to attack sans-culotte militants and close down the Paris Jacobin club, but the muscadins soon developed their own counter-revolutionary agenda – becoming gang-like hooligans – and provoked the popular revolts of Germinal and Prairial in 1795.[61]

The muscadins were the antithesis of the sans-culottes. Numbering about 3000 men, they were often the sons of middle-class minor officials and small shopkeepers, and formed an odd mix of ex-prisoners, draft dodgers, hack writers, notaries, theater types, and white-collar clerks. They were unified by their young age (they called themselves the 'French youth') and hung out in the Palais Royal and the Tuileries.[62] These gangs even had their own female counterparts, called the *merveilleuses*, who also adopted a sexually-charged style.[63]

Like the Jacobins and sans-culottes, the muscadins turned fashion into a political uniform, but here they inverted radical ideas about masculinity. In the context of economic collapse and famine, the muscadins flouted a luxurious and decadent style, a fact noticed by observers like L.-S. Mercier.[64] Imitating fashionable and reactionary icons, the muscadins wore closely fitted coats and they had long, braided hair. They wore powdered wigs, half-moon hats, wide cravats, black velvet collars, big lapels, ribbons, tight breeches, stockings, and open shoes – and they finished this attire with powder, perfume, and monocles (perhaps an 'in' joke because many had procured military deferment on grounds of poor eyesight).[65] This gender-bending was more than symbolic, as many muscadins escaped round-ups by cross-dressing as women.[66]

Though foppish in style, the muscadins were violent. They carried heavy clubs and attacked known terrorists or anyone dressed in radical attire. In carnivalesque fashion, they defaced revolutionary symbols, smashing busts of Marat and Lepeletier, and smeared Jacobin images with excrement. They called for peace instead of 'fraternity or death' and forced government authorities to remove Marat and Lepeletier from the Panthéon. The muscadins also used sexual violence by threatening to rape daughters and associates of Jacobin leaders; on one occasion, they assaulted a young girl in the Convention. On the streets, they stripped Jacobins and female sans-culottes and beat them on the posterior. The reactionary press sometimes made off-color remarks about these events, implying that radicalism should be punished with rape and sodomy.[67]

Another case appears within the artistic community. In the Thermidorean period, painters reconsidered the artist's status as an individual and member of a larger artistic community. After the government dissolved the Academy of Arts in 1793, artists were no longer governed by formal rules of training, exhibition, and commissions.[68] As atomized agents in the art market, artists sought new forms of sociability to remake individual and collective identity. To do so, they presented themselves as members of the middle-class elite, as savvy professionals on a par with disciplines such as medicine, law, and engineering. Artists thus justified their vocation by casting themselves as a masculine ideal: art was a manly occupation that combined style, business and family values. The artist exemplified a new kind of bohemian bourgeois, but his fashionable sensibilities never outweighed his commitment to the social and moral order.[69]

At the same time, artists also transformed their studios into fraternal spaces. More than just a workshop, the studio allowed like-minded men to congregate and offer their wares to the public. One striking example is J.-L. David's studio work after his release from prison in 1794. Traditionally, David had encouraged a more egalitarian relationship between student and teacher to undermine the aristocratic practices of old regime academies.[70] After the Terror, however, these master–teacher relations were colored by the masculine experiences of the Jacobin republic. This change emerges in David's new approach to the male nude, which resurfaced as a kind of memento of the Jacobin Hercules. According to Delafontaine, who studied under David, his pupils started each work day by drawing the male nude. When the group could not pay models, the best-looking men would pose nude for their colleagues. In part, David had become interested in anatomical realism and wanted to portray the male figure more accurately, but there were other prerogatives. According to Ewa Lajer-Burcharth, David put the male body at the center of a whole network of interpersonal relations involving training, ideal objects, and sociability. In a nostalgic way, David took his experiences with Jacobin masculinity and put them in the private studio, creating 'a surrogate world replacing what the artist had lost with the fall of the Jacobins.'[71]

These ideas spilled into medical circles. Like artists, young doctors gathered around a central male personage who served as both teacher and leader – not exactly a father figure, but rather as a first among male equals. This trend appears with the brilliant and charismatic Xavier Bichat, who is remembered today for his work on histology and experimental physiology.[72] After 1796, Bichat offered his own private courses on anatomy and surgery (he attracted several hundred students), replacing an older medical paternalism with a fraternal esprit de corps. Joined by his young cohorts, Bichat pioneered ingenious but ghoulish experiments. Beyond accepted medical norms, Bichat's life revolved around dismembered bodies: his apartment was littered with human specimens; his group attended guillotinings to study violent death; and they raided graveyards for cadavers. Bichat's attachment and drive emerge in his few private letters and later obituaries, which portrayed him as a dutiful son and brotherly teacher.[73] When Bichat died suddenly in 1803, his youthful circle experienced the loss as an irreparable calamity, and they cast him as a feverish romantic who had given body and soul to satisfy his genius – views captured in Louis Hersent's passionate painting, *La mort de Xavier Bichat* (1817).[74]

In some cases, artistic and medical practices overlapped. The best example is Dr Jean-Galbert Salvage's book on the anatomy of the Borghese Gladiator, the famed Greek sculpture from the first century BCE. Art critics had long identified the Gladiator as a paragon of male beauty and anatomical realism.[75] In the 1790s, Salvage wanted to test these claims and enlisted a group of young artists to help him. In a scene befitting Mary Shelley's *Frankenstein*, they scavenged the Paris morgues for beautiful male bodies and, using pieces of these corpses, they sculpted two gladiators and other antique pieces. Salvage published a folio edition with stunning engravings in 1812 (four years after Napoleon Bonaparte installed the original at the Louvre),[76] and it was acclaimed by J.-L. David and the art historian Emeric-David.[77]

Salvage's fascinating but macabre work embodied the interplay between projections of ideal manhood, on the one hand, and efforts to live out new fraternal feelings in associational life, on the other. Foremost, Salvage wanted to test the art historian Joachim Winckelmann's famous theory that Greco-Roman sculptures projected ideal beauty and did not realistically represent actual bodies of the past (a point that was being furiously debated in intellectual circles).[78] Salvage's detailed anatomical work suggested otherwise: Greek sculptors, it seemed, dissected human corpses, took the best parts of these bodies, and made a composite figure. The beauty was not ideal, but material and real. In implicit ways, his work promised that men could mold their present-day bodies into the beautiful, sensual bodies of Antiquity. The revolution could still make a utopian society of ideal manhood, free and beautiful. But the homosocial world of private associations, not mass politics, would realize these ideals.

* * *

The French Revolution challenged gendered structures of power, and produced competing and conflicting experiences of masculinity. It opened serious debate about what it meant to be a man and it gave revolutionaries new opportunities to experiment with these new ideas in their daily life. In this psychosocial context, men reacted in a variety of ways. In extreme cases, revolutionary men suffered social and psychological anxieties, driving them towards 'backlash' politics against women, shutting women out of public life and limiting their rights. By contrast, other men found the breakdown of old social hierarchies to be profoundly liberating, because it allowed them to change their lives and experiment with new affective behavior. For some, the revolution promoted pro-woman sentiments: they believed in universal egalitarianism and wanted to share this new political world with revolutionary sisters. At the same time, revolutionaries also sought more egalitarian relations with other men, rooted in new fraternal bonds of freedom. Though these spaces were often segregated by gender, they remained potentially subversive because they allowed men to coexist outside patriarchal authority in bonds that were sometimes deeply affective, if not homoerotic. Given the range of diverse experiences, it was most likely the search for social stability that drove men back to traditional paternalism and separate spheres, effectively rebuilding a more conservative society at the expense of women's rights. But during the revolution, the alternatives had been clearly laid out.

Notes

1. For the essential studies, see George L. Mosse, *The Image of Man: the Creation of Modern Masculinity* (New York: Oxford University Press, 1996); and Robert A. Nye, *Masculinity and Male Codes of Honor in Modern France* (New York: Oxford University Press, 1993). On the exclusion of women, see Joan Landes, *Women and the Public Sphere in the Age of the French Revolution* (Ithaca: Cornell University Press, 1988); and Dorinda Outram, *The Body and the French Revolution: Sex, Class, and Political Culture* (New Haven: Yale University Press, 1989). On biological incommensurability, see Thomas Laqueur, *Maxing Sex: Body and Gender from the Greeks to Freud* (Cambridge, MA: Harvard University Press, 1990); and Londa Schiebinger, *Nature's Body: Gender in the Making of Modern Science* (Boston: Beacon Press, 1993).
2. R.W. Connell, *Masculinities*, 2nd edn (Berkeley: University of California Press, 2005), p. 77.
3. Clifford Geertz, 'Centers, Kings, and Charisma: Reflections on the Symbolics of Power,' in *Culture and its Creators: Essays in Honor of Edward Shils*, eds Joseph Ben-David and Terry Nichols Clark (Chicago: University of Chicago Press, 1977), p. 171.
4. Lynn Hunt, *The Family Romance of the French Revolution* (Berkeley: University of California Press, 1992), ch. 3.
5. See Joan Landes, 'Republican Citizenship and Heterosocial Desire: Concepts of Masculinity in Revolutionary France,' in *Masculinities in Politics and War: Gendering Modern History*, eds Stefan Dudink, Karen Hagemann, and John Tosh (Manchester: Manchester University Press, 2004), p. 112.
6. Lynn Hunt and Margaret Hunt, 'The Affective Revolution in 1790s Britain,' *Eighteenth-century Studies*, 34 (2001): 497.
7. Quoted in Patrice Higonnet, *Goodness beyond Virtue: Jacobins during the French Revolution* (Cambridge, MA: Harvard University Press, 1998), p. 136.
8. Jean-Claude Bonnet, *Naissance du Panthéon: essai sur le culte des grands hommes* (Paris: Fayard, 1998), pp. 18–27.
9. Hunt, *Family Romance*, ch. 2. On these literary dimensions, see Katherine Astbury and Marie-Emmanuelle Plagnol-Diéval (eds), *Le mâle en France, 1715–1830: représentations de la masculinité* (Oxford: Peter Lang, 2004).
10. Robert Favre, *La mort dans la littérature et la pensée françaises au siècle des Lumières* (Lyon: Presses Universitaires de Lyon, 1978), pp. 275–331; and Harvey Chisick, *The Limits of Reform in the Enlightenment: Attitudes toward the Education of the Lower Classes in Eighteenth-century France* (Princeton, NJ: Princeton University Press, 1981), pp. 185–97.
11. Warren Roberts, *Morality and Social Class in Eighteenth-century French Literature and Painting* (Toronto: University of Toronto Press, 1974).
12. Landes, *Women and the Public Sphere*, pt. 1.
13. Mona Ozouf, *L'homme régénéré: essais sur la Révolution française* (Paris: Gallimard, 1989), pp. 116–57.
14. Ibid., pp. 158–82.
15. Marcel David, *Fraternité et Révolution française, 1789–1799* (Paris: Aubier, 1987), p. 12.
16. See especially Philippe Bordes, *Le serment du jeu de paume de Jacques-Louis David: le peintre, son milieu et son temps de 1789 à 1792* (Paris: Editions de la Réunion des musées nationaux, 1983).

17. Dorothy Johnson, *Jacques-Louis David: Art in Metamorphosis* (Princeton, NJ: Princeton University Press, 1993), pp. 77–81.
18. Ewa Lajer-Burcharth, *Necklines: the Art of Jacques-Louis David after the Terror* (New Haven, CT: Yale University Press, 1999), p. 106.
19. Antoine de Baecque, *Le corps de l'histoire: métaphores et politique* (Paris: Calmann-Lévy, 1993), pp. 227–53. See also Alex Potts, 'Beautiful Bodies and Dying Heroes: Images of Ideal Manhood in the French Revolution,' *History Workshop*, 30 (Autumn 1990): 1–20.
20. Eve Kosofsky Sedgwick, *Between Men: English Literature and Male Homosocial Desire* (New York: Columbia University Press, 1985).
21. Landes, *Women and the Public Sphere*, pp. 152–58.
22. Warren Roberts, *Jacques-Louis David and Jean-Louis Prieur, Revolutionary Artists: the Public, the Populace, and Images of the French Revolution* (Albany: State University of New York Press, 2000), p. 236.
23. Louis Bergeron, 'Évolution de la fête révolutionnaire: chronologie et typologie,' *Les fêtes de la Révolution*, eds Jean and Paul Viallaneix Ehrand (Paris: Société des Études Robespierristes), p. 127.
24. See Serge Bianchi, *La révolution culturelle de l'an II: élites et peuple, 1789–1799* (Paris: Aubie, 1982); Lynn Hunt, *Politics, Culture, and Class in the French Revolution* (Berkeley: University of California Press, 1984).
25. Alan I. Forrest, *Conscripts and Deserters: the Army and French Society during the Revolution and Empire* (New York: Oxford University Press, 1989).
26. Mosse, *Image of Man*, pp. 50–1.
27. See André Rauch, *Le premier sexe: mutations et crise de l'identité masculine* (Paris: Hachette, 2000), p. 48; and Alan I. Forrest, *The Soldiers of the French Revolution* (Durham: Duke University Press, 1990).
28. Jean Paul Bertaud, *The Army of the French Revolution: from Citizen-Soldiers to Instrument of Power* (Princeton, NJ: Princeton University Press, 1988), pp. 121, 212.
29. Edmund Burke, *Thoughts on French Affairs* (1791), in *Edmund Burke on Revolution*, ed. Robert A. Smith (New York: Harper & Row, 1968), p. 190, as quoted in Hunt, *Politics*, p. 125.
30. Higonnet, *Goodness*, p. 187.
31. Ibid., pp. 186, 193, 197–8.
32. Dominique Godineau, *Citoyenne tricoteuses: les femmes du peuple à Pairs pendant la Révolution française* (Aix-en-Province: Alinea, 1988), pp. 143–77, 199–219.
33. Ibid., pp. 163–77.
34. Albert Soboul, *Les sans-culottes parisiens en l'an II: mouvement populaire et gouvernement révolutionnaire, 2 Juin 1793–9 Thermidor An II* (Paris: Librairie Clavreuil, 1958), pp. 451, 475.
35. Richard Andrews, 'Social Structures, Political Elites, and Ideology in Revolutionary Paris, 1792–1794: a Critical Evaluation of Albert Soboul's *Les sans-culottes parisiens en l'An II*,' *Journal of Social History*, 19 (1985): 71–112.
36. William H. Sewell, *Work and Revolution in France: the Language of Labor from the Old Regime to 1848* (New York: Cambridge University Press, 1980), pp. 96–8.
37. On this culture, see Daniel Roche, *Le peuple de Paris: essai sur la culture populaire au XVIIIe siècle* (Paris: Fayard, 1981), pp. 135–267.
38. Godineau, *Citoyennes tricoteuses*, pp. 33–63; Sewell, *Work*, pp. 109–11.
39. Soboul, *Les sans-culottes*, pp. 491–6, 673–77.
40. Aileen Ribeiro, *Fashion in the French Revolution* (New York: Holmes & Meier, 1988), p. 86.

41. See the comments in Richard Wrigley, 'The Formation and Currency of a Vesti-mentary Stereotype: the Sans-culottes in Revolutionary France', in *Fashioning the Body Politic: Dress, Gender, Citizenship*, ed. Wendy Parkins (Oxford: Berg, 2002), pp. 19–47.
42. Soboul, *Les sans-culottes*, pp. 581–648, 649–59.
43. Sewell, *Work*, pp. 102, 104–5.
44. Soboul, *Les sans-culottes*, pp. 570–6.
45. T.J. Clark, 'Painting in the Year Two,' *Representations*, 47 (1994): 13–63.
46. 'David propose à la Convention l'érection d'un monument consacré à la gloire du peuple français sur le terre-plein du Pont Neuf,' in Daniel Wildenstein and Guy Wildenstein, *Documents complémentaires au catalogue de l'Oeuvre de Louis David* (Paris: Fondation Wildenstein, 1973), p. 70.
47. See L.-S. Mercier, *Le nouveau Paris*, ed. Jean-Claude Bonnet (Paris: Mercure de France, 1994), pp. 858–77.
48. Édouard Pommier, *L'art de la liberté: doctrines et débats de la Révolution française* (Paris: Gallimard, 1991), pp. 167–74.
49. J.-L. David, 'Son rapport sur la fête héroïque,' *Journal des débats* (no. 659): 301, in Wildenstein and Wildenstein, *Documents*, p. 108. See Jean-Claude Bonnet, 'Les formes de célébration', in *La mort de Marat*, ed. J.-C. Bonnet (Paris: Flammarion, 1986), pp. 10–28; and Johnson, *Jacques-Louis David: Art in Metamorphosis*, p. 74.
50. De Baecque, *Le corps*, pp. 345–51.
51. Ibid., pp. 351–62.
52. J.-R. Mantion, 'Enveloppes à Marat David,' in *La mort de Marat*, ed. Bonnet, pp. 187–203.
53. De Baecque, *Le corps*, pp. 352–60.
54. Léonard Bourdon and A.-C. Thibaudeau, *Recueil des actions héroïques et civiques des républicains français* (Paris: Impr. nationale, an II).
55. François Furet, *Interpreting the French Revolution*, trans. Elborn Forster (Cambridge: Cambridge University Press, 1981), pp. 58, 72, 74–8.
56. See especially S. Desan, 'Reconstituting the Social after the Terror: Family, Property, and the Law in Popular Politics,' *Past and Present*, 164 (1999): 81–121.
57. On the Idéologues, see Sergio Moravia, *Il pensiero degli Idéologues: scienza e filosofia in Francia (1780–1815)* (Florence: La Nuova Italia, 1974); and Martin Staum, *Minerva's Message: Stabilizing the French Revolution* (Montreal: McGill-Queen's University Press, 1996).
58. C.-F. Volney, *La loi naturelle, ou catéchisme du citoyen française* (1793 [Year II]; Paris: Armand Colin, 1934), pp. 108, 113, 138–9, 148; and P.-J.-G. Cabanis, *Rapports du physique et du moral de l'homme*, 2 vols (Paris: Crapart, Year X [1802]).
59. Quoted in Geneviève Fraisse, *Le controverse des sexes* (Paris: Presses universitaires de France, 2001), p. 86.
60. For a contemporary perspective, see Mercier, *Le nouveau Paris*, pp. 337–40, 400–18. On style and taste, see Ribeiro, *Fashion*, pp. 113–19; and Bianchi, *La révolution culturelle*.
61. François Gendron, *The Gilded Youth of Thermidor* (Montreal: McGill-Queen's University Press, 1993), pp. 3, 5, 165.
62. Ibid., pp. 3, 10, 82.
63. Ewa Lajer-Burcharth, 'The Muscadins and Merveilleuses: Body and Fashion in Public Space under the Directory, 1795–99,' in *Repression and Expression: Literary and Social Coding in Nineteenth-Century France*, ed. Carrol F. Coates (New York: Peter Lang, 1996), pp. 137–46.

64. Mercier, *Le nouveau Paris*, pp. 504–5.
65. *Memoirs of the Duchesse d'Abrantès*, 8 vols (London, 1831–35), 1: p. 115, quoted in Ribeiro, *Fashion*, p. 117.
66. Gendron, *Gilded Youth*, p. 203.
67. Ibid., pp. 29, 43, 63.
68. On this context, see Thomas E. Crow, *Emulation: Making Artists for Revolutionary France* (New Haven, CT: Yale University Press, 1995).
69. Lajer-Burcharth, *Necklines*, p. 213.
70. Thomas Crow, 'Revolutionary Activism and the Cult of Male Beauty in the Studio of David,' in *Fictions of the French Revolution*, ed. Bernadette Fort (Evanston: Northwestern University Press, 1991), p. 55.
71. Lajer-Burcharth, *Necklines*, pp. 220–1.
72. On Bichat, see Elizabeth Haigh, *Xavier Bichat and the Medical Theory of the Eighteenth Century* (London: Wellcome Institute for the History of Medicine, 1984); and John E. Lesch, *Science and Medicine in France: the Emergence of Experimental Physiology, 1790–1855* (Cambridge, MA: Harvard University Press, 1984).
73. Pierre Sue, *Éloge historique de Marie-Français-Xavier Bichat* (Paris: Delance, 1803); and *Notice sur Marie-François-Xavier Bichat* (Paris: Giguet et Michaud, 1802).
74. Henri-Marie Husson, *Notice historique sur la vie et les travaux de Marie-Fr.-Xav. Bichat* (Paris: Stoupe, 1802), pp. 20–1; and E.-F. Miel, *Essai sur le Salon de 1817* (Paris: Delaunay, 1817), p. 117. On this image, see Robert Rosenblum, *Transformations in Late Eighteenth Century Art* (Princeton, NJ: Princeton University Press, 1967), pp. 38–9.
75. Esprit-Antoine Gibelin, 'Mémoire sur la statue antique dénommé le Gladiateur de Borghèse,' *Mémoires de l'Institut national des sciences et arts*: 3e classe: *Littérature et beaux arts* (Year XI), p. 492.
76. Jean-Galbert Salvage, *Anatomie du gladiateur combattant, applicable aux beaux arts* (Paris: chez l'auteur, 1812).
77. See Philippe Sénéchal, 'L'*Anatomie du Gladiateur combattant* de Jean-Galbert Salvage: science et art à Paris sous l'Empire,' in *Curiosité: études d'histoire de l'art*, eds Olivier Bonfait, Véronique Gerald Powell and Philippe Sénéchal (Paris: Flammarion, 1998), pp. 119–228; and Meredith Shedd, 'Prometheus the Primeval Sculptor: Archaeology and Anatomy in Emeric-David's *Recherches sur l'art statuaire*,' *Zeitschrift für Kunstgeschichte*, 1 (1991): 81–106.
78. Archives de l'Institut, 3A4, séance publique du 15 vendémaire, an X.

3
Making Frenchmen into Warriors: Martial Masculinity in Napoleonic France

Michael J. Hughes

In September 1808, the soldiers of the victorious Grande Armée attended a banquet in Paris held in their honor. The banquet was part of a series of celebrations that had been organized by the Imperial government and Napoleon Bonaparte himself. The army was marching from Germany to Spain to suppress the rebellion against French rule assisted by the British, and it would be fêted in major cities as it traversed France. Napoleon intended to use the celebrations to reward his soldiers for their past victories and to encourage them to new triumphs. At the banquet in Paris, just as in the banquets held elsewhere, songs were sung to the troops. In the capital, the famous singing and drinking society, the *Caveau moderne*, performed for the army. One of the songs that it sang was entitled, *Aux braves de la Grande Armée*. Like so many Napoleonic military songs, the song expressed admiration for the martial and sexual prowess of French soldiers. It proclaimed, 'For protecting the honor of his name / For doing honor to the taverns / For dancing to the sound of the cannon / For getting their hands on the girls / And then leaving them for their muskets / There is only the French.'[1] In all likelihood, the soldiers present were invited to sing along or joined in on their own. While the song was composed by one of the *Caveau*'s songwriters, it was actually the product of orders issued directly by the Emperor.[2] Moreover, it did more than sing the praises of Napoleon's soldiers; the song also promoted a distinctly martial vision of French manhood.

As the preceding chapters have shown, masculinity in France has frequently been associated with war and the military. In the Old Regime, the image of the aristocratic military hero existed alongside the *honnête homme*, and the cult of the great military man increasingly dominated the later phases of the French Revolution. During these periods, however, discourses that defined manhood in martial terms were often overshadowed by other forms of masculinity. The Napoleonic era witnessed a reversal of this trend. Under Napoleon's rule, the warrior-Frenchman who emerged in *Aux braves de la Grande Armée* became the masculine ideal. The Napoleonic regime and its supporters sought to cultivate a form of manhood that is best described as martial masculinity. Napoleonic martial masculinity presented the French soldier and the martial virtues that he possessed as the epitome of manhood. The attributes ascribed to this masculine archetype included the war-like tendencies traditionally associated with the French aristocracy, the desire for military honor and glory, and devotion to the defense of the *patrie* and its reputation. In official discourse, the Napoleonic soldier was also defined by a virile and aggressive heterosexuality. Napoleon and his supporters promoted this representation of the soldier as a model to which all French males should aspire. In so doing, they sought to militarize masculinity in France and transform all Frenchmen into warriors. The armies of the Consulate and the Empire would become the principal site in which this process was carried out. Martial masculinity, however, was not confined to the military. The Napoleonic regime likewise endeavored to inculcate it in the civilian population.

To claim that the Napoleonic state promoted a martial form of masculinity may seem like a rather banal statement of the obvious. Virtually ever since the coup of 18 Brumaire, Napoleonic France has been portrayed as a militaristic state that glorified war, conquest and the military. The historical literature on the Napoleonic period contains numerous accounts of Napoleon's efforts to spread military values in France.[3] Historians of masculinity likewise acknowledge that the Napoleonic era produced a rise in militarism. Robert A. Nye and George L. Mosse identify the revolutionary and Napoleonic periods as a key stage in the history of masculinity in which the militarization of European manhood took place.[4] They claim that the changes wrought by the French Revolution and the wars it generated led to the extension of the martial values traditionally associated with the aristocracy to all classes of men, and especially to the bourgeoisie. This development resulted in the emergence of a modern masculinity that linked manhood to military service to the nation-state. Since Nye and Mosse focus primarily on developments in the late nineteenth and twentieth centuries, neither actually explains how this process occurred, nor fully explores the contours of the militaristic masculinity constructed during the revolutionary and Napoleonic eras. Karen Hagemann's crucial research on Prussia illustrates the validity of their arguments for masculinity in Germany.[5] The impact of the Napoleonic wars on French masculinity, however, has not received the same attention. The voluminous literature on Napoleonic military history and the military values of the Napoleonic regime does not explicitly address the relationship between war and manhood. Furthermore, the gender historians who have made such essential contributions to our understanding of the French Revolution and the Napoleonic period tend to neglect war and the military. This chapter therefore ventures once more over the well-trodden terrain of Napoleonic warfare and Napoleon's armies. It is a particularly important task because war, the military, and the phenomena associated with them, which one scholar defines as the 'war system', constitute essential sites not only for the construction of masculinity, but for gender identities as a whole.[6]

Soon after Napoleon secured control of the French government in 1799, he began to spread martial virtues in France. A republican general, he was educated in military academies and spent most of his life in the army. He believed that the values that he had acquired in the military were the source of his own accomplishments, and had produced the great military victories of the revolution that allowed France to regain the position of power and grandeur that it lost earlier in the eighteenth century. To further his own ambitions and maintain French dominance in Europe, Napoleon felt that it was necessary to propagate the warrior virtues that resided in the army. He therefore instructed his officials to foster the development of 'the military spirit' in France, and encouraged them to 'do things that inspire heroic sentiments in the nation, in the youth, and in the army'.[7] Napoleon was not alone in the belief that the interests of the nation would be best served in this manner. Others in the political, social, intellectual and military elite, such as Carrion de Nizas, eagerly assisted him. De Nizas was a member of the Tribunate, a political assembly established during the Consulate. Assigned by the government to defend the creation of the Legion of Honor before his fellow tribunes, he implored them, 'Let us watch over and conserve with care this warrior attitude, this spirit of military honor, in which our true grandeur resides . . . All the arts have their excellence and their beauty, without a doubt; but the arts of honor and victory are the true [arts] of the French people.'[8]

Although de Nizas and Napoleon undoubtedly hoped that French women would develop an appreciation for war and help them inspire heroic sentiments in their menfolk and children, the Napoleonic regime was primarily concerned with the military spirit of the male population. Napoleon and his supporters did not think that it would be necessary to teach French men martial virtues. Rather, they intended to nurture the war-like qualities that inhered in them. Napoleon himself believed that French men possessed a natural affinity for war and military service. As he explained in a letter to his minister of the interior, he regarded the military profession as a 'career natural to all Frenchmen.'[9] Such beliefs had deep roots in France. Since the Middle Ages, the French nobility had been defined by its military functions. Over time, these military functions became synonymous with noble masculinity in the figure of the aristocratic military hero. French male aristocrats, and especially the *noblesse d'épée*, were literally considered to have war in their blood. They were believed to inherit the martial traits passed on by their warrior forebears who had ruled and defended France since the time of Clovis.[10] Inside and outside France, French nobles were reputed to be natural warriors who aggressively pursued opportunities to prove their physical courage and military skills.

Admirers and critics of the aristocracy's war-like spirit believed that one of its fundamental sources was an honor code based upon two attributes: honor, and the desire for *gloire*, or glory. Honor constituted the need to be esteemed and respected in the eyes of others, and the yearning for personal distinctions and privileges. Related to honor, glory can be defined as the prestige, fame, or renown acquired through extraordinary actions or achievements. Although both traits remained tied to the individual's reputation, they could be obtained in different ways. Glory could only be derived from exceptional accomplishments whereas honor could be secured through more mundane means such as honest conduct, loyal service to one's superiors, and professional competence. Honor and glory could also be gained through non-military endeavors, including noteworthy displays of intellectual or artistic talents. For the male noble, however, the most coveted forms accrued from feats of arms. Notable demonstrations of martial prowess enhanced individual honor and provided glory to a degree unmatched by any other activity. To prove their aristocratic manhood, French noblemen therefore intrigued for commissions in the army, tried to distinguish themselves in battle, and routinely killed one another in duels.[11]

Honor escaped the confines of the aristocracy in the eighteenth century. After the death of Louis XIV, a group of intellectuals, reformers and social commentators (who Jay Smith refers to as patriot writers) increasingly ascribed honor to all French men. They were part of a movement to create a *patrie* patterned after classical models, and their writings generated a vigorous debate about how a spirit of patriotism should be developed in France. The source of inspiration was the concept of virtue that existed in ancient Greece and Republican Rome, 'a selfless devotion to the political community at large.'[12] However, since virtue seemed incompatible with the French character and monarchy, patriot writers relied on honor, which was considered a truly French sentiment, as a source of patriotism. They proposed that the best means to stimulate devotion to the *patrie* would be to appeal to a pure kind of honor in which the individual would only be esteemed for actions that benefited the public good. While conservatives maintained that only noblemen possessed the honor necessary for genuine patriotism, more and more writers appropriated honor for French men in general. They claimed that honor was not simply a noble trait, but a French one. Such ideas even led reformers to formulate projects in which schools and the army would cultivate the honor of French men for patriotic purposes. They sparked much discussion, but were never put into practice.[13]

In contrast to the royal government, revolutionary politicians made deliberate use of schools and the army to effect a transformation of French men. They employed these institutions, as well as festivals, symbols, and various kinds of propaganda, to promote the virtue that many patriot writers considered ill-suited to France. The most extensive efforts to cultivate virtue took place in the revolutionary armies. Between 1792 and 1794, the French government and political radicals transformed the army into an *école du jacobinisme*. The military culture created by the Jacobin Republic to indoctrinate its citizen-soldiers transferred the martial prowess long associated with the nobleman to the common Frenchman. It portrayed him as a natural soldier whose innate élan and patriotism rendered his attacks, and especially those with cold steel, irresistible.[14]

While the revolutionaries celebrated the martial prowess of the French male, they held more ambivalent views toward traditional military values such as honor and glory.[15] Many revolutionary leaders regarded them with hostility because they were linked to the nobility and violated the principle of equality by creating distinctions between men. Jacobin radicals in particular singled out military honor as a danger to the Republic and sought to purge it from the army. Since honor was believed to encourage the pursuit of personal interests instead of devotion to the common good, politicians such as Robespierre feared that it would produce soldiers who could be used by counter-revolutionary forces to overturn the revolution. Despite the efforts of radicals to eliminate honor, it persisted in the army and re-emerged following the Terror. Under the Directory, republican generals such as Napoleon began to reward soldiers with special, decorated military items known as *Armes d'honneur* that were intended to honor the individual and his accomplishments.[16]

When General Bonaparte became the ruler of France, he restored the warrior virtues of the aristocracy to the army. The changes that he introduced into the military became part of his broader program to inspire heroic sentiments in the French nation. Much like patriot writers and Jacobin radicals, Napoleon recognized the potential of the army to effect far-reaching changes in French society and culture. He and his collaborators, however, possessed far more power and resources than the patriot writers, and more time and greater internal stability than the Jacobins to turn their plans into reality. The means by which the Napoleonic regime would transform the army into a instrument of social engineering was its official military culture. This military culture was a set of ideas and practices employed to directly influence the army. It was intended to produce an army and soldiers that were highly motivated, imbued with the martial virtues cherished by Napoleon and, above all, loyal to the Napoleonic state and its ruler.

The Napoleonic regime assembled its official military culture from numerous components. One of the most important components was written and print media, which included proclamations to the army, orders of the day, and military bulletins. Orders of the day were military orders issued by the army's leadership that were read aloud to the troops. Military bulletins such as the famous *Bulletin de la Grande Armée* were newsletters that provided accounts of Napoleon's military campaigns. As this chapter has already shown, the Napoleonic regime also relied on songs and festivals to shape its soldiery. Songs were sung and distributed to soldiers during fêtes and other special occasions. Soldiers could also buy song-sheets with officially approved military songs from *colporteurs*, or songbooks compiled from such songs. The festivals at which these songs might be sung consisted of the anniversary of the founding of the Republic, Napoleon's birthday and the feast of Saint Napoleon on 15 August, the anniversary of Napoleon's coronation and the battle of Austerlitz, and the birth of Napoleon's heir, the King of Rome. The French government also held celebrations for the army when the Imperial Guard returned to Paris in 1807, during the Grande Armée's march to Spain in 1808, and at the *Champ de Mai* ceremony in 1815. The *Champ de mai* celebration was intended to rally the army to defend Napoleon's recently restored government from the Allies. In these fêtes, French soldiers often received the rewards that formed another element of Napoleonic military culture. An array of rewards was established for the army, ranging from simple words of praise from Napoleon, to battlefield promotions, to titles of nobility, and perhaps the most coveted reward of all, the Legion of Honor. Finally, the Napoleonic regime constructed its military culture through a variety of ceremonies and symbolic activities. French military leaders had their troops build monuments in honor of Napoleon, circulated petitions expressing their support for him, and organized ceremonies that commemorated French military heroes who died in battle. Moreover, Napoleon devoted countless hours to reviewing his soldiers, utilizing such occasions to establish the personal bond with them that would form such a prominent part of his legend.[17]

This military culture formed a vital component of a broader program to cultivate martial masculinity in France. It was designed to transform French men and adolescents into soldiers who embodied the military values and masculinity that the Napoleonic regime sought to disseminate in France. It accomplished this task by pressuring and persuading the hundreds of thousands of men serving in the army to conform to an idealized vision of the French soldier. Then, each year, Napoleon's government sent tens of thousands of new recruits from every part of France to the army. There, they were immersed in Napoleonic military culture, compelled to adapt to its soldier ideal, exposed to veterans who had internalized it, and subjected to the rigors, dangers, and pleasures of military life for several years. Through these measures, Napoleon and his supporters intended to make military service a rite of passage that would develop the natural military qualities of the French male, and forge him into a warrior, the truest and best kind of Frenchman.

The process of militarization did not end with the soldier's return to civilian life. The Napoleonic regime expected him to marry, have children, and become a respected member of his community. In this role, he would transmit his martial virtues to his descendants, the young males of his community, and his fellow citizens. General Junot communicated these expectations to a gathering of soldiers who received the Legion of Honor in 1803. He explained that Napoleon 'hoped that in your old age, seated in the middle of your children, you would tell them how you acquired an *Arme d'honneur*, and how they would be able to win one. He foresaw that a sign of esteem, in perpetuating your memory, would become an obligation for your descendants, and never an exemption from imitating you.'[18] Inspired by their fathers' example, the offspring of soldiers would follow in their footsteps, preserving and perpetually augmenting the *esprit militaire* in France. Napoleon even admitted to his valet that he hoped to make military service synonymous with manhood to the point 'where a girl will not want a boy who has not paid his debt toward the *patrie*.'[19]

The key to the transformation of French manhood was the archetype of the French soldier disseminated in the army. Napoleonic military culture portrayed the ideal French soldier as an enthusiastic warrior who loved to fight, greeted war as an opportunity to distinguish himself, and hoped to win fame and fortune in battle. Military bulletins featured numerous images of this kind. A bulletin from 1807 offers a good example. It described an encounter between Marshal Murat and a colonel of cavalry during the battle of Heilsberg. The latter, his sword 'dripping with blood', exultantly announced to Murat, 'Prince, review my regiment, you will see that there is no soldier whose saber is not like mine.'[20] Similar, though less sanguinary, representations appeared in Napoleonic military songs. In songs, French troops were 'proud children of victory,' whose 'warrior ardor' always 'aspires to some great feat.'[21]

The official military culture of the Consulate and the Empire likewise attributed another characteristic that had belonged to the aristocracy to the Napoleonic soldier: the love of glory. *La gloire* saturated Napoleonic military culture. Its prominence reflected Napoleon's personal vision for the army. On different occasions, he explicitly instructed civilian and military officials to maintain his soldiers' 'love of glory.'[22] These instructions and the interest in glory that persisted among military and civilian elites produced a continuous supply of propaganda materials that emphasized the soldiery's need for glory.[23] Songs described French soldiers as 'daring warriors' who 'only breathe for glory,' and claimed that 'glory is dear / To French soldiers.'[24] The monuments built for and by Napoleon's troops reminded them of the glory they cherished. The 51st regiment of infantry erected a pyramid in its camp near the English Channel that bore a sundial and the inscription, 'every hour of the soldier belongs to glory.'[25] In addition, military glory remained one of the predominant themes in the rhetoric employed in the army. As he distributed the Legion of Honor to his troops, General Marmont told them that those who had not yet received the award would 'one day receive a similar honor.' The only proof that he needed, was their 'love of glory.'[26] Napoleon's famous proclamations to the army breathed the same glory that his troops allegedly did. While the Grande Armée marched to Spain, he issued a proclamation that invoked its soldiers' desire for glory by challenging them to win still more: 'Soldiers, you surpassed the renown of modern armies; but have you equaled the glory of the armies of Rome, who, in the same campaign, triumphed on the Rhine and on the Euphrates, in Illyria and on the Tagus?'[27]

In addition to his obsession with glory, the Napoleonic soldier was defined by his honor. This was another trait that Napoleon wished to develop among his troops. He expressed this goal in deliberations about the creation of the Legion of Honor among his advisors. He countered objections to the award by arguing, 'the French are not changed by ten years of revolution . . . They have only one sentiment: honor; it is therefore necessary to give encouragement to this sentiment; they need distinctions.'[28] To nourish honor in the army, different forms of propaganda presented images of soldiers who were 'moved only by honor,' or who 'honor alone leads to glory,' but rewards were the primary means used to accomplish Napoleon's objective.[29]

The Legion of Honor was the most important of these rewards. Napoleon created the award in 1802 to honor individuals who had rendered exceptional service to the state and the *patrie*. While the Legion was available to civilians, it was conceived mainly as a military reward, and soldiers dominated its membership. Along with a stipend and other privileges, legionnaires received a medal which featured Napoleon's profile, the imperial eagle and the motto, '*Honneur et Patrie.*' Upon admission into the Legion of Honor, members swore an oath of allegiance to Napoleon and the Empire. The Legion formed an essential component of Napoleonic military culture. The distribution of its medals was a noteworthy event in the army, and Napoleon and his military commanders organized special ceremonies to award the decoration. They further enhanced the prestige of the award by presenting accounts of these events in military bulletins and orders of the day, which reached a wider audience than the men who witnessed the ceremonies. In their writings and in awards ceremonies, army leaders highlighted the value of the award for French soldiers and encouraged them to perform feats of arms that would earn it. For example, General Dorsner delivered a speech in the army camps near Brest that proclaimed, 'The glorious institution to which you belong will attest to the great deeds of warriors, the grandeur of the nation and the valor of its chief . . . What Frenchman would not glory in being a Member of the Legion of Honor, of this Legion of brave men that its august founder calls the elite of the nation!'[30]

Dorsner closed his speech by calling upon the troops present to swear the 'sacred words, henceforth inseparable and dear to all French: honor, *patrie*, Napoleon.'[31] In doing so, he revealed a crucial aspect of Napoleonic military culture. Napoleon did attempt to restore honor and glory to the army and French manhood, but the forms that they took resembled the honor espoused by the patriot writers of the eighteenth century. Combining the martial virtues of the Old Regime with the civic virtue of the revolution, the Napoleonic regime harnessed honor and glory to patriotism. The Legion of Honor best exemplifies this trend. The honor that the Legion was intended to encourage, like the honor of the nobleman, was 'the desire and the hope for public esteem.'[32] Yet according to the officials who helped Napoleon establish the Legion, which included generals from the army, Napoleonic honor was a 'republican' or 'national' honor that would inspire Frenchmen to serve the *patrie*.[33] They acknowledged that 'virtue alone is not, for common men, a sufficient reward for virtue,' and therefore contended that it was necessary to offer them incentives to dedicate themselves to the *patrie*.[34] The honor conferred by the Legion of Honor would provide this incentive. In the words of Counselor of State Roederer, the government's spokesman for the institution, through honor ('this passion of the French') the Legion would 'fix the bond that must unite citizens to the *patrie*.'[35] Furthermore, in their efforts to combine honor with virtue, Napoleonic officials ridiculed the selfish, aristocratic 'honor of the court,' and portrayed the honor that the Legion of Honor was designed to nourish, the 'national honor' that 'wishes to be . . . intimately engaged in the public interest,' as pure 'French honor.'[36]

These ideas were not limited to political circles. French military leaders communicated this vision of honor to their troops. In a speech to his soldiers, Marshal Davout explained that Napoleon created the Legion of Honor 'to bind more intimately to the *patrie* all of the soldiers and citizens who merited this honorable reward.' He continued, proclaiming that true honor would only be obtained through actions that benefited the *patrie*: 'Under the reign of Napoleon, there will be no other titles except those from personal services rendered to the *patrie*, no other source of renown than that of national gratitude, and no other distinction than that of honor. . . .'[37] Over time, the Legion of Honor, like the honors dispensed by the Bourbon monarchy, was increasingly associated with personal service to Napoleon and his dynasty rather than devotion to the *patrie*, but for most of the Napoleonic era, it promoted a virtuous honor.[38]

Along with tying honor to virtue, the Napoleonic regime made more direct appeals to the army's patriotism. Devotion to the *patrie*, and Napoleon, who represented it, defined the ideal soldier as much as his love of war, glory, and honor. Representations of patriotic soldiers emerged in numerous facets of Napoleonic military culture. Portraying Napoleon's soldiers as devoted servants of the nation, a song honoring the Imperial Guard claimed that 'Each friend of the *patrie* / Embraces its defenders.'[39] The speeches given to the army in the military celebrations in 1808 also emphasized that good French soldiers gladly honored their obligations to the *patrie*. In Paris, the Prefect of the Department of the Seine greeted Marshal Victor's troops by thanking them for the 'services that you have rendered to the *patrie*' and praised them for their 'zeal for the national cause.'[40] As Napoleon's government became increasingly monarchical in the later years of the Empire, allusions to political entities that linked Napoleon to the revolution, like the *patrie*, the nation, and the French people became rare.[41] They never completely disappeared, however, and resurfaced with renewed intensity during the Hundred Days. On the eve of Waterloo, a proclamation by Napoleon invoked the willingness of the French soldier to sacrifice himself for the nation. It promised that with a victory, 'the rights, honor and welfare of the *patrie* will be reconquered. For every Frenchman who has courage, the moment has come to conquer or perish!'[42]

As this proclamation indicates, Napoleonic soldiers not only protected the physical existence of the *patrie*, they also defended its reputation. The French nation resembled its soldiers. In the official military culture of the Consulate and the Empire, France emerged as a warrior nation characterized by its resolve to maintain its prominence and prestige in Europe, and its need to increase its honor and glory through demonstrations of military prowess. Through their proclamations, orders of the day, and bulletins, Napoleon and French military leaders explained that the Empire's wars were necessary to defend the reputation and position that France had acquired during the revolution. It had become the 'Grande Nation,' the dominant power in Europe, and its people the 'First people of the world.'[43] Napoleon could not allow France to be defeated by the Allies, or accede to their conditions for peace because they would compel the French to relinquish these titles, and humiliate the Great Nation. An Allied triumph, declared a bulletin in 1805, would 'dishonor France, make it submit to the yoke of England, make it abandon Belgium, and force the Emperor to hand his crown of iron [of the Kingdom of Italy] to the degenerate race of the Kings of Sardinia.'[44] Since the loss of primacy and reputation constituted the greatest threat to the nation, the Napoleonic regime insisted that France needed to avenge insults to its national honor through warfare and secure its national glory through new military triumphs. These themes dominated Napoleon's initial proclamation for the Russian campaign of 1812. War was imperative because Russia's behavior 'places us between dishonor and war: the choice cannot be doubtful . . . let us take the war into her territory. The second war of Poland will be glorious to French arms like the first.'[45] As the soldiers of the warrior nation, Napoleon's troops were repeatedly reminded that it was their duty to maintain the honor and glory of France. According to Napoleon's proclamations, they were the 'worthy defenders of the honor of my crown and the glory of the Great People,' who were willing to sacrifice their lives 'against those who would attack our honor.'[46]

Napoleon's soldiers were not only heroes who defended the honor of France; they were also 'young heroes . . . in bed.'[47] The most neglected aspects of Napoleonic military culture are its intensely sexual content and highly gendered imagery. One of the ways that the Napoleonic regime encouraged the men in the army to conform to its soldier model was to link its attributes to French masculinity. Numerous types of Napoleonic propaganda identified the soldier's martial virtues with manliness, but none more so than songs. Gender discourses constituted one of the dominant features of these songs, and they employed representations of both masculinity and femininity to reinforce the warlike character of French manhood. Echoing ideas about French men that existed among the Napoleonic elite, songs such as *Ronde adressée à la Grande Armée, à son passage à Paris*, celebrated the military qualities of the French male: 'Each of you, good-hearted fellow [*franc luron*], / loves the table and war, / And runs to the sound of the cannon / Like he runs to the sound of the glass.'[48] Napoleonic songs likewise portrayed the love of glory and patriotism as essential elements of French masculinity. A song about a conscript departing for the Grande Armée in 1805 illustrates this tendency. In it, a recruit bids farewell to his lover, justifying his departure by invoking his manly responsibilities:

> Rose, believe me, dry your tears;
> In the camps I will face the risks,
> Because a God protects our arms;
> Moreover, a Frenchman each day

> For glory risks his life:
> Before being born for love
> He was born for his *patrie*.[49]

The image of the despairing woman left behind that emerges in this song was a common theme in Napoleonic songs. Numerous songs contained scenes in which men tried to console tearful lovers as they eagerly marched off to war. Napoleon's soldiers, however, did not only leave distressed mistresses in their wake. One of the songs sung during the celebrations for the Imperial Guard in 1807 referred to the sadness of wives and mothers whose husbands and sons left for the army. This song declared that the Frenchman's first step in his military career was 'triumphing' over the tears of such women.[50]

These representations of women were particularly important because they reinforced the martial character of French masculinity. The presentation of the military ardor that typified the response of men to war, in tandem with the sadness and fear that it generated in women, expressed an implicit comparison between the genders. Whereas war elicited despair and anxiety in women, men embraced the opportunities and obligations that it provided. War and the army were portrayed as the natural element for the masculine, allowing men to achieve their full potential. The implications of this comparison would have been clear to soldiers and civilians in Napoleonic France. Masculinity entailed a love of combat, the desire for glory and an eagerness to answer the call of the *patrie*. On the other hand, the absence of military qualities was associated with femininity. Furthermore, the faint-hearted women of Napoleonic songs accentuated the warlike tendencies of the Frenchman by implying that French women required men to protect them.

In reality, women may have needed protection *from* Napoleon's soldiers, for songs encouraged them to pursue sex as vigorously as they pursued military victories. Songs from the Consulate and the Empire repeatedly mentioned and praised the sexual exploits of French troops, portraying aggressive heterosexuality as another attribute of the Napoleonic soldier. Many songs proposed that military service enhanced the sex appeal of French men. This allure would then lead to sexual encounters and cause women to become the lovers and wives of French soldiers when they returned home. One song expressed this message to the troops of the Grande Armée by asking them, 'What fort has resisted you? What beauty resists you?' Another told them, 'When these foreign hordes will have perished under your blows, you will come to your mistresses to offer sweeter combats.'[51] Women were not only charmed by Napoleon's soldiers, however. As these songs suggest, they were also conquered. A song for the troops marching to Spain proudly declared, 'Defying all resistance, / you know how in your combats / to conquer and populate states.'[52] Images of the French soldier's sexual conquests appear almost as frequently as their military conquests in songs, highlighting the importance of sex for the soldier. Unfortunately, since sex was such a necessity, Consular and Imperial songs sometimes endorsed the use of force to obtain it. In what can only be characterized as a rape fantasy, the song *Ran plan plan tambour battant, chanson de caserne* describes a sexual encounter in Pomerania in which a French soldier drags a scared young girl off into the woods and begins to have sex with her. The girl soon overcomes her inhibitions, and even begs the soldier for another 'screw': ' "You beat the retreat too soon", / she said to me sighing ... / "Enemy that I love so much, / make another drum roll".' The soldier, of course, obliged.[53]

Although it may be shocking to modern sensibilities, such men were celebrated as heroes. Through its official military culture, the Napoleonic regime portrayed the Napoleonic soldier and the qualities that he possessed as the masculine ideal. It continuously presented the French soldier – the warrior who prized war, valued honor and military glory, dedicated himself to his *patrie* and its honor, and displayed his sexual virility – as the best kind of Frenchman. Speeches, songs, bulletins, orders of the day, and proclamations acclaimed Napoleon's soldiers as 'heroes,' the 'honor of France,' the 'elite of the nation,' and the 'intrepid elite of the French.'[54] Napoleon even informed his troops after the victorious campaign of 1805, 'my people will treat with you as it should toward its heroes and its defenders.'[55] The military festivals which were designed to accomplish this goal likewise held up the soldier as an object of reverence. In the celebrations organized in 1808, officials representing the city of Paris honored the troops of the Grande Armée with a speech that declared that 'it is for the citizens, it is fitting for us to celebrate' the virtues of France's soldiers and 'it is important for us to show them as an example to our children who will pass into your ranks.'[56] Such discourses took place in an atmosphere of cheering crowds, orchestras playing military music, and a profusion of military trophies decorated with images and inscriptions praising the army, all of which reminded the men in the ranks of the exalted position of the soldier in French culture and society.[57] Moreover, members of the military were the principal recipients of the two most prestigious awards granted by the Napoleonic state: the Legion of Honor and titles of Imperial nobility.[58]

Much like the gendered images in military songs, the identification of the soldier as the epitome of French manhood encouraged the men serving in the army to adopt the martial attributes associated with the soldier archetype and become the warriors that the Napoleonic regime strove to produce. By 1815, approximately 1,660,000 Frenchmen served in Napoleon's armies, making the French army and Napoleonic military culture powerful instruments for the transformation of masculinity.[59] As Napoleon and his supporters planned, the soldiers who survived their military service could and did carry their martial values and masculinity into the civilian population. However, the Napoleonic regime also attempted to make Frenchmen into warriors through other means. It relied on many of the same propaganda measures used in the army to shape civilian public opinion. Priests read military bulletins from the pulpit, and government newspapers like the *Moniteur universel* published them and Napoleon's proclamations to the army. Napoleonic newspapers also contained detailed accounts of the celebrations organized for the army, which multitudes of civilians all over France attended. Military songs, including those sung to soldiers at festivals, were both handed out to civilians and made available for sale to them.[60] In addition, Napoleon's government distributed propaganda pamphlets to facilitate conscription which contained the heroic depictions of the French soldier circulating in its official military culture. Moreover, it encouraged the production of artwork, popular prints, and plays that contained similar imagery. While civilian men were not exposed to the pressures to conform to the soldier archetype that existed in the army, they were nevertheless constantly encouraged to venerate and imitate the warriors who appeared in Consular and Imperial propaganda.[61]

In its attempts to construct a martial masculinity in France, the Napoleonic regime endeavored to transfer the military values that were traditionally associated with the French aristocracy to all men. It assumed that all males in France, regardless of birth, occupation, or social status, were natural warriors, and encouraged them to imitate the soldiers who appeared in the army's official military culture and in government propaganda. The masculine ideal of Consular and Imperial France also combined the nobleman's warlike tendencies and his need for honor and glory with the patriotism of eighteenth-century reformers and the revolutionaries. To this mixture, it added a predatory heterosexuality. This combination made martial masculinity a particularly potent tool. It gave Napoleon and his supporters a powerful source of military motivation for the army, an invaluable resource for mobilizing the French population in support of Napoleon's wars, and a means to uphold the intensely patriarchal social and political order established by Napoleon. In addition, it allowed the Napoleonic regime to continue the nation-building process that began under the Republic, for it communicated its vision of a hyper-masculine warrior nation composed of a warlike citizenry to every corner of France for more than a decade.[62] Voltaire famously quipped that eighteenth-century Prussia was an army with a state. Had Napoleon won the Napoleonic wars, the comment might equally have applied to France. Even with Napoleon's defeat, Napoleonic martial masculinity lived on. The swaggering, grumbling Napoleonic soldier, or *grognard*, remained a powerful masculine icon throughout the nineteenth century, gaining new life during the July Monarchy and Second Empire. Eventually, he would even serve as a vehicle for the extreme nationalism identified with the mythological Nicolas Chauvin, a Napoleonic soldier who would have the dubious distinction of being immortalized in the word chauvinism.[63]

Notes

1. *Hommage du caveau moderne à la Grande Armée, ou chansons et couplets chantés à Tivoli pendant les Diners donnés par la ville de Paris aux Braves qui ont traversé cette*

64   *French Masculinities*

capitale dans le courant de Septembre 1808 (Paris: Imprimerie de Brasseur Aîné, 1808), p. 12.

2. Napoleon Bonaparte, *Correspondance de Napoléon Ier publiée par ordre de l'Empereur Napoléon III*, 32 vols (Paris, 1858–1869), piece number [hereafter no.] 14331, 17: 518–19; no. 14291, 17: 486–7.
3. See especially Jean-Paul Bertaud, 'Napoleon's Officers,' *Past and Present*, 112 (August 1986): 91–111; idem., *Guerre et société en France de Louis XIV à Napoléon Ier* (Paris: Armand Colin, 1998), pp. 52–65, 135–83; Annie Jourdan, *Napoléon: héros, imperator, mécène* (Paris: Aubier, 1998); Alan Forrest, 'The Military Culture of Napoleonic France,' in Philip G. Dwyer (ed.), *Napoleon and Europe* (Harlow: Pearson Education, 2001), pp. 43–59.
4. Robert A. Nye, *Masculinity and Male Codes of Honor in Modern France* (Berkeley: University of California Press, 1993); George L. Mosse, *The Image of Man: the Creation of Modern Masculinity* (New York: Oxford University Press, 1996).
5. Karen Hagemann, *'Mannlicher Muth und Teutsche Ehre': Nation, Militär und Geschlecht zur Zeit der Antinapoleonischen Kriege Preußens* (Paderborn: Ferdinand Schöningh, 2002); idem., 'German Heroes: the Cult of the Death for the Fatherland in Nineteenth-century Germany,' in Stefan Dudink, Karen Hagemann, and John Tosh (eds), *Masculinities in Politics and War: Gendering Modern History* (Manchester: Manchester University Press, 2004), pp. 116–34.
6. For a definition of the 'war system' and its relationship to gender, see Joshua S. Goldstein, *War and Gender: How Gender Shapes the War System and Vice Versa* (Cambridge: Cambridge University Press, 2001). For the role of war in the construction of gender identities, see Graham Dawson, *Soldier Heroes: British Adventure, Empire and the Imagining of Masculinities* (London and New York: Routledge, 1994); John A. Lynn, 'The Embattled Future of Academic Military History,' *Journal of Military History*, 61 (October 1997): 777–89; Leo Braudy, *From Chivalry to Terrorism: War and the Changing Nature of Masculinity* (New York: Alfred A. Knopf, 2003); Dudink, Hagemann, and Tosh (eds), *Masculinities in Politics and War*.
7. Napoleon, *Correspondance*, no. 9832, 12: 55; no. 13567, 16: 335; no. 11644, 14: 203.
8. *Gazette nationale ou le Moniteur universel précédé d'une introduction historique remontant au 5 mai 1789, contenant un abrégé des anciens États-généraux des assemblées des notables et des principaux événemens qui ont amené la révolution* (hereafter *Moniteur*) (Paris: Chez Selier, 1802–1815): no. 240, 30 floréal, an 10 (20 May 1802).
9. Napoleon, *Correspondance*, no. 10876, 13: 259.
10. Nye, *Masculinity and Male Codes of Honor*, pp. 15–30.
11. Ibid., pp. 15–30; John A. Lynn, 'Toward an Army of Honor: the Moral Evolution of the French Army, 1789–1815,' *French Historical Studies*, 16(1) (Spring 1989): 152–82; idem., *Giant of the Grand Siècle: the French Army, 1610–1715* (Cambridge: Cambridge University Press, 1997), pp. 248–318; Guy Rowlands, *The Dynastic State and the Army under Louis XIV: Royal Service and Private Interest, 1661–1701* (Cambridge: Cambridge University Press, 2002), pp. 156–8, 222–5, 318–35; Jay M. Smith, *Nobility Reimagined: the Patriotic Nation in Eighteenth-century France* (Ithaca, NY: Cornell University Press, 2005).
12. Smith, *Nobility Reimagined*, p. 28.
13. For the transformation of honor, see ibid.
14. Jean-Paul Bertaud, *La Révolution armée: Les soldats-citoyens et la Révolution français* (Paris: Editions Robert Lafont, 1979), pp. 109–229; John A. Lynn, *The Bayonets of the Republic: Motivation and Tactics in the Army of Revolutionary France, 1791–1794* (1984; Boulder, CO: Westview 1996), pp. 119–82; idem., 'Toward an Army of Honor';

Alan Forrest, *The Soldiers of the French Revolution* (Durham, NC: Duke University Press, 1990), pp. 89–124.

15. Lynn, 'Toward an Army of Honor,' pp. 154–5.
16. L. Bonneville de Marsangy, *La Légion d'Honneur 1802–1900* (Paris: Librairie Renouard, 1907), pp. 14–15; Lynn, 'Toward an Army of Honor', pp. 168–9.
17. Michael J. Hughes, ' "Vive la République!, Vive l'Empereur!": Military Culture and Motivation in the Armies of Napoleon, 1803–1808' (PhD diss., University of Illinois at Urbana-Champaign, 2005); Jean Morvan, *Le soldat impérial (1800–1814)*, 2 vols (1904; repr. Paris: Librairie Historique F. Teissèdre, 1999), 2: pp. 474–520; Maurice Choury, *Les grognards et Napoléon* (Paris: Librairie Académique Perrin, 1968); J. Lucas-Dubreton, *Les soldats de Napoléon* (Paris: Librairie Jules Tallandier, 1977); John R. Elting, *Swords around a Throne: Napoleon's Grande Armée* (New York: The Free Press, 1988; repr. New York: Da Capo Press, 1997), pp. 589–603; Lynn, 'Toward an Army of Honor'; Alan Forrest, *Napoleon's Men: the Soldiers of the Revolution and Empire* (London, New York: Hambledon and London, 2002), pp. 53–78.
18. *Moniteur*, no. 12, 12 vendémiaire, an 12 (5 October 1803).
19. Louis Joseph, Comte Marchand, *Mémoires de Marchand, premier valet de chambre et exécuteur testamentaire de l'Empereur, publiée d'après le manuscrit original*, ed. Jean Bourguignon, 2 vols (Paris: Plon, n.d.), 1: p. 98, quoted in Gérard de Puymège, *Chauvin, Le Soldat-Laboureur: Contribution à l'étude des nationalismes* (Paris: Éditions Gallimard, 1993), p. 39.
20. Napoleon, *Correspondance*, no. 12793, 15: 356.
21. *Hommage du caveau moderne*, pp. 23, 18.
22. Napoleon, *Correspondance*, no. 11855, 14: 324; no. 14291, 17: 486.
23. Steven Englund, *Napoleon: a Political Life* (Cambridge, MA: Harvard University Press, 2004), pp. 142–50, 243–69, 332–9.
24. Pierre François Palloy, 'Le banquet de famille,' in *Le troubador des armées françaises, ou les chants de la victoire aux armées françaises* (Paris: Pelletier, n.d.), p. 33.
25. *Moniteur*, no. 333, 8 fructidor, an 12 (26 August 1804).
26. Order of the day, Camp of Utrecht, 23 fructidor, an 12 (10 September 1804), C^1 19, Service historique de l'armée de Terre, Archives de guerre, Château de Vincennes, Vincennes (hereafter AG).
27. Napoleon, *Correspondance*, no. 14338, 17: 521.
28. Antoine-Claire, Comte Thibaudeau, *Mémoires sur le Consulat. 1799 à 1804. Par un ancien conseiller d'état* (Paris: Chez Ponthieu et Cie, Libraires, 1827), p. 83.
29. Napoleon, *Correspondance*, no. 11737, 14: 263; *Le chansonnier de la Grande Armée, ou choix de chansons militaires, dédié aux braves, (C'est-à-dire à tous les Soldats Français)* (Paris: Chez Marchand, 1809), p. 36.
30. General Donzelot to Marshal Augereau, Brest, 2 vendémiaire, an 13 (24 September 1804), C^1 19, AG.
31. Ibid.
32. See the speech by General Mathieu Dumas in *Moniteur*, no. 241, 1 prairial, an 10 (21 May 1802).
33. See the speech by Carrion de Nizas in ibid., no. 240, 30 floréal, an 10 (20 May 1802); and by Pierre Louis Roederer in ibid., no. 241, 1 prairial, an 10 (21 May 1802).
34. See the speech by General Dumas in ibid.
35. See the speech by Roederer in ibid.
36. Ibid.
37. Marshal Davout to the Minister of War, 8 thermidor, an 12 (27 July 1804), Ostende, I^1 83, AG.

38. See, for example, the new oath for the Legion of Honor in 1811, in Jean Daniel, *La Légion d'Honneur: Histoire et organisation de l'ordre national* (Paris: Éditions André Bonne, 1948), p. 184.
39. Pierre François Palloy, 'Hommage à la Garde Impérial, A son entrée triomphale à Paris, le 25 Novembre 1807,' in *Le troubador des armées françaises.*
40. *Moniteur*, no. 267, 23 September 1808.
41. Lynn, 'Toward an Army of Honor'; Forrest, *Napoleon's Men*, pp. 53–78.
42. Napoleon Bonaparte, *Proclamations, ordres du jour, et bulletins de la Grande Armée*, ed. Jean Tulard (Paris: Union générale d'éditions, 1964), p. 174.
43. General Vandamme to the general officers and to all of the grades of the 2nd Division, Landsberg, 20 vendémiaire, an 14 (12 October 1805), C² 5, AG; Proclamation, Schonbrunn, 6 nivôse, an 14 (25 December 1805), C² 11, AG.
44. Napoleon, *Correspondance*, no. 9550, 11: 464.
45. Napoleon, *Proclamations, ordres du jour, et bulletins*, 129.
46. Proclamation of the Emperor and King, Potsdam, 26 October 1806, C² 11, AG; Proclamation, Schonbronn, 6 nivôse, an 14 (25 December 1805), C² 11, AG.
47. *Hommage du caveau moderne*, p. 23.
48. Ibid., p. 40.
49. *Le chansonnier de la Grande Armée*, p. 4.
50. *Moniteur*, no. 331, 27 novembre 1807.
51. *Hommage du caveau moderne*, pp. 40, 30.
52. Ibid., p. 44.
53. Ibid., pp. 96–7.
54. See the speech given to General Marchand's troops in *Moniteur*, no. 273, 29 September 1808; see also the speech given to the Imperial Guard in ibid., no. 330, 26 November 1807; General Vandamme to the general officers and to all of the grades of the 2nd Division, Landsberg, 20 vendémiaire, an 14 (12 October 1805), C² 5, AG; see the 'chant guerrier improvisée par M.M. Arnault et Méhul,' in *Moniteur*, no. 267, 23 September 1808.
55. Proclamation, Schonbronn, 6 nivôse, an 14 (25 December 1805), C² 11, AG.
56. See the speech to Victor's troops in *Moniteur*, no. 267, 23 September 1808.
57. Hughes, ' "Vive la République!, Vive l'Empereur!" ' pp. 107–9, 144–64.
58. Daniel, *La Légion d'Honneur*, pp. 113–20; Natalie Petiteau, *Élites et mobilités: la noblesse d'Empire au XIXe siècle (1808–1914)* (Paris: La Boutique de l'Histoire, 1997), p. 458.
59. Natalie Petiteau, *Lendemains d'empire: les soldats de Napoléon dans la France du XIXe siècle* (Paris: Boutique de l'Histoire, 2003), p. 39.
60. Hughes, ' "Vive la République!, Vive l'Empereur!",' pp. 187–96.
61. Robert B. Holtman, *Napoleonic Propaganda* (Baton Rouge: Louisiana State University Press, 1950); Bertaud, *Guerre et société en France*, pp. 52–65, 135–83; Forrest, 'The Military Culture of Napoleonic France,' pp. 43–59.
62. For nation-building during the revolution, see David A. Bell, *The Cult of the Nation in France: Inventing Nationalism, 1680–1800* (Cambridge, MA: Harvard University Press, 2001).
63. De Puymège, *Chauvin, Le Soldat-Laboureur*; David M. Hopkin, *Soldier and Peasant in French Popular Culture, 1766–1870* (Rochester, NY: The Boydell Press for the Royal Historical Society, 2003), pp. 215–352.

4
Neighborhood Boys and Men: the Changing Spaces of Masculine Identity in France, 1848–71

Bertrand Taithe

The translation of Eugen Weber's *Peasants into Frenchmen* as *La fin des terroirs* removed the gendered undertone of the original title but introduced in its stead a sense of place which was not clear in the original wording.[1] The relationship between place and masculine identity is one of the recurrent issues of nineteenth-century explorations of masculinity in its broader social and cultural implications. The sense of place which relates to the locality and local customs as well as to a sense of belonging in the social hierarchy determined how gender identity might be performed in a mostly rural country. The boundaries of the locality affected how male sociability could develop and how identity and masculine deportment might become almost synonymous. In a country marked by extreme regional diversity, including linguistic and geographical differences, French men were primarily regional men. They were perceived as determined by local racial attributes and social customs but also affected by climatic or even telluric influences. This geographical determinism evolved from an impressionistic sentiment into a science which retains its hold over French self-perception to this day.[2]

In Weber's argument the modernizing move towards a national cultural space gradually eroded these differences and eased the birth of a national sense of identity, implicitly a masculine one, through a long yet mostly smooth process led from above but operating through structural homogenization.

While it is not the purpose of this chapter to engage with this modernization narrative, a gendered perspective on these differences highlights the complexity of any abstract sense of identity such as national identity.[3] Regional determinism affected not only the stability of the national category of the 'Frenchman', but also the viability of a polity based on universal *male* suffrage.[4] Beyond the regionalist perspectives which still dominated any form of detailed political or social analysis in the nineteenth century, a number of anxieties remained about the discrepancies (whether physical or moral) between the regions and the likelihood that any genuine assimilation of all the positive strands could be accomplished in any form of homogeneous social organization.[5] Building on Abbé Grégoire's alarmed awareness of cultural differences, education programs from the 1830s onwards set themselves the task of educating and forming worthy French men. Often in opposition to local mores and vernacular idioms of masculinity, they proposed different approaches to masculine role models. Through education a 'rough' rural boy might be transformed into a more polite man and, depending on his aptitude, attain a position in society matching his '*capacités*.' Beyond regional or local variations, French masculine roles were further divided along certain cultural binaries, especially, for example, bourgeois/bohemians, city dwellers/rural folk, and boyhood/manhood. In spite of these binaries, none of these conflicting subcategories were in themselves stable and their boundaries were porous.

There were many potential pitfalls in this quest for a unitary French masculine identity, the main one being that such a generalized sense of manhood – free of original corruption and uprooted from any narrow sense of locality – did not exist anywhere and would never be found except in myths of the bourgeoisie or aristocracy (which often transcended the national). Even the local might break down to reveal further parochial perspectives: in the countryside local differences extended down to the hamlet, while in cities these variations were reducible to the neighborhood. Much recent historiography has particularly emphasized how individuals identified with the narrow circles that circumscribed their abodes. Yet, this strong sense of place could also be a weakness.[6] For instance, the psychiatric disease known as 'nostalgia' represented a key challenge to the displacement of men across space, in particular in the colonial enterprise. If nineteenth-century society offered a number of bourgeois sites of sociability which might counteract the dangers of immaturity or cocoon the displaced in a masculine way, these forms of sociability (clubs, Masonic lodges, National Guard units) mostly remained elitist and emphasized the combination of education and wealth. For those lacking wealth, social or cultural capital these sites often remained unattainable, and their lower-class ersatz, the café or political groups, offered more unstable homosocial spaces and often riotous transitions. For the poor, the rites of passage between boyhood and manhood could take place in dangerous settings. Working-class male groups had their own codes of masculinity which made lesser demands on costly appearances while often remaining as exclusive as their bourgeois counterparts. Rural origins allied to their professions constituted the identity of workers and required the performance of specific manly acts.[7]

Among the more socially mobile educated youth, incomplete access to cultural and social capital presented the danger of falling between two classes and of being denied manly attributes. In large urban centers, the Bohemians, usually provincials in danger of being *déclassé*, presented an attractive countermodel of masculinity based around dynamic notions of creativity, youth and even revolutionary enthusiasm. Yet even Bohemians, students or the educated underclass had their own quarters and limited horizons beyond which they seldom ventured.

This chapter will explore these issues by considering in turn the question of the sense of place and its psycho-geographical meanings as exemplified in the psychiatric disease of nostalgia. If Frenchmen remained, almost pathologically, the men of their native locality, they nevertheless increasingly congregated in urban centers, often remote from their origins. Clubs and homosocial groups sought to address the transitions from rural to urban, from boyhood to manhood, far from the original context of their members. These responses were varied, and French masculinity took different forms from class to class and place to place. Ultimately these real divisions in the habitus of masculinity undermined any national generalization produced in large cities, particularly Paris. Over the period, 1848–70, the politics of class and revolutionary solidarities found gendered expressions in the organization of manly displays of strength, notably through the National Guard. Yet these gendered class differences were themselves fractured by the question of origins, and Martin Nadaud gives a good example of how working-class men opposed each other in ritualized manners.[8] Finally the defeat of 1870 and the subsequent civil war of 1871 further highlighted the weakness of an abstract category of men which denied the divided realities of French masculinity.

The province of immature men

In French culture, being 'provincial' was and remains the attribute of the lesser educated. Yet the notion of the province was highly abstract, since it related to large geographical entities, such as Corsica or Limousin or departmental identities that gradually coalesced after the major reorganization of the French state during the revolutionary years. Small as a region could be, the notorious *esprit de clocher* described by Ted Margadant and Alain Corbin, related to ever narrower spheres, usually those of a village, a small town, and occasionally a 'canton.'[9] As Corbin points out, this geographical unit was literally a space of sounds, a sense of place limited in space by familiar noises. The church bells that were reconditioned after the revolution marked the local time. The rituals of the parish – sociable gatherings with peers met in the local school, especially after the 1830s social celebrations and common work, after 1848 the electoral rituals which could emphasize the sense of belonging to a group of citizens, and annual village fêtes – marked a familiar landscape of childhood which could contain an entire life. While some disagree about the extent of the closed nature of French rural life or peasant identity, there is evidence that much of France remained relatively impervious to national events or showed long-lasting regional variations.[10] Within the rural setting, rites of masculinity varied according to local traditions, and from the mid-nineteenth century onwards they were studied with increasing precision by folklorists who tended to write down and solidify customs that were in reality often more fluid. By the mid-nineteenth century, the predominantly male riotous charivaris of the *Ancien Régime* were usually domesticated into more festive modes. Festive violence only occasionally erupted as spectacularly as in the 'village of cannibals' when a local notable was murdered by the men of the village who associated him with the Prussian invasion.[11] Nevertheless, clog dancing, performance at the harvest, and occasional demonstrations of strength all functioned as complex rites of passage as well as rituals of seduction.

In a crowded rural environment (French rural densities reached their apex in the mid-nineteenth century) boys could remain boys for their entire lives if they could not find the means of sustaining a family. In some complex but impoverished societies, it was not unusual for a brother to remain single and to spend his life as a farm boy working on his elder brother's land. Manhood and financial autonomy had become more closely associated in the postfeudal rural landscape composed largely of small rural holdings. Farm hands and long-term servants who did not settle were forever the '*garçons de ferme*,' that is, incomplete men.

The sexual tensions of enforced celibacy as well as the harsh economic fate of rural men were the stuff of a range of telling fictional accounts. French romantics, such as George Sand, attempted to idealize French rural menfolk, and this imagery was used particularly stridently in 1848 when they became included in the political culture.[12] Yet this idealism never entirely attenuated the harsh images of life on the breadline or the occasional accounts of sexual violence in the countryside. At the end of the Second Empire and in the early Third Republic, naturalists such as Émile Zola or Guy de Maupassant could exploit to better effect the difficult situation of men on the margins of propertied society.[13]

The binary representation of archaism and modernity arose particularly during the Second Republic (1848–51) and Second Empire (1851–70), when technocratic ideals were more forcefully deployed. The enforced modernization of 'insalubrious swamps' (such as the Landes region in the south-west of France) was accompanied by a constant denunciation of the degrading conditions of life in the countryside, where men were portrayed as living barely better than the beasts who often shared their basic accommodation. As opposed to the idealized rustic incarnation of French manhood, peasants were more often portrayed with both feet stuck in manure. While the myth of the peasant soldier, simple, earthy and upright, was occasionally evoked in the town, in the countryside, conscription was perceived less as a test of aptitude (*bon pour le service*) than as a calamity.[14] Throughout the mid-nineteenth century, the French state used a lottery to select the men serving in its armies. Men who had reached the age of military service age (twenty) were invited to pull a number from a box. The unlucky ones were then enrolled for up to seven years. The ritual of conscription, *la classe*, went well beyond the selection event, and involved manly socialization over the entire year. As David Hopkin points out, this male society presented some appearance of equality before fate, in spite of a generalized system of replacements which enabled the wealthy to buy themselves out of military service.[15] Decorated and covered with ribbons, young men roamed the locality for weeks before the lottery took place. Later on, reunions and mutual societies created enduring networks of sociability organized around this experience of being a twenty-year-old man in the locality. The conscription rituals, which varied from place to place and remain particularly strong in Beaujolais even today (in spite of the abolition of conscription), operated as a bridge between a national process sponsored by the state and localized forms of masculinity.[16]

Yet this masculine pride could be severely tested if one obtained the wrong number. Joining the army between 1848 and 1871 was no sinecure, as the French military engaged in numerous wars from the Crimea, Italy, Mexico and China to the always restless Algerian hinterland. Even though most of these wars were relatively successful, the experience of war was universally miserable for men who had been aggregated in diverse units comprising soldiers from many regions. For military men, the disease of nostalgia, an ailment rife during the Napoleonic wars, could offer a deadly embrace.[17] This disease had a contested and moveable role in the nosology of mania throughout the nineteenth century, but was kept alive in the medical literature through often plagiarized medical theses.[18] The notion of nostalgia was grounded in this French provincial experience.

While the disease has been described as a disease of memory,[19] it was really one that focused on the desire to return, to travel back or even, in some cases, to discover the real *'pays.'*[20] The emphasis on *pays* (close here in meaning to the German *Heimat*) made it a disease of the motherland narrowly defined. In the military, especially among those stationed overseas, the land of nostalgia also remained specific down to a village or a region, and authors took great pains to distinguish patriotism from nostalgia. The former was lofty and conceptual, while the latter remained grounded in childhood experiences, tastes and flavors, magnified by distance into a phantasmagoria. Among urban-dwelling physicians writing on the topic, this lower form of 'childish' attachment to the land explained why Savoyards, Bretons, Flemish and Corsicans seemed to be most sensitive to nostalgia's devastating influence on their constitution.[21]

Doctors persistently denounced the immaturity implicit in nostalgia, and emphasized that the soldier or colonist's complex relationship to the nation had to transcend the *petit pays* to emphasize the *grand pays*.[22] While both locations were remote from the soldier, one was related to 'mature' concepts such as civilization, civility, and hygiene, while the other suggested the petty residue of youth. Some colonials born in Algeria thus explained how they had to return to France in spite of being born and bred in Algeria to cure nostalgia unattached to childhood experiences. As the colonial doctor Saint-Vel put it, the disease slowly sets in even in an attractive environment:

> beautiful as the tropical sky might be it is not always enough to dissipate the regrets and sadness of the immigrant, the first symptoms of nostalgia.

It does not normally appear in the first few weeks, but later, when the curiosity dulls as the body begins languishing. First of all everything is new, unpredictable and alien: the vegetation, the flowers, the fruits, animals, customs and costumes; so the first feeling is often this feeling of ill-defined trouble, mixing pleasure and uneasiness of the unknown. Later the immigrant feels isolated amidst a people with whom he does not share any joys or prejudices, obliged as he is to lead a monotonous and retired life because of the lack of public distractions.[23]

Soon it leads to delusions whereby the body accepted illnesses like the reminders of a former life. The classic case was reported by Ruftz in 1850 when he described a migrant taking pleasure in the cold shivers of malaria, which made him fondly recall cold winters at home.[24]

Epidemic forms affecting the vitality of entire communities could then appear in spite of heterogeneous origins.[25] The effects of the ailment on the digestive system were particularly noticeable together with the inflammation of the brain first noted by Larrey and Pinel during the revolutionary wars. In three or four stages, the disease led to suicide or collapse by nervous exhaustion and decline of the vital system as a whole.[26] In the often repeated words of the naval surgeon Thévenot, who had pessimistic views on French suitability for the colonial task, 'nostalgia is nothing but the expression of a vital need to return home to the soil where one had grown up.'[27] This combination of primitive sensibility and attachment to the land meant that the men displaced by the whim of the state also suffered increased mortality through nostalgia. Considered a malady that mostly afflicted 'primitive' rural men, nostalgia was thus said to have decimated the Arabs who had been removed from Muslim lands.[28] Even though medical experts predicted that the Communards deported to New Caledonia would be immune – 'these criminals who do not believe in anything and who have no homeland, religion or families'[29] and might, paradoxically, be therefore ideal material for colonization – the deported perished in great numbers due to nostalgia.[30] This medical typology did not explain everything. Other explanations existed. Fromentin, like many Orientalist painters after him, blamed nostalgia on the soldiers' lack of aesthetic sensibility when faced with the 'radiant immobility of the Sahara.'[31]

At a fundamental level, these 'immature' men needed their own locality and childhood peers in order to behave like men. Provincial identities framed the range of masculine cultural responses. Metropolitan critiques of country men often targeted the more 'backward' provinces. In the national press Bretons were routinely described as primitive and violent, while Corsicans were routinely denounced for their excessive sense of honor and their customary use of weapons in brawls or honor killings.[32] Yet all of these stereotypes were reversible and prone to counter-generalizations: the Corsicans were thus allegedly predisposed by their land to 'male virtues' that made them well-suited for state or military service.[33] These stereotypes were made particularly salient in 1870–71 when the hastily mobilized provincial armies, organized in regional units, reinforced the defense of Paris.[34] The Bretons, isolated by their linguistic inaptitude to communicate with the Parisians, were widely perceived to form a praetorian guard for the government. In the eyes of the more radical republicans, they were the embodiment of the backward-looking Frenchmen whose violence and brutality were obstacles to the Republic's civilizing mission. On the other hand, their idealized rurality also made them the favorites of reactionary Catholics such as Louis Veuillot, who identified the Breton with the simplicity of authentic French manhood nurtured in the Catholic faith.[35] In Paris itself, these provincial conscripts presented a salient contrast to the politically educated and socialized urbanites. The elections of February 1871, which returned a largely reactionary assembly, were perceived by the city dwellers as the revenge of the rural and uneducated citizens (*ruraux*) unable to comprehend where the national interest lay or even to have any political and national sense. The theme was exploited by the Versailles government to highlight differences between 'real' and 'decadent' Frenchmen.[36] For the revolutionary republicans, these provincial men were seen as the opposite of citizens, and even staunch republicans came to doubt the virtue of universal male suffrage in February 1871 when provincial men returned mostly conservative members of parliament.

The city of fractious masculinities

1870 was undoubtedly the year when city and citizen were most closely associated, and when urban masculinity was most closely linked to revolutionary attitudes, though this was sometimes pathologized as 'obsidional fever,' or the madness of the besieged.[37] During the Franco-Prussian War, besieged cities like Paris and Belfort, or revolutionary cities like Lyon and Marseille, were largely governed by young revolutionary men whose political clubs called for war to the last and, occasionally, social upheaval.[38] Even in their short-lived moment of triumph, these urban revolutionaries had to contest their cultural role in relation to the bourgeoisie whose sociability they often mimicked.

Away from the French countryside, where the bourgeois were isolated and often absentee landlords (even when they were supposedly in positions of leadership such as appointed mayors), the French male bourgeois found their identity in urban cultural institutions.[39] Only within the urban environment could they find the social institutions which would enable men to perform their role, to negotiate the move from boyhood to adulthood, from bachelor to pater familias.[40] The period from 1848–71 witnessed the rise of a greater diversity of social contexts in which masculine codes could be developed and tested. The rise of a developed civil society offering many sites of club-based sociability dates from the Second Empire. In the larger cities there were many groups that opened themselves to young men, either born in the locality or introduced to it. If military men had their *cercles*, civilians had their cafés, billiard rooms, learned societies, *comices agricoles*, professional chambers (*chambre des notaires*, for instance), and musical groups (*harmonies*), as well as religious *conférences* (like the *Conférence de Saint-Vincent de Paul* created in 1833 by Frédéric Ozanam) and Masonic lodges. All of these offered different spaces for comradeship, decorum or familiarity. While male clubs could range from theological discussion groups to trivial singing clubs specializing in obscene songs, they were nevertheless central to the performance of male attitudes, and always included rituals and rites of passage.[41] The fact that so many of these sites remained under strict police surveillance for any trace of seditious comments until at least the mid-1860s meant that the emphasis was on discreet and interiorized forms of political expression which could be displayed physically and in myriad non-verbal ways.[42]

Demeanor was codified with increasing rigidity over the period while subtle class distinctions often violated the apparent class equality of the clubs devoted to the discussion of ideas. The Freemasons in particular have been the object of considerable scholarly scrutiny, thanks largely to their good record-keeping of attendance and the police records they generated.[43] While most of the historiography is concerned with the political and social implications of these societies in which open debates occasionally took place, one could also consider their gendered attributes.[44] All these groups were strictly male and codified masculine attitudes. In Freemasonry the initiation rituals were literally rites of passage between obscurity and the light. They associated weapons in their rituals while they structured their sense of belonging around secrets and revelations. While some lodges were open to working-class men, these were the ones most likely to be closed down by the authorities, and few comprised genuinely mixed social classes.

In lodges as in the clubs, male bourgeois sociability was marked by formal hierarchies (presidents and secretaries) and codes of honor. The performance of bourgeois masculinity increasingly mimicked military virtues and poses. As Robert Nye has noted, dueling had become an acceptable urban bourgeois practice where honor was represented simultaneously as a form of capital (something that could be lost, gained or topped up), and a presentation of a social self that was almost extraneous to the person and which was enhanced through feats of courage.[45] Beyond the athletic clubs that developed primarily after 1870, there was one national network of bourgeois clubs in which masculine codes could be tested using military tropes: the National Guard. The National Guard was a remnant of the French Revolution which had lost most of its key revolutionary attributes.[46] This bourgeois militia had had its heyday under Louis-Philippe (1830–48), the bourgeois king who often wore its uniform. Its social role was primarily that of a peacekeeping force, composed of bourgeois volunteers who kept their own equipment and uniform at home and paraded and trained on Sundays at the Champs de Mars. Subject to much ridicule and easy prey to caricatures such as Daumier's, the national guardsmen nevertheless embodied citizenship in its fullest sense by being armed and trained stakeholders in law and order. They could associate with military modes of masculinity without being tainted as coarse *soldatesque*.

Uncommon in the countryside, the national guardsmen were primarily urban and exclusive, from the age of service to later middle age. They were primarily organized by neighborhood rather than in larger groupings and offered a strictly hierarchical setting for comradeship. The citizens' primary roles as defenders of social order, and men of order were embodied in the National Guard even though conservatives sometimes portrayed them as 'legions of libertines, mocking the cult of the flag.'[47] The association of full citizenship with National Guard service was potent, and throughout the period there were calls for working-class men to be able to join in. This militia of essentially civilian men was appropriated by the bourgeoisie in every conservative regime and expanded to the working class in revolutionary eras. Thus membership in the National Guard was extended to the working class in 1848 and withdrawn under the Second Empire. With the democratization of the regime, the status of the Guard arose once again. The reorganization of the army in 1868 seemed to answer calls to use all the vital forces of the nation and created a three-tiered military structure with two reserves: the *gardes mobiles*, composed of men who had drawn lucky numbers at the military service lottery, and the National Guard, which was composed of older men.[48] In the emergency of the war of 1870, the Guard became a genuinely militarized force against the Prussian invasion and opened itself once more to working-class men.

The events of 1870 forced the *mobiles* to the front line and led to the extension of National Guard service to all men and to the partial mobilization of some of them into frontline units.[49] In besieged Paris all men were, at least nominally, attached to a neighborhood unit. The uniform became the attire of masculinity while boys as young as fourteen could join in and enjoy some rights of adult citizens. In 1870 the government of national defense felt compelled to restore the inner democracy of the National Guard. In its final incarnation, the National Guard had become a synthesis of bourgeois and working-class modes of sociability and this heady mix proved intoxicating for some bourgeois men relishing the masculine comradeship transcending class boundaries.[50]

Class masculinities

The boundaries between urban and rural were often vague or porous in nineteenth-century France. Not only were many working-class areas located so far on the outskirts of the city that they were almost rural, but many working-class men either had been, or would again become agricultural laborers. Like Savoyards, Breton navvies, and Auvergnat coal merchants, Limousin migrant workers from Creuse and Corrèze specialized mostly in one trade (construction) which they practiced over seasons of one or several years primarily in the Paris, Lyon and Bordeaux areas. When boys had come of age, they would travel with their fathers to the city, and live there, often miserably, in order to save some money that would be put back into the land or used to pay debts and taxes. This wave of immigrants had social and consumption patterns close to those practiced a hundred years later by North African immigrants. Martin Nadaud, who was to become one of the first workers elected to the National Assembly in 1849, made his first move to Paris at the age of fifteen, to work as a *limousinant*, mixing the rough cement that would bind loose stonework. At seventeen he began his apprenticeship as a builder and entered the adult male group, with its rites and duties. On the first day on a new job, one had to pay for a round of drinks and take unflinchingly the practical jokes that accompanied initiation into the circle. Contacts were key to finding employment, and networks of sociability from the countryside were of practical use in the city.[51] Thus the locality followed the migrant worker to Paris, and his reputation at home could be made or unmade by his behavior in closely-knit groups.

On his return from his first 'season' of three years, Nadaud noted that his new clothes contrasted with the 'the harsh drugget cloth [*le droguet*] which made us peasants so heavy and slow, moving with difficulty and clumsily.' These peasants in urban attires might have been mocked by the local bourgeois, but for Nadaud the young men represented 'habits of loyalty and honesty that intelligent workers acquire by rubbing against social superiors that one meets at every moment in a large town,' which contrasted with the 'avaricious and ignorant petty bourgeoisie of the villages and [provincial] towns.'[52] Victims of constant discrimination, the migrant workers turned towards *chausson* or French kick-boxing, training in regularly established *salles* under masters only to practice the noble art in punch-ups and ballroom brawls: '[my critics] had forgotten that my motive for my acts was like that of a duelist, the point of honor. We had never accepted hearing the stonemasons of Creuse insulted.'[53] In his autobiography, Nadaud explained the ways in which a fight was set up between two groups from different regions practicing different professions:

> one of the lads, in agreement with his comrades, pushed the joke too far. He chose to unbutton himself [to defecate] in front of the entrance of our worksite while we were having lunch. His friends were in stitches when they saw us come back from the greasy spoon. This shame we could not, we should not accept it. We decided that one of us would go and challenge them.[54]

In contrast to the individual honor disputes which were characteristic of bourgeois social codes, most fights and boxing duels were presented as interprofessional rivalries, testimony, in Nadaud's view, to the divided condition of the working class, but in reality more revealing of discrimination against and between migrant workers from the provinces. The masculine traits of the workplace were to be defended in ritualized brawls with the tacit support of the employer. In some cases Nadaud's employer was also a sparring partner in the boxing club. The *Compagnons* societies, which formed the elite of artisan workers, which were then in severe decline, also partook in a culture of extreme rivalry and violence focused on the regional identity of their members.[55]

The issue of honesty, proclaimed as a regional as well as a professional quality, was nevertheless relativized in practice. To finance their pleasures, some men attempted to cut corners, for instance, selling scrap metal stolen from building sites to raise money to hire prostitutes.

> He was sentenced and died in prison. As F was almost a neighbour, and that all our comrades knew him as a friendly, affable and obliging man, his humiliating end, while deserved, made us sad; as a matter of fact, he belonged to a very respectable family of peasants. To add to the unhappy circumstances, he had married a young woman of exemplary conduct.[56]

Honor was contextualized in relation to the home group (the family, the wife, the regional neighborhood) and to the male social group: he was an obliging comrade. While Nadaud's particular republican stance emphasized the self-help and autodidactic aspects of his republican education, his entire career as a local politician was founded on his home (the Creuse department) and the men of his profession (in Paris). His rise to eminence among his peers and the attributes of his education impacted only within the narrow circles of his local social networks. Even after 1851, when his exile took him to England, he remained involved in the social networks of his region over and above those of the republican emigrants.[57] The role of neighborhoods in revolutionary masculinities has been analyzed controversially by Gould in an effort to quantify the networks and posit a possible change in class culture.[58] In spite of his overall argument of a reinforcement of neighborhood solidarities over the period at the expense of class solidarity, the evidence of the insurrections of 1848–49 showed men most willing to take arms to defend a close community of associates. During the Commune of Paris, in addition to the well-known examples of foreigners joining in the insurrection, most Communards defended themselves best in their own neighborhoods, through their locally-organized National Guard units.[59] The heroes were local, and much Communard revolutionary activity had an intensely local dimension.

Similarly marked by their origins and the difficulty of overcoming them, there were other archetypes of troublesome groups in what their contemporaries called *déclassés* or Bohemians, after the sentimental novel of Henry Murger, *Scènes de la vie de Bohème*.[60] In the novel, Bohemians survived from hand to mouth in almost entirely male circles, occasionally associating themselves with *grisettes*, themselves on the margins of registered prostitution.[61]

Some twenty years later, the darker Vingtras series of autobiographical novels penned by Jules Vallès portrayed the harsh realities of a bitterly dissatisfied crowd of educated but penniless youths living off expedients.[62] What another journalist called the 'ridiculous black jackets' (*habit noirs ridicules*) were attempting to ape bourgeois respectability while mending or sharing a single jacket, dyed with writing ink where the thread was showing.[63] These characters, following the literary trail of Balzac's heroes, were violent and prickly on matters of honor. Vallès shared a room, and even his clothes, with his friend Legrand with whom he constantly bickered. This close friendship reinforced their identity and ensured that they remained attached to their puritan ideals of virtue and their hatred of the 'fat ones' (*les gras*).[64] Yet the bourgeois lifestyle appealed to the impoverished Bohemians:

> now that our wallet is full and that we have freshened up, that we almost look respectable with our new clothes on, now that we have had a haircut and our beard is under control, we dare to return to café Mariage and we even get drunk on the first day! We get drunk to show our money, to kill our poor gold coins, to make them ring, to show up, to be admired! Legrand, at one stage stands up and says:
> 'We are men of good company – we are two gentlemen. . . .'[65]

On a relentless alcohol-driven self-destructive journey, Vallès and his friend unsuccessfully seek fights and end up dueling with each other. Characteristically, Vallès represented the conflict between the lodgers as springing mainly from their different origins: 'our flat was too small for our personalities, one Breton, one from Auvergne.' Later on the friends borrow money to afford the tools of the duel while enjoying the sexual thrill and self-assurance that a virile duel can give:

> I feel that my timidity, the natural daughter of an impoverished and harsh lifestyle, which makes the poor man look vulgar, that shyness is gone at the prospect of a fight we will wage like gentlemen, and I feel free facing the nobility of danger; I, who was so scared of a coal merchant's bill, will put myself ten feet away from the muzzle of a gun.

The masculinity of the duel was primarily interiorized since even the witnesses challenged the duelist's serious intents, 'slapping my back, making a face and talking to me as if I was a brat.' The entertaining of these irreverent witnesses proved to be another necessary expense of the dueling trial: 'they won't come without cigars and they are never satisfied unless they can drink Madeira wine and chartreuse.' Yet, without witnesses, a duel would lose its meaning and decorum. Eventually the students pawned their collective wealth to raise the money to rent two dueling pistols and to ride to the field in a carriage. At the end of a fierce duel, Legrand was maimed while Vallès had to mend his coat, pierced by a bullet: 'it forces me to enter left shoulder first in the homes where I teach. They think I have a tic or that I am a hunchback.'[66]

The later years of the Second Empire, especially after the liberalization of the press in 1868, were marked by increasingly diverse views expressed in violent terms, and dueling was presented to Vallès as a career opener.[67] Journalists and politicians practiced aggressive language as weapons and were often rude to each other in a spirit of *'blague'* which could end in duels. Literary over-investment in masculine role-playing revealed the insecurities of unsettled young men. Even the leading stars, among them the author of *Frenchmen of the Decadence*, Henri Rochefort, could never aspire to respectability or even to full manhood because of their strident opposition to the military regime of Louis Napoléon: 'if the army is the elite of the nation, it is obvious that I, who never had any taste for the military condition, I belong to the lowest orders of Frenchmen, what they call the "chuck" in the butchers' trade slang.'[68] These aspiring men were nevertheless to emerge as the revolutionary leaders of 1870–71, and their grandiloquent extolling of hyper-masculine warrior behavior was to be tested to destruction in civil war.

Paris 1870–71: a crisis of masculinity?

The war of 1870, the revolution of September 1870, the numerous insurrections that took place in Paris and major provincial cities, and eventually the Commune of Paris in March 1871, were all perceived as major tests of endurance and worth for class-divided, parochial and hot-headed Frenchmen. Yet the picture was confused. On the one hand, as a moment of crisis, the French military defeats of summer 1870 were perceived less as a crisis of masculinity than as the revelation of structural problems in the French military and social organization. The professional soldiers of that summer had not been inferior to their German foes, and much mythologizing surrounded some glorious defeats.[69] Urban insurrections and the Commune of Paris, on the other hand, highlighted afresh current concerns about decadence. The calls to arms of Gambetta, unlike those of Danton three generations earlier, had not unleashed the revolutionary strength of men able to face the whole of Europe for twenty-five years.[70] At the end of the civil war which followed the Franco-Prussian war, the defeated revolutionaries of the Commune were seldom represented as worthy opponents or as full men. Apart from the singular figure of Delescluze, who was renowned for his suicidal courage but who really belonged to the generation of 1848 revolutionaries, the Communards were routinely denounced as mere hot-headed fools, cowards or even as boys. The emblematic figure of this revolutionary boyhood was Raoul Rigault, aged twenty-five, who had been the leader of the Communard police and whose cruelty and *blague* were identified as the product of Bohemian excess associated with the animal impulses of working-class men.[71] Bearded, loud, boisterous, cynical, middle-class and educated, Rigault embodied the evolutionary excesses of the Commune and was directly responsible for the execution of its hostages. Rigault resembled the most notorious murderer of the last year of the Second Empire, the deluded *déclassé* Troppman, whose murders had highlighted the savagery at the heart of class jealousy.[72]

In spite of his many flaws, most commentators noted and deplored Rigault's wasted youth, and ultimately it was the boy rather than the man that was summarily executed in a street.[73] The revolutionary posturing of 1870–71 was portrayed as parody rather than authentic enthusiasm. The men of the Commune, compared with their revolutionary elders, seemed pale imitators of defunct ways. Their outlandish Bohemian masculinity and posturing, their beards and immorality, were denounced throughout Europe as the expression of antisocial instincts. When some of the leaders of the Commune escaped in May 1871, they had to take care to shave and disguise themselves as bourgeois.

On the other side of the conflict, in the Communard texts and press, the Versailles armies were painted as provincial savages equally excessive and brutal, or even sadistic.[74] The *année terrible* and particularly the Commune of Paris were portrayed in deeply gendered terms.[75] The failings of individual men were associated with pre-existing concerns about the French race, and later fed a more general interpretation of decadence in the *fin de siècle*.[76] Even though there were few instances of direct discussions of masculinity per se, the cult of action that developed among the veterans of the Commune and of the war itself, for instance in the works of the arch-nationalist Déroulède, emphasized the need to find new foundations for French male identity. The post-war aims were to create Frenchmen solidly bonded to each other by virile comradeship that would transcend the differences of regional origins or of class.[77]

Émile Zola reflected this projection into masculine ideals in the concluding scene of *La Débâcle*. In the last melodramatic chapter, Jean, the rural hero of the novel, considers Maurice, the revolutionary young man whom he had mortally wounded in the re-conquest of Paris:

> Jean approached the body of Maurice. He looked at him, with his large forehead that seemed even bigger, his long thin face, his empty eyes, a little crazy before where his madness had died too. He would have liked to cuddle him, his dear little one, as he had called him so often, and he dared not. He could see himself covered with his blood . . .[78]

Jean remained the manly archetype, rooted in rural and provincial values. Maurice, the urban effete man, ended up looking like a boy that has never managed to mature into a real Frenchman. Following well-established tropes of political sacrifice, it was only in killing the revolutionary boy that the provincial man could be entrusted with the task of rebuilding France and its honor in the final sentences of the novel. Ultimately the divisive masculinities of the Second Empire were set against each other in a sacrificial drama, and the myth of salvation was articulated around, not a singular providential man but rather new, provincial, yet patriotic Frenchmen.[79] Set against the corrupted urban culture of revolutionary France, the conservative republican creed of the decades following the wars highlighted the role of education in re-shaping this masculine model and emphatically asserted the earthy values of its model of civilization.[80]

Notes

1. Eugen Weber, *Peasants into Frenchmen* (London: Chatto and Windus, 1977).
2. See André Siegfried's use of topography to establish cultural boundaries, *Tableau Politique de la France de l'Ouest* (1913; Paris: Imprimerie Nationale, 1995).
3. Ted W. Margadant, 'Tradition and Modernity in Rural France during the Nineteenth Century,' *Journal of Modern History*, 56 (1984): 667–97; Charles Tilly, 'Did the Cake of Custom Break?' in *Consciousness and Class Experience in Nineteenth Century Europe*, ed. John Merriman (New York: Holmes and Meier, 1979), pp. 17–44.
4. See Pierre Rosanvallon, *Le Sacre du citoyen* (Paris: Gallimard, 1992).
5. Jean-Charles Chenu, *Recruitement de l'Armée et population de la France* (Paris: Dentu, 1867).
6. Stéphane Gerson, *The Pride of Place* (Ithaca: Cornell University Press, 2003).
7. W. Scott Haine ' "Café Friend": Friendship and Fraternity in Parisian Working-Class Cafés, 1850–1914,' *Journal of Contemporary History*, 27 (4) (1992): 607–26.
8. Martin Nadaud, *Mémoires de Léonard, ancien garçon maçon*, ed. Maurice Agulhon (Limoges: Lucien Souny, 1998).
9. Margadant, 'Tradition and Modernity'; Margadant, *Urban Rivalries in the French Revolution* (Princeton, NJ: Princeton University Press, 1992); Alain Corbin, *Les Cloches de la terre* (Paris: Albin Michel, 1994).
10. See the classic text of the geographer Hervé le Bras, *Les Trois France* (Paris: Seuil, 1986).
11. A. Corbin, *The Village of Cannibals: Rage and Murder in France, 1870* (Cambridge, MA: Harvard University Press, 1992).
12. George Sand, *La Mare au Diable* (1846; Paris: Flammarion, 1964).
13. See for instance, Émile Zola, *La Terre* (Paris: C. Marpon and E. Flammarion, 1889), which was condemned for obscenity.
14. Gérard de Puymège, *Chauvin, le Soldat Laboureur* (Paris: Gallimard, 1993), pp. 208–25.
15. David Hopkin, *Soldier and Peasant in French Popular Culture* (Rochester, NY: Boydell Press for the Royal Historical Society, 2003), pp. 136–47.
16. Jean-Claude Pignard, *Les Conscrits de Villefranche en Beaujolais* (Lyon: Éditions de Trévoux, 1988).
17. For a subtle analysis see Lisa O'Sullivan, 'Dying for Home' (Doctoral Dissertation, University of London, 2006).
18. Bill Bynum defined it as a discarded diagnosis: 'Discarded Diagnoses: Nostalgia,' *Lancet*, 358 (9299) (22–29 December 2001): 2176; George Rosen, 'Nostalgie, a Forgotten Psychological Disorder,' *Clio Medica*, 10 (1975): 29–52; Von Klaus Brunnet, *Nostalgie in der Geschichte des Medizin* (Düsseldorf: Tritsch, 1984). The topic has long been a favorite of medical doctoral theses, for example, Denis Guerbois, 'Essai sur la nostalgie' (Paris, 1803); Louis Tailhade, 'Quelques Considéra-tions sur la nostalgie' (Montpellier, 1850); Oscar Devic, 'La Nostalgie ou mal du pays' (Montpellier, 1855); Emmanuel Eugène Blache, 'Dissertation sur la nostalgie' (Strasbourg, 1860); Auguste Benoist de la Grandière, *De la Nostalgie ou mal du pays*

(Paris: Adrien Delahaye, 1873); Charles François Geit, 'Quelques considérations sur la nature de la nostalgie' (Montpellier, 1874).

19. Michael S. Roth, 'Dying of the Past: Medical Studies of Nostalgia in Nineteenth Century France,' *History and Memory*, 3 (1991): 5–29.
20. Eugène Fritsch, *La Nostalgie du Soldat* (Paris: Jouaust, 1876), pp. 4–6.
21. Fritsch, *La Nostalgie*, pp. 6–12.
22. Benoist de la Grandière, *De la Nostalgie*, p. 3.
23. O. Saint-Vel, *Hygiène des européens dans les climats tropicaux* (Paris: A. Delahaye, 1872), p. 18.
24. Ruftz, *État statistique et historique sur la population de la Martinique* (Paris: Masson, 1850); also Benoist de la Grandière, *De la Nostalgie*, pp. 20–1.
25. Fritsch, *La Nostalgie*, p. 11.
26. Édouard Tubiana, *La Nostalgie dans les Armées de la Révolution* (Paris: Vézin, 1958), pp. 11–12.
27. Thévenot, *Traité des maladies des européens dans les pays chauds* (Paris: Baillière, 1840); also quoted in Auguste Haspel, *De la Nostalgie* (Paris: Masson, 1874), p. 43.
28. Haspel, *De la Nostalgie*, pp. 34–5.
29. Benoist de la Grandière, *De la Nostalgie*, pp. 60–1.
30. Alice Bullard, *Exile to Paradise* (Stanford, CA: Stanford University Press, 2000).
31. Eugène Fromentin, *Un été dans le Sahara* (1856; Paris: Plon, 1912), pp. 182–4.
32. Jean de la Rocca, *La Corse calomniée, réponse à M Clavé, de la Revue des Deux Mondes* (Ajaccio: n.p., 1864).
33. Dr F.-M. Costa (de Bastelica), *La Corse et son recrutement, études historiques, statistiques et médicales* (Paris: Victor Rozier, 1873), p. 70.
34. Edmond Fuzier-Herman, *La Province au siège de Paris* (Paris: Librairie Militaire de J. Dumaine, 1871).
35. Louis Veuillot, *Paris pendant les deux sièges* (Paris: Victor Palmé, 1871; 2 vols, 1872); G. D'Éthampes, *Bretons et Vendéens* (Paris: Briday, 1884), pp. 12–13.
36. Paul Bourgeois, *Les Ruraux* (Versailles: n.p., 1871).
37. Bertrand Taithe, *Defeated Flesh* (Manchester: Manchester University Press, 1999), p. 213.
38. L. Greenberg, *Sisters of Liberty* (Cambridge, MA: Harvard University Press, 1971); Bertrand Taithe, 'Slow Revolutionary Deaths,' *French History*, 17 (3) (2003): 280–306.
39. Adeline Daumard, *La Bourgeoisie Parisienne de 1815–1848* (1963; Paris: Albin Michel, 1996), pp. 391–8.
40. Carol E Harrison, *The Bourgeois Citizen in Nineteenth-century France* (Oxford: Oxford University Press, 1999).
41. Marie-Véronique Gauthier, *Chanson, sociabilité et grivoiserie au xixe siècle* (Paris: Aubier, 1992).
42. Sudhir Hazareesingh and Vincent Wright, *Francs-maçons sous le Second Empire* (Rennes: PUR, 2001); Luis Martin (ed.), *Les Francs-maçons dans la cité* (Rennes: PUR, 2000).
43. Philip Nord, 'Republicanism and Utopian Vision: French Freemasonry in the 1860s and 1870s,' *Journal of Modern History*, 63 (June 1991): 213–29.
44. Alain Dalotel, Alain Faure and Jean-Claude Freiermuth, *Aux Origines de la Commune* (Paris: François Maspéro, 1980).
45. Robert A. Nye, *Masculinity and Male Codes of Honor in Modern France* (Berkeley: University of California Press, 1993), pp. 132–47.
46. Georges Carrot, 'La Garde Nationale 1789–1871, une institution de la Nation' (Thèse de Doctorat de 3ième cycle, Université de Nice, 1979); Bertrand Taithe, *Citizenship and Wars: France in Turmoil 1870–1871* (London: Routledge, 2001), ch. 3.

47. A. Du Laz, *Les Provinces à la capitale, autorité-provincialité* (Paris: Charpentier, 1850), p. 93.
48. *Nouveau Manuel de la Garde Nationale* (Paris: Hachette, 1870); *Organisation de la Garde Nationale* (Paris: Librairie Administrative Dupont, 1870); Jean Casevitz, *Une Loi manquée: la loi Niel 1866–1868* (Paris: Presses Universitaires de France, 1959).
49. Taithe, *Citizenship and Wars*, pp. 38–53.
50. P. Lary (ed.), *Lettres d'un homme [Victor Desplats] à la femme qu'il aime pendant le siège de Paris et la Commune* (Paris: Jean-Claude Lattès, 1980).
51. Alan R.H. Baker, *Fraternity among the French Peasantry* (Cambridge: Cambridge University Press, 1999).
52. Nadaud, *Mémoires*, pp. 79–82.
53. Ibid., pp. 99–101.
54. Ibid., pp. 118–19.
55. Frédéric Chavaud, *De Pierre Rivière à Landru* (Brussels: Brepols, 1991), pp. 78–83.
56. Nadaud, *Mémoires*, p. 121.
57. Daniel Dayen, *Martin Nadaud: ouvrier maçon et député, 1815–1898* (Limoges: Lucien Souny, 1998); Gillian Tindall, *The Journey of Martin Nadaud: a Life in Turbulent Times* (London: Pimlico, 2000).
58. Roger Gould, *Insurgent Identities* (Chicago: University of Chicago Press, 1996).
59. Le Marquis de la Rochethulon, *Du Rôle de la garde nationale et de l'armée de Paris dans les préparatifs de l'insurrection du 18 mars* (Paris: Léon Techener, 1872).
60. Henry Murger, *Scènes de la vie de Bohème* (Paris: Garnier, 1929).
61. Victoria E. Thompson, *The Virtuous Marketplace* (Baltimore: Johns Hopkins University Press, 2000), ch. 4.
62. Vallès, Jules, *Souvenirs d'un étudiant pauvre, le candidat des pauvres, lettre à Jules Mirès* (Paris: Oeuvres complètes, Éditeurs Français Réunis, 1972), pp. 108–14; Rachael Langford, *Jules Vallès and the Narration of History* (Bern: Peter Lang, 1999).
63. B. Maurice, 'La Misère en habit noir,' in *Les Français peints par eux-mêmes* (Paris: Philippaut, 1861), pp. 294–6.
64. Vallès, *Le Candidat*, pp. 270–7.
65. Ibid., p. 282.
66. Ibid., pp. 287–307.
67. Vallès contributed to *Le Figaro*'s reviewing section from the time of the duel onwards.
68. Henri Rochefort, *Les Français de la décadence* (Paris: Librairie Centrale, 1867), p. 107.
69. See Taithe, *Defeated Flesh*, chs 1–3; Habert de Ginestet, *Souvenirs d'un prisonnier de guerre en Allemagne* (Paris: Flammarion, n.d., *c.* 1879).
70. Richard D. Challener, *The French Theory of the Nation in Arms, 1866–1939* (New York: Columbia University Press, 1965).
71. Charles Prolès, *Les Hommes de la révolution de 1871* (Paris: Chamuel, 1898); Maxime Vuillaume, H. Bellenger and L. de Marancour, *Hommes et choses du temps de la Commune* (Geneva: n.p., 1871).
72. Roger Williams, *Manners and Murders in the World of Louis Napoleon* (Seattle: University of Washington Press, 1975), pp. 112–27.
73. Cattelain, *Souvenirs inédits du chef de la sûreté sous la Commune* (Paris: Juven, 1900), p. 69.
74. E. Monteil, *Souvenirs de la Commune, 1871* (Paris: Charavay Frères, 1883), p. 188.
75. Eugene Schulkind, 'Socialist Women during the 1871 Paris Commune,' *Past and Present*, 106 (1985): 124–63; Gay Gullickson, *Unruly Women of Paris* (Ithaca: Cornell University Press, 1996); David Barry, 'Community, Tradition and Memory among Rebel Working-class Women of Paris: 1830, 1848, 1871,' *European Review of History/Revue européenne d'histoire*, 7 (2) (2000): 261–76.

76. Daniel Pick, *Faces of Degeneration: a European Disorder, c. 1848–c. 1918* (Cambridge: Cambridge University Press, 1989); Robert Elliot Kaplan, *Forgotten Crisis: the Fin-de-siècle Crisis of Democracy in France* (Oxford: Berg, 1995).
77. Maurice Larkin, ' "La République en danger"? The Pretenders, the Army and Deroulede, 1898–1899,' *English Historical Review*, 100 (394) (1985): 85–105.
78. Émile Zola, *La Débâcle* (Paris: Charpentier, 1892), p. 635.
79. The sacrificial discourse was obviously a trope of religious discourses, but also a recurrent theme in republican representations. See for instance: Richard D.E. Burton's *Blood in the City* (Ithaca: Cornell University Press, 2001); Ivan Strenski, *Contesting Sacrifice* (Chicago: University of Chicago Press, 1997).
80. See, for instance, G. Bruno's textbook: *Le Tour de France par deux enfants* (Paris: Belin, 1877); John Strachan, 'Romance, Religion and the Republic: Bruno's *Le tour de la France par deux enfants*,' *French History*, 18 (1) (2004): 96–118.

5

La Civilisation and its Discontents: Modernity, Manhood and the Body in the Early Third Republic

Christopher E. Forth

> France has been the center, the *foyer* of civilization in Europe.
>
> François Guizot (1828)

> What should we think of a 'civilization' that promises us, in the near future, a race of dwarfs with flabby and undefined muscles, thin limbs, the faces of inferior anthropoids, with big hydrocephalus heads . . . ?
>
> Georges Rouhet (1904)

One might expect that there would be differences between François Guizot and Georges Rouhet. Guizot, a well-known historian and statesman of the early nineteenth century, helped to reinforce France's reputation as the centre of *civilisation* in the Western world. Rouhet, a bodybuilder and physical culture instructor whose words reached a more restricted readership decades later, was just one of many who asked some hard questions about civilization's effects upon the body, especially the bodies of French men. The fact that the masculinity of those who aligned themselves with civilization could be challenged may come as some surprise to contemporary scholars. After all, many of the qualities implicit in the concept of civilization in the West have been identified as being inherently masculinist and ethnocentric, thus allowing white male elites to exercise misogynist and racist practices on grand scales. In broad terms, this is the understanding of civilization implicit in the secular *mission civilisatrice* that animated the 'new imperialism' of the Third Republic. As Alice Conklin shows, a 'mission to civilize' informed the official doctrine used for the elevation of 'primitive' peoples in overseas colonies. Conklin suggests that the rhetoric of French *civilisation* basically consisted of a sense of mastery or freedom from specific forms of tyranny, whether of geography, disease, instinct or despotism. What was to be eradicated in West African colonies was to some extent mirrored in the reforms that republicans also carried out within France itself, namely local languages (or dialects, in the case of the mainland), regional customs and organizations, which would be replaced with 'republican' virtues such as a common language, freedom, social equality (among men) and liberal justice. In this framework the provinces appeared as vast 'savage' regions desperately in need of the civilizing mission that functioned as a form of 'inner colonization.'[1]

Some scholars have viewed this rationalist project as an expression of a broader imposition of the demands of white, bourgeois males over a host of subjected populations, from women and proletarians to indigenous peoples across the globe. Indeed, many have come to view the rationality that was so often celebrated as central to civilization as being closely bound up with French concepts of masculinity generally.[2] According to Annelise Maugue, around 1900, bourgeois men repudiated in themselves qualities thought to be too closely associated with the feminine, particularly sexuality and sentimentality, which she describes as a double disavowal of *le corps* and *le coeur*. Just as female identity was usually reduced to the dominance of the womb, masculinity was often presented as being crystallized in the brain. Maugue argues that the flight to abstraction was a compensation for men troubled by the repeated incursions of women into traditionally male domains. 'What is more revealing of this terrible anxiety than the exclusive identification of man with the brain, this organ perched up high, invisible, protected by the cranial case from all direct contact with the external world?' Although acknowledging the specifically bourgeois nature of this masculinization of rationality, Maugue agrees that 'intellectual activity unquestionably seems constitutive of male identity' in a model that 'remains unchanged.'[3]

There is much to recommend this association of manhood with reason, technology and development. In nineteenth-century France, liberal philosophers, sociologists and educators, from François Guizot and Victor Cousin to Charles Renouvier and Émile Durkheim, articulated a model of civic manhood largely predicated on reason and morality, thus proposing a gendered dualism that situated women and 'the feminine' on the side of the body and nature. According to an influential thinker like Victor Cousin, whose spiritualist philosophy left its stamp on *lycée* education throughout the century, it was the ability to transcend the sensations and limitations of the body that distinguished elite males from men of the lower orders as well as from all women.[4] While many of these affirmations of rational manhood were enshrined in educational institutions, they were also rivalled by discourses that refused any simple disconnection of 'masculine' minds from 'feminine' bodies, particularly those articulated in medicine and allied sciences that, whether inflected by evolutionary or degeneration theory, emphasized the centrality of the body to the health and sanity of the individual and the race. In these largely materialist discourses, the male body was not only an essential precondition for the exercise of reason and morality (famously summed up in the nineteenth-century motto of holistic health, *mens sana in corpus sano*), but it was the medium through which men literally embodied the strength, endurance and bellicosity that allowed them to be effective soldiers, whether on the field of battle or, figuratively speaking, the 'battlefield' of everyday life.

To be sure, these two broad approaches to masculinity shared a great deal of common ground, not least when it came to affirming the bourgeois male's superior strength and capacity for reason and morality, and thus the legitimacy of his domination over women, proletarians and non-Western peoples. In medical and psychiatric terms, intellectual work has traditionally been seen as so quintessentially male that it threatened to virilize women who used their minds excessively, depriving them of their 'natural' feminine charms when it did not drive them to hysteria, lesbianism or insanity. This celebration of masculine intellect is also central to the definition of 'civilization' proposed by François Guizot, which called for the concurrent and unified development of social well-being and intellectual life. Although Guizot contended that the signs of civilization were everywhere across Europe, he accorded his own country a privileged role in relation to the progressive advance of the human race.[5] As Victor Hugo later pronounced, France was 'the missionary of civilization in Europe', suggesting that the *mission civilisatrice* reflected French leadership in a much broader Western development.[6]

Yet if liberal thinkers of the post-revolutionary era celebrated civilization while largely bracketing the body from civic masculinity, medical discourses continued to level their gaze on the interplay between the body and its conditions of life, and thus turned a critical eye upon the environment that created and was created by civilized manhood. Physicians, psychiatrists and anthropologists called attention to the precarious position of male bodies under the circumstances of modern society. As a polyphony of competing (yet authoritative) voices, the bourgeois discourse of civilization was capable of affirming the intellectual and corporeal superiority of French elites over women and men from other social and racial groups while asserting, in a different register, that the same 'superior' civilization also promoted physical and moral decay that diminished the very men who created it. Defined largely in terms of reason, culture and the professions, bourgeois manhood was potentially undone by the lifestyles and habits that defined it and made it possible.

Alice Bullard notes that, for French elites in the nineteenth century, 'the ideal of civilization acted as a sort of talisman that kept at bay the crisis of meaning generated by modernity.'[7] I would go further, to argue that when approached from the perspectives of gender and lifestyle, civilization was itself an internally contradictory ideal that challenged many forms of masculinity on the bodily level. The irony of civilization does not simply reside in its role as a shield behind which French men hypocritically concealed their 'uncivilized' impulses and agendas. Rather it was also a deeply problematic development that worked through a double logic that at once bolstered the status of white, middle-class males while promoting the conditions that threatened their masculinity.[8] Depending on how one viewed the matter, the opposite of 'civilization' was not merely 'barbarism', but *virilité* as well. By focusing on the medical (and medicalized) discourses that took the male body as their object, this chapter probes the gendered tensions that troubled the French engagement with civilization during the early Third Republic. By approaching masculinity as an intrinsically unstable construct – what Judith Surkis describes as a contingent norm 'constituted by ever-present possibilities of abnormal deviation' – this chapter argues that the lifestyles, habits and temptations of modern civilization posed the greatest challenge to middle-class manhood by throwing into relief the gulf between the corporeal weaknesses of civic masculinity and the more robust martial ideal that continued to haunt it through the outbreak of World War I and beyond.[9]

Civilisation and masculinity

When it is not considered suspiciously freighted with ethnocentric assumptions, 'civilization' seems a rather quaint concept these days. Yet, historically speaking, civilization and Frenchness go together, and for good reason. The French not only literally invented the term, but for centuries they have been considered the most refined, cultured and educated of Western countries. While a distinction between 'civilized' and 'coarse' peoples has been around for millennia, the notion of *la civilisation* did not come into general usage until the 1750s, when, as Jean Starobinski points out, 'it drew together the diverse expressions of a preexisting concept [that is, *le civilisé*]. That concept included such notions as improvements in comfort, advances in education, politer manners, cultivation of the arts and sciences, growth of commerce and industry, and acquisition of material goods and luxuries.'[10] As a moral ideal, civilization was implicitly 'patriarchal,' and by insisting upon the domestication of women, it transformed mothers and wives into the moralizing agents of society while refusing them access to the world of politics, the professions and ideas.[11] Yet since even the least 'manly' of men is capable of exercising (or benefiting from) control over women, patriarchy is not necessarily co-extensive with masculinity. Although the idea of civilization ultimately mutated and became open to a variety of interpretations and applications in the nineteenth century, middle-class masculinity has remained haunted by developments implicit to the experience and conceptualization of civilization described by Starobinski: refined manners, education and culture, and material comfort and luxuries. Sedentary lifestyles constitute a fourth development pertaining to the body that has accompanied modern civilization, less as a value to be celebrated than as a common denominator of the other three.

Emerging as lived realities for Western elites from the early modern era onward, these four overlapping aspects of civilization have formed the principal terms against which modern men have expressed their dissatisfaction with the world they have created and which in turn has shaped them. While the notion of civilization would be employed in a variety of ways from the eighteenth century, these core features would continue to be counted among its most distinctive attributes.[12] When they were not being condemned for encouraging deception and manipulation, the refined manners that greased the wheels of sociability were frequently contrasted to the more direct emotional expressions of simpler times, when less inhibited men expressed their aggression and lust more freely and happily.[13] For centuries the cerebral regimens that constitute the training ground for most modern professions have been counterposed, both morally and medically, to more physically active and risky male occupations. Indeed, excessive study has been repeatedly identified as causing a range of illnesses and unhealthy practices, from nervousness, masturbation and constipation to same-sex vice. Despite being defended as a spur to industry, the consumer indulgence that inevitably accompanies material abundance is frequently denigrated as fostering an 'effeminate' submission to appetite, appearances and immorality supposedly absent in earlier, simpler times. Luxury has been historically identified as softening male bodies in a way that led to masturbation, sodomy, obesity, laziness and weakness. Finally, the sedentary existence that seems implicit to these polite, cerebral and consumer-oriented lifestyles is almost always condemned as the exact opposite of manly action and health, a main cause of the obesity and muscular atrophy that promised to be 'cured' through sports and military training at the end of the nineteenth century. Whether condemned together or individually, these four aspects of civilization have been cited across the Western world as the main environmental factors that threaten to turn men into weak and 'effeminate' creatures. At stake in this critique was not merely the fact that cerebral, comfortable and sedentary lifestyles made many noble and middle-class men ill-suited to the rigors of war, but that, if left unchecked, they threatened to create beings whose gender was undecidable under any circumstances.

In light of these recurring misgivings about civilization, the close French connection with this concept generated some problematic gender effects, notably on the international scene. The gradual refinement of noble manners that Norbert Elias describes as part of the 'civilizing process' emerged during the sixteenth century and was most clearly manifested in the courts of France and the Italian states, and in time spread across Europe. In the seventeenth century many European elites acknowledged the superior refinement and education that was present in France, and, in an attempt to polish their own 'rough' ways, submitted to lessons in civility from the French. Hence the rise of the *Kavalierstour* or 'grand tour' which could lead young aristocrats from Britain and the German states to Italy and France as part of their development as proper gentlemen.[14] Yet this nod to the superiority of French *civilisation* was under fire by the mid-1700s. Reason and culture were fine things, most agreed, but across Europe (and in France as well), reform-minded nobles and members of the emerging middle classes grew increasingly concerned about how luxury, manners and culture threatened to soften the bodies and minds of the citizenry.[15] A benefit to sociability and commerce, civilization also promoted soft men at the expense of more robust types. Identifying France as the embodiment of the feminizing ills of civilization was a common strategy in the nation-building movements of the late eighteenth and early nineteenth centuries, all of which were only sharpened during the revolutionary and Napoleonic wars. If by the early nineteenth century few countries envied France its missionary role in civilization, it was not because they had abandoned the project of modernity or had embraced 'barbarism' as its desirable opposite. Rather, in the name of preserving certain 'traditional' male traits associated with the warrior societies of ancient times, reformers in those countries sought ways of introjecting doses of the 'primitive' as a means of counteracting the softening effects of modern society by promoting coarser manners, diminished sensibility, physical hardiness and a greater ability to endure pain. For many Western countries, the deleterious effects of modern society could be offset by some encounter with the 'primitivity' of simpler and hardier societies.

What Gail Bederman usefully describes as the 'inoculation' of middle-class men with doses of 'barbarism' was thus not merely a preoccupation of anglophone countries, nor was it a strictly *fin-de-siècle* phenomenon.[16] Rather, it reflects a deeper, almost structural anxiety about the relationship between the 'civilizing process' and the rougher forms of masculinity that have been marginalized since the emergence of centralized monarchies in the sixteenth century. The perceived need to recapture aspects of this 'lost' male world flowered in the neoclassical and primitivist movements of the eighteenth century, many of which proposed means of strengthening enfeebled male bodies so they could better withstand privation and fatigue. The French themselves were aware of the double logic of civilization, and in the ferment of the revolutionary era many took steps toward mitigating its feminizing potential, which was at that time closely associated with the corruption of the Old Regime. The latter's eradication could be imagined as, among other things, a brave new world for men who had hitherto been weakened by despotism, luxury, idleness and the 'rule of women.'[17] As the national body usurped the privileged image of the royal body as the centre of political attention, this collective organism required personal bodies of a particular type, molded into shape and accustomed to perform arduous new tasks through rigorous training.[18]

This vigorous male ideal, which flowered during the Napoleonic era, did not survive the Restoration's strong emphasis on civility and a return to order. In the 1820s, Victor Cousin's highly influential rationalist conception of the self offered an attractive alternative to the body-based sensationalist models of the person that had reigned in the eighteenth century (and which some said had caused the violent passions unleashed during the revolution). By bracketing the body from his concept of the *moi*, Cousin had indeed found a way of leaving passions and imagination to the side; yet, by suggesting that the mind has no sex, he also left men without a corporeal basis for explaining just why this rational self was a primarily *male* prerogative.[19] Deprived of a robust physical foundation that would distinguish male and female minds, the liberal conception of manhood remained a fragile edifice propped up by sexist social relationships and some fancy discursive footwork. The robust male body thus continued to haunt middle-class men whose professions and lifestyles seemed divorced from strenuous effort and risk-taking. In his sweeping history of European civilization, even François Guizot acknowledged the superior virility of the rough, vibrant and bellicose Germanic 'barbarians,' whose 'male character' and 'obstinate energy' had been lost while the bourgeoisie retained the timidity and modesty it had developed in the twelfth century. Such was the fate of those engaged in what Guizot called 'the soft activity of modern times.'[20]

Philosophy's gendered mind/body dualism may have been incorporated into the *lycées* that trained the nation's elite, but it was not taken seriously in the medical discourses that gained in power and influence throughout the nineteenth century.[21] Since at least the seventeenth century, intellectual work, and the sedentariness that accompanies it, has been viewed as detrimental to physical health and, by extension, to robust masculinity. In the 1760s, the influential Swiss physician Samuel-Auguste Tissot spoke for many when he condemned the hygienic carelessness that seemed to mark many men of letters, whose health problems so clearly called into question their claims to virility. 'It is necessary to be a savant without ceasing to be a man,' Tissot asserted, and male scholars ever since have tried to find ways of accomplishing both.[22] Rejecting as dogmatic the dualism inherent in academic philosophy, physicians of the early nineteenth century reiterated many of the points made earlier about the pitfalls of the life of the mind. Jean-Etienne-Dominique Esquirol contended that a sedentary life was a common cause of insanity, which he considered a 'disease of civilization.' The number of insane, he claimed, 'is in direct proportion to its progress.' Scipion Pinel (son of the famous Philippe) not only corroborated this point, but, in his survey of the relative lack of mental disorders among 'savage' people, declared madness the 'privileged affliction of peoples who think.' It was 'the thermometer of their state of advancement; it rises or falls with it.'[23]

What Pinel and Esquirol identified as twin causes of insanity – the sedentary life and cerebral pursuits – were in fact lifestyle traits of the very bourgeois elite that rose to prominence in the nineteenth century. In his widely-cited *Physiologie et hygiène des hommes livrés aux travaux de l'esprit* (1834), which was reprinted throughout the century, the popular physician Joseph Henri Réveillé-Parise observed that the nervous temperament of men engaged in intellectual professions was aggravated by the strain they placed on themselves through immoderate mental work, lack of exercise, solitude, late hours, and neglecting basic hygienic precepts. His advice pertained to a range of men whose work was primarily cerebral rather than physical – from artists, writers and scientists to administrators, businessmen, politicians and functionaries.[24] From this medical perspective, lofty works of genius and complex affairs of state sprang from a common condition of intellectual fatigue and muscular inactivity. This problem was compounded by the connection that other physicians made between the top-heaviness of bourgeois existence and sexual impotence. 'Condemned to a very long period of complete repose,' claimed the best-selling

Hygiène et physiologie du mariage (1848), 'the genital organs lose their capacity to function.' Significantly, this was not a problem one generally encountered among men of the lower orders (that is, the 'savages' of the city and country-side); rather 'that's what happens to savants and men constantly immersed in deep meditation; all their vital energy is carried to the brain; they forget that they are men, and let their virility fall into complete atrophy.'[25] Something similar happened with gastronomy, the art of good taste that is often viewed as quintessentially French. When taken to extremes, it too threatened to redirect the 'vital force' from the genitals to the digestive tract.[26] Gastronomes like Brillat-Savarin may have smugly declared that obesity 'is never found either among the savages, or in those classes of society in which men work to eat, and eat only to live,' but such claims merely reinforced the assumption that refine-ments of the table hardly rendered men fit enough to defend their country.[27] Whether through mental work, culinary excess or sedentary lifestyles, modern civilization posed challenges to the male supremacy it so often celebrated.

Republican manhood

If the Third Republic embarked upon a 'mission to civilize' the provinces and other parts of the world, in terms of masculinity this was an ambiguous project indeed. However strongly it may have been endorsed by the state, civilization continued to be an unstable concept during the Third Republic. Claims that civilization was an unmitigated blessing were constructed in the face of counter-assertions that present-day society needed to be purged of its unhealthy tendencies if 'true' civilization was to be possible. Against the 'savagery' of the Communards of 1870–71, the Third Republic threw its official weight behind the notion of civilization as a largely moralizing force.

There is now a considerable body of work on how the anxieties that gripped the French following the Franco-Prussian War were linked to a spectrum of corporeal dangers, most of which were bound up with the insalubrious devel-opments of the modern world. Alcohol, sexual licentiousness, excessive study, and a general lack of physical hardiness: all had counted among the most disturbing by-products of civilization since the eighteenth century, where the decline of fighting virtues was widely identified as the most common result of such softening experiences. The seeds of the 1870 military defeat were found across the landscape of modern life. Drunkenness and syphilis, vices often asso-ciated with urban existence, received considerable attention for their capacity to diminish strength and erode the will one needed on the field of battle. Yet so too did the state of the *lycées*, the very institutions upon which the greatness of modern French civilization had been erected.[28] In the eyes of critics, then, most aspects of modern civilized existence played some role in the decadence that precipitated the fall of France.

As I have argued elsewhere, *les intellectuels*, a social category that broadly comprised men engaged in largely cerebral and sedentary professions as well as academics, aesthetes and men of letters, crystallized many of these concerns about the effects of modern lifestyles upon the bodies of republican elites. As was the case in other countries, it was the state functionary and office clerk who were most frequently ridiculed. A refugee from the proletariat and a parvenu among the solidly middle class, the functionary was the epitome of what American physician George Beard described as the top-heavy 'brain worker' with weak muscles and tightly-wound nerves.[29] If not rendered impotent as a result of his professional life, his career ambitions would surely encourage him to postpone or forgo having children, a dangerous prospect in an age fraught with anxieties about national depopulation. As the pro-natalist writings of Arsène Dumont and Alphonse Bertillon suggested, 'civilization' exercised a deleterious influence over 'natural' male sexual desires by encouraging men selfishly to indulge their consumer dreams while postponing or forgoing reproduction altogether.[30]

The stresses and stimuli of modern life had a curious effect upon urban dwellers whose mental powers and nervous sensibilities distinguished them from the 'coarse' multitudes. Overstimulated by the stresses and temptations of modern life, degenerate individuals were considered less capable of controlling base impulses through the use of their 'higher faculties,' and were thus increasingly left slaves to their physical urges. Thus, as modernization unfolded, its tendency was to make people more and more 'primitive' in their tastes, manners and morality.[31] Even anthropologists like Francis Pruner-Bey claimed that, while indigenous societies are structured by complex laws and institutions, the 'real savages' were those who pursued personal pleasures or who abandoned the metropole for the apparent lawlessness of the colonies.[32] For many physicians the eighteenth century remained an important reference for the disorders that afflicted men a century later, which is why one doctor explained that neurasthenia 'recalls the vapors of our ancestors.'[33] After all, explained Maurice Potel, 'Neurasthenia is not a sickness of the century [*mal de siècle*]; it is rather a sickness of civilization and [according to another expert] "it increases in intensity at the rate of the progress of the latter; it progresses insofar as man becomes more sedentary, more active intellectually, a principal cause of the development of this neurosis".'[34]

Among those who saw masculinity (and thus human superiority) reflected in a large brain, outspoken and intelligent women were easily caricatured by showing them with comically enlarged heads; yet the same could be done for those men whose physiques were not as developed as their minds. A modern Parisian might have a larger brain than 'savages,' explained the alienist Alexandre Cullerre, but as this brain became perfected over the generations it also became 'more fragile, more impressionable, and thus more susceptible to the causes of disorganization.' In an echo of Esquirol, Cullerre reminded readers that 'the history of madness is the history of civilization.'[35] Thus in his book *La Vie éléctrique* (1892), the French illustrator and futurologist, Albert Robida, could present his darkly comic vision of the eventual 'physical degeneration of overly refined races' by depicting a family gathering around an infant's crib (Figure 5.1). Not only does everyone in the scene wear eyeglasses (indeed, vision was widely thought to diminish as civilization progressed), but all possess comically enlarged and conical heads that are stark contrasts to the slightness of their arms and chests. Moreover, they are all avidly engaged in the very activities that had caused such physical transformations over time: reading and debating. Looming on the wall behind them is a portrait of a hale and hearty army officer, presumably some ancestor whose closer acquaintance with physical exertion, endurance and combat has little place in this dubious future age. This tension between mind and manhood was reinforced in the numerous caricatures of egg-headed intellectuals during the Dreyfus Affair, thus fueling George's Rouhet's concerns about a future populated by 'a race of dwarfs with flabby and undefined muscles, thin limbs . . . with big hydrocephalus heads.'[36] Mental powers without a corresponding muscular development were less of an advance than a weakness.

Robida's coneheads may have come from France, but their physiognomies reflected similar problems faced in other countries. Fears of intellectual advancement at the expense of physical development circulated widely around 1900. Across the Western world, adventure, aggression and physical exercise (in the form of boxing, team sports or gymnastics) were prescribed as therapy for weakened men subjected to deadening routines or top-heavy cerebral existence. Yet while English public schoolboys were being hardened on the playing fields, French students continued to be taught the virtues of intellect and civilization over barbarism, especially those in *lycées* where Victor Cousin's dualistic philosophy reigned supreme. This is evident in the attention that textbooks accorded the undisciplined and barbaric Gauls, whose hot blood, schoolboys were told, still ran in their veins. While expected to polish their manners and submit to the pedagogical mission of the state, schoolboys were also expected to retain the more laudable of barbaric qualities, notably the courage, heroism and intelligence evinced by Vercingetorix, who unified the Gauls in their unsuccessful rebellion against the Romans in 53–52 BCE. This defeat allowed the unruly Gauls to become perfected by adopting the polish of Roman civilization. Like the boorish Gauls, a child-race that was assimilated into the more disciplined Roman empire, schoolboys too must overcome their barbaric tendencies to become civilized adults without losing their warrior spirit.[37]

School textbooks certainly impressed upon students the importance of these ideals; yet how were boys to develop the courage and heroism they supposedly inherited from their Gallic ancestors unless their education extended beyond the development of their minds? The lifestyles of boys thus became of understandable concern throughout this period. During the 1880s the strict regimen to which French schoolboys were subject, which combined aspects of military and monastic discipline, provoked an outcry about intellectual over-taxation (*surmenage intellectuel*) that exhausted boys as it deprived them of physical exercise. Although medical experts and pedagogues alike called for greater attention

Figure 5.1 Albert Robida, 'Déchéance physique des races trop affinées,' *La vie éléctrique* (Paris: La librairie illustrée, 1892), p. 153

to gymnastics and sport to offset the strains of excessive study, attempts to promote physical fitness were thwarted for years by institutional limitations as well as parental resistance. Hygienic advice for children encouraged parents to give them plenty of exercise, ideally in the fresh air of the country, and to get them used to curbing their appetites; mature males were encouraged to exercise vigorously and overcome the tendency to treat their bodies as 'precious' things.[38] In France as elsewhere, the fact that these messages had to be continually reinforced suggests the general disinclination of elites to heed this advice.

It is for these reasons that *lycées* were often viewed as hotbeds of vice. When set loose in the modern city, many claimed, young men had no will to resist its seductive pleasures. The closing decades of the century were thus rife with campaigns aimed at protecting boys and adolescents from the corrupting influences of the city, from dancing, smoking and drinking to dime novels and pornography, all of which were thought capable of inciting a heterosexual excess that could lead to outright homosexuality.[39] The alienist Charles Féré thus concurred with sexologists elsewhere that sexual 'inversion' was a form of hereditary degeneration that would necessarily increase as society became more civilized. For him and for many others, same-sex vice continued to be closely connected to environment and heredity.[40]

Masturbation too continued to be linked to the conditions of an advanced society. In 1897, Dr Thésée Pouillet described the habit of blaming civilization as something that had been 'accepted without question and reproduced, like a tradition, by the majority of physicians and moralists.' Despite criticizing this tendency, Pouillet himself subscribed to a moderate version of this thesis, arguing that civilization played a powerful but secondary role in the etiology of solitary sex that would be ameliorated once the moral advances of civilization caught up with development of material life.[41] Even if some physicians condemned masturbators as exercising a contaminating influence that made them 'destroyers of civilization,' the factors that most believed to be *causes* of solitary sex remained to some extent connected to the unique lifestyles promoted in the modern city.[42] It too was an effect of civilization that threatened to destroy civilization.

It is not surprising to learn that inoculations of the primitive were widely prescribed in the sporting and health reform movements that gained in popularity around 1900. The initiatives of Pierre de Coubertin and others to promote British-style team sports may be viewed as attempts to follow the English lead by crafting more robust bodies through strenuous exercise and effort. Physical culture encouraged the adoption of hardier regimens in order to ensure the health of the race, notably by returning to 'the simple and patriarchal life of yesteryear.'[43] This was part of what Albert Surier called 'a warrior education' that aimed 'to remake France in its very flesh.'[44] Here was indeed a new Spartan ethic that would harden men against the elements. 'The well-balanced man, in short, the true athlete, should be as indifferent to the cold as to the heat, should take the days and seasons as they come, accept the rain without grumbling and the sun with joy.'[45]

If republican discourses often depicted the backwaters of France as 'savage' regions awaiting the polishing influence of civilization, one never needed to leave Paris to encounter primitivity. It was during these decades that the street gangs known as *les apaches* provoked the consternation of the bourgeoisie as well as some approval from Bohemian and anarchist circles. Here was a 'barbarism' that revealed the limitations of bourgeois men more accustomed to the formal niceties (and relatively low mortality rate) of the duel. Edmond Vary's self-defense manual, *Comment on se defend dans la rue et chez soi* (1909), encouraged middle-class men to overcome their reticence about hand-to-hand combat in order to deal appropriately with ruffians on the street. Rather than transform his readers into urban vigilantes, Vary imparted fighting techniques and tricks to give men confidence when facing adversaries. Notably, this required forgetting what one had come to expect about combat under civilized circumstances. 'In the course of an altercation there is nothing more ridiculous than to say to the individual in question: "do you know who I am?" . . . This gives an impression of cowardice and aggravates the adversary.' When all else fails, Vary suggested that one should 'put yourself into a mad anger. A furious madman has the strength of many men . . . If you are endowed with a strong voice, you could intimidate your adversary by emitting savage screams, as Turkish wrestlers do.'[46]

As one might expect, representations of the non-Western world played an important role in negotiating the tensions between civilization and manhood, and, in an age of ever-expanding bureaucracies, many contended that a stint in the colonies was a worthier male pursuit than becoming a mere clerk or functionary. Many colonists raved about how a hard life in Indochina, West Africa or Algeria played a rejuvenating role for Frenchmen, representing what Marshal Hubert Lyautey called 'the finest school of energy.'[47] Others warned about the drift into sodomy and other vices that many soldiers acquired while overseas and which they continued to practice even after their return, or expressed concerns that men would become *décivilisé* as a result of being immersed in foreign cultures and climates.[48] New Caledonia and other colonies were sometimes presented as sites for the creation of 'new men', especially for those Communards, habitual criminals and *apaches* whose 'atavistic' tendencies rendered rehabilitation in modern urban contexts quite useless. By being relocated to 'primitive' conditions, these modern throwbacks to the prehistoric savage would be compelled to evolve. Forced to produce their own food and shelter, 'savage' prisoners would need to submit to an agricultural routine that would tie them to the land and thus to the rudiments of civilization itself. In other words, they would recapitulate in their own lives the transition from nomadic to sedentary that was 'the veritable departure point of civilization.'[49] For already refined bourgeois men, the risk of succumbing to the rough environment of the colonies was also a threat. Hence the oases of European luxury and refinement that were constructed in the higher elevations of Indochina, the famous hill stations and resorts that tried to emulate even the temperatures of home along with many of its comforts and luxuries.[50]

If lower-class 'savages' needed agricultural labor to make them civilized, men who were already polished needed the trappings of civilization to keep them from 'going native.'

Despite these encounters with primitivity, it became clear to many that Frenchmen, in the face of mounting international tensions, were reluctant or unable to harness the 'savage within' in order to face the challenges of war. Since attempts to reverse the country's dwindling birthrate had failed since the 1870s, new measures were needed to compensate for the shortage of Frenchmen. This shortfall was not merely a demographic matter. According to Lieutenant-Colonel Charles Mangin, an officer in the French Colonial Army, depopulation was mainly the result of couples who, afflicted with an 'egoistic sentiment of well-being' and 'the aspiration towards an easy life,' confused civilization with material progress and selfishly decided not to have children. Amounting to the abandonment of the warrior ethic of disciplined hardness, the pursuit of well-being was often cited as a main reason for the apparent decline of French manhood around 1900. As war with Germany began to seem inevitable after 1905, Mangin suggested that Senegalese and Sudanese men could be conscripted in order to swell the ranks of the French army. The arguments he mobilized to support this thesis were enlisted from the racist assumptions of the day. Centuries of endless struggle, he claimed, have 'impressed upon the black race . . . a warrior character' that could be readily subject to military control for the French army: 'Not only do they love danger and a life of adventures, but they are above all capable of being disciplined.' Because the reflexes 'are very easy to train in primitives,' Mangin explained, the education of black recruits can proceed through imitation and 'suggestion.'

Above all, black men possessed what over-refined white men lacked: a well-developed ability to withstand 'fatigue and privations.' Whereas Europeans could only cope with foreign climates 'with great hygienic precautions and on the condition that they invigorate themselves periodically in their native air,' black soldiers were thought capable of enduring just about any environment. Their 'savagery' also made them a frightening spectacle to behold, their mere presence alone possessing 'incomparable shock power. Their arrival on the field of battle will produce in the enemy a considerable moral effect.' If all of this made Africans seem like little more than frighteningly powerful and easily programmed robots, the contrast they posed to flagging French manhood was quite telling. In effect, Mangin presented black masculinity as a substitute for, as well as a potential rejuvenator of, Gallic masculinity. 'In future battles these primitives, for whom life matters so little and whose young blood boils with so much ardor, as if it is eager to be spilled, will certainly measure up to the ancient "French fury" and arouse it if need be.' Although such arguments generated some controversy in France, they acquired greater credence once it became clear the war was going to be a long one. From 1916 onward, 140,000 West African troops were drafted to fight on the Western Front.[51]

Conclusion

The mobilization of colonial troops drives home the notion that, from the perspective of masculinity, the lifestyles wrought by modern civilization were often viewed with ambivalence, not least because they threw into relief the gulf that separated fighting manhood from less impressive civic masculinities. Aside from the racist assumptions that allowed Africans to be viewed as largely disposable beings, black soldiers were enlisted precisely because they possessed the warrior instincts that Mangin and many others believed had been muted by the habits, comforts and egoism of modern French society. Even if there was some hope that Frenchmen might recapture the 'fury' of their ancestors, in the meantime African men would supply the 'savagery' they so sorely lacked. Most commentators, however, insisted that French manhood needed to be completely overhauled if it was to survive the conflict that seemed increasingly likely in the decade before 1914. As the writer Étienne Rey insisted, 'France will cease to exist if she should only be the delicate flower of Latin culture.'[52] Rey's voice was not merely part of the chorus that demanded a reform of virility in the years before the Great War, but one of many that warned of the physical and moral dangers of *civilisation*, above all for the very bourgeois males who most actively promoted and benefited from this sociocultural ideal. Even though the Great War itself would be framed through the lens of a benevolent French *civilisation* versus a barbaric German *Kultur*, for military purposes a bit of primitivity remained a good thing to have.[53]

The *civilisation* that enthused many French men is thus subject to the same paradox that Marshall Berman identifies at the heart of modernity: 'To be modern is to find ourselves in an environment that promises us adventure, power, joy, growth, transformation of ourselves and the world – and, at the same time, that threatens to destroy everything we have, everything we know, everything we are.'[54] Gender scholarship that fails to address the complexity of *civilisation* not only risks oversimplifying the instabilities at the heart of modern masculinity, but has little way of accounting for the fact that feminism itself was often viewed as the fruit of a civilization whose internal contradictions incessantly propelled it towards gender trouble.

Mary Louise Roberts rightly shows how many people in the post-1918 era found a 'civilization without sexes' either frightening or liberating.[55] Yet, from a different perspective, such a prospect was also slightly redundant. If protofascist critics like Pierre Drieu la Rochelle declared that their's was a civilization 'that no longer has sexes,' their immediate concerns about how the war had destabilized gender distinctions may also be viewed against *la longue durée* of ongoing misgivings about civilization as a process that feminized men as it virilized women. Drieu did not feel that the war alone had brought about this state of affairs, for the carefree hedonism of the 1920s was in many respects just an acceleration of the material comforts and sensual pleasures that modern civilization already facilitated and promoted. So if the nationalist

Drieu became a willing collaborator once the Nazis conquered France in June 1940, it had much to do with his admiration for the 'force' that seemed to have been embodied in the German soldiers who smashed through every French defense. In his view, the French could only hope to rejuvenate their virility by emulating their conquerors. Drieu concurred with Robert Brasillach's claim that the fascist man needed to continue resisting the 'touching feminine meek-nesses' of civilization and instead seek refuge in the medieval past. After all, Drieu claimed, ever since the sixteenth century and the rise of modern civiliza-tion 'the French had lost their sense of the body.'[56]

Notes

1. Alice Conklin, *A Mission to Civilize: the Republican Idea of Empire in France and West Africa, 1895–1930* (Stanford, CA: Stanford University Press, 1997), pp. 6, 9–10; Eugen Weber, *Peasants into Frenchmen: the Modernization of Rural France, 1870–1914* (Stanford, CA: Stanford University Press, 1976), pp. 3–22, 485–96.
2. Mary Louise Roberts, *Civilization without Sexes: Reconstructing Gender in Postwar France, 1917–1927* (Chicago: University of Chicago Press, 1994).
3. Annelise Maugue, *L'identité masculine en crise au tournant du siècle, 1871–1914* (Paris: Éditions Rivages, 1987), pp. 32–3.
4. Jan Goldstein, *The Post-revolutionary Self: Politics and Psyche in France, 1750–1850* (Cambridge, MA: Harvard University Press, 2005), pp. 174, 202, 205–6, 231, 235.
5. François Guizot, *Histoire de la civilization en France depuis la chute de l'empire Romain*, in *Oeuvres de Guizot* (6th edn; Paris: Victor Masson, 1851), 1: 6.
6. Quoted in Jean Starobinski, *Blessings in Disguise; or the Morality of Evil*, trans Arthur Goldhammer (Cambridge, MA: Harvard University Press, 1993), p. 20.
7. Alice Bullard, *Exile to Paradise: Savagery and Civilization in Paris and the South Pacific, 1790–1900* (Stanford, CA: Stanford University Press, 2000), p. 2.
8. For a fuller discussion of these ideas in a wider context, see Christopher E. Forth, *Civilization and its Malcontents: Masculinity and the Body in the Modern West* (Basingstoke: Palgrave, forthcoming).
9. Judith Surkis, *Sexing the Citizen: Morality and Masculinity in France, 1870–1920* (Ithaca, NY: Cornell University Press, 2006), p. 12.
10. Starobinski, *Blessings in Disguise*, p. 3.
11. Bullard, *Exile to Paradise*, pp. 14–15.
12. As Starobinski explains, 'the word could take on a pluralist, ethnological, relativistic meaning yet still retain certain implications of the most generalist sort.' Starobinski, *Blessings in Disguise*, p. 6.
13. Michèle Cohen, ' "Manners" Make the Man: Politeness, Chivalry, and the Con-struction of Masculinity, 1750–1830,' *Journal of British Studies*, 44 (April 2005): 312–29.
14. Ronald G. Asch, *Nobilities in Transition, 1550–1700: Courtiers and Rebels in Britain and Europe* (London: Arnold, 2003), pp. 56–60.
15. Philip Carter, *Men and the Emergence of Polite Society, Britain 1660–1800* (London: Pearson, 2001); Teresa Sanislo, 'Models of Manliness and Femininity: the Physical Culture of the Enlightenment and Early National Movement in Germany, 1770–1819' (Doctoral Dissertation in History, University of Michigan, 2001). See also Anne C. Vila, Chapter 1 in this volume.

16. Gail Bederman, *Manliness and Civilization: a Cultural History of Gender and Race in the United States, 1880–1917* (Chicago: University of Chicago Press, 1995), p. 97.
17. Jean-Jacques Rousseau, *A Discourse on the Arts and Sciences*, in *The Social Contract and Other Discourses*, trans. G.D.H. Cole (London: Everyman, 1993), p. 5.
18. Antoine de Baecque, *The Body Politic: Corporeal Metaphor in France, 1770–1800*, trans. Charlotte Mandell (Stanford, CA: Stanford University Press), p. 142; see also Bullard, *Exile to Paradise*, pp. 15–16.
19. Goldstein, *Post-revolutionary Self*.
20. François Guizot, *Cours d'histoire moderne* (Paris: Pichon et Didier, 1828), p. 35.
21. Ian R. Dowbiggin, *Inheriting Madness: Professionalization and Psychiatric Knowledge in Nineteenth-century France* (Berkeley: University of California Press, 1991), pp. 36, 60–1.
22. Samuel Auguste Tissot, *De la santé des gens de lettres* (1768; Geneva: Slatkine, 1981), p. 56.
23. J.E.D. Esquirol, *Mental Maladies: a Treatise on Insanity* (1845; English edition: New York: Hafner Publishing Company, 1965), p. 40; Scipion Pinel, *Physiologie de l'homme aliéné* (Paris: J. Rouvier et E. Le Bouvier, 1833), p. 73.
24. J.H. Réveillé-Parise, *Physiologie et hygiéne des hommes livrés aux travaux de l'esprit* (1834; 4th edn: Paris: G.-A. Dentu, 1845).
25. A. Debay, *Hygiène et physiologie du mariage* (1848; 29th edn, Paris: E. Dentu, 1862), pp. 40, 270–3.
26. Robert A. Nye, *Masculinity and Male Codes of Honor in Modern France* (New York: Oxford University Press, 1993), p. 70.
27. Jean-Anthelme Brillat-Savarin, *The Physiology of Taste*, trans. Anne Drayton (1825; London: Penguin, 1994), p. 208.
28. Bertrand Taithe, *Defeated Flesh: Welfare, Warfare and the Making of Modern France* (Manchester: Manchester University Press, 1999), pp. 208–32; Surkis, *Sexing the Citizen*.
29. Christopher E. Forth, *The Dreyfus Affair and the Crisis of French Manhood* (Baltimore: Johns Hopkins University Press, 2004).
30. This fear of how a 'taste for luxury' generated egoism among men and women animated natalists during the 1920s as well. Surkis, *Sexing the Citizen*, pp. 118–20; Roberts, *Civilization without Sexes*, 124–5.
31. Harry Oosterhuis, 'Medical Science and the Modernization of Sexuality,' in *Sexual Cultures in Europe: National Histories*, eds Franz X. Eder, Lesley Hall, and Gert Hekma (Manchester: Manchester University Press, 1999), p. 228.
32. Bullard, *Exile to Paradise*, p. 23.
33. Henry Labonne, *Comment on se défend des maladies nerveuses: La lutte contre la neurasthénie et les névroses* (Paris: Société d'éditions scientifiques, n.d.), pp. 32–3.
34. Maurice Potel, 'Neurasthénie,' *La Grande encyclopédie* (Paris: Société anonyme de la Grande encyclopédie, 1898–99), 24: 986.
35. Alexandre Cullerre, *Les frontières de la folie* (Paris: Baillière et fils, 1888), p. 318.
36. Georges Rouhet, 'De la nécessité de la culture physique,' *La Culture physique*,1 (March 1904): 28–9; Venita Datta, *Birth of a National Icon: the Literary Avant-garde and the Emergence of the Modern Intellectual* (Albany: State University of New York Press, 1999), pp. 135–82; Forth, *Dreyfus Affair*, pp. 74–7.
37. Dominique Maingueneau, *Les livres d'école de la république, 1870–1914* (Paris: Le Sycomore, 1979), pp. 51–71. For a recent discussion, see Denis M. Provencher and Luke L. Eilderts, 'The Nation According to Lavisse: Teaching Masculinity and Male Citizenship in Third-Republic France,' *French Cultural Studies*, 18(1) (2007): 31–57.
38. Alexandre Donné, *Hygiène des gens du monde* (Paris: Baillière, 1879), pp. 18–20, 21–2.

39. Angus McLaren, *The Trials of Masculinity: Policing Sexual Boundaries, 1870–1930* (Chicago: University of Chicago Press, 1997), pp. 30–1; Surkis, *Sexing the Citizen.*

40. Antony Copley, *Sexual Moralities in France, 1780–1980* (London: Routledge, 1989), 147; Harry Oosterhuis, *Stepchildren of Nature: Krafft-Ebing, Psychiatry, and the Making of Sexual Identity* (Chicago: University of Chicago Press, 2000), p. 54.

41. Thésée Pouillet, *De l'onanisme chez l'homme* (Paris: Vigor frères, 1897), pp. 41–2.

42. Vernon A. Rosario, *The Erotic Imagination: French Histories of Perversity* (New York: Oxford University Press, 1997), pp. 20–8.

43. Georges Rouhet, 'De la nécessité de la culture physique (suite),' *La Culture physique,* 1 (June 1904): 75.

44. Albert Surier, 'La guerre et le sport,' *La Culture physique,* 1 (October 1904): 162.

45. Albert Surier, 'Propos d'été,' *La Culture physique,* 3 (38) (1 August 1906): 605.

46. Edmond Vary, *Comment on se defend dans la rue et chez soi* (Paris: La Nouvelle Populaire, 1909), pp. 9, 11, 13.

47. Robert Aldrich, *Colonialism and Homosexuality* (London: Routledge, 2003), p. 67.

48. Rudi C. Bleys, *The Geography of Perversion: Male-to-male Sexual Behavior outside the West and the Ethnographic Imagination, 1759–1918* (New York: NYU Press, 1995), pp. 148–9. See Robert Aldrich, Chapter 7 in this volume.

49. Matt K. Matsuda, *The Memory of the Modern* (New York: Oxford University Press, 1996), pp. 147–8, 152.

50. Eric T. Jennings, 'From *Indochine* to *Indochic:* the Lang Bian/Dalat Palace Hotel and French Colonial Leisure, Power and Culture,' *Modern Asian Studies,* 37 (1) (February 2003): 159–94. On the civilizing role of women in the colonies, see Penny Edwards, 'On Home Ground: Settling Land and Domesticating Difference in the "Non-settler" Colonies of Burma and Cambodia,' *Journal of Colonialism and Colonial History,* 4 (3) (2003): paragraphs 12, 25.

51. Lieutenant-Colonel Mangin, *La force noire* (Paris: Hachette, 1910), pp. 23, 30, 36, 228, 234, 236, 247–8, 252, 258, 343; Joe Lunn, ' "Les Races Guerrières": Racial Preconceptions in the French Military about West African Soldiers during the First World War,' *Journal of Contemporary History,* 34 (4) (1999): 517–26.

52. Étienne Rey, *La renaissance de l'orgueil français* (Paris: Grasset, 1912), pp. 31–2.

53. Martha Hanna, *The Mobilization of Intellect: French Scholars and Writers during the Great War* (Cambridge, MA: Harvard University Press, 1996).

54. Marshall Berman, *All that is Solid Melts into Air: the Experience of Modernity* (London: Verso, 1995), p. 15.

55. Roberts, *Civilization without Sexes.*

56. Quoted in Robert Soucy, *Fascist Intellectual: Drieu La Rochelle* (Berkeley: University of California Press, 1979), p. 188.

6
Enemies Within: Venereal Disease and the Defense of French Masculinity between the Wars

Judith Surkis

'In ten years syphilis has killed 1,500,000 Frenchmen, as many as the war in four years.'[1] So ran the refrain of social hygienists, who, in the wake of the First World War, worked to remobilize energies against France's 'inner enemies' – social diseases such as tuberculosis, alcoholism, and syphilis. In the course of the war and in its aftermath, social hygiene emerged as a powerful metaphor for and practice of French national reconstruction. As the radical politician, Senator, Mayor of Lyon and eventual Prime Minister Edouard Herriot proclaimed in his work *Créer*, a guidebook of sorts to the remaking of France, 'Physiology appears to us, from now on, as an essential element of politics.'[2] The preservation of human life was at the heart of politics in interwar France. Sexual health and its implications for the health of the family and hence what was increasingly referred to as the 'race' was at the core of these concerns.

Social experts often figured the war as a crucible of new approaches to life. Hygienic politics would hence 'draw from war itself all that it might contain that is favourable to the maintenance and improvement of life.'[3] In wartime, hygiene, including sexual hygiene, had been 'militarized.'[4] As one Ministry of War flier from the early twenties ominously warned army recruits: 'Frenchmen! Be aware, the Germans are beaten, but the greatest enemies still need to be fought. Most of all Alcohol, Tuberculosis, and Venereal Diseases.'[5]

Already before 1914, military physicians and the ministries of the army and navy had been receptive to the propaganda efforts of venereal disease specialists, instituting new prophylactic educational programs as well as procedures to detect and prevent syphilis in the rank and file. These measures were imagined as supplements to France's notorious system of regulated prostitution.[6] The outbreak of hostilities brought a more stringent policing of prostitution, which persisted though the war and afterwards.[7] Justified by the need to maintain the moral and physical health of the army, these measures targeted prostitutes and homosexuals [*individus de moeurs spéciales*] as traitors and threats to the military effort. A law of 1 October 1917 thus made the owners of drinking establishments who housed these suspect characters subject to fines and imprisonment.[8] As the war dragged on, concerned physicians called

103

attention to the inadequacy of mere policing. The moral, social and physical disruption created by the war had brought an apparent increase in venereal infections. As Ernest Gaucher commented in his report to the Academy of Medicine, 'Venereal contagion results from the easy and suspicious encounters that men, in civilian life, would carefully avoid.' And women, 'ordinary' ones included, abandoned on the home front, similarly 'let themselves go.'[9] The distinctions upon which regulated prostitution, in theory, relied had been eroded. Continual troop movements broke down social and geographic boundaries, creating a veritable 'brew of men, who can, in this way carry the germs of venereal disease into the smallest villages.'[10] Justin Godart, the Ministry of War's Under-secretary of State for Health responded to the urgent calls of these physicians. A series of circulars issued in 1916 and 1917 established both stricter procedures for inspecting the venereal condition of troops and for treating infected soldiers and civilians alike in a new system of 'annex services.'[11] While new methods of treatment for syphilis by arsenic injection had been developed in 1909, it was only during the war that they began to receive widespread, publicly-funded application. Godart's wartime measures contained the lineaments of subsequent policies of prevention and treatment, put into place in part under his direction as Minister of Work and Hygiene in 1924 and of Public Health in 1932.[12]

While medical and social concerns with syphilis were by no means new, the postwar 'venereal peril' assumed specific symbolic resonances. Embodying an erosion of boundaries and corporeal permeability, venereal disease, like the unregulated prostitution and homosexuality with which it was associated, threatened the moral and physical fiber upon which victory and national recovery would depend. Now imagined as an uncanny 'inner enemy,' syphilis corporealized perceived threats to the integrity of French masculinity. In the nineteenth century, prostitution and venereal disease worked as an exemplary 'regulatory couplet.' In the post-war context, however, the threat of disease did not just come from suspect women.[13] Other men, and foreign, racially marked men in particular, were imagined as agents of infection. In combating this menace, sexual hygiene was haunted by the very specters that it aimed to dispel. Like other projects devoted to the post-war reconstruction of French masculinity, it both conjured and managed these threats.[14] This ambivalent dynamic lent sexual hygiene metaphorical and practical efficacy. By symbolizing the fragile boundary between a corporeally sound, sexually potent French male citizen and threats to that body by implicitly foreign men, the interwar battle against the 'venereal peril' articulated and enforced the distinction.

Physiological politics

With over a million war dead and millions more injured and disabled, the problem of population was at the core of policies aimed at reconstruction.

'Depopulation' took on both new meanings and new urgency in the wake of the war.[15] It was integral to a vast array of interwar governmental and social concerns – education, labor, immigration, sanitary, military, welfare, and colonial policy. While similarly underwritten by national and natalist concerns, approaches to these policies were flexible and varied rather than uniform; they took both punitive and productive forms. This flexibility accounted for both the power and pervasiveness of hygienic thought. While appealing to social solidarity and national unity, it also enabled a production of differences between men and women, subjects and citizens, foreigners and nationals, all in the name of public health.

At one extreme was a law of 31 July 1920, which outlawed the advertisement and sale of contraceptives, with the notable exception of condoms due to their importance as venereal preservatives; it also banned advertisements for abortions (which were already illegal). A second measure, passed in 1923, made women who sought abortions subject to criminal prosecution. Laden with references to the trauma and losses of the war, these laws focused their punitive and regulatory efforts on women's bodies, drawing a clear corollary between contraception and abortion. Like regulated prostitution, these measures conceived of women not as autonomous subjects, capable of conducting themselves as hygienic citizens, but as objects of state control. By figuring women as reckless, egoistic, and inattentive to the national needs, which superseded their own, the measures sought to recontain the social and sexual threat iconically embodied by the 'new woman,' with her taste for new fashions, a boyish haircut, fast cars, exotic music – and the men who played and danced to it.[16] In these same years, attempts to pass legislation granting women's suffrage, while upheld in the Chamber of Deputies, were blocked on multiple occasions by the Senate.[17] Full citizenship, in the interwar period, remained the province of men. As the exception made for condoms in the 1920 law made clear, attitudes towards the regulation and protection of presumptively heterosexual men and their bodies took a markedly different and less overtly punitive form.

If the 1920 law limited speech, the battle against venereal disease sought to provoke it. Propaganda designed by the *Société française de prophylaxie sanitaire et morale (SFPSM)* and eventually, the *Ligue nationale contre le péril vénérien* was one of its principle 'arms.' Already during the war, lectures to soldiers stated that venereal infections were not 'shameful' and urged soldiers to present themselves 'without delay at a doctor's visit in case of accident.'[18] These palliative rather than punitive measures conceived of men's heterosexual desires as natural, and as hence vulnerable to contamination. Presentations aimed at young men regularly recommended deferred gratification. But they worked, as well, to normalize and indeed celebrate their heterosexual desires; this would not be so in lectures designed for young women.[19]

As Dr Paul Faivre, a Ministry of the Interior official, explained in one report, both girls and boys would benefit from hygienic instruction as long as it used 'the right language, which cannot be the same for everyone.' For soldiers this language included advice on 'individual prophylactic' procedures.[20] 'Is not morality itself highly interested in having individuals keep themselves healthy, so that they can found a home and propagate the race?' asked Faivre.[21] In the case of young women, there would be no mention of prophylactic techniques. Their sexual education, which worked in tandem with new approaches to infant health, focused on 'the study of the physiological functions of women, maternity, breast feeding, and childcare.'[22]

Sexual education aimed at young men likewise upheld the 'productive and reproductive' citizen as their ideal. While always haunted by the very refusal that it sought to overcome, this education, like other contemporary measures designed to revalorize paternity, figured fatherhood as both a social privilege and as a duty.[23] Clearly the focus of Catholic social reformers' 'sentimental education,' these themes were present in hygienists' programs as well.[24] As the childcare expert Adolphe Pinard urged his young auditors, 'In order to be a real man, a *complete citizen*, you must be a *père de famille*.'[25] Model lectures edited by the *Ligue national* thus promoted sexual continence until marriage as the embodiment of virility.[26] For hygienists, this ideal was based on the dissemination of rational sexual knowledge. In highlighting the inadequacy, and indeed, danger of silence and repression, their approaches were fueled by the visibility of sexual pleasure in post-war public culture itself – in the cinema, advertising, and the dance hall. Sexual 'enlightenment' provided the basis for anti-venereal treatment and propaganda and, in turn, for the masculinity it sought to protect (Figure 6.1).

Created with the aid of funds budgeted by parliament beginning in 1920, new public dispensaries were on the frontline in the battle against venereal disease. Some 1697 such centers, offering 3,754,419 consultations in 1931 alone, also disseminated information.[27] In addition to fliers, propaganda experts distributed films and radio conferences on 'France's venereal armament,' including dramatic productions with titles such as 'The kiss that kills' and 'Once upon a time, three friends.'[28] Their mission, according to Lucien Viborel, the director of anti-venereal propaganda for the *Office national d'hygiène sociale*, was clear. 'It is not in hiding one's face that one destroys an enemy or learns how to defend oneself. It is, on the contrary, in striving, early on, to know it in its smallest details, that one can measure its vulnerability, attack it effectively, and, at the very least, arm oneself in order to undo it.'[29] The martial metaphors that pervaded sexual hygiene texts had evident rhetorical force. But what, exactly, was the enemy that they were fighting?

Their target was certainly not men's sexual instincts themselves or, at least, those that took on purportedly 'normal' and 'healthy' form. Even Dr Laignel-Lavastine's highly cautionary *Vénus et ses dangers* figured young men's presumptively heterosexual desires to be the natural 'psychic expression of the reproductive instinct.'[30] Filled with ubiquitous injunctions to young men to be at once productive and *reproductive* citizens, hygiene tracts

Figure 6.1   André Cavaillon, *L'armement anti-vénérien en France* (Paris: Mouvement Sanitaire, 1928), p. 174

took men's heterosexual desires to be a constitutive component of their citizenship. Enlightenment, and not repression, would make men 'whole' citizens. According to childcare expert Pinard, 'from darkness, light must follow, from barbarism must come true civilization.'[31] Hygiene advocates situated their aims within a progressive and, importantly, a civilizational narrative, one that followed France's projected rebirth from the horrors and sacrifice of war. Theirs was a battle against primitive 'ignorance,' the 'principal cause of the propagation of venereal diseases and of the disastrous consequences to which they lead,' as Just Sicard de Plauzoles explained in a lecture to students at the elite Ecole polytechnique.[32] Ignorance was a synecdoche for perverse and disorderly secret knowledge, exemplified by pornography and the deviant, implicitly homosexual 'corrupting friend.' Much better, as Viborel explained, 'to learn about the normal functions of the human organism in a natural history lesson than in the course of a discussion with a perverted comrade or one-on-one with an idiotic, pornographic publication.'[33]

The existence of these surreptitious threats made outright sexual repression dangerous. As the prominent hygienist Léon Bernard commented in his introduction to a manual of anti-venereal propaganda, the 'absolute, apostolic' preaching of chastity (a nod to the dangers of Catholic orthodoxy) was misguided. Chastity prepared the way for deviance, in which the 'taunting offers of some will meet the immoral inversions of others.'[34] Ignorance and repression led to perversion. In order to guard against this threat, here metonymically linked to venereal contagion, practical measures were necessary for male youths who might be incapable of abstinence.

The implications of this position were not lost on conservative moralists who attacked state-funded anti-venereal propaganda as tantamount to pornography. Social Catholic Abbé Jean Viollet denounced 'official hygienists' for propagating 'debauchery in giving youth a way to protect themselves against the dangers of misconduct.'[35] A 1922 congress against pornography likewise condemned the army's anti-venereal tracts for leading young soldiers to believe that 'debauchery is inevitable at their age and that venereal diseases are unimportant, because remedies render them harmless.'[36] While always suspicious of secular state-supported efforts, purity reformers similarly promoted education, rather than outright repression. As social Protestant Pasteur Elie Gounelle commented at the congress, 'a sewer blocked on one side, mounts at the other.'[37]

In doing battle against 'ignorance,' sexual hygienists named the perverse potential of men's sexual instincts and offered a rational solution to that problem. Their initiatives imagined a 'civilized' male citizen whose desires could be avowed and hence ideally severed from secrecy, disease, and perversity. As more traditional moralists were keen to point out, however, this project of enlightenment was risky. Because structured by the revelation of, to use Pinard's terms, 'dark' and 'barbaric' instincts, the sexual 'civilization' that formed the basis of post-war French masculinity and citizenship was precarious.

This ambivalence towards the revelation of 'primitive' instincts helps to explain how the popularity of overtly sexualized 'exoticism' in post-war French culture – from jazz to surrealism – was shadowed, as we will see, by anxieties surrounding racially marked foreign men.[38] As an incitement to and alibi for sexual pleasure, exoticism was touted as a source of invigorating release and renewal. But the fashionable 'rage' for things exotic was, simultaneously, figured as a force of contagion. The ironic preface to *Le tumulte noir*, which featured iconic images of Josephine Baker and the *Revue nègre*, thus described Parisians as being 'since the armistice . . . stricken with Negropathy.' Its author's faux-hygienism exonerated the artist, Paul Colin, who was depicted as a medical illustrator of sorts, documenting the *'delirium tremens* of Negromania.'[39] The equivocal text both celebrated the profound, sexualized energies of primitivism and reinforced its association with uncontrolled – and devirilizing – illness.

In this context, publicly visible 'foreign' men in metropolitan France were constituted as an uncanny 'primitive' presence. Imagined, in different ways, as repositories of sexual contagion, the African-American jazz man, the colonial worker, and, increasingly in the 1930s, the 'Jew' represented at once somatic and symbolic threats to the integrity of the French citizen's masculinity. Given the contemporary currency of hygienic discourse and practice, the regulation of venereal disease both avowed and administered this threat. It served as one important way in which to reassert differences between French and foreign men, citizens and subjects, which had been seemingly eroded by the war.

Production and reproduction

In response to the nation's perceived demographic deficit, interwar policies of production and reproduction were closely aligned. New approaches to men's sexual instincts coincided with new methods of work science, which similarly identified and stabilized individual differences in the name of rational organization and social harmony.[40] The study of gender and civilization differences, with respect to both work and sex, informed these interrelated projects of national – and masculine – restoration.[41]

Alongside natalism and social hygiene, immigrant labor was vital to France's post-war renewal, even as it challenged the meaning of the nation and its masculinity. Allied concerns about French norms of productivity, reproductivity, and hygiene, in turn, shaped immigration policy in multiple ways.[42] In this context, the 'venereal peril' articulated and managed a perceived erosion of national boundaries and the uncanny presence of 'foreign' colonial men within 'domestic' French space. By positioning male foreigners as somatic and sexual threats, it justified new forms of sanitary control. Like the new approaches to venereal disease more generally, these attitudes initially took shape during the war.

France famously called upon its colonies for the war effort. Hundreds of thousands of soldiers were conscripted, often by force, from West and North Africa, as well as Indochina. And over half a million immigrant workers met wartime labor shortages, some 300,000 of whom traveled to the metropole from French colonies and protectorates as well as China. According to a perverse logic which abjected the men on whose labor the nation's survival in part depended, they were isolated in separate facilities and subject to separate regulations. Claims that 'indigenous' subjects were vulnerable to moral, sexual, and political contagion underwrote this segregation.[43]

Before the war, physicians who had worked in the colonies and with colonial troops warned against their endemic syphilis as well as their irrational resistance to treatment. Following this expert advice, Justin Godart's 25 September 1916 circular addressed the case of 'indigenes called to work in factories' by ordering that they be subject to a 'very attentive visit' when they disembarked in France, and again when they arrived at the military establishment or factory to which they were assigned. A follow-up circular urged that 'it has been observed that colonial workers and foreigners of diverse provenance (Algeria, Tunisia, Morocco, Indochina, China, etc.) employed in different work centers frequently arrive affected by venereal infections, and especially serious and highly contagious incidents of syphilis.' Because they posed 'a serious danger to the metropole,' Godart urged that they be subject to monthly or bi-monthly examinations during their tenure. French workers, and those who were assimilated to them, were not required to undergo these examinations.[44] This surveillance was underwritten by these subjects' presumptive insensitivity to moral instruction. As one physician noted, 'How can we expect that such teaching can reach the spirit of a Negro from the Sudan or even that of a more cultivated Muslim, whose moral shape is, thanks to the Koran, notably different?'[45] Resistance to sexual enlightenment became one way to distinguish between French and foreign men, to represent the threat the latter posed to national integrity, and to justify their differential treatment.

After the war, racist policies towards non-European migrants, especially those from North Africa, drew on just such sexualized fears about contagious, corruptible men, who were – as critics were keen to point out – overwhelmingly single. One analyst, for example, estimated that women made up only 2 per cent of those from 'Africa,' in contrast to 42 per cent of Italians.[46] For natalist immigration specialists these statistics demonstrated the greater desirability and assimilability of Europeans, especially Catholic Italians and Poles, who embodied an ideally reproductive paternity.[47]

Opponents of North African migration, meanwhile, played up the demoralizing effects of metropolitan life on indigenous soldiers and workers. Colonel Paul Azan thus explained how the North African 'only meets up with the lowest class of the masculine and feminine population; he gets into the habit of drinking, which he didn't have before, and learns to disdain the French woman, who he respected in Algeria.' According to this logic, the indigene would threaten the colonial racial and sexual order upon his return. While in the metropole, he sowed his diseases, especially tuberculosis and syphilis, and committed crimes, because dominated by his 'savage instincts.'[48] Immigration specialists often echoed these sentiments.[49] For Norbert Gomar, 'sexual liberty' was what attracted Algerian immigrants to metropolitan France in the first place. He thus warned against 'these terrible germ carriers . . . the syphilitic Kabyles, who come to the metropole to spread their terrible microbe.'[50] According to Georges Mauco, prostitution and traditional healers ruined 'the moral and physical health of these unfortunates, among whom tuberculosis and syphilis do frightening damage.'[51] These moralizing arguments about sexual dissipation and contagion served a clear political function; they delegitimated post-war challenges posed by colonial subjects to the identity of the French citizen – and his masculinity – by figuring them in sexual, rather than political terms.

By concretizing and corporealizing racial and sexual fears, invocations of the venereal peril drew implicit distinctions between French men, on the one hand, and colonial and foreign subjects on the other. For, if French men's sexual instincts were imagined as amenable to education, experts on immigration consistently portrayed North Africans, with their violent and excessive passions, as resistant to and indeed incapable of sexual enlightenment. Immigration experts thus highlighted particular sexual proclivities – including polygamy and pederasty ('it seems to be accepted by all as almost normal,' according to one expert on Moroccan immigration) – as evidence of this excess and difference.[52] And, following the 1919 Jonnart Law, the charge of polygamy was notoriously used to disqualify Algerian indigenes from full citizenship.[53] While serving a clear political function, the fixation on Algerian men's polygamy was also a projective fantasy and uncanny echo of debates about polygamy as a rational solution to the shortage of *French* men.[54] This 'shortage' of French men fueled anxieties about North Africans as sexual threats to French women and justified calls for the 'selection' and regulation of those who arrived on metropolitan soil.

In an atmosphere of moral panic following the murders of two women by an unemployed Kabyle immigrant in Paris, new procedures regulating Algerian immigration were passed in 1924.[55] National sanitary defense was a crucial component of the new restrictions, which instituted screening for diseases prior to immigrants' departure. While, in theory, motivated by the sexual and hygienic threat posed by single men, the same circular established that indigenous Algerians who wanted to bring their families with them had to provide proof of adequate resources and lodging.[56] According to this evident double bind, Algerian migrants were consigned to the mobile – and hence dangerous – bachelor status, which justified the restrictions in the first place.

For those migrants already living in the capital, the Paris Municipal Council established special venereal disease and tuberculosis clinics, exclusively for 'North Africans,' in 1925. The threat of social disease articulated the sanitary, moral, and political fears which drove this police project of 'protection and surveillance.'[57] Pierre Godin, who launched the initiative, contended that 'syphilis is, for North Africans, the leprosy of today.'[58] Octave Depont, a seasoned colonial administrator and spirited advocate of the venture, deplored 'Berbers' atavistic taste for promiscuity,' which 'the open air of their mountains attenuates, but which, in Paris, is excessively dangerous for public health.' Abject images of dirty, drunken, and diseased single men, living together in excessively close quarters, were a staple of texts calling for the need to carefully regulate North African immigration.[59] These men's imagined susceptibility to disease underwrote the political surveillance that accompanied the project's mission of 'assistance.' And it also delegitimated their politicization by figuring it as a form of contagion. As Depont explained, 'Africans are very receptive . . . One can never without danger excite men who are as impressionable as Berbers, who have such rough and roving minds.'[60] Venereal disease, associated as it was with primitive sexual contagion, symbolized these men's menacing difference in hygienic rather than overtly political terms. Their susceptibility to syphilis was an index of their incapacity for citizenship and, inversely, of French men's purported sexual and political enlightenment.

Advocates for Algerian rights clearly identified the hypocrisy of the claims made in order to justify these regulations. The 'young Algerian' Ferhat Abbas, at the time an advocate for assimilation, denounced the 1924 ministerial circular restricting travel to the metropole. By invoking 'the criminality of "sidis" and the danger for France of these reservoirs of viruses,' he explained, it constituted a 'cabal mounted against the poor indigenous worker.'[61] As *Sidi de banlieue*, the 1937 novel by Jean Damase depicting the ravages of a syphilitic North African immigrant drawn to the metropole by his sexual desires, made clear, these fears – at once hygienic, political, and sexual – were only exacerbated in the following decade.[62]

Corporeal citizenship

In the 1920s, sanitary considerations underwrote policies that directly correlated national and corporeal boundaries. A 15 February 1927 circular, for example, made medical verification of the 'absence of active infectious diseases,' including 'venereal diseases,' a visa requirement for foreign nationals who sought to work in France.[63] As concerns about the presence of foreigners on French national soil sharpened in the 1930s with the onset of the depression, Hitler's rise to power, and the arrival of thousands of refugees, this conflation of corporeal and national integrity assumed even greater force. Hygiene offered a potent way to articulate both immigrants' difference and their potentially corrosive effect on the nation's integrity – and its masculinity. The permeability of the nation's territorial and corporeal boundaries symbolized its feminization. While figures on the radical right were the most vocal and virulent in their calls to restore the nation's borders, progressive, 'republican' population specialists addressed the question as well.

For example, the liberal *Association des études sexologiques*, founded by Édouard Toulouse in 1931, advocated a rationalist model of population and sexual management. Its members included prominent anti-venereal activists, such as Sicard de Plauzoles, feminists like Bertie Albrecht, the President of the *Ligue des droits de l'homme*, Victor Basch, and Justin Godart, its honorary president.[64] Founded on 'rational' hygienic principles, the association's proposed programs combined liberatory and regulatory components. They thus claimed that sexual needs, including those of women, should be satisfied 'in the interest of the neuro-biological equilibrium.' By creating more sexual opportunities for men, this liberation would reduce prostitution (and hence contamination). While encouraging such freedom of heterosexual expression, they also promoted premarital syphilis screening (which was eventually adopted under Vichy) and mandatory treatment, measures which clearly infringed on men's legally protected (sexual) privacy.[65] In keeping with this regulatory approach, the association recommended that the 'selection' of immigrants 'be attentively researched.'[66]

Sicard's approach to immigration similarly combined incitation and regulation. In his social hygiene lectures at the Sorbonne in 1937, he described immigration as 'necessary and good' and ethnic mixing as formative of the 'French nation.' He however cautioned against 'crossings' between 'races that are very different, such as, for example, black and white, black and yellow, white and yellow,' and hence advocated selective immigration.[67] As is clear in Sicard's case, racialist thinking could be integrated into sexual hygiene's purportedly rational determination of which sexual relations were a source of national strength, and which might result in implicitly devirilizing 'degeneration.'

This tendency was especially pronounced in the sinister writings of Sicard's fellow hygienist, René Martial, who, by the end of the 1930s, had become one of the foremost theorists of 'race' in France.[68] A vocal critic of 'métissage,' or unhealthy racial mixing in the 1930s, Martial began his career as a hygienist in a venereal disease clinic in 1902. As an SFPSM member, he promoted sexual 'enlightenment' and a rational approach to syphilis treatment.[69] From the mid-1920s onward, Martial refocused his thinking about sexual instincts on the supposed science of 'inter-racial' grafting. Conflating racial health with a vital, implicitly virile sexual instinct, Martial argued that 'races' remained constant 'naturally' and 'spontaneously.' This integrity, he claimed, was under siege because of the large-scale population movements associated with both colonization and 'anarchic' immigration. According to a tautological argument, 'disharmonious' *métissage* bred more *métissage*. This created a 'weakening of the race's instinct of conservation; its lapse [*relâchement*] facilitates incoherent mixing.'[70] Figured in terms of deficiency and disorder, *métissage* symbolized corporeal and national devirilization, a depletion which the *métis*, characterized as 'timorous or indecisive, dissimulating or perfidious,' seemingly embodied.[71] Symptomatic of this dissipation, 'feminism' and social diseases such as syphilis were, for Martial, so many signs that the 'French' race and its sexual instincts were no longer capable of self-preservation.

Analogous concerns about devirilization as the inevitable result of eroded racial and sexual identities animated contemporary political discourse. Critics of the Republic increasingly drew correlations between moral and sexual confusion and contemporary political disorder. Writing in the wake of the 6 February 1934 anti-parliamentary riots in Paris, the political editor of the conservative weekly *Gringoire*, attributed post-war French disarray to, among other causes, inflation, money changers, jazz nudists, cocktail orgies, gangster films, bailed-out crooks, old *garçonnes*, and literary pederasts.[72] For its detractors, the Republic's internally corrupt and feminized leaders were incapable of holding firm in the face of powerful external threats; the parliamentary system itself appeared to be an 'inner enemy' of the nation. Images of France as weak and deficient, colonized and contaminated by foreigners and Jews reached a fever pitch with the election of Léon Blum's socialist-led Popular Front government in 1936. For right-wing critics, Blum embodied a decadent, Jewified, hybrid, and sexually perverted nation, at once threatened from beyond its borders and fatally undermined from within.[73] References to disease, including venereal diseases, suffused anti-republican and anti-Semitic accounts of France's decline, of the 'Judeo-Masonic' threat and the 'Bolshevik microbe.' This visceral rhetoric and its powers of horror rendered perceptible the secret maladies supposedly sapping the virile forces of the nation at its very source.[74]

Laurent Viguier, for example, described Blum's leadership of France as a kind of venereal contagion. 'Since the marriage with Blum,' he wrote, 'the young bride [that is, France] is devoured by a canker.'[75] He quoted at length from Blum's recently republished 1907 text *On Marriage* alongside passages from Leviticus, in order to figure Blum – and hence 'Jews' – as a libertine and sexual deviant, a defender of incest, onanism, bestiality, and pederasty. For the reactionary press, *On Marriage* proved that Blum was incapable of (sexual) self-government and hence unfit to lead the nation.[76] His recommendation that young women be granted more sexual freedom (again, with the hopes of reducing prostitution) appeared to confirm the fears of the regime's most radical critics – that the 'Republic' was a slut (*la gueuse*), its ministers, her pimps and clients.[77] (Figure 6.2.)

Contemporary anti-Semitic writings followed a derepressive logic of their own, by revealing the 'secret maladies' purportedly plaguing the nation. Taking the 'Protocols of the Elders of Zion' as its playbook, the Catholic-run *Revue internationale des sociétés secrètes*, for example, denounced nudism, sexual education, the abolition of prostitution, feminism, Popular Front family policy, and the World Sex Reform Congress as so many Judeo-Masonic threats to the integrity of French masculinity. One writer, castigating the abolition of prostitution in several socialist municipalities, proclaimed, 'To pretend to defend morality and public health by imposing a system which will increase demoralization and aggravate the venereal peril. There it is, caught red handed [*saisie sur le vif*], the machine to bestialize [*abrutir*] the "Goys"!'[78]

Figure 6.2 Roger Roy, 'De le théorie à la pratique ou le ménage à trois,' *Le Gringoire* (14 May 1937), p. 1

The populist far-right journal, *Gringoire*, meanwhile, took another tack. It sought to cleave French men's sexuality from that of deviant and foreign others through a strategy of incitement and disavowal.[79] Salacious travelogues by the likes of Louis Charles Royer offered first-hand accounts of sexual exploits in faraway places – Germany, the Soviet Union, and Algeria – allowing its readers to participate in these pleasures, while distancing themselves from them. Cartoons regularly hinted at the connections between Jews, Freemasons, and homosexuals whose secret associations purportedly threatened the heterosexual integrity of the French national body. Advertisements for hormonal replacement therapies and hygienic regimes, meanwhile, promised to restore men's sexual potency and hence to overcome France's presumptively decadent and diminished state.

The associations between disease, racial corruption, and deficient masculinity also found pointed expression in the works of Louis-Ferdinand Céline and Pierre Drieu la Rochelle.[80] Based on his service as a doctor in the poor suburbs of Paris, Céline's early novels portrayed France as eaten away by disease and 'occupied' by foreigners.[81] His later, virulently anti-Semitic pamphlets likewise depicted a failed French masculinity ravaged by the interconnected ills of venereal disease, homosexuality, and racial mixing. Foreign men, 'Jews, afro-asiatic hybrids . . . relentless fornicators,' were the source of this corruption, 'contaminators of our most degrading poxes [*vérole*, a colloquial term for venereal disease], insatiable.' In Céline's paranoid fantasy, they sought to destroy France by creating 'a confusion of the sexes by all the dicks [*bites*] of all possible colors.' Here, the syphilitic man, 'everywhere dilapidated, eaten away, testicles, scrotum' epitomized France's degraded condition.[82]

This dense figurative nexus appears as well in Drieu la Rochelle's fascist Bildungsroman, *Gilles*. On a visit to a now emptied countryside, Gilles's mentor explains how France, unable to reproduce itself, was left with only a passion for self-destruction. 'The very source of life is affected,' he commented. 'No more sperm [*foutre*], or it goes into the bidet.' The implications were dire: 'They will be invaded. They are already invaded. Poles, Czechs, dirty Arabs [*des bicots*].' Gilles summed up the current state of affairs: 'There is a power of syphilis in France.'[83]

Conclusion

There was indeed a 'power of syphilis' in interwar France. Since the end of World War I, the 'venereal peril' had embodied an internal threat to the nation's sexual health, which served to justify concrete measures to maintain and police its corporeal integrity. The simultaneously symbolic and practical power of venereal disease was by no means new to the interwar period. What was new, however, was the way in which this perceived threat worked to construct differences, not just between men and women, but also between French and foreign men. Venereal disease was not merely a convenient metaphor for the fragility, permeability, and instability of French masculinity. Its figurative possibility, as a sign and symptom of sexual confusion and contagion, anchored diffuse concerns about who could and should qualify as a French man in specific bodies. Hygienists worked to expose this 'inner enemy,' whose perniciousness was metonymically linked to a secrecy and perversion that their sexual education programs were designed to combat. This project of enlightenment ideally cleaved French masculinity from its association with the treacherous and traitorous foreigners in its midst. And indeed, hygienists and immigration specialists designated 'foreign' men, North Africans, in particular, as dangerous repositories of contagion, who were all the more threatening because incapable of or resistant to sexual enlightenment. The sexual and somatic threat posed by these men underwrote their administrative regulation as well as their exclusion from French citizenship. Even progressive advocates of immigration took recourse to sanitary concerns in order to describe France's sexual and corporeal limits. The prominence of the rhetoric of sexual contagion among the Republic's most virulent right-wing critics is, given this context, unsurprising. My point here is not to efface important distinctions between republicans and their critics. The pervasiveness of these concerns across the political spectrum instead illustrates just how much traction they actually had.[84] Right-wing opponents of progressive sexual hygiene, and of the Republic more generally, also figured their enemies as forces of hidden contagion, whose disfiguring and devirilizing potential they ceaselessly sought to reveal. They too sought to cleave French masculinity from its associations with secret perversity, by bringing to light how foreign men were undermining the nation from within. And they likewise drew on the symbolic power of the venereal peril in order to articulate and manage that threat.

Notes

1. Henri Gougerot, 'Un danger national a combattre,' *Bulletin de la Société française de prophylaxie sanitaire et morale (BSFPSM)* (May 1920): 82.
2. Edouard Herriot, *Créer* (Paris: Payot, 1919), p. 171.
3. Emile Boutroux in Alliance d'hygiene sociale, *La guerre et la vie de demain, conférences de l'alliance de l'hygiène sociale (1914–1916)*, Vol. 1 (Paris: Félix Alcan, 1916), p. 17.
4. Lion Murard and Patrick Zylberman, 'L'autre guerre (1914–1918): La santé publique en France sous l'oeil de l'Amérique,' *Revue historique*, 276 (1986): 368–98, 370.
5. Auguste Queyrat and Just Sicard de Plauzoles (eds), *Manuel d'éducation prophylactique contre les maladies vénériennes* (Paris: Maloine, 1922).
6. For an account of these developments, see Judith Surkis, *Sexing the Citizen: Morality and Masculinity in France, 1870–1920* (Ithaca: Cornell University Press, 2006). On the regulation of prostitution, Alain Corbin, *Les filles de noce* (Paris: Aubier, 1978).
7. Jean-Yves Le Naour, *Misères et tourments de la chair durant la Grande Guerre: les moeurs sexuelles des Français, 1914–1918* (Paris: Aubier, 2002), pp. 162–79; Michelle K. Rhoades, ' "No safe women": Prostitution, Masculinity, and Disease in France during the Great War' (PhD History, University of Iowa, 2001).
8. André Cavaillon, *L'armement anti-vénérien en France* (Paris: Mouvement sanitaire, 1928), p. 53. On the homosexual as threat to the war effort, Florence Tamagne, *Histoire de l'homosexualité en Europe: Berlin, Londres, Paris 1919–1939* (Paris: Seuil, 2000), pp. 30–5.
9. E. Gaucher, 'Les maladies vénériennes pendant la guerre à l'hôpital Villemin et dans ses annexes,' *Bulletin de l'Académie de médicine*, 75 (28 March 1916): 337–8.
10. E. Gaucher and L. Bizard, 'Statisique des syphilis contractées par les militaires depuis la mobilisation,' *Annales de Maladies vénériennes (AMV)*, 11 (March 1916): 131–2.
11. Ministère de la Guerre, Sous-secretariat d'Etat du service de santé militaire, Circulaire 251 Ci/7, 25 September 1916; Ministère de l'Intérieur, Direction de l'Assistance de l'hygiène publique, Circulaire 57, 5 June 1917. See also, Le Naour, *Misères*, pp. 190–98; Michelle K. Rhoades, 'Renegotiating French Masculinity: Medicine and Venereal Disease during the Great War,' *French Historical Studies*, 29 (2) (2006): 293–327; Surkis, *Sexing the Citizen*, Chapter 8.
12. Lion Murard and Patrick Zylberman, ' "Au-dessus des individus et des groupements de politique pure" Justin Godart et la Santé publique,' in *Justin Godart: Un homme dans son siècle (1871–1956)*, ed. Annette Wieviorka (Paris: CNRS Editions, 2004), pp. 169–80; Claude Quétel, *History of Syphilis* (Baltimore: Johns Hopkins University Press, 1990).
13. On this regulatory dynamic, Andrew R. Aisenberg, 'Syphilis and Prostitution: a Regulatory Couplet in Nineteenth-century France,' in *Sex, Sin and Suffering: Venereal*

Disease and European Society since 1870, eds Roger Davidson and Lesley A. Hall (London: Routledge, 2001), pp. 15–28.

14. See, for example, Carolyn J. Dean, *The Frail Social Body: Pornography, Homosexuality and other Fantasies in Interwar France* (Berkeley: University of California Press, 2000); Roxanne Panchasi, 'Reconstructions: Prosthetics and the Rehabilitation of the Male Body in World War I France,' *differences*, 7 (3) (1995): 109–39; Mary Louise Roberts, *Civilization without Sexes: Reconstructing Gender in Postwar France, 1917–1927* (Chicago: Chicago University Press, 1994); Daniel J. Sherman, 'Monuments, Mourning and Masculinity in France after World War I,' *Gender and History*, 8 (1) (1996): 82–107.

15. Marie-Monique Huss, 'Pronatalism in the Inter-war Period in France,' *Journal of Contemporary History*, 25 (1) (1990): 39–68; Sîan Reynolds, *France between the Wars: Gender and Politics* (New York: Routledge, 1996), pp. 18–37; Roberts, *Civilization without Sexes*, 93–8. On natalist concerns prior to the First World War, see Joshua Cole, *The Power of Large Numbers: Population, Politics, and Gender in Nineteenth-century France* (Ithaca: Cornell University Press, 2000).

16. Jean Elisabeth Pedersen, 'Regulating Abortion and Birth Control: Gender, Medicine, and Republican Politics in France, 1870–1920,' *French Historical Studies*, 19 (3) (1996): 673–98; Roberts, *Civilization without Sexes*, p. 109.

17. Paul Smith, *Feminism and the Third Republic: Women's Political and Civil Rights in France, 1918–1945* (New York: Oxford University Press, 1996).

18. Circulaire 251 Ci/7, 2.

19. On the celebration of the soldier's heterosexuality Marie-Monique Huss, 'Pronatalism and the Popular Ideology of the Child in Wartime France: the Evidence of the Picture Postcard,' in *The Upheaval of War: Family, Work, and Welfare in Europe, 1914–1918*, eds Richard Wall and Jay Winter (Cambridge: Cambridge University Press, 1988), pp. 329–67; Rhoades, 'Renegotiating.'

20. For advice to soldiers, see: 'Circulaire relative à la propagande antivénérienne dans l'armée,' n. 5740/C, Ministère de la Guerre, reprinted in Queyrat and Sicard de Plauzoles, *Manuel d'éducation*, pp. 167–75.

21. Paul Faivre, 'Exposé d'ensemble de l'organisation de la lutte antivénérienne en France,' *Revue d'hygiène*, 44 (1922): 290–1.

22. 'A propos de l'éducation sexuelle: voeux de la Société,' *BSFPSM* (July 1922): 126. On the development of sexual education for girls, see Yvonne Knibiehler, 'L'éducation sexuelle des filles ax XXe siècle,' *Clio*, 4 (1996): 139–60; Roberts, *Civilization without Sexes;* Mary Lynn Stewart, ' "Science is always chaste": Sexual Initiation and Sex Education in France, 1880s–1920s,' *Journal of Contemporary History*, 32 (3) (1997): 381–93. On maternal health, see Françoise Thebaud, *Quand nos grand-mères donnaient la vie: la maternité en France dans l'entre-deux-guerres* (Lyon: Presses Universitaires de Lyon, 1986).

23. See, for example, Kristen Stromberg Childers, *Fathers, Families, and the State in France, 1914–1945* (Ithaca: Cornell University Press, 2003), pp. 49–53; Cheryl Koos, 'Fascism, Fatherhood, and the Family in Interwar France: the Case of Antoine Redier and the Legion,' *Journal of Family History*, 24, (3) (1999): 317–29.

24. On Catholic approaches to sexual knowledge in the interwar period, see Martine Sevegrand, *Les Enfants du bon dieu: les catholiques français et la procréation au XXe siècle* (Paris: Albin Michel, 1995).

25. Dr Adolphe Pinard, *A la jeunesse, pour l'avenir de la race francaise* (Paris: Persan, 1925), p. 8.

26. See, for example, Dr Laignel-Lavastine, *Vénus et ses dangers* (Paris: Persan-Beaumont, 1926); Pinard, *A la jeunesse.*

27. For these and other statistics, see Ministère de Santé publique, *L'organisation antivénérienne en France* (Paris: Office national d'hygiène sociale, 1930); Ministère de Santé publique, *Compte rendu statistique de l'activité antivénérien pour l'annéé* (Paris: 1931); 'Les maladies vénériennes devant la Chambre des deputés,' *Prophylaxie antivénérienne (PA)* (January 1930): 24–36.
28. Lucien Viborel, *La technique moderne de la propagande d'hygiène sociale* (Paris: Editions de 'la vie saine', 1930), pp. 216–17. See, for example, Louis Forest, *Ils étaient trois: histoire de trois jeunes hommes de notre siècle* (Paris: Société de publications modernes, 1928).
29. Lucien Viborel, 'L'éducation publique contre le péril vénérien,' in Ministère de Santé publique, *L'organisation*, p. xv.
30. Laignel-Lavastine, *Vénus*, p. 5.
31. Pinard, *A la jeunesse*, p. 8.
32. Just Sicard de Plauzoles, *Les maladies vénériennes: plan d'une conférence faite aux élèves de l'Ecole Polytechnique* (Paris, 1928), p. 3.
33. Ministère de Santé publique, *L'organisation*, pp. xvi–xvii. On countering repression as the best way to battle the contagiousness of both pornography and homosexuality, see Dean, *The Frail Social Body*.
34. Léon Bernard, 'Le rôle de l'éducation populaire dans la défense contre les maladies vénériennes,' in Queyrat and Sicard de Plauzoles (eds), *Manuel d'éducation*, p. 14.
35. Abbé J. Viollet, 'De l'autorité de l'Etat sur le terrain de la famille et de l'éducation,' in Association du mariage chrétien, *L'autorité et la liberté dans la famille et autour de la famille* (Paris, 1924), p. 83.
36. See the discussion and vote in: Fédération française des sociétés contre l'immoralité publique, 'Rapports, Discussions et Voeux,' *3e Congrès National contre la Pornographie* (1922), p. 123. Letter reprinted in *BSFPSM* (April 1922), p. 66.
37. Fédération française, 'Rapports, Discussions et Voeux,' p. 68.
38. See Tyler Stovall, 'National Identity and Shifting Imperial Frontiers: Whiteness and the Exclusion of Colonial Labor after World War I,' *Representations*, 84 (52) (2004): 52–72.
39. Cited in Karen C.C. Dalton and Henry Louis Gates, 'Josephine Baker and Paul Colin: African American Dance Seen through Parisian Eyes,' *Critical Inquiry*, 24 (2) (1998): 933–4. On the racial and sexual dynamics of exoticism, see Brett A. Berliner, *Ambivalent Desire: the Exotic Black Other in Jazz Age France* (Amherst: University of Massachusetts Press, 2002); Elizabeth Ezra, *The Colonial Unconscious: Race and Culture in Interwar France* (Ithaca: Cornell University Press, 2000); Jeffrey Jackson, *Making Jazz French: Music and Modern Life in Interwar Paris* (Durham: Duke University Press, 2003).
40. On French work science, Jackie Clarke, 'Engineering a New Order in the 1930s: the Case of Jean Coutrot,' *French Historical Studies*, 24 (1) (2001): 63–86; William H. Schneider, 'The Scientific Study of Labor in Interwar France,' *French Historical Studies*, 17 (2) (1991): 410–46. For an account of the role of industry in family policy, see Susan Pedersen, *Family, Dependence, and the Origins of the Welfare State: Britain and France, 1915–1945* (Cambridge: Cambridge University Press, 1993).
41. Laura Lee Downs, *Manufacturing Inequality: Gender Division in the French and British Metalworking Industries, 1914–1939* (Ithaca: Cornell University Press, 1995); Laura Levine Frader, 'From Muscles to Nerves: Gender, "Race," and the Body at Work in France, 1919–1939,' *International Review of Social History*, 44 (Supplement) (1999): 123–147; Reynolds, *France between the Wars*, pp. 92–114; Roberts, *Civilization without Sexes*, pp. 188–96.
42. Elisa Camiscioli, 'Producing Citizens, Reproducing the "French Race": Immigration, Demography, and Pronatalism in Early Twentieth-century France,' *Gender and*

History, 13 (3) (2001): 593–621; Gary S. Cross, *Immigrant Workers in Industrial France: the Making of a New Laboring Class* (Philadelphia: Temple University Press, 1983); Stovall, 'National Identity.'

43. Neil MacMaster, *Colonial Migrants and Racism: Algerians in France, 1900–62* (London: Macmillan, 1997); Tyler Stovall, 'The Color Line behind the Lines: Racial Violence in France during the Great War,' *American Historical Review*, 103 (3) (1998): 741. On the recruitment of soldiers in West Africa, see Alice L. Conklin, *A Mission to Civilize: the Republican Idea of Empire in France and West Africa* (Stanford, CA: Stanford University Press, 1997).

44. Circulaire 251 Ci/7, 2; and Sous-secrétariat du Service de santé militaire, Circular 399 Ci/7, 10 January 1917. See also Surkis, *Sexing the Citizen*, pp. 237–8.

45. Charles Soulier, 'Voeu en faveur d'une loi sur la repression du racolage et contre la contamination vénérienne,' *AMV*, 12 (April 1917): 369. On racist attitudes and sexual anxiety toward colonial subjects, see Le Naour, *Misères*, pp. 260–72; Julia Miller, 'The "Romance of regulation": the Movement against State-regulated Prostitution in France, 1871–1948' (PhD History, New York University, 2000), pp. 409–42; Stovall, 'Color Line'; Tyler Stovall, 'Love, Labor, and Race: Colonial Men and White Women in France during the Great War,' in *French Civilization and its Discontents*, eds Tyler Stovall and Georges Van Den Abbeele (Lanham: Lexington Books, 2003), pp. 297–321.

46. Georges Mauco, *Les étrangers en France: Leur rôle dans l'activité économique* (Paris: Armand Colin, 1932), p. 175.

47. Camiscioli, 'Producing Citizens.'

48. Paul (Colonel) Azan, *L'armée indigene nord africaine* (Charles-Lavaulzelle: Paris, 1925), pp. 27, 32–3.

49. Ralph Schor, *L'opinion française et les étrangers en France, 1919–1939* (Paris: Publications de la Sorbonne, 1985), pp. 165–8, 419–21.

50. Norbert Gomar, 'L'émigration algérienne en France' (Doctorat en droit, Université de Paris, 1931), pp. 45–6.

51. Mauco, *Les étrangers*, pp. 347–9.

52. Joanny Ray, 'Les marocains en France' (Doctorat en droit, Université de Paris, 1937), p. 203.

53. Patrick Weil, *Qu'est-ce qu'un Français? Histoire de la nationalité française depuis la révolution* (Paris: Bernard Grasset, 2002), p. 240. Analogous policies applied in French West Africa, see Gary Wilder, *The French Imperial Nation-state: Negritude and Colonial Humanism between the Wars* (Chicago: University of Chicago Press, 2005), pp. 132–3.

54. Le Naour, *Misères*, pp. 118–22. On polygamy as a remedy for prostitution, homosexuality, and venereal disease: M Georges-Anquétil, *La Maîtresse légitime: essai sur le mariage polygamique de demain* (Paris: Les Editions Georges-Anquetil, 1923).

55. MacMaster, *Colonial Migrants*; Neil MacMaster, 'The rue Fondary Murders of 1923 and the Origins of Anti-Arab Racism,' in *Violence and Conflict in the Politics and Society of Modern France*, eds Jan Windebank and Renate Gunther (Lewiston, NY: Edwin Mellon Press, 1995), pp. 149–60.

56. Gomar, 'L'émigration algérienne en France,' p. 87. These measures were reasserted by decree in 1926 and 1928. Hygienic considerations were central to their remaining in place (pp. 93–107).

57. Ibid., pp. 115–19, Clifford Rosenberg, 'The Colonial Politics of Health Care Provision in Interwar Paris,' *French Historical Studies*, 27 (3) (2004): 637–68.

58. Cited in Schor, *L'opinion*, 420.

59. Octave Depont, *L'Algérie du centenaire* (Paris: Recueil Sirey, 1928), p. 135.

60. Ibid., p. 122.

61. Ferhat Abbas, *Le jeune algérien* (Paris: Editions de la Jeune Parque, 1931), p. 118.

62. Jean Damase, *Sidi de banlieue* (Paris: Fasquelle, 1937). See also Miller, ' "Romance of Regulation" ', pp. 413–15.

63. M. Valet, 'Les restrictions à l'immigration' (Doctorat en droit, Université de Paris, 1930), p. 207.

64. 'Déclaration de l'Association d'études sexologiques,' *PA*, 3 (9) (September 1931): 599. On Toulouse and mental hygiene, Carolyn J. Dean, *The Self and its Pleasures: Bataille, Lacan and the History of the Decentered Subject* (Ithaca: Cornell University Press, 1992).

65. William H. Schneider, *Quantity and Quality: the Search for Biological Regeneration in Twentieth Century France* (Cambridge: Cambridge University Press, 1990), pp. 177–86. On pre-marital screening, Anne Carol, *Histoire de l'eugénisme en France: les médecins et la procréation 19e–20e siècle* (Paris: Seuil, 1996), pp. 312–39.

66. 'Déclaration de l'Association d'études sexologiques,' *PA*, 3 (9) (September 1931): 604.

67. Just Sicard de Plauzoles, 'La situation démographique en France,' *PA*, 9 (4) (April 1937): 237–8.

68. On Martial, Benoît Laribou, 'René Martial, 1873–1955: De l'hygiènisme à la raciologie, une trajectoire possible,' *Genèses* (2005): 98–120; Schneider, *Quantity and Quality*, pp. 230–55.

69. 'Conférence programme pour les élèves des Ecoles normales d'instituteurs,' *BSFPSM* (July 1924): 67–8. See also, René Martial, 'A propos de la discussion du rapport de M. Bobin, *L'éducation sexuelle*,' *BSFPSM* (May 1922): 76.

70. René Martial, *Vie et constance des races* (Paris: Mercure de France, 1939), pp. 247–8. On the role of *métissage* in the sexual and racial construction of citizenship, Emmanuelle Saada, 'Race and Sociological Reason in the Republic: Inquiries on the Métis in the French Empire (1908–1937),' *International Sociology*, 17 (3) (2002): 361–91; Ann Laura Stoler, 'Sexual Affronts and Racial Frontiers: European Identities and the Cultural Politics of Exclusion in Colonial Southeast Asia,' *Comparative Studies in Society and History*, 34 (3) (1992): 514–51.

71. Martial, *Vie*, p. 246.

72. Henri Beraud, 'L'oeuf,' *Gringoire* (20 April 1934).

73. On Jewishness, sexual perversity, and Blum, Pierre Birnbaum, *Anti-Semitism in France: a Political History from Leon Blum to the Present* (Oxford: Basil Blackwell, 1992), pp. 147–77; Sandrine Sanos, ' "Marianne and the Jew": Far-right Intellectuals and antisemitism in the 1930s' (PhD History, Rutgers, 2004); Ralph Schor, *L'antisemitisme en France pendant les années trente* (Paris: Editions complexe, 1992), pp. 176–7.

74. Schor, *L'antisemitisme*, p. 59. See, for example, Jean Jacoby, 'L'enfance rouge en U.R.S.S.,' *Gringoire* (23 March 1934); 'L'homme malade,' *Gringoire* (16 April 1937). On the history of these metaphors, Martha Hanna, 'Metaphors of Malaise and Misogyny in the Rhetoric of the Action Française,' *Historical Reflections/Reflexions historiques*, 20 (1) (1994): 29–55; William Kidd, 'Marianne: from Medusa to Messalina, Psycho-sexual Imagery and Political Propaganda in France, 1789–1945,' *Journal of European Studies*, 34 (4) (2004): 334–48.

75. Laurent Viguier, *Les juifs à travers Léon Blum* (Paris: Editions Baudinière, 1938), p. 24.

76. 'Le Mariage selon M. Léon Blum,' *Gringoire* (7 May 1937); and 'M. Blum expose a "Je suis partout" ses idées,' *Je suis partout* (12 May 1937).

77. For his discussion of prostitution, see Léon Blum, *L'oeuvre de Léon Blum*, vol. 2 (1905–14) (Paris: Albin Michel, 1962), pp. 157–60. See also, Max-Bridge (Louise

Anne Marie Morel Mehu), *Réponse au livre de M. Blum intitulé 'Du mariage'* (Lyon: Editions Max-Bridge, 1937); Marcel Thiébaut, *En lisant M. Léon Blum* (Paris: Gallimard, 1937); and Yves Tamaris, 'L'amoralité juive,' *Revue internationale des sociétés secretes (RISS)* (15 December 1937): 701–703.

78. 'La Contre-Morale maçonnique,' *RISS* (13 September 1931): 951. See also 'Nudisme: le Juif a commence, le Judéo-Maçon continue,' *RISS* (10 August, 1930): 762–5.

79. On this double strategy in German fascism, Dagmar Herzog, *Sex after Fascism: Memory and Morality in Twentieth-century Germany* (Princeton: Princeton University Press, 2005).

80. On Céline, see David Carroll, *French Literary Fascism: Nationalism, Anti-Semitism, and Ideology of Culture* (Princeton: Princeton University Press, 1995), pp. 186–95; Alice Yaeger Kaplan, *Reproductions of Banality: Fascism, Literature, and French Intellectual Life* (Minneapolis: University of Minnesota Press, 1986); Sanos, ' "Marianne," ' Chapter 4.

81. See, for example, Louis-Ferdinand Céline, *Mort à crédit* (Paris: Gallimard, 1952), pp. 28–29. On the place of hygienic discourse in Céline's writing, see Philippe Roussin, *Misère de la literature, terreur de l'histoire: Céline et la litérature contemporaine* (Paris: Gallimard, 2005), pp. 132–40, 542–52.

82. Louis Ferdinand Céline, *L'école des cadavres* (Paris: Denoël, 1938), pp. 128, 204 and 109.

83. Pierre Drieu la Rochelle, *Gilles* (Paris: Gallimard, 1939), pp. 493–4.

84. For a comparable analysis, Mark Meyers, 'Feminizing Fascist Men: Crowd Psychology, Gender, and Sexuality in French Anti-Fascism, 1929–1945,' *French Historical Studies*, 29 (1) (2006): 109–42.

7
Colonial Man

Robert Aldrich

'Empire was a man's business,' writes John Tosh about the British Empire,[1] and the same characterization applies to French colonialism. Especially in the early stages of expansion, men vastly outnumbered women among the explorers, soldiers and sailors, merchants and planters, administrators and missionaries who created 'greater France,' though later propaganda promoted recruitment of women, particularly as potential wives and mothers. Typically 'masculine' virtues – duty, bravery, physical prowess, and stamina – were seen as necessary to imperial vocations. Adventure, exercise of authority, sexual licence, even a latitude for violence (to use Tosh's list) counted among the manly rewards of empire.[2] Empire reinforced patriarchy and was a test of a nation's virility.

The 'manliness' of imperial ventures seemed too obvious to colonial actors and many later historians to be interrogated. However, recent research has provided a more nuanced understanding of the roles played by men and women in the making of empire.[3] Commonly held views about manliness formed part of the core of imperial sentiment, and such male-dominated institutions as the public school and the sports team, the 'boy's own' adventure stories and the Boy Scouts movement served as conduits for formation of imperial agents and stimulus for colonialist support. Colonies provided sexual opportunism for European men, but the imperial 'gaze' at natives provoked racial and gender stereotyping not devoid of political intention.[4] Inter-ethnic sexual attractions destabilized cultural and sexual segregation, and mixed-raced children remained visible reminders of derogation from masculine and European continence.[5] A 'disjuncture between prescription and practice' occurred in situations where domesticity, inviolate morality, and gender obedience were meant to recreate and reinforce European norms of civilization.[6] Yet the colonial experience helped form ideas about sexuality, gender and morality, including dissident sexualities.[7] Colonialist 'manifest manhood' could inflect international policy, even to the point of provoking colonial wars.[8]

Such issues are intriguing in the case of French masculinity, especially in the late nineteenth and early twentieth centuries when, as Robert Nye has argued, new models of masculinity were linked to articulation of sexual typologies, normative sexual behavior was related to strategies of bourgeois reproduction, depopulation and degeneration created intensely felt threats, and a culture of masculine honor reigned.[9] Debates on homosexuality and women's rights symbolized shifting identities and expectations. Key episodes of public life, such as the Dreyfus Affair, revealed sexual tensions, circulated discussion of racial and ethnic stereotypes, and reprised underlying concerns about fecundity, virility, and morality, including the 'crisis' in *fin-de-siècle* French manhood analyzed by Christopher Forth.[10]

A short step led from the Jewish 'other' to the colonial 'other,' and from France to the empire. France during the Dreyfus Affair was consolidating the world's second largest overseas empire, covering 11 million square kilometers; 100 million people lived in France and its domains by the 1930s. France had lost most of its old colonies in wars with Britain in the late 1700s and with the defeat of Napoleon. However, in 1830, France conquered Algiers, the beginning of a takeover of Algeria, Tunisia (made a protectorate in 1881), and Morocco (a protectorate in 1912) in North Africa. From the 1840s, France acquired strategic islands, from Mayotte in the Indian Ocean to Tahiti and New Caledonia in the Pacific. Seeking a toehold in Southeast Asia, French troops landed in Cochinchina in the late 1850s, and French Indochina by the 1880s included Vietnam, Cambodia, and Laos. In Africa, France expanded from coastal trading posts to conquer much of western and equatorial Africa, from Mauritania to the Congo, as well as the large island of Madagascar. Finally, after the First World War, France gained a League of Nations mandate over Syria and Lebanon. The empire weathered the world wars, but subsequent anti-colonial challenges proved successful. After an eight-year war, France was forced to evacuate Indochina in 1954. An even more bitter anti-colonial war in Algeria began the same year, strongly resisted by the *pieds-noirs* in France's only major settler colony, but in 1962 France had to retreat from that outpost. Meanwhile, most of the other colonies had achieved independence, leaving only 'confetti of empire' under French control.[11]

The colonies provided not just a 'greater France' but another sort of France. They constituted an extension of the hexagon, but also – at least according to promoters – a place where the essence of Frenchness could be distilled. Here the French could escape mediocrity, degeneration, debilitating ideologies, the hyperaesthesia and anomie of modern urban life. Here the true man was at home, and the real man could find his vocation. Marshal Lyautey, France's most revered colonial patriot,[12] expressed this male ambition in a speech to students in Oran, Algeria: 'Not only because of a taste for adventure and travel am I a committed colonialist . . . I have found in our colonies . . . the finest practical school where, as in a crucible, our race can be tempered and recast.' Colonials such as soldiers could, quite literally, sire a newly revivified French race: 'Underneath their uniforms . . . you find men, real men (*des hommes, des hommes complets*).' Lyautey rediscovered the Renaissance ideal in French youths and soldiers in North Africa, 'the terrain *par excellence* of energy, rejuvenation and fecundity.' The 'complete man,' in short, was the colonial man.[13]

Lyautey's assertion invites reflection on colonial masculinity, a comprehensive history of which has yet to be written.[14] This chapter provides observations on three themes: the national ideal of the colonial man and the reality compared to the image; dangers to manhood posed by colonial conditions; and the juxtaposition of French and native manhood. It argues that colonial masculinity and its actions – conquest, pacification, the building of new countries, settlement, promotion of traditional virtues – was seen as compensation for a deficit of manliness in France, as evidenced by military defeat in 1870–71, a falling birth rate and depopulation, fears of degeneration, and contestatory social and cultural currents. With inevitable comparisons between French and native masculinity, however, the French had to claim a 'higher' manhood, shaped by civilization as well as racial superiority. The dream of masculine victory in the colonies nevertheless ultimately turned into nightmare with the defeat of French manhood during the wars of decolonization.

Images and ideals

Ideal colonial men peer beckoningly from a 1930s recruitment poster for the *troupes coloniales*. Three officers arrive in the African bush, native sailors waiting in the boat that has brought them to the new posting. One officer sits with his traveling case, another bargains for fruit, but the third, standing on a makeshift pontoon with his arms akimbo, seems most emblematic of the colonial enterprise. He is dressed in neatly pressed khaki trousers and knee-length shorts, sturdy shoes and long socks. His pith helmet provides a necessary accoutrement in the harsh sun and the quintessential marker of his colonizing status; the wristwatch intimates the bringing of Western order to primitive societies. This well-built specimen of European manhood is the boy-next-door sent on a civilizing mission. He looks forthrightly towards his new domain, body language suggestive of authority and strong will, even if the face bears bewilderment disguised as stern readiness to complete his duty.[15]

Similar images adorned other *affiches* as incentives to French men to broaden their horizons and take part in a great national endeavor. Changing scenes underlined the breadth of the empire, and slogans trumpeted colonial service. Young soldiers in immaculate tropical whites stand on the banks of the Perfume River, 'Annamites' walking on the shore with sampans in the water before the gates to the imperial palace in Hué, or the scene is changed to the desert with two officers next to a richly caparisoned camel. Though the posters exhort 'Join up to the colonial troops,' there is no hint of conquest, fighting or 'pacification'; yet another poster bears the anodyne wording, 'Travel – the colonial troops invite you,' as two smiling officers chat with Africans at the mosque of Djenné, as if colonial military service were little different from a summer holiday.[16]

In a more muscular fashion, a poster for the Légion Etrangère arranges two figures against the emblematic flame of France's most famous overseas force, one in military uniform with rifle, the other, stripped to the waist and wielding a pick-axe: 'Legionnaire, soldier and builder,' reads an inscription echoing Lyautey's imperative. A later poster, from the 1950s, in the midst of the Indochinese war, however, pulls no punches. An angry soldier in red beret, a machine-gun slung across his chest, points to an unseen battlefield with one hand, while the other gives the thumbs-up salute; the alarming slogan for the 'colonial parachutists' reads, 'Glory is my reward, and a fight my forum.'[17] Another poster proclaimed: 'You are a man. Go to Indochina and defend liberty. You'll come back a leader.' The sentences say much about ideals of masculinity and colonialism. Maleness, warfare, liberty, colonialism, patriotism, and success conjoin in an unquestioned nexus of personal commitment and nationalism that mark the red-blooded male ready to fight for the Tricolor.

Times changed between the days when empire seemed secure (at least from a distance), and the years after 1945 when France fought in Indochina and North Africa (and carried out brutal repressions elsewhere, notably in Madagascar) to keep hold of the *outre-mer*. Newspaper readers were riveted to stories of parachutists who tried in vain to save comrades, and France's imperial glory, in the doomed redout of Dien Bien Phu. Soon the public were reading accusations of French use of torture in Algeria, alongside pictures of French soldiers gunned down by 'terrorists.' Journalists described French soldiers whose genitals had been cut off and stuffed into their mouths – no more nightmarish assault on French manhood could be imagined.

Soldiers, whether victorious or defeated, noble workers for *mise en valeur* of colonial domains, or hardened fighters against anti-French rebellion, provided the most vivid symbol of colonial masculinity. However, they were not the only men featured in colonial iconography; a gallery of *scènes et types* illustrated varieties of manhood. Particularly important in the early decades of colonialism, more than a century before those distressing scenes of the end of empire in the early 1960s, were images of conquerors in the 1830s and 1840s. Commissioned artists painted dramatic renditions of advances in North Africa, battles in Algeria, the taking of the smalah, the defeat of Abd el-Kader. Swords flying, guns smoking, the cavalry and the infantry battle bravely and die gloriously in tableaux that consecrate military manhood.

Explorers represented a somewhat different view of manhood. Metropolitan readers of *L'Illustration* and *Tour du monde* thrilled to the exploits of men charting paths across territory previously unknown to Europeans, fighting off wild beasts and no less savage natives, suffering horrifically to carry forward the flag. Drawings and engravings pictured iconic figures such as Francis Garnier making his way up the Mekong River in Indochina in the 1870s and Jean-Baptiste Marchand traversing the Sahel for his encounter with the British at Fashoda in 1898. The new medium of photography also recorded adventures, though technical difficulties meant that studio portraits sometimes had to be arranged to bring home local color: a widely-circulated 1880s picture of Pierre Savorgnan de Brazza shows the explorer of the Congo clad in a ragged outfit with an Arab-looking headdress, his travel pack near his incongruously bare feet.[18]

The missionary was a different type of colonial man, the celibate priest who renounced those twin signifiers of traditional masculinity, fornication and fatherhood, for love of God. Recruiting colonial workers no less avidly than did the military, the church distributed pictures of benevolent priests saying mass, teaching, and healing in distant climes. They wore black cassocks or richly embroidered chasubles, though from time to time, with ordinary sleeves rolled up, tending the faithful or tending their gardens. Their male heroism was not military action but evangelization, though the end might also be martyrdom – many paintings depict saintly clerics, eyes cast heavenward as they endure unspeakable tortures.

By the early 1900s, men called to colonial service, whether by church or state, entered a world different from that of the pioneers. In the Great War, colonials and native troopers were called upon to defend France, and by the tens of thousands, colonial *poilus* fought on the battlefields of Europe. *Spahis, zouaves, marsouins,* and *Légionnaires* were sent to the trenches of Flanders, joined by *tirailleurs sénégalais* and soldiers from Indochina, the Antilles and Oceania, fighting not for the extension of France's imperium, but for the salvation of France itself. War memorials throughout the overseas dominions, just as in every French city and hamlet at home, testified to the masculine sacrifice of colonials and colonized alike.[19] For those who rendered glorious service to France, citizenship – parsimoniously granted by French authorities – might provide a reward to survivors: masculine valor on the *champs d'honneur* provided apprenticeship and qualification for the rights of the male citizen to whom the vote was reserved.

By the 1920s, the war won and 'pacification' being achieved (as the French naively hoped), a new type of colonial man was needed. The explorer and the soldier were now joined in the pantheon by the man armed with a diploma from the École Coloniale or a contract from a business firm.[20] Administrators – the 'rois de la brousse' – governed vast districts, engineers built highways, railways and dams, architects designed modernist cities from Rabat to Hanoi. Traditional masculine virtues still proved necessary, but with brains as vital as brawn. Important too were settlers, hardy migrants who rooted French civilization in the new soil and founded families to perpetuate the race. Settlers in the bush might not differ so much from their nineteenth-century forebears, but urban colonial men took on trappings of civility, gathering at fashionable cafés and clubs, playing sport or attending concerts.[21]

Explorer, conqueror, soldier, cleric, settler: such are the men who populate the imperial imagery. These stereotypes do not exhaust the gallery of Frenchmen abroad, who were not all so glamorous or noble. Brutalities committed by some conquerors shocked even the metropolitan public, and anti-colonialists underlined the excesses of soldiers with power of life and death over their subjects far from the niceties of European justice and the 'rules of engagement.' Although the French retained a soft spot for the Foreign Legion, and the notion that it was composed of criminals escaping their past does not entirely conform to reality, nevertheless a certain suspicion surrounded foreign mercenaries fighting for France.[22] Other corps also had a dubious reputation, especially the bataillons d'Afrique to which prisoners were sent, rumored to harbor near unbearable punishment and ungodly vice.

Some of the French overseas meanwhile integrated all too well into colonial life, 'going native,' dressing and living like locals, marrying (not just cohabiting with) indigenous women. A few, such as the painter Étienne Dinet – who lived in Algeria, converted to Islam, completed the *hajj*, translated Arabic tales and shared lodgings with an Arabic companion and his spouse – managed to keep compatriots' respect.[23] Others were viewed with amusement or disapproval, or castigated as *décivilisés* and traitors to their race.[24]

Frenchmen in the colonies also included *bagnards,* malefactors incarcerated in the 'green hell' of Guyana. Dreyfus and 'Papillon' gained fame, but most remained simple criminals transported to South America. Others were sent to New Caledonia, France's other penal colony, including recidivist criminals, rebels of the Paris Commune of 1871, and participants in an Algerian insurrection in 1870. France dispatched prisoners to New Caledonia from the 1860s to the 1890s, and continued to transport convicts to Guyana until after the Second World War. Convicts, especially inmates of Devil's Island, achieved folkloric notoriety, but the men – the vast majority – nevertheless represented a reprobate image of manhood: murderers, thieves, rebels, social misfits. Paradoxically, however, authorities hoped that miscreants would be regenerated and transformed into honest and dedicated pillars of settler colonies in South America and the South Pacific.[25]

A final image was the degenerate colonial, who had succumbed to alcohol, drugs and vice, wasting his life in cheap bordellos, opium dens or louche bars, depraved and ruined. Pictures of such men understandably did not end up on recruitment posters or in imperial propaganda, but this 'type' underlines the disparity between ideal and reality that sometimes existed in the colonies. It revealed the fragile position of manhood overseas, and suggested the dangers to masculinity posed by colonial situations.

Colonial manhood and its dangers

The ideal of manhood in the colonies was clear, explicitly and implicitly, to those who discussed imperial issues. One Dr Barot, in a 1902 guide for intending colonials, sketched a prototype of the complete colonial man, while warning of dangers overseas. He championed colonial life as a form of character development:

> The true colonial must be intelligent, and thus moral, educated, patient and observant. He must speak well, remain controlled in his actions, and

be just in his evaluations, and firm in his decisions . . . A European in the colonies, according to circumstances, must be by turns an administrator, surveyor, engineer, mason, gunsmith, restaurant-keeper, accountant, customs inspector, magistrate, farmer, doctor and soldier! Obliged to face new demands at any moment, the colonialist contrives to be a jack-of-all-trades, and in this virile scramble – where he must combat nature, humans and disease – only strongly cast characters will be able to resist and to impose themselves. Life in the bush, with its dangers, fatigue and surprises, its wild charm and its breadth of action, emancipates, revivifies and consecrates the energies that lie dormant in the well-springs of European civilization.[26]

A man embarking on a colonial career must be healthy, brave, long-suffering, and full of endurance to survive its rigors. He should have knowledge of arms to defend himself and his property against insurrection and crime. Ability to handle guns would also allow him to enjoy hunting, one of the most popular colonial recreations, bagging big game, and thus symbolically subduing the wild environment. He must be dutiful, loyal to his country, and willing to uphold the best principles of his race. Renegade ideas were not welcome where *esprit de corps* was vital for national and racial cohesion. The colonialist must be guided by astute morals, though even prudish colonial promoters realized that robust men need be allowed rest and recreation, wine and women; lust for life and its pleasures proved a man fit for colonial service.

These criteria set out late nineteenth- and early twentieth-century masculine virtues of a vernacular and rustic sort. The intellectual, the Bohemian, and the dandy, though common in Paris, were relatively rare species in the colonies, though many administrators and clerics became accomplished ethnographers, and a lively if limited cultural life developed in such centers as Algiers and Hanoi. The colonial might well have to engage in certain 'feminine' pursuits – cooking, mending clothes, caring for the ill – especially on expeditions, but the model demanded a masculine man in the traditional mold.

Many colonials aspired to, and fulfilled, the high ambitions and lofty ideals. Letters, memoirs, and autobiographies recount intrepid accomplishments, even if reminiscences are no doubt self-serving. Misdeeds, such as ill treatment of indigenous peoples, are glossed over or justified as crucial to the furtherance of the colonial order. Many, too, are rather coy about the pleasures of private life, especially sexual liaisons that superannuated colonials might not wish publicized at home.[27] Memoirs reveal a sense of mission, pleasure in surmounting the difficulties of colonial existence, satisfaction at turning hands to a variety of chores. The autobiography of Hubert Deschamps, an interwar colonial governor and ethnographer of leftist political orientation, provides an example: 'Colonization offered me a noble ideal of dedication to progress. Furthermore, it answered basic needs, curiosity, the urge to flee banality and oneself for *dépaysement*, to live in tune with nature and to find poetry in everyday life. Simple, unencumbered happiness could thus be found in one's chosen profession.'[28]

The image of the versatile, heroic (and often erotic) colonial and soldier 'played' well in France. Interwar films, such as Jacques Feyder's *Le Grand jeu* and Julien Duvivier's *La Bandéra* screened the dashing adventures of French (and Spanish) Legionnaires. As David Henry Slavin points out, they perpetuated both the 'war myth' of valor and sacrifice in service of the motherland and the notion of colonies as a 'male fantasy world where human will and courage could change the course of history.'[29] Popular music also reproduced the image of virile soldiery, fighting in the field, building new countries or frolicking on furlough. Raymond Asso's 1936 'Le Fanion de la Légion,' complete with 'Moorish' melodies, recounted 'the fine story' of thirty soldiers besieged in a Maghrebin *bled*, perishing as the 'scoundrels' approach but faithful to their post, 'Stripped to the waist, but covered with Glory / Bloody, bruised and in rags / Lacking bread and water, lacking munitions.' Even their banner is ripped down by the assailants, but the Legionnaires in their dying moment draw flags onto their chests with their blood. Asso's 'Mon Légionnaire,' also from 1936, most famous of all colonial songs in Édith Piaf's performance, recalls a woman's night of love with a tattooed Legionnaire – 'He was slender, he was handsome / He smelled of the desert sand' – before he, too, met his destiny in the desert.[30]

Popular culture, as songs about troopers' dire fates suggest, did not always paint a portrait of colonial felicity. Stories of colonial sex and love, as Alain Ruscio remarks, were tales of sadness: separation from lovers at home, ill-fated affairs in the colonies.[31] Novels treated colonial men as pioneers, heroes, modern centurions, but also as men whom the jungle or the desert could destroy. Arguably the most famous works centering on colonial manhood were the novels of the naval officer and *académicien* Pierre Loti. *Le Mariage de Loti* chronicled a romance in Polynesia, while a similarly tragic encounter in Japan featured in *Madame Chrysanthème*.[32]

Loti's *Le Roman d'un spahi*, published in 1881, provided the most complete portrait of the ill-fated colonial man. Jean Peyral, a peasant from the Cévennes, is the standard pin-up, 'a man of tall proportions who carried his head high and proud ... extremely handsome, of a male and serious sort of beauty, with large clear eyes.' Despite limited intellectual endowment but with great ambition, Jean becomes a *spahi*, joining a legendary corps of colonial soldiers,[33] and ends up in Senegal. 'The foreignness of this country struck his novice imagination,' and Jean is entranced. Landscapes 'bespoke a land of exile and of remove from the homeland,' but Africa offers 'magic in its tropical sunrises, with such limpidity in the morning air and such a well-being in its unaccustomed coolness.' Jean quickly adapts to the hard-living, hard-drinking life of the colonial ranker, and has his first sexual fling with a Creole woman. Soon after, fever almost kills him, but he recovers to immerse himself again in colonial life, now attracted by 'local color,' the songs and dances that 'had something heavily voluptuous and animalistically sensual.' Soon he is involved with Fatou-gaye, a Senegalese he describes as his 'little monkey.'

As letters from his mother worry about his health and morals, and report the tears of a pining girlfriend at home, Jean plunges ever deeper into a life that changes him body and soul. After five years, 'his features were sharper, and he was tanner and thinner; he had taken on a military and Arabic air; his shoulders and his chest were much broader, though his waist remained narrow and supple; he donned his fez and twirled his long moustache with the coquettishness of a soldier that suited him perfectly.' In the unknown hinterland, he then dies in battle, and Fatou-gaye, in a delirium of loss and violence, strangles their child and commits suicide.

The unexpected and shocking end to *Le Roman d'un spahi* suggests multiple interpretations that resonate with themes of masculinity in France and the colonies. Jean is a typical peasant destined to a masculine life of agricultural labor before he is drawn to wider horizons. Loti returns time and again to the physical beauty of a man who finds natural fulfillment in sexual conquest amidst the cafés and bordellos of Saint-Louis. There lies the danger: disease, vice, seduction by temptresses, miscegenation. Jean succumbs and, abandoning family and fiancée, seems to 'go native,' as suggested by darkening skin and jaunty fez.[34] Finally, ruin and death await Jean, his lover and their child. Loti's *spahi*, therefore, exemplifies provincial manhood, colonial adventure and its rewards, but also the tragic fate of self-destruction on exotic shores.[35] Few works better typify the splendors and miseries of colonial manhood than Loti's 'narratives of ambiguity,' in Hélène de Burgh's formulation.[36]

The empire provided a theatre where masculine virtues, achievements, pleasures, and excesses could be performed. Indeed colonies served as the perfect environment in which adventure, duty, and accomplishment – imbued in males through up-bringing, education, compulsory military service, and civic propaganda – could show themselves off. Colonial lobbyists promoted an imperial world where manliness could best be deployed, developed, and rewarded, away from the flaccid over-refined life of European cities and the limited opportunities of the countryside. However, if the colonies were the parade ground for manliness, they were also the testing ground for masculinity.

Many dangers awaited men (and women) overseas, including the obvious hazards of warfare with the injuries and incapacitation that might result even if death were avoided. There were also environmental dangers, which Dr Barot listed in his 1902 guide: heat, unsanitary water, microbes, insects, malaria-bearing mosquitoes. To those perils he added the dangers of alcohol, which he opined had greater and more deleterious effects in tropical countries than in Europe, and women, carriers of venereal diseases and other maladies. Disease ran rife in conditions of poor sanitation and rudimentary medical care. In the 1860s, the death rate for soldiers in Algeria was 14.76 per thousand compared to 9.95 in the metropole; half of those who died in Algeria fell victim to malaria, and a third to intestinal infections. The death rate fell during the rest of the century, but from 1902 to 1906, was still almost twice as high in Algeria as in France.[37] Far more French soldiers died from disease than from fighting in the conquest of Madagascar; from 1894 to 1895, 5756 soldiers of an expedition of 21,600 died – twenty perished from combat, and the rest were victims of disease.[38] Alcohol was also a major danger for men who sought camaraderie in drinking and for whom wine and spirits helped dull loneliness and physical hardship. One doctor stated that 'at the outset of the Algerian conquest, there were more victims of absinthe than of the sun or fever.'[39] Not only would alcohol wreak unfortunate physical effects, it was a temptation to laxity and immoderation. Alcohol joined drugs, particularly opium in Indochina, as an instigation to vice, undermining manly resolve to resist evil.[40]

One 1890s manual warned troopers about the dangers of alcohol and sex, then proceeded to practical suggestions: 'Little soldier, the two worst enemies are alcohol and the prostitute. If you want to keep vigorous and healthy, to be a good soldier and a free citizen, and to live to see your children . . . abstain [from sex] when you have drunk too much, have sex with a suspect partner only with a condom, smear your member with Vaseline or, for lack of anything better, with any sort of grease (lamp oil), urinate immediately after coition, etc.'[41] Such counsel responded to mounting concern about venereal disease – an 1893 thesis calculated that VD was twice as common in colonial troops as in the regular metropolitan army. The sexual desires of lusty soldiers, failure to regulate prostitution, and sexual license promoted (as was widely believed) by hot climates aggravated the menace of infection. The prevalence of VD led to stricter examinations of soldiers and prostitutes, and to establishment of officially sanctioned brothels and red-light districts.[42]

Sex was one of the dangers and temptations to colonials, though authorities and doctors were not wholly averse to prostitution and were sympathetic to concubinage, particularly in the early years. Dr Villedary, writing in the 1890s, said that 'the physiologist does not aim to become an implacable censor and to forbid our brilliant officers and our hot-blooded colonials all frequentation of that part of the population commonly known – not always rightly, at least in certain colonies – as the finer sex. All of our needs have a right to be satisfied. But use is not abuse.' He counseled 'wise moderation.'[43] Some writers gave advice on why the taking of a concubine would be helpful. Dr Barot advised soldiers who could not abstain completely for a two-year tour of duty to establish a 'temporary union,' enumerating the benefits: avoidance of venereal disease, aid in pacifying the local population and establishing contact with natives, avoidance of affairs with married women, companionship and emotional satisfaction (since a native woman, 'if she is not too unintelligent,' would help distract him from his cares, relieve his boredom and 'keep him from giving himself over to alcoholism or to the sexual depravities that are unfortunately so frequent in hot climates') and instruction in local languages and customs.[44] *Mariage à la mode du pays*, where a newly arriving colonial cohabited with a native woman during his stay, was endemic in the early colonial period, though later viewed with disapprobation.

Dr Villedary's mention of 'depravity' makes an intriguing reference to 'perversions' flaunted in the colonies, ranging from 'kinky' heterosexual practices to homosexuality. Colonials were reminded, repeating a belief dating to Antiquity, that hot climates sparked sexual excesses, and that sodomy flourished in North Africa and the Middle East, while the effeminacy ascribed to Asian men supposedly made them androgynously seductive. Furthermore, homosexual practices were often connected with the army – situational homosexuality in barracks and on military campaigns – and rumored to be so widespread in the navy that *le vice marin* served as a euphemism for sodomy. Soldiers and sailors on home leave sometimes found in homosexual prostitution a source of income.[45]

Although it is impossible to know how widespread homosexuality was among colonials, observers regularly remarked on 'vice.' Many said that soldiers taking part in the conquest of Algeria had enjoyed homosexual sex, and brought the foreign habit home with them. One July Monarchy observer ironically lamented, 'A frightening pederastic outbreak seems the only real benefit to come from the war in Algeria'; another stated that homosexuality had 'invaded' the metropole from the Maghreb.[46] Dr Kermogant talked of the 'vast scale' of pederasty in the penal colony of New Caledonia.[47] Several studies devoted great attention to homosexual sex, and even homosexual 'marriages,' among soldiers in the bataillons d'Afrique.[48] A naval doctor, Jacobus X, in *L'Art d'aimer aux colonies,* a mixture of travelogue, serious commentary, and titillating descriptions, detailed the easy availability of young men for sex everywhere from Algeria to Vietnam. Close emotional bonding of soldiers formed part of military comradeship, with the homoerotic undertones never far distant. Several well-known officers were suspected of homosexuality – Lyautey's inclination was an open secret.[49] Fictional writing, such as the novels of the bisexual Loti, popularized the view of overseas sexual license that included homosexual dalliance.[50]

If colonial men avoided death and disease, vice and depravity, they might still fall prey to the *cafard,* a malaise induced by homesickness, hot climates, and the pressures of colonial life and isolation. Tropical neurasthenia could be symptomatic of the fragilities of both white masculinity and colonial order.[51] Dr Barot diagnosed mental 'anaemia' and morbid psychology that made a man either hyperactive or lethargic, caused him to become bitter and complaining, or led to a persecution complex; it could also lead – predictably – to immoderate use of alcohol or sex, and result in exhaustion and apathy. In short, this threatened loss of moral manhood to a man who could not resist tropical rigors and the seductions preferred to assuage them.[52]

French men and native men

Paternalist advice hints at defensiveness about masculine virtues and behavior, despite the macho strutting and swagger characterizing soldiers and settlers.

French masculinity, inevitably, was juxtaposed with other prototypes of manliness around the world. The physical endowments of natives fascinated explorers, ethnographers, artists, and writers. Europeans and others could hardly avoid a mutually curious gaze at each other's bodies and the behaviors and moral attributes that somatotypes were thought to present, especially with the emergence of craniometry, phrenology, and other 'scientific' investigations of race. Eighteenth-century seafarers in the Pacific wrote lengthily about the bodies of 'savages' and practices such as tattooing and scarification. Even sober accounts of Oceania lingered on the 'classical' physical beauty of Polynesian warriors, though observers considered Melanesians less attractive. In the nineteenth century, racializing typologies created hierarchies of ethnic groups with ascribed virtues and vices. In caricatured form, the French found Arabs, Africans, and Polynesians powerfully masculine, though touched with degeneration or barbarity, while the men of southern and eastern Asia were less manly. Physical size, muscularity, and genital endowments entered into the equations – phalloplethsysmographers such as Jacobus X did not hesitate to make assertions about the penis size of different races with unstated links to virility and manliness.[53]

Conjunctions between somatotype, morality, and civilization were implicit in colonial writing, stereotypes useful in domination of subject peoples. An assertion of the African's physical strength and endurance was necessary to underpin arguments about the suitability of black slaves for plantation labor and tropical employment. (The presumption of Asian men's lack of prowess had to be glossed when the French needed plantation labor in Indochina and, after the abolition of slavery, recruited indentured labor throughout Asia.) Yet physical size and strength also intimated dangerous physicality, above all unconstrained sexual lust, including a supposed danger to white women. Arabic masculinity incorporated the pleasures of the harem and a penchant for pederasty, while the Asian was said to be drawn to arcane sexual behaviors, from the refinements of the *Kama Sutra* to the fetishism of the Orient.

Colonial discourse explicitly and implicitly compared French and native in terms of body, mind, and soul. The best known, and most provocative, post-colonial psychological analysis of male racial self-juxtaposition came from Frantz Fanon: 'For the majority of white men the Negro represents the sexual instinct (in its raw state). The Negro is the incarnation of a genital potency beyond all moralities and prohibitions.' In the Western imaginary, 'the Negro is the genital,' and blacks, rumored to possess outsized penises, are associated with unbridled lust, carefree passion, and rape. This stereotype created antipathy, since 'when a white man hates black men, is he not yielding to a feeling of impotence and of sexual inferiority? Since his ideal is an infinite virility, is there not a phenomenon of diminution in relation to the Negro, who is viewed as a penis symbol?' Such hatred expressed itself in sadistic exploitation of the black man. The racial penis inferiority complex also produced fears of black sexual power and of its attraction to white women. However, European male sentiments were mixed, too, with yearning for the supposed sexual freedom of blacks: 'The civilized white man retains an irrational longing for unusual eras of sexual license, of orgiastic scenes, of unpunished rapes, of unrepressed incest . . . Projecting his own desires onto the Negro, the white man behaves "as if" the Negro really had them.' Rather enigmatically, Fanon added that 'the Negrophobic man is a repressed homosexual.'[54]

Fanon's arguments remain tantalizing, and some aspects of colonial history – preoccupation with morphology, fears about miscegenation and rape, the eroticization of Africans – give credence to his perspectives, though only a psychologist could offer due consideration.[55] Nevertheless, one might suggest that the French ideal of colonial (and indeed metropolitan) manliness was a 'higher' masculinity, where wild sexual impulses have been tamed, and the genitals do not monopolize passion. The complete colonial man, unlike the stereotype of the African, Asian, or Oceanian, is one who, in Greco-Roman and Judeo-Christian style, can master his base urges and subsume lust to the superior goals of civilization: a 'higher' masculinity reserved for the white man.

A racially-based monopoly of 'higher' masculinity clearly conflicted with aims to create 'black Frenchmen' through assimilation and acculturation. Caricatured assumptions about native masculinity indeed came to regular tests during the colonial period. The First World War presented the foreign man not as barbaric fighter but as brave warrior, battling not against but for France. Older notions did not disappear – Indochinese brought to France were thought more adapted to factory work than front-line fighting, though thousands died in battle.[56] The vernacular masculine virtues of bravery, loyalty, discipline, and endurance were now positively credited to colonial soldiers harnessed to the war effort alongside French comrades. Suitably clothed in a military uniform, the native soldier stood shoulder to shoulder with the soldierly manliness of the *poilu*.

Juxtaposition between French and foreign manhood would later occasionally revert to old stereotypes, as propaganda stripped off the garb of civility when referring to soldiers fighting against France during wars of decolonization. In Indochina, nationalists using guerrilla tactics were accused of not fighting in true manly fashion, while in North Africa, the employment of terrorist tactics was seen as contravention of the rules of war and of manliness. Engagement on the battlefield retained the afterglow of chivalric combat, but other tactics – irrespective of use of irregular warfare by the French themselves – were condemned as little less than abdication of manliness. Images of French soldiers in Vietnam and Algeria emphasized masculine physical and moral virtues; pictorials delighted in photographs of shirtless soldiers, the cream of French manhood bravely fighting against ignoble enemies. Demonized images of Vietnamese and Algerian opponents – with racialized cartoons suggesting dishonesty, duplicity, and outright barbarity – contrasted with the pictures of French boys. Images of captured enemies, often bound, prostrate and forced into submission, intrinsically provided further contrast with the upright, victorious and manly French defenders of the imperial *patrie*.

Imperialism and the crisis of French manhood

The relation between French and native masculinity, though changing with political circumstances, nonetheless lies in the background of colonial views of manhood. So, too, does the contrast between a pessimistic perspective inspired by the crisis besetting manhood in the metropole, and an uplifting vision of redemptive colonial manliness. With attacks on traditional manhood in France from the late 1800s, colonial masculinity could be compensatory. Degeneration at home weakened Europeans, while colonial actions regenerated the race. The constraints of urban life hindered exercise of manhood, but the freedom of the colonies liberated a man to ford rivers, hack through jungles, and traverse deserts. The 'new woman' was born in Europe, but the old-fashioned man thrived in the colonies. Pacifism, socialism, and lack of military preparedness threatened the homeland, but colonials would come to the rescue. Europeans might refuse to reproduce, but the colonial man would father new Frances overseas. With the erection of a myth of compensatory masculinity, it was hardly surprising that wars of independence – with defeated soldiers and mutilated corpses – constituted an attack on French manhood, and on the soldiers and settlers who incarnated it. Having been emasculated through manly colonial dominance, the rebels symbolically redeemed their own masculinity.[57]

The colonies provided a forum for a 'real' French man to stretch his legs and flex his muscles. He conquered territory, defeated enemies, built bustling cities, and sired new societies. Manly virtues provided the mettle of empire, with manly pleasures as its rewards. Nevertheless, the colonial man had to brave disease and death, debilitation, and degeneration. Alcohol, drugs, vice, and the *cafard* could compromise manliness. The colonial man had to stand up to men of different 'races' who might oppose or thwart his ambitions or challenge the very assumptions of his masculinity. The French man had constantly to promote and defend his manliness as the brave soldier, the wise administrator, the hard-working colonist, and to cast himself into the role of the *civilized* man juxtaposed to the savage one. Everywhere the French man was favorably compared to the native, who ultimately proved a formidable and triumphant opponent. The radiant image of men in the glory days of empire contrasted with photographs of defeated men evacuated from Dien Bien Phu, abused cadavers in Algeria and thousands of disheveled and disoriented *pieds-noirs* awaiting 'repatriation' from North Africa. The men of empire, the soldiers and settlers leaving the imperial outposts wrested from French control, arrived in a *mère-patrie* in the throes of 'sexual revolution.'[58] Second-wave feminism, homosexual emancipation, and the social and intellectual changes of the 1950s and 1960s would bring into question the gender certainties that had been paraded, but also tested, in the imperial arena.

Notes

1. John Tosh, *Manliness and Masculinities in Nineteenth-century Britain* (Harlow: Pearson/Longman, 2005), p. 193.
2. Ibid., p. 203.
3. Angela Woollacott, *Gender and Empire* (London: Palgrave Macmillan, 2006); Philippa Levine (ed.), *Gender and Empire* (Oxford: Oxford University Press, 2004).
4. Mrinalinhi Sinha, *Colonial Masculinity: the 'Manly Englishman' and the 'Effeminate Bengali' in the Nineteenth Century* (Manchester: Manchester University Press, 1995).
5. Owen White, *Children of the French Empire: Miscegenation and Colonial Society in French West Africa, 1895–1960* (Oxford: Oxford University Press, 1999).
6. Ann Laura Stoler, *Carnal Knowledge and Imperial Power: Race and the Intimate in Colonial Rule* (Berkeley: University of California Press, 2002), pp. 1–2.
7. Rudi Bleys, *The Geography of Perversion: Male-to-male Sexual Behaviour outside the West and the Ethnographic Imagination, 1750–1918* (New York: New York University Press, 1995). Nevertheless, for Ann Laura Stoler, in *Race and the Education of Desire: Foucault's History of Sexuality and the Colonial Order of Things* (Durham, NC: University of North Carolina Press, 1995), Western theorizing about sexuality did not always take account of the colonial experience.
8. Amy S. Greenberg, *Manifest Manhood and the Antebellum American Empire* (Cambridge: Cambridge University Press, 2005); Kristin L. Hoganson, *Fighting for American Manhood: How Gender Politics Provoked the Spanish-American and Philippine-American Wars* (New Haven: Yale University Press, 1998).
9. Robert A. Nye, *Masculinity and Male Codes of Honor in Modern France* (Oxford: Oxford University Press, 1993).
10. Christopher E. Forth, *The Dreyfus Affair and the Crisis of French Manhood* (Baltimore: Johns Hopkins University Press, 2004).
11. See Pascal Blanchard and Sandrine Lemaire (eds), *Culture impériale. Les colonies au coeur de la République* (Paris: Autrement, 2003), and *Culture coloniale. La France conquise par son empire* (Paris: Autrement, 2004), and Martin Evans (ed.), *Empire and Culture: the French Experience, 1830–1940* (London: Palgrave Macmillan, 2004).
12. Hubert Lyautey (1854–1934) served in Algeria as a young soldier, then was posted to Tonkin. He administered part of Madagascar and subsequently became the first Resident-General of Morocco, the territory with which he is most associated. He also organised the 1931 International Colonial Exhibition in Paris. Lyautey wrote widely on his colonial activities, and championed the military officer as a model for national regeneration.
13. Hubert Lyautey, speech at the 'Distribution des prix au lycée,' Oran, 17 July 1907, in *Paroles d'action*, ed. Jean-Louis Miège (Paris: Imprimerie Nationale, 1995), pp. 72–80.
14. See Julia Clancy-Smith and Frances Gouda (eds), *Domesticating the Empire: Race, Gender, and Family Life in French and Dutch Colonialism* (Charlottesville, VA: University Press of Virginia, 1998).
15. The poster is reproduced in Eric Deroo, Gabrielle Deroo, and Marie-Cécile de Taillac, *Aux Colonies, où l'on découvre les vestiges d'un empire englouti* (Paris: Hors Collection/Presses de la Cité, 1992), p. 23. A cropped version appears on the cover of my *Greater France: a History of French Overseas Expansion* (London: Macmillan, 1996).
16. The images are reproduced in Deroo, Deroo and de Taillac, *Aux Colonies*, and Pascal Blanchard and Armelle Chatelier (eds), *Images et colonies* (Paris: La Découverte, 1993).

17. For colonialism in museums, see Robert Aldrich, *Vestiges of the Colonial Empire in France: Monuments, Museums and Colonial Memories* (London: Palgrave Macmillan, 2005).
18. The photograph by Paul Nadar is in the collection of the Bibliothèque Nationale de France.
19. The heroization of colonial soldiers should not obscure the complexity of perspectives on 'natives' recruited for France. See Joe Lunn, ' "Les Races Guerrières": Racial Preconceptions in the French Military about West African Soldiers during the First World War,' *Journal of Contemporary History*, 34 (4) (1999): 517–36. On the racism that troopers faced in France, see Tyler Stovall, 'The Color Line behind the Lines: Racial Violence in France during the First World War,' *American Historical Review*, 103 (3) (1998): 739–69. The recriminations in Germany about the French use of colonial forces is discussed in Jean Yves Le Naour, *La Honte noire. L'Allemagne et les troupes coloniales françaises, 1914–1945* (Paris: Hachette, 2003).
20. The École Coloniale trained men in political theory, administrative procedure, law, literary Arabic and other languages, and the fundamentals of economics and engineering. See William B. Cohen, *Rulers of Empire: the French Colonial Service in Africa* (Stanford, CA: Hoover Institution Press, 1971).
21. To further complicate the issue, the differences between types of settler men might be drawn out: *Béké* planters in the West Indies, third- or fourth-generation *Français d'Algérie*, former convicts in New Caledonia, and so on. New arrivals from the metropole lived alongside long-term settlers, Creoles alongside *métis*. Inter-colonial migration – 'Syrians' to the West Indies and Africa, Martinican and Guadelouopean administrators in Africa, Asian laborers in New Caledonia, *tirailleurs sénégalais* posted around the colonies – was also common. In Algeria, the settler population comprised a spectrum of ancestral origins – French, Italian, Spanish, Maltese.
22. Douglas Porch, *The French Foreign Legion: a Complete History of the Legendary Fighting Force* (New York: HarperCollins Publishers, 1991).
23. François Pouillon, *Les Deux Vies d'Étienne Dinet, peintre en Islam. L'Algérie et l'héritage colonial* (Paris: Balland, 1997).
24. See Owen White, 'The Decivilizing Mission: Auguste Dupuis-Yakouba and French Timbuktu,' *French Historical Studies*, 27 (3) (Summer 2004): 541–68.
25. Isabelle Merle, *Expériences coloniales. La Nouvelle-Calédonie, 1853–1920* (Paris: Belin, 1995).
26. Dr Barot, *Guide pratique de l'Européen dans l'Afrique occidentale* (Paris: Flammarion, 1902), pp. 510–11.
27. One exception is Roger Curel, whose *Éloge de la colonie. Un usuel de la destruction* (Paris: Editions Climats, 1992) discusses bordellos, pp. 17–28.
28. Hubert Deschamps, *Roi de la brousse. Mémoires d'autres mondes* (Paris: Berger-Levrault, 1975), p. 92.
29. David Henry Slavin, *Colonial Cinema and Imperial France, 1919–1939* (Baltimore: Johns Hopkins University Press, 2001), esp. ch. 7; quotation from p. 151.
30. The lyrics are reprinted in Alain Ruscio, *Que la France était belle au temps des colonies ... Anthologie de chansons coloniales et exotiques françaises* (Paris: Maisonneuve & Larose, 2001), esp. ch. 10.
31. Alain Ruscio (ed.), *Amours coloniales* (Brussels: Editions Complexe, 1996).
32. See Matt K. Matsuda, *Empires of Love: Histories of France and the Pacific* (New York: Oxford University Press, 2005).
33. See Raymond Noulens (ed.), *Les Spahis. Cavaliers de l'armée d'Afrique* (Paris: Musée de l'Armée, 1997).

34. Playing dress-up was a common pastime for colonial men. Brazza's Arabic garb was mentioned earlier, Loti often had himself photographed in native clothing, and there are pictures of Lyautey in North African robes. French soldiers in North Africa, especially the *spahis* and *zouaves*, wore hybrid uniforms.

35. Pierre Loti, *Le Roman d'un spahi* (Paris: Folio, 1992), pp. 49, 63, 141, 108.

36. Hélène de Burgh, *Sex, Sailors and Colonies: Narratives of Ambiguity in the Works of Pierre Loti* (Bern: Peter Lang, 2005).

37. Philip D. Curtin, *Death by Migration: Europe's Encounter with the Tropical World in the Nineteenth Century* (Cambridge: Cambridge University Press, 1989), from tables, pp. 188–93.

38. Brigadier David Bernard, cited by Deroo, Deroo, and de Taillac, *Aux Colonies*, p. 20.

39. Dr Villedary, *Guide sanitaire des troupes et du colon aux colonies* (Paris: Société d'Editions Scientifiques, 1893).

40. Frank Proschan, ' "Syphilis, opiomania, and pederasty": Colonial Constructions of Vietnamese (and French) Social Diseases,' *Journal of the History of Sexuality*, 11 (4) (2002): 610–36.

41. Ernest-Jean-François Pichon, *Les Maladies vénériennes aux colonies* (Bordeaux: University of Bordeaux, 1905), p. 39.

42. See Jean Mathier and P.-H. Maury, *Bousbir, La Prostitution dans le Maroc coloniale. Ethnographie d'un quartier réservé*, ed. Abdelmajid Arrif (Paris: Paris-Méditerranée, 2003), a 1951 study of Casablanca; and Christelle Taraud, *La Prostitution coloniale. Algérie, Tunisie, Maroc (1830–1962)* (Paris: Payot, 2003).

43. Villedary, *Guide sanitaire*, pp. 66–7.

44. Barot, *Guide pratique*, pp. 556–7.

45. Régis Revenin, *Homosexualité et prostitution masculines à Paris, 1870–1918* (Paris: L'Harmattan, 2005), pp. 128–38.

46. Quoted in ibid., p. 110.

47. M.A. Kermogant, *Aperçu sur les maladies vénériennes dans les colonies françaises* (Paris: Imprimerie Nationale, 1903).

48. Dr Paul Rebierre, *'Joyeux' et demi-fous* (Paris: Maloine, 1909), 41ff.; René Jude, *Les Dégénérés dans les Bataillons d'Afrique* (Vannes: LeBeau, 1907).

49. Christian Gury, *Lyautey-Charlus* (Paris: Kimé, 1998).

50. See Robert Aldrich, *Colonialism and Homosexuality* (London: Routledge, 2003), esp. ch. 11 on the French and North Africa.

51. On the medical phenomenon in America's outposts, see Warwick Anderson, 'The Trespass Speaks: White Masculinity and Colonial Breakdown,' *American Historical Review*, 102 (5) (December 1997): 1343–70.

52. See Eugène Jung, *L'Initiation coloniale. Guide à l'usage de tous les futurs coloniaux* (Paris: Puyforcat, 1931).

53. *L'Art d'aimer aux colonies* went through various editions – with different titles and noms de plume; see Aldrich, *Colonialism and Sexuality*; Proschan ' "Syphilis, opiomania, and pederasty".' Phalloplethsygmography was the measurement of genitals, see the glossary in Ronald Hyam's, *Empire and Sexuality: the British Experience* (Manchester: Manchester University Press, 1990).

54. Frantz Fanon, *Black Skin, White Masks*, trans. Charles Lam Markmann (1952; London: Grove, 1986), quotations from pp. 177, 180, 165, 157, 156.

55. Compare Ashis Nandy's arguments about the 'unconscious homo-eroticized bonding' in *The Intimate Enemy: Loss and Recovery of Self under Colonialism* (Delhi: Oxford University Press, 1983), p. 10.

56. See note 15, above.

57. Nandy, *The Intimate Enemy*, talks about 'redemption' of masculinity in anti-colonial movements (and its rejection in Gandhi's 'non-cooperation'). This is explored in the Dutch East Indies by Frances Gouda, 'Gender and "Hyper-masculinity" as Post-colonial Modernity during Indonesia's Struggle for Independence, 1945 to 1949,' in *Gender, Sexuality and Colonial Modernities*, ed. Antoinette Burton (London: Routledge, 1999), pp. 161–74.

58. Simone de Beauvoir's *Le Deuxième sexe* dates from 1949; Arcadie, the first homophile organization, was set up in 1954.

8
In the Name of the Father: Male Masculinities in Vichy France

Miranda Pollard

MASCULIN, -INE
Qui est propre à l'homme en tant qu'être humain du sexe doué du pouvoir de fécondation . . . 1. Qui appartient à un homme . . . 2. Qui est considéré comme caractéristique des hommes . . . Qui rappelle un homme, qui ressemble à un homme. **Masculinité**, caractère masculin, ensemble des caractères spécifiques – ou considérés comme tels – de l'homme; synonyme. *virilité*; antonyme, *féminité*.

MASCULINISER, verbe trans. Conférer un aspect masculine (à quelqu'un); Synon. viriliser; Anton. Féminiser
Trésor de la Langue Française.[1]

Gender is not exactly what one 'is' or what one 'has.' Gender is the apparatus by which the production and normalization of masculine and feminine takes place . . . The conflation of gender with masculine/feminine, man/woman, male/female, thus performs the very naturalization that the notion of gender is meant to forestall.
Judith Butler, *Undoing Gender* (2004)[2]

Introduction

On a hot summer day in June 1940, following a six-week campaign and the worst military rout in French history, Maréchal Philippe Henri Pétain spoke to France by radio. He announced that he had assumed the direction of the new government. In so doing he gave the gift of his person to his country to alleviate its suffering. Pétain proclaimed the end of the government's defense against the German invasion. He spoke of the heroism of the French army, its magnificent resistance, the support of the veterans whom he was proud to have commanded, and the misfortune of the millions of civilian refugees who had in desperation taken to the roads and fled southwards hopelessly trying to get ahead of the Wehrmacht's lightning advance. Balancing the specter of (masculine and male) soldiers, past and present, with the pitiful plight of (female and feminized) refugees, the eighty-four year old Maréchal addressed these chaotic masses in terms of 'compassion and concern.' The writer Jean Guéhenno noted:

> June 17 1940. It's over. An old man who no longer has the voice of a man but speaks like an old woman has told us at 12:30 tonight that he has asked for peace. I think about all the young people. It was terrible to see them go off to war. But is it less terrible to see them forced to live in a dishonored country?[3]

Pétain betrayed not only his defeatist instincts but also his paternalist relationship to the hordes of undisciplined civilians and soldiers who were his immediate audience. Passive and shocked, the French public waited to learn the outcome of their new leader's promise to seek terms with Hitler, 'soldier to soldier, after an honorable fight . . . to put an end to the hostilities.' Few politicians, soldiers, civilians – men or women – could imagine that Pétain, the revered victor of Verdun, would accept the humiliating armistice terms which Hitler decreed, any more than they could envisage a vicious German occupation of over four years duration. For the majority, Pétain's voice was an authoritative masculine one, both fatherly and benign.

The triangle of masculinities

Vichy France's efforts to naturalize femininity and to mobilize gender politically have already been well-documented.[4] This chapter merely continues that process, but specifically within the compass of masculinity and men as political leaders.

A country humiliated by military defeat and led by an octogenarian WWI veteran, a state truncated into seven zones occupied by a foreign enemy, a nation without autonomy in economic or political matters, whose sovereignty was unequivocally compromised, and a society deprived of over a million and a half POWs held hostage in the Reich, surely presuppose a lack of mastery, a failure of the totality of manly attributes, a 'crisis in masculinity.' On German time and paying German-imposed rates for the franc, the very coin which was used to fund the German military occupation of France, the Etat Français appeared to be an impotent force in its own destiny. But, if neither clock nor currency was within its power and its sovereign 'virility' was frail, was Vichy France inescapably in the grip of gender incoherence? Had 'the production and normalization of [the] masculine' failed?

In the context of Vichy France, that which is 'proper to the male' and especially the power of the male 'as a procreative being' was unclear. Could the requisite binary of sexual difference, masculine/male versus feminine/female, be rescued? The 'whore' known as the Third Republic was dead, but the New Order was as yet unknown in 1940. Indeed, in face of the Germans, the rejection by French men of their fellow French men as 'imbeciles,' 'bemonocled dandies or sword-rattlers,' 'cretins,' 'dumb men' and scoundrels' boded ill for a new beginning.[5]

Pétain's assertion of paternal power was not the only way in which masculinity was made visible in the struggle to mobilize and command the forces of gendered order on behalf of a bewildered France. In 1940, the topographical markers of Pétainism at Vichy, resistance in London and collaborationism in Paris, seemed to create a geometry of male struggle, masculinist claims to authority, and male-dominated discourse. The war for gender's coherence was being organized in vastly different circumstances. If Maréchal Pétain marked one point of this political triangle of troubled masculinity, de Gaulle was another, and the competing voices of de Brinon, Déat, Deloncle, and Doriot another, there were further points within this triangle representing overlapping references of political masculinity. These included the two prime ministers, Pierre Laval and Admiral François Darlan, and their various ministerial appointees, such as Adrien Marquet and then Pierre Pucheu, as Minister of the Interior, George Lamirand, Minister of Youth, Philippe Renaudin, Commissioner for the Family; of the heads of Vichy's anti-Semitic Commissariat on Jewish Affairs, Xavier Vallat and Darquier de la Pellepoix; but also ardent collaborationist latecomers to the government such as Joseph Darnand, the head of the *Milice*, and Philippe Henriot, Vichy's propaganda genius.

From the Nord to the Alpes-Maritimes, from Brittany to the Midi-Pyrénées, the communist resistance and the various underground groups linked in the National Resistance Council (CNR) formed another – perhaps the most – significant set of reference points. Because of their diversity and clandestine nature, resistance movements fit uneasily within any equations of political geometry. If Jean Moulin is a masculine icon (better known in death than he ever was in 1940 when he was a prefect at Chartres, or in 1943 when he was betrayed to the Gestapo), then others like Jean Texier, Gabriel Péri, Henry Frénay, or Emmanuel Astier de la Vigérie, and the Manouchian Group, also represent markers of masculinity. But the resistance within France was never exclusively marked by individual men. Group identity and affiliations, and the participation of women in all aspects of the opposition to Vichy and the Germans, gave the resistance a more diffuse masculine identity. In Vichy, Paris, and London (and subsequently Gaullist strongholds such as Algiers and Dakar), *men* were recognizable public claimants to (masculine) authority, in style, message, and medium of communication. In the resistance, voices of dissent were less easily rendered exclusively male or masculine. Yet women resisters were always at war within an ideology whose parameters were restrictive, especially after the shift to armed conflict.[6]

Mapping the coordinates of political masculinity in WWII France, therefore, will never follow a straight line. Yet how Frenchmen's masculinity was articulated and mobilized at Vichy, in Paris, and in London, gives us information not just about the rhetoric of male authority, but also about the very workings of masculine and male power. In ideological terms, masculinity was mobilized both consciously and/or by default, being the very grammar of political struggle. The paternalist appeals of Pétain reflected and constituted Vichy's familial and familiar claim to obedience. De Gaulle's hold on the French opposition's aspirations – and his Allies' confidence – resided in his traditionalist masculinist and militarist discourse. Collaborationists such as Jacques Doriot and Marcel Déat looked to a virile pro-German fascism (both for their material support and their ideological values). Finally, whether armed and organized or civilian and non-violent, and whether or not they were committed to the formal equality of women, the leaders of resistance groups, from the communists through the ex-radicals and right-wing nationalists, all shared a common lexicon of a strong anti-German, new France. Men were in charge of the terms in which the war for political power and the soul of France was fought. Their hold on *potentially* hegemonic (not to mention forceful, or resonant) masculinity was constantly contested, shifting according to the chronology of the war, and the vagaries of public opinion. Pétain's 'fathering' of the French people, for example, was more persuasive in the summer of 1940 than at any time afterwards. De Gaulle's status as traitor and expatriate soldier, while represented in terms of (masculine) honor and duty, did not take on the proper gravitas of masculine leadership until sanctified by Allied support and the fealty of clandestine opposition within France. Wartime masculinity had multiple points of reference. Furthermore, some gendered identities can scarcely be mapped among these various discourses of French masculinity. French and foreign Jews, Spanish republican refugees and gypsy internees, further complicate the meanings of masculinity in this period, as do the hundreds of thousands of French households where women became the de facto and legal *chefs de famille.*[7]

Above all, the impact of daily and ever-increasing violence connoted the impossibility of counting on anything or anybody in occupied France, especially not French men and French masculinity. Ideologically and materially, the pretensions of masculine and male sovereignty collapsed when confronted with both German power and coerced collaboration. Nor was masculinity about symbols and allegories that floated freely above or beyond material realities. Masculinity was a key circuit of power, and a grid through which politics could be drawn to scale. There was no innocent French masculinity, no way to separate a 'protective' masculine Vichy from a murderous German masculinity. Hundreds of thousands of men fell outside the 'legitimate' Vichy family and were as likely to be rounded up, arrested, and imprisoned by the French gendarmes, police, or the men of the SOL or *Milice*, as by German forces. Arguably the *female* victims of the Vichy regime and the German conqueror were caught between a representational schema which portrayed them as masculinized subjects (terrorists) or essentially passive feminized victims (deportees with children, who vanished from France altogether) or, alternatively, as *sub-stitute* men in the family and workplace, called up for a temporary national service which would end with the return of real men and the end of the real war. Of course, Pétain's calculation – that Germany would defeat Britain and the war would end soon – was a costly mistake. By August 1942 at the latest, Pétain's 'gift of his person' was revealed as a cruel and empty gesture. Vichy was facilitating the near starvation of French families, the expropriation of the French economy for the Third Reich's war machine, and the military stability of Hitler's western front. Moreover, it was actively complicit in torture, murder, and genocide. As thousands of terrorized women, men, and children were dragged away to detention centers, internment camps, and the transit accom-modations of Drancy en route to Auschwitz, it was hard for even Vichy's most loyal subjects (even the most die-hard anti-Semites) to believe in France's delivery from evil.

The following sections sketch out the histories of French masculinity from a variety of geographical and political coordinates. They provide a very brief survey of how political masculinity was assumed, invented, re-staged or re-constructed.

Vertex I: Vichy

The well-known photograph of Pétain's Cabinet in November 1940 squeezed into what looks like a wall-papered bedroom in the Hôtel du Parc, gives a clue to Vichy's male masculine credentials.[8] A group of mostly balding men (apart from Paul Baudouin and Yves Bouthillier) in dark suits (apart from Pierre Laval and Marcel Peyrouton) smile awkwardly as they hunch up around a narrow table, four to a side with Admiral Darlan and Pierre Caziot elbowing each other at the table's end. Did these men share common char-acteristics of masculinity? Yes, obviously. But their embodiment of mas-culinity is literally limited and pared down: deprived even of the props of republican parliamentary life (the Chamber of Deputies) or the seat of tradi-tional power (the Elysée, the Matignon, and the Quai d'Orsay), the French state is being governed from a *salon*. (One is tempted to see *salonnières*.) The boxed-in civilian paternity of Vichy is all too obvious, a paternity which is not granted the (prosthetic) apparatus of high politics and aesthetics, or, most importantly, of military sanction. The armistice agreed to by these men of Vichy has deprived them of the masculine authority of the French army, of civic Paris, as well as the kind of political spectacle to which the French public were habituated. In the summer of 1940, the men of Vichy looked very tame. Pétain had to put distance between himself and these male politi-cians. He had to put himself above and apart from other men.

As Gérard Miller sardonically remarked, 'Pétainist discourse made the Maréchal the center (Father, Master, God) the most central (loving, powerful, neutral), such that he became each point of the circumference.'[9] With a near monopoly on public political discourse in the aftermath of defeat, Vichy portrayed itself as not only the sole legitimate public authority, but also as the incarnation of a glorious (if temporarily bowed) history to which all members of the 'real' French national community could proffer allegiance. That both aspects of this portrait – French state and French history – were coded masculine was hardly surprising. Pétain's solution to the defeat was represented as both rational and commonsensical, thus as quintessentially masculine in substance. The more pertinent question, then, was which form of masculinity would prevail? How would Vichy authorize itself as the centrifugal force of French sovereignty, and how would majority support – the infamous forty million French men [sic] of 1940 – be rallied toward a new political center and maintained as a centrist unity of political opinion?

Pétain was now the sovereign and constitutionally-endowed center of French public life; the new symbolic father who held, according to his earthly 'maker,' Pierre Laval, more legal authority than any Louis XIV. This 'father of the nation' would speak for – and to – his subject children in the familiar and family-rooted language of public/private command. Although the resonance of fatherly solicitude may be understandable in the context of military rout, the exodus of 6–10 million civilians before the invading Wehrmacht, and the confusion of parliamentary prerogatives in June, July and August 1940, the continued valence of patriarchal imagery may seem implausible. Yet in the following years, Pétainism relied on the fathering metaphor and a uniquely patriarchal agenda.

Whether on behalf of the National Revolution, in the sphere of negotiations with Nazi Germany, in domestic political matters such as educational policy, in championing the Chantiers de la Jeunesse, in official propaganda on the family, on the radio, or in his tours of southern cities to meet with prelates, notables, and adoring crowds, the last living Maréchal of France consistently posed as the ultimate 'Father of Fathers, the Father-Gold standard,' to use Miller's words. It was a short step to a familiar incantation:

Our Father
Who is our Head
May your name be glorified
May your rule commence
May your will be done
On earth, so that we may live . . .
Allow us not
To fall back into
Futile dreaming
And falsehoods
Deliver us from evil
O Maréchal![10]

The cult and iconography of Marshal Pétain have been comprehensively documented, and a vast body of photographs, posters, written speeches, folk artifacts, music, and official archives attest both to the extraordinary popularity of the head of state and to the acuity with which the administration exploited that popularity, ever conscious – especially thanks to the tight surveillance and censorship of public opinion – of the necessity of maintaining a Pétainist *élan* that would disguise the failures of the collaborationist state. This popular 'maréchalisme de masse' (Pechanski) had its 'golden age' in 1940–41, when the whole country seemed to be singing 'Maréchal, Nous Voilà,' the latest paean to the 'Savior of France.'[11] Although 'les gars' bore little relation to the young men of the Hitler *Jügend*, their masculinity was rooted in an anti-democratic political culture, heavily inflected toward Maurassian nationalism and Roman Catholic piety. Vichy France's male masculinity relied upon social hierarchy, the embracing – not renunciation – of bourgeois traditions, the breezy enthusiasm of the scouts and the sober, sentimental attachment of WWI veterans. Both men and boys turned out in their hundreds of thousands to hail their hero.[12] Pétain's restrained masculinity was not seen by the majority of the country as a problem. It was certainly not unfavorably compared to the virile energy of Hitler and Mussolini (except by the pro-German Paris collaborationists). The fascist dictators' performance of masculinity still struck many French people as somewhat ludicrous. In *Sept Étoiles*, René Benjamin (Pétain's hagiographer) asserted 'The Maréchal has nothing of the dictator who overturns the present by prophesizing the future. He is simply *the* Father of his country.'[13]

Yet in 1940, Pétain was eighty-four years old, a childless hero of the Great War, and a man of the traditional right who had not married his female companion, Eugénie. Not only did his representation of 'good enough fathering' not rest on any literal reality, but his claims to father the nation relied on the actions of a previous generation, an intervention at Verdun in 1917 which had become as mythical as Pétain's physical vigor was to become in the four years of occupation. The hero of Verdun myth glorified stubborn endurance at the price of capturing its protagonist in a drama that was nearly a quarter of a century old. Here was an old veteran, an old man. Pétain speaking as a father was almost rejuvenating himself then, and using the lexicon of fatherhood allowed him to evoke masculine virtues without virility, to pose as national protector without nationalist militarism.

There was inattention and disobedience, of course. As early as October 1940, Pétain had to admonish his 'children,' some of whom had begun to question his authority after his infamous handshake with Hitler. 'Up to now I have used the language of a father,' Pétain reminded his 'family'; 'Today I use the language of a leader.' Yet even this shift in roles worked within the same conceptual framework, with the same masculine authorial voice. Conjugating fatherhood provided an explicit linguistic and historical link to Latin-French male authority, again emphasizing the indigenous and well-rooted traditions of a previously invincible France. Speaking in the language of a leader (*chef*) the week after Montoire was intended to connect the political dots in Pétain's portrait of the new France: 'It is with honor and to maintain French unity – a unity of ten centuries – in the framework of building a new European order, that I enter today on the path of collaboration.'[14]

Yet if the key characteristics of fatherhood are that of male progenitor and male provider, then Pétain represented an already compromised masculinity: this was a mismatch between male-ness and masculinity, a symbol of masculinity that was weakened by material failures. Even before workers, food, fuel, and textiles became so scarce,[15] repopulating France and providing for French families was not a task either Pétain or the average French 'father' (or mother-provider) could easily accomplish in occupied France. Pétain could not regenerate France. These failures (of fathering) meant not only that Pétain's patriarchal legitimacy was fatally undermined, but the naturalized relationship of masculinity and fatherhood was also severed. In 1940–44, French fathers could be neither progenitors nor protectors, neither natural leaders nor natural providers.

To be sure, the National Revolution did not fail because of the lack of fathering or because French masculinity was compromised. The demise of Vichy was a complex process, its chronology differentiated by region and community. The image of Pétain waving to an enthusiastic crowd in front of Notre Dame, Paris, in April 1944 is notoriously placed beside the enthusiastic photographs of General de Gaulle being greeted by perhaps the very same crowds in August 1944, to illustrate the fickle nature of public opinion. But the other obvious interpretation is one centered on masculinist authority and the seduction of father figures, the bridge between the aging and impotent Maréchal and the male heir presumptive General, prodigal son of the national military family. The irony of their previous personal relationship, paternal and filial, in no way negated the reality of their total hostility (following de Gaulle's call to oppose Vichy and a Vichy court sentencing this son of France to death for treason). Symbolically this new competitive fathering was further complicated by the rebellious discourse of delinquent sons, or what Bertram Gordon has called Vichy's 'alter ego': the French collaborationists. These men believed that they 'were asserting the existence of a virile French manhood that would form the elite corps of a new fascist France.'[16]

Vertex II: Paris

If the forms of Vichy's masculinity were unmistakably patriarchal, the collaborationists of Paris articulated a more conflicted masculinity which alternated between the strident tones of those who envied Nazism's unambiguous virility, and those who preached intimate cooperation with Germany in the service of a French third way between bourgeois democracy and Bolshevism.

In Paris, home to the SS, the German Embassy, and the French representatives of the German Army's High Command, the arc of masculinity was clearly marked. The occupier had apparently unfettered scope for domination, but the French proponents of collaboration also had their manly and male outlets. Paris collaborationists used paramilitary gatherings, marches, uniforms, salutes, symbols, and pugilistic threats, to assert their virile relationship both with Vichy and with Germany, urging French men to support Pétain's National Revolution in the context of an imminent Axis victory in war, thereby situating themselves for their desired more equal fraternal relationship with Germany.

Alice Kaplan provides a nuanced reading of Sartre's famous essay, 'What is a collaborator?' which presents the French fascist as an outsider, foreign to French traditions, a 'womanly' figure who provides the ultimate metaphor of collaboration as a 'sexual union where France plays the role of the Woman.'[17] Kaplan suggests that Robert Brasillach reversed the age-old 'myth of Germany and France as a male-female couple' when he stated in 1943: 'Like it or not, we have lived together; French[men] of some reflection during these years will have more or less slept with Germany, and the memory of it will remain sweet to them.' This fascination with German 'otherness' is, then, open to the possibility that seduction is potentially homosexual. If French heterosexuality is open to erasure, then masculinity also needs to be re-imagined. What masculinist discourse could encompass so many contradictions?[18]

Cardinal Baudrillart, the aged Catholic prelate and Director of the Institut Catholique in Paris, enthusiastically embraced collaboration. Despite prior antipathy to Germany, he now saw collaboration as an integral part of the new 'crusade' against godless Bolshevism. Referring to Pétain's Montoire meeting with Hitler, Baudrillart thanked God for the gift of Maréchal Pétain 'in the hour when everything seemed lost.'

> As a priest and a Frenchman, I will tell you that these Légionnaires [French volunteers against Bolshevism] . . . represent . . . a new chivalry . . . May their weapons be blessed, may the tomb of Christ be delivered into safety.[19]

Hyberbolic or not, this church leader was heaping praise on those 'warriors,' in French and German uniform (the latter eventually numbering about 40,000),[20] who were prepared to die on the eastern front for their cause. Among these new 'twentieth century crusaders' was the ex-communist, Jacques Doriot, leader of the Parti populaire français (PPF). In the words of one of his ardent supporters, the collaborationist masculinity of Doriot – who was to be killed near Sigmaringen, Germany – was inextricable from his tough proletarian credentials:

> Where would we be if the best cadres of the communist party had not found themselves in the PPF; if we had not opposed communism by force; if Doriot had not torn 100,000 workers from Moscow's grip . . . the

man of St. Denis, the man who is the great working-class hope . . . It so happens that Doriot is a worker and that France needs to be put back to work . . . Doriot . . . is the great worker of France . . . He knows how to strike hard and fast.[21]

Vichy's last Minister of Education, Abel Bonnard,[22] usually identified as a homosexual and a collaborationist, preferred the leadership of Joseph Darnand. This decorated WWI veteran and founder of the *Milice*, the Gestapo's French ally in brutally repressing resistance and hunting down Jewish men, women, and children, was, for Bonnard, 'the model of the French man we need, because he is simultaneously a man of substance and a man of passion.' Who cared if violent masculinity was not popular? Addressing the *Miliciens*, Bonnard asserted 'Opinion is nothing other than an enormous female [creature]. I recognize and salute you, the male of the nation.'[23]

The theme of masculinity as action, and thus as opposed to feminine passivity, underlined the virtues of collaborationism for most of the Parisian collaborators. Eugène Deloncle, an ex-Cagoulard, founded the *Mouvement social révolutionnaire* to militate for a resolutely pro-German National Revolution, led by 'a group of men of action, decisive, not big talkers, whose past has included sacrifices which are a sure guarantee of the future.' These activists wanted 'the bastards now in power to be swept away; that there be no more Jews or Freemasons to harm us; that the policies of Montoire be applied so that France can take her place in the new Europe; that the country's healthy and French elements be united.'[24]

Vertex III: London

While many of the right-wing collaborationists had cut their teeth in fascist leagues and anti-democratic politics of the 1930s, the man who was to become the leader of the alliance of French resistance movements had little obvious background to prepare him. If Paris was the location for muscular and unapologetic collaborationism, charted in the colors of fascist masculinity, then London was the location for an equally unapologetic but oppositional nationalism, a robust nationalism that more quietly asserted a seemingly natural – and arguably more stable – French masculinity. Well established in his military career under the Third Republic, where he was recognized for his advocacy of mechanized mobile warfare, Charles de Gaulle had been included in Paul Reynaud's last cabinet, had been promoted to the rank of (provisional) general, and had led a successful defense in the field against the German invasion. Even if inexperienced politically, in June 1940 he had the right credentials to embody a recognizable French masculinity – that of a courageous and loyal soldier, who at 50 years old was the youthful face of the French military high command. His famous radio address of 18 June 1940, urging French men and women to continue the war, was significant both for its audacious optimism and its explicit disobedience to his superior officer, Maréchal Pétain, an erstwhile patron. Situated in London, with precious little money, few followers, and the often hostile skepticism of his would-be allies, de Gaulle assumed the mantle of the next great French hero as though by accident. Yet his language and audacity are only comprehensible within the parameters of contemporary masculinity. Could any French woman have taken this stand? Could another type of Frenchman? It was the combination of military status, a non-partisan record, and manly French chauvinism that provided de Gaulle with potential authority. His gift was the ability to convert that potential into extraordinary political and military value on behalf of an anti-collaborationist France, a France still at war.

De Gaulle did not speak for, inspire or control all the diverse forms of resistance that flourished within the occupied and (until November 1942) unoccupied zones either in June 1940 or August 1944 (when Paris was liberated by the advance forces of the Free French Army). But this particular locus of masculinity had a unique resonance. France has lost a battle, de Gaulle famously declared, but France has not lost the war. The formula that a 'makeshift government had capitulated and given way to panic' neatly summed up his reasonable opposition to events. But although strategically prescient about a world war – 'In the free universe, immense forces have not yet swung into operation. Some day these forces will crush the enemy' – de Gaulle's calculations relied on one overriding value: honor. This panicked government had delivered France 'into bondage,' 'forgetting honor.' France must be ready to fight on and ultimately to take her place among the victors. On that day, France 'would regain its liberty and its greatness.'[25] De Gaulle invited French*men* (soldiers, sailors, airman, engineers, technicians . . .) to join *him* with the rallying cry 'Our country is in mortal danger. Let us all fight to save *her*. Long live France!' De Gaulle met and raised the stakes on the discourse of masculine patriotism (emphasis added).

In a Christmas message from London (24 December 1941), for example, de Gaulle – at this stage himself a father of three – tells French children a 'tale' about their country's history. This resistance history succeeds in several ways. The national 'domestic realm' is claimed (an important feat for a foreign-based leader) in a way that legitimizes Gaullism as a Christian and homely phenomenon.[26] Is this not the type of exciting story the children might be treated to on Christmas Eve, in the dark hours of anticipation before Midnight Mass? The 'tale of glory' also delivers an optimistic version of the French past and future. While acknowledging the difficulty of the present, de Gaulle speaks of heroes, honor, and triumphs, thus restoring French glory via a heterosexual romance narrative whose terms are unassailable and in which his own role is thus well-grounded. It is a fatherly address without the chiding and shaming of Pétain's messages in 1941. There was no need to read between the lines, to imagine the content of a 'double game' which Pétain might be playing. These were simple truths, fit for children. De Gaulle's parental message is in a masculine register, but one that is transparent, without equivocation and without threats. The good and the bad characters are easily identified. This surely mobilizes what Sonya Rose, in her work on England during the Second World War, has called a 'tempered masculinity,' a version of political discourse which does not equate with 'hegemonic masculinity,' although it may be its catalyst.[27]

> Once upon a time, there was a country called France. Nations, you know, are like great ladies. They vary in beauty, goodness, and bravery. Well, children, of all these lady-nations, none was more beautiful, better, or braver than our Lady France. But she had a cruel neighbor, crafty and jealous, called Germany. Now one day Germany, crazy with vanity and wickedness, decided to turn all her neighbors into slaves.[28]

France and her friends had beaten the nasty neighbor in 1918, but soon, '[t]aking advantage of their simplicity, she prepared to invade anew. Soon she hurled herself once more against France, and this time she won the battle.' In this story the good, simple French people are not to blame. As though de Gaulle were turning the pages of a much nicer story book, the tale continues:

> The enemy and his friends say that France deserved to be beaten. But the French nation is made up of your Daddies and Mummies, your brothers and sisters, and you, children, know very well they were not to blame. If our army was beaten, it was certainly not because our soldiers were lacking in courage or discipline.

Nothing was as it might seem. Why were papa and maman unhappy?

> Dear children of France, you go hungry because the enemy is eating our bread and our meat; you are cold because the enemy is stealing our coal and our logs; you are unhappy because the enemy tells you, and gets other people to tell you, that you are the sons and daughters of conquered men.

Masculinity is thus summoned in a variety of images, both subliminal and explicit. The wicked neighbor is cruel – he eats children's food; he is a thief – he steals children's warmth away; he is devious – he tells children terrible lies and gets other grown-ups to do the same. But the good men fight to protect French children and Mother France. This chivalric tale ends in a 'solemn promise':

> You will have a visit soon, dear children of France, a visit from a lady called Victory . . . and then you will see how beautiful she is!

If de Gaulle's story drew on masculine and feminine elements to construct a narrative simple enough for French children, it also revealed the equation of nationalism and resistance to be capable of solution via diverse formulae: paternalism, patriarchy, parentalism/familialism, chivalry, militarism, and so on. The common denominator is a masculinity whose value extends to female embodiments: Lady France, beautiful and brave, and Victory France, whose presence was ever imminent.

We know from popular and scholarly representations of this period that no one image or language of masculinity became hegemonic, either for Vichy or for the resistance, for rural *résistants* or city *collabos*, for women or for men, French or foreign in France. Luc Capdevila has usefully documented the ways in which French women and French femininity were jointly mobilized in the discourses of resistance.[29] The identifiable points of a triangle of political masculinities sketched above exist in tension with the larger blueprint of historical masculinities within and beyond metropolitan France. The German (and Italian) takeover of the nominally 'free' zone in November 1942, the STO (foreign labor draft) of February 1943, the Gestapo round-up of Jews in Nice in September–October 1943, the CNR Charter of March 1944 or the Allied bombing of Marseilles in May 1944 – any of these places and moments would reveal a distinct narrative for material and symbolic masculinities. And neither men nor women had a stable or exclusive hold on those masculinities.

The hexagon divided

Historians debate the timing, scale, and momentum of the growth of opposition to Vichy, the support for armed resistance, and the nature of French people's expectations about an Allied victory and post-war French political settlement. Celebrations in August 1944 were, as Rod Kedward remarks, 'both carefree and laden with anxiety.'

> Liberation as a beginning divided those who saw the moment of liberation itself as the opportunity for change from those who cautioned the need to wait for the new government, the end of the war, the return of the prisoners and deportees, and the first post-war elections.

For quite different reasons, de Gaulle and the Communist Party opted to support the re-establishment of 'order,' asserting, respectively, the primacy of the national interest and the primacy of a continuing war in Europe. Men, male leaders, and masculinist agendas re-emerged in familiar configuration despite the potentially revolutionary moment.[30] Of all the enactments of violence and masculinity in this period of 'liberation,' perhaps the most conspicuous and sexualized was the phenomenon of '*la tonte*' (head-shearing) which Fabrice Virgili has so brilliantly analyzed in *Shorn Women: Gender and Punishment in Liberation France*.[31] Of approximately 20,000 victims of this violent retribution for presumed collaboration, the vast majority were women – and none of the male victims were punished for sexual reasons. In a masculine political and sexual economy, these were simultaneously the fallen woman, worthy of violent retribution, and the new woman citizen, worthy of the vote. Political masculinities thus continued to be in flux.

Every aspect of French society in 'the dark years' is a potential site for exploring the fluctuating meanings and representations of masculinity: bureaucracy, cinema, school curricula, family life, Maquis group, local café, internment camp, the markets of cities and villages throughout France, and the factories and farms of the Nord and Paris, of Normandie and Provence. Although an invidiously selective list, locations from which to explore the discourses of French masculinity in 1944–45, for example, would have to include not just Vichy and Paris, but also the sites of formal and spontaneous resistance, of 'outlaw culture,' of survival, and of rescue, as well as of repression, violence, and atrocity, as well as the sites of the purge and *la tonte*. The diversity of locations would be significant: the Cévennes, the Côtes-du-Nord, the Alpes-Maritimes and Le Chambon-sur-Lignon, Oradour-sur-Glane, Bayeux, and Corsica. But, as Karen Adler has documented with remarkable sensitivity in *Jews and Gender in Liberation France*, the 'long liberation' proved contradictory and painful for those returning and those marginalized by the new assertions of masculinist republican French identity.[32] These points of memory and representation serve to remind us of the open-ended nature of masculinity and its relationship to French wartime history.

The historians: the arc of masculinity

Vichy historiography has undergone many major interpretive and empirical shifts since the earliest days of the post-war period. While Robert Paxton's *Vichy France: Old Guard and New Order* (1972)[33] is a unique marker in this process, it is safe to say that the development of research in all areas of WWII France has grown exponentially in the last quarter century, from singular studies like that of Henry Rousso's *The Vichy Syndrome* to edited collections such as *Vichy and the Historians* (edited by Sarah Fishman et al.) which honored Paxton's retirement from Columbia University.[34] Where does masculinity figure in this vast literature? The subject of women and gender was, through the 1980s and 1990s, slowly forced on the mostly hostile mainstream establishment of Vichy experts.[35] Françine Muel-Dreyfus's *Vichy et l'éternel féminin* (1996) and my own *Reign of Virtue* (1998) were primarily concerned with the gender politics and sexed discourse of the Pétainist state. While the fascisms of Italy and Germany have attracted popular and scholarly attention precisely for their mobilization of misogynistic war veterans, radical anti-feminist ideology and an aesthetic of hyper-virility, French fascism and ultra-right movements have been the subject of heated exchanges about nomenclature and political significance, with the historiographical 'pendulum' swinging from a renunciation of fascist credentials for Vichy to an embracing of the same, to a further refinement of terms and emphasis on ambiguity. Whether in Paris, London,

Vichy, or in the French provinces, at the level of political organizations, social institutions, the state or national ideologies, homosexuality, homosocial bonding, and hetero-normative discourses are only some of the areas which deserve more historical attention. Building on the work of feminist historians of Vichy on the apparatus of gender in France, this chapter has merely highlighted some of the elements of political discourse in which masculinity is present, troubling and portentous. More systematic and comprehensive research on male identity, masculinity and male sexuality as identities in flux will surely yield plenty of insights into the politics of Vichy and life under the occupation. French WWII historiography has yet to have its historian of masculinity.

Notes

1. *Dictionnaire da la langue française du XIXe et du XXe siecle (1789–1960)* (Paris: CNRS, Gallimard, 1985).
2. Judith Butler, *Undoing Gender* (London: Routledge Press, 2004), pp. 42–3.
3. Guéhenno, as quoted in W.D. Halls, *The Youth of Vichy France* (New York: Oxford University Press, 1981), p. v.
4. See Miranda Pollard, *Reign of Virtue: Mobilizing Gender in Vichy France* (Chicago: University of Chicago Press, 1998); and Francine Muel-Dreyfus, *Vichy and the Eternal Feminine: a Contribution to a Political Sociology of Gender*, trans. Kathleen A. Johnson (Durham, NC: Duke University Press, 2001).
5. See Philipp Burrin, *Living with Defeat: France under the German Occupation, 1940–1944*, trans. Janet Lloyd (London: Arnold, 1996), pp. 32ff.
6. See Paula Schwartz, '*Partisanes* and Gender Politics in Vichy France,' *French Historical Studies*, 16 (1) (Spring 1989): 121–51.
7. Sarah Fishman, *We Will Wait: Wives of French Prisoners of War* (New Haven: Yale University Press, 1991).
8. See illustration 1 in *La Propagande sous Vichy, 1940–1944*, eds Laurent Gervereau and Denis Peschanski (Paris: Editions BDIC, 1990), p. 14.
9. Gérard Miller, *Les Pousse-au-jouir du Maréchal Pétain* (Paris: Editions du Seuil, 1975), Preface by Roland Barthes, p. 70.
10. Georges Gérard, as cited by Miller, *Les pousse-au-jouir*, p. 54.
11. 'Maréchal Nous Voilà.' Women and girls were also enthusiastic choir members for this song, yet the beat and lyrics arguably render the song properly masculine. *Francais, vous chantiez: Chansons de l'Occupation* (Arcadia Chansons, 1999).
12. See 'Des relais,' in Gervereau and Peschanski, *La Propagande sous Vichy, 1940–1944*, pp. 32–81.
13. René Benjamin, *Les Sept Étoiles de France* (Paris: Plon, 1942).
14. Philippe Pétain, 'Message du 30 octobre 1940,' in *Discours aux Français (17 juin 1940–20 août 1944)*, ed. Jean-Claude Barbas (Paris: Albin Michel, 1989) pp. 94–6.
15. On this vital aspect of occupation life and male/female roles, see Dominique Veillon, *Vivre et Survivre en France, 1939–1947* (Paris: Payot, 1995).
16. Bertram M. Gordon, *Collaborationism in France during the Second World War* (Ithaca, NY: Cornell University Press, 1980), p. 39.
17. Alice Yaeger Kaplan, *Reproductions of Banality: Fascism, Literature and French Intellectual Life* (Minneapolis: University of Minnesota Press, 1986), p. 14.

18. It is worth noting that women formed a sizable number of the collaborationist organizations' members. See Burrin, *Living with Defeat*, p. 429. On the general background, see Melanie Hawthorne and Richard J. Golsan, *Gender and Fascism in Modern France* (Hanover: Dartmouth University Press, 1997).
19. Cardinal Baudrillart as cited in Pascal Ory's *La France Allemande: Paroles du collaborationisme* (Paris: Archives Gallimard, 1977).
20. Burrin, *Living with Defeat*, p. 436.
21. Maurice Yves Sicard, *Doriot contre Moscou* (Paris: Editions populaires françaises, n.d. [1941?]), as cited in Ory, *La France Allemande*, p. 112. On the social composition of the different collaborationist organizations, see Burrin, *Living With Defeat*, pp. 436ff.
22. On Bonnard's educational agenda for cultivating separate sexes, even as late as June 1944, see Pollard, *Reign of Virtue*, p. 83.
23. Abel Bonnard, 'Allocution . . . aux chefs miliciens (30 janvier 1943)', cited in Ory *La France Allemande*, p. 142.
24. Deloncle quoted in Ory, *La France Allemande*, p. 114.
25. Général Charles de Gaulle, *Appel du 18 juin 1940*. For all the broadcasts of the French service of the BBC, see Jean-Louis Crémieux-Brilhac (ed.), *Les Voix de la Liberté. Ici Londres, 1940–1944* (Paris: La Documentation Française, 1975).
26. This metaphorical construction of Christian France, hardly surprising given de Gaulle's own Roman Catholic education and the necessity of wresting legitimacy from Vichy, nonetheless serves to erase Jewish children from the patriotic narratives of belonging. Renée Poznanski's *Jews in France during World War II*, trans. Nathan Bracher (Waltham, MA: Brandeis University Press, 2001) provides an indispensable introduction to the experience of foreign and French Jews throughout wartime France.
27. Sonya O. Rose, 'Temperate Heroes: Concepts of Masculinity in Second World War Britain,' in *Masculinities in Politics and War: Gendering Modern History*, eds Stefan Dudink, Karen Hagemann, and John Tosh (Manchester: Manchester University Press, 2004), pp. 177–95.
28. Charles de Gaulle, *Christmas Message to the Children of France* (24 December 1941).
29. Luc Capdevila, 'La Mobilization des femmes dans la France combattante, 1940–1945,' *Clio*, 12 (2000): 57–80. See also, Capdevila, 'The Quest for Masculinity in a Defeated France (1940–1945),' *Contemporary European History*, 3 (10) (2001): 423–45.
30. Ron Kedward, *La Vie en Bleu: France and the French since 1900* (Harmondsworth: Penguin, 2006), pp. 302–9.
31. Fabrice Virgili, *Shorn Women: Gender and Punishment in Liberation France*, trans. John Flower (Oxford: Berg, 2002).
32. K.H. Adler, *Jews and Gender in Liberation France* (Cambridge: Cambridge University Press, 2003).
33. Robert O. Paxton, *Vichy France: Old Guard and New Order* (New York: Knopf, 1972).
34. Henry Rousso, *The Vichy Syndrome: History and Memory in France since 1944*, trans. Arthur Goldhammer (Cambridge, MA: Harvard University Press, 1991); Sarah Fishman et al., *Vichy and the Historians* (Oxford: Berg, 2000).
35. The proceedings of the 1990 international conference hosted by the IHTP-CNRS, 'Le Régime de Vichy et les français' (published in 1992 under the same name in an 800-page Fayard collection, edited by Jean-Pierre Azèma and François Bédarida) brought these tensions into the open. For an account sympathetic to this author's interventions on gender and Vichy, see Robert Gildea's review in *Journal of Modern History*, 73 (1) (March 2001): 184.

9
Revolt and Recuperation: Masculinities and the *Roman Noir* in Immediate Post-war France

Claire Gorrara

The Second World War, commonly referred to as *les années noires*, was a period during which French people endured not only material hardship and deprivation but also the violent disruption of national identities. As with other moments of national crisis, gender identities were mobilized to make sense of such radical dislocations. This occurred at the level of historical experience and material reality, perhaps most visibly evidenced in the wave of head-shearings of women suspected of collaboration at the liberation. At the level of representation, such experiences were to be embedded in cultural narratives that continue to inflect gender relations in France today, such as the femininity of betrayal and submission to the occupier and the masculine prerogative of resistance. Such sexed narratives would have an enormous impact on the ways in which France would reconstruct itself in the aftermath of defeat, occupation, and bloody liberation. They provided the linguistic coordinates for the rhetoric of reconstruction centered on the masculinist paradigm of a 'virile' rebirth and the return of women to the hearth and domestic responsibilities. Indeed, it could be said that 'regendering the nation' in 1944–45 proved to be one of the most formative moments in the evolution of not only sexual but social identities in twentieth-century France.

This chapter will focus on the reconstruction of French masculinities in the immediate post-war era through the prism of crime fiction. It will briefly outline the wartime context in order to examine the late 1940s as a period that witnessed the consolidation of a masculinist ethos, firmly rooted in the heroic images of male resistance and sacrifice for the greater good of the nation. However, at the same moment that such 'hegemonic' masculinities were being harnessed to the project of nation-building and the drive for modernization, other voices were articulating far more troubling visions of post-war French manhood. These visions both bore the imprint of unresolved traumas from the recent past and projected deeply felt and collective anxieties over the 'event' of modernization, as Kristin Ross has termed it.[1] Such voices strove to highlight the violent contortions of the body politic demanded by the economic miracle of the 'trente glorieuses.' This was achieved mainly through the depiction of 'criminal' working-class masculinities, represented as doomed to obsolescence by social, political, and economic processes from which they were excluded. In exploring the work of two of the founding fathers of the French *roman noir*, Léo Malet and André Héléna, this chapter will consider the ways in which the *roman noir* operated as a site of counter-cultural politics, challenging the myths of a seamless and ahistorical process of modernization.

Regendering the nation

The Second World War stands as a watershed for French masculinities, a period when one of the most enduring couplings of nation and gender, war and masculinity, was put to the test and found wanting. French men and connotations of masculinity were radically undermined by the experience of rapid and ignominious defeat in less than four weeks in May–June 1940, followed by the surrender and dissolution of the Third Republic. By 1945, over 1,700,000 French men were living on German soil, either as prisoners of war or as conscripts or volunteers for the STO (*service du travail obligatoire*) forced labor scheme in Germany, while many thousands had been deported to concentration and extermination camps in the east. The campaign for liberation of the national territory in the final months of the war was overwhelmingly a foreign affair as Allied troops evicted the invader with the support of French resistance units, incorporating men from both the internal resistance and de Gaulle's Free French. Yet, as Luc Capdevila has persuasively argued, it was precisely at such a time of crisis for male identity that 'the myth of virility' was most ardently mobilized.[2] Appeals that called upon age-old idealizations of the masculine resonated in almost every area of social, cultural, and political life during the war years: from Vichy's construction of the French man as the linchpin of the National Revolution and its credo of 'famille, travail, patrie' to the resistance's call for 'free' Frenchmen who would take up arms to defend the nation. As Capdevila notes, with the intensification of the ideological battles of the war years, multiple representations of the masculine converged on the figure of the armed volunteer.

It was during the struggles for order and legitimation at the liberation that such a model of the 'virile warrior' was to reach its apotheosis, manifested most spectacularly in the head-shearings of women accused of relations with the enemy. Such public acts of humiliation were sexed punishments, a ritualized debasing of women who were perceived to have sullied France.[3] In a very real sense, women's bodies stood in metonymically for the nation. Their bodily desecration was above all an attempt to cleanse and purify the nation, to remove the bodily stain or blemish of collaboration and to enact a kind of *tabula rasa* that would erase the past from national memory. The agents of such physical and symbolical removal of the enemy's trace on French soil were French men, primarily those claiming an affiliation with the resistance. Hence, as Capdevila and others have argued, the head-shearings could be interpreted as part of a 'male backlash,' a reassertion of male power and prestige after the dishonor of defeat, and would feed into a highly gendered process of post-war reconstruction.[4]

In the immediate post-war period, France's ruling elites were acutely aware of the need to promote the connections between nationhood and masculinity. Michael Kelly eloquently points to the ideological 'sleight of hand' whereby the values and project of post-war humanism were suffused with masculine connotations, making the human-masculine the primary motor of identification for post-war recovery.[5] In more prosaic terms, this reassertion of masculine identities at a national level took the form of the armed male resistance fighter at the moment of the bloody battles for liberation. In the late 1940s, this circumscribed and highly selective image of the resistance would be the one given official endorsement and celebrated in the renaming of roads, the erection of war monuments and commemorative plaques.[6] The contribution of women resisters was marginalized, even though a sizable proportion of the new generation of women *députés* elected to the first Constituent Assembly in October 1945 attested to the importance of the resistance in their political formation.[7] Meanwhile, the wider 'culture of resistance', which had supported and sustained the more spectacular paramilitary activities of sabotage and armed combat was relegated to the background. By instating rituals and ceremonies that celebrated the *fraternité* of the resistance, the emergent Fourth Republic exploited the image of the male combatant to legitimize its origins and its fledgling institutions.

Yet, as R.W. Connell has stressed, 'hegemonic' masculinities are subject to challenge and contestation. Such 'culturally exalted' identities are dominant at the expense of other marginalized and subordinate masculinities and exist in an uneasy relation to changing patterns of female emancipation and autonomy.[8] Sexual identities and gendered patterns of behavior are responsive to, as well as constructed by, historical conditions and subject to internal contradictions that disrupt social practices. In this context, it is fair to ask to what extent such dominant masculine ideals became embedded in wider post-war French culture. For while France's post-war political and cultural elites may have invested in particular ideological formulations of the masculine, other arenas of cultural activity offer a markedly different picture.

Dark fictions

Crime fiction, in its more hard-boiled variant as the *roman noir*, has been a staple of twentieth-century popular culture in France. A steady flow of translated American classics, such as novels by Dashiell Hammett and Horace McCoy, were imported into France in the interwar years and were generally well received by the French intelligentsia and the general reading public. These novels were not relegated to the literary margins but read, in some instances, as acclaimed novels of bleak despair, alienation, and transgression that drew on pre-existing themes in French popular culture, as well as anticipating the philosophical and aesthetic project of existentialism. Indeed, it was French critics who were some of the first to give the *roman noir* its literary credentials, analyzing the connections between the modernist writing of authors such as Hemingway and Faulkner and the behaviorist technique of Hammett, a stylist of the hard-boiled school.[9] Boundaries between high and popular culture, that were later to become so entrenched, were more permeable in the late 1940s and encouraged the wide circulation of crime fiction novels within French society.

However, it was the years immediately following the Second World War that saw an explosion of *noir* fiction and film in France. After the retreat of the German occupier and an enforced deprivation of all things American, crime fiction became one of the cultural products synonymous with the development of an American-style consumer culture and the attendant challenges it posed to French cultural identities. A wave of hugely influential *films noirs* hit France in these years, with the release of classics such as *The Maltese Falcon* (1941) and *Double Indemnity* (1944), films that were to define the genre for a generation of writers and critics. The crime novel itself was boosted by the creation of the *Série noire* under the editorship of former surrealist Marcel Duhamel. This now iconic series came to embody the newly emerging *roman noir* with its early listings dominated by translations of American and British writers, such as Raymond Chandler, James M. Cain, and Peter Cheyney. Yet such cultural exports were not always welcomed with open arms. For critics such as Thomas Narcejac, himself a detective fiction writer, the imported *roman noir* and its French counterpart represented the worst excesses of sensationalism and voyeurism. Crudely exploitative, such a form was destined to drive indigenous French detective fiction to the margins and lead to the advent of a dumbed-down and standardized crime novel that would be a travesty of French traditions.[10]

Such perceptions of early French *roman noir* production persist today. While it is certainly true that the vast majority of French-authored texts in the late 1940s were derivative, this is by no means the whole story. A number of French writers adapted the American model as a formative cultural narrative of their times. For, as Lee Horsley has cogently argued, what she terms 'literary noir' is far more than the stereotypical figure of the hard-boiled private eye, captured most enduringly in Raymond Chandler's depiction of the 'mean streets' and 'the man of honor.'[11] Horsley's study focuses on both the aesthetics and politics of such a protean form of representation, with particular emphasis on the shifting identities and world vision that characterize different cycles of *noir* production. She identifies some constant character types, but her work is far more revealing of the ways in which *noir* fiction seeks to destabilize normative patterns of behavior and understanding. This is often achieved via the creation of disturbed 'centres of consciousness' whose fractured stories throw back frightening images of social disorder.[12] For, as Horsley emphasizes, by focalizing the narrative through the minds of such dislocated individuals, these authors compel readers to consider the relationship between the individual and society. What role have societal institutions played in the molding of such morally ambivalent beings? How far is the damaged narrator a mirror of the world that s/he inhabits? Indeed, to what extent is the violence in the text generated by social (dis)order rather than inimical to its functioning? Such questions subtend the potential of the *roman noir* to operate as a form of socio-political critique, a disabused voice from the margins that comments on the ubiquitous deceptions of its times. In the context of immediate post-war France, it was this counter-cultural perspective that would attract some of the most accomplished early practitioners of the form.

Revolt and recuperation

In the late 1940s, the *roman noir* was adopted by a number of French writers as a vehicle for presenting a highly critical view of the post-war world order. Some chose to assume the identity of their American counterparts and wrote evocative tales of social and political breakdown in a darkly transposed America.[13] Others, like Léo Malet and André Héléna, chose to set their novels in a recognizable French context. This choice to locate disturbing tales of violence and transgression on home soil was one that both authors recognized went against the national mood of recovery and would earn them the reprobation of the cultural establishment. In his *avant propos* to *La Vie est dégueulasse* (1948), Malet anticipates alienated reader responses to his book and notes how his novel does not fit 'le goût du jour 1947–8' [the tastes of 1947–8].[14] Héléna engages in a full frontal assault on reader sensibilities in his *Défense du roman noir* published in 1951. Here, Héléna castigates the post-war literary elites for their moral outrage at a form of writing whose mission it was to 'montrer l'humanité telle qu'elle est et non telle qu'elle devrait être' [show humanity as it is and not as it should be].[15] In a spirited riposte to those who decried the moral bankruptcy of the *noir* universe, he ends with a stinging assertion that such writing is but the product of its times and as such cannot be held responsible for its dark and desolate vision: 'la littérature n'est pas responsable de son époque, c'est l'époque qui est responsable de sa littérature' [literature is not responsible for its times, rather it is the times that are responsible for their literature].[16] For in the late 1940s, Héléna and Malet were two authors who used the *roman noir* as a means of exploring some of the tensions and anxieties confronting France at a time of unprecedented economic, social, and political change. Filtered through the consciousness of damaged and brutalized narrators, texts such as Malet's *La Vie est dégueulasse* (1948) and Héléna's *Le Bon Dieu s'en fout* (1949) chart the rise and fall of working-class male protagonists who stand in stark contrast to the 'myth of modernization' as Kristin Ross has described it in relation to France in the 1950s and 1960s. In these texts, we do not have 'a perfect reconciliation of past and future in an endless present, a world where all sedimentation of social experience has been leveled out or smoothed away.'[17] Rather, such male protagonists force a consideration of the messy human business of transition from wartime deprivation to post-war consumerism and the historically contingent factors that shaped the early years of France's rapid modernization.

Léo Malet is often considered the father of the French *roman noir*. A former surrealist poet with anarchist sympathies, he began writing pastiche American crime novels during the occupation in order to supplement his income.[18] However, the defining moment in his career came in 1943 with the publication of *120, rue de la gare*, featuring the first ever French hard-boiled detective, Nestor 'Dynamite' Burma. Set during the dark years of the occupation, Malet's tale of double identities and lost pearls charts the recovery of its central character from repatriated prisoner of war to successful detective, Dynamite Burma. His resolution of the mysteries central to the narrative projects an image of France hopeful of victory and renewal.[19] Burma was to become Malet's most endearing creation, acting as the central character in his acclaimed series *Les Nouveaux Mystères de Paris* (1954–59), each set in a different *arrondissement* of Paris, and earning him the plaudits of the French crime writing community.[20] Yet, at the same time as he was embarking on the Burma mysteries, Malet was also elaborating a far more disturbing set of *roman noirs* that drew on his surrealist and anarchist preoccupations. The *Trilogie noire*, written between 1947 and 1949, was the antithesis of the humorous and largely positive Burma adventures. *La Vie est dégueulasse* (1948), *Le Soleil n'est pas pour nous* (1949), and *Sueurs aux tripes*, finally published in 1969, all indicate by their titles the nihilistic tendencies of the novelist and an overwhelming sense of the entropic forces at work in French society of the late 1940s.

La Vie est dégueulasse is narrated from the perspective of Jean Fraiger, the leader of an armed gang charged with bolstering a miners' strike with direct action, an obvious reference to the wave of strikes and industrial action that hit France in 1947–48. In the opening pages, the group commits a bank robbery in order to support the families of the strikers but it quickly degenerates into bloody chaos with two guards killed and the money rendered useless as the serial numbers on the bank notes are known to the authorities. The strike committee, which had initially commissioned the robbery, condemns the group's actions and what began as politically sanctioned violence descends into a killing spree as Jean and his accomplices proceed to rob and murder for personal gain and public notoriety. Jean's coldly clinical perspective on his actions depicts violence as spectacle, a theatrical display with himself as central artistic sensibility.

While the group terrorizes the general populace as 'the mysterious bloody trio,' Jean's sense of ascendancy and mastery in the public sphere is contrasted with his inability to consummate his relationship with Gloria, the epitome of bourgeois values and prosperity and the symbol of his sexual inadequacy. With the elimination of Gloria's husband as a rival for her affections,

Jean's quest for sexual fulfillment seems attained and his relationship with Gloria is consummated, but the narrator is still assailed by doubts over his sexual prowess and virility. Finally driven to consult a psychoanalyst, Mr Clapas, Jean's disturbing psycho-sexual predilections are diagnosed as the symptoms of lifelong grieving for the loss of his mother as a child. Jean dies in a bloody shoot-out at a police station and the novel ends on press reports that promise to publish the rambling 'confession' found on the narrator's dead body, alongside Clapas's psychological evaluation of his patient.

By the end of the text, the rampaging violence associated with Jean and his gang would appear to have been safely disassociated from the social order. With the intervention of the psychoanalyst, a *deus ex machina* figure of authority, Jean's sexual neuroses and the connections between his aberrant behavior and wider social and economic forces have been dismissed as 'ce cas particulier de complexe d'infériorité' [this interesting case of an inferiority complex].[21] Masculinity disorder is reduced to a 'condition' that can be diagnosed, if not cured, creating an image of working-class French masculinity as violent and criminal, unassimilable into mainstream society. Yet such representations serve their purpose in the teleology of the text. Jean's bloody demise is recuperated by those in power to stand as a salutary tale for others who might be tempted to follow his example. Textual strategies reinforce this neutering of Jean's rebellion against conformism and the social order. Have we been in fact reading his 'confession' as promised in the final newspaper report and its coda in Clapas's dispassionate analysis? If so, has the extraordinary narrative of the violent psychopath been reduced to yet another example of a sensationalist *fait divers*, repackaged to meet the insatiable appetites of readers for tales of gore and violence? While the official discourse is predicated on denying the individual male criminal's implication in the social fabric, symbolic and metaphorical layers of meaning in the text highlight his status as a privileged voice that represents the wartime, and indeed pre-war, masculine identities to be demolished in order to make way for the new 'virile' France.

During a period when masculine ideals and values were marshaled to support the project of nation-building, Malet builds his text around a narrator-protagonist who embodies masculine failure, humiliation, and despair. Yet this figure is traversed by the history of his times as, on one level, Jean Fraiger can be interpreted as a darkly inverted image of the armed resister, the powerful symbol of dominant masculinity in the late 1940s. In the opening pages of the novel, he positions himself and his fellow bank robbers as following in a long line of political insurrectionists, prepared and willing to take direct action to champion the cause of the poor and oppressed. Like the populist images of the armed male resister, violence is to be used to challenge a 'criminal' order, here represented by state troops who charge the striking miners, killing a young girl.

However, these images of masculine self-assertion through decisive action swiftly break down in the text. From the principled agent of social change, Jean's narrative degenerates into one where masculine power and force is perverted to satisfy increasingly sado-masochistic desires. These are represented most powerfully in the dream world of the text which comes to overwhelm Jean's waking reality as the demarcations between fantasy and reality collapse. Central to these scenes is Jean's troubled sexual identity, which surfaces in a variety of forms: from paralysis in the presence of the object of his desire to a far more disturbing image of necrophilia as the dreaming consciousness imagines a scene of sterile lovemaking that ends in the sudden recognition of the decomposing body in his arms. Intense anxiety and neurosis over sexual performance haunt the main protagonist as markers of his personal humiliation as a man.

Such individual male failure and impotency are extended in the novel to encompass the whole body politic, and are closely associated with class inequalities. For Jean's outbursts of violence and depravity are inescapably connected to the functioning of the social order. Images of male powerlessness and victimization pepper the text, from the brutal mutilation of a gang member's body early on to the numerous male guards, policemen, and bank employees who are killed in the act of robbery. In the novel, working-class 'criminals' impose a reign of terror on the middle-class privileges of the rich as banks, factories, and other capitalist institutions are targeted. Yet while they hold the public in thrall, their exploits salaciously reported in the press, the gang members themselves inhabit the transient spaces and places of dingy hotels, rented rooms, bars, and cafés, in an image of working-class exclusion and marginalization. To a great extent, they represent pre-war traditions of organized gang culture, codes of 'honor' that were on the wane in these years as international crime networks transformed the French *milieu*. Anachronistic both in terms of their political inspiration and their methods, Jean and his gang are destined to be eliminated from post-war histories as surplus to requirements.

The anxieties and insecurities of working-class masculinity are also represented in the text through Jean's deeply ambivalent relationship with Gloria. Gloria represents the seductions of middle-class prosperity and conformism. Presented almost exclusively in her well-appointed apartment, Gloria symbolizes the consumer dreams of the *cadre* generation. She is the 'parfaite maîtresse de maison, soucieuse des aises de ses hôtes' [the perfect hostess, attentive to her guests' needs][22] and is viewed by her husband, Laubier, as the embodiment of his aspirational lifestyle. This is perhaps most tellingly observed in his description of her as the luxury car he could never afford to buy: 'personnellement, je n'ai jamais eu les moyens d'acheter une voiture digne de Gloria' [personally, I have never had the means to buy a car worthy of Gloria].[23] Jean's pursuit of her is, therefore, at once a quest for sexual fulfillment and an attempt to invest in 'the cult of comfort centered on the home' so central to the leisured time of the ambitious young *cadre*.[24] What is striking about the text is the ways in which such a feminine-invested dream of modernization is overlaid with wartime images of collaboration. These betray the legacy of the recent historical past that was to be so carefully edited out of immediate post-war accounts.

The most arresting scene in the novel is Jean's dreamscape of revolutionary insurrection which carries with it the familiar tropes of the liberation: 'Dans la rue, on s'exterminait ferme. Ça tirait de tous les côtés. Des bombes explosaient. Des immeubles flambaient' [In the street, people were killing one another. Shots came from all sides. Bombs exploded and buildings were in flames].[25] As the narrator enters the headquarters of the striking miners, he is faced with a series of mannequins in glass coffins, straight out of the fashion plates of the day. As he approaches one, his co-conspirator lifts one of the bleeding heads to meet him. It is the decapitated head of Gloria, bearing the marks of her violent demise. Its serpent hair, bloody mouth and petrifying look all signal the image's debt to the mythological figure of Medusa, the ultimate castrating woman. [26] This composite image draws on a number of the themes that have been so central to the novel and which foretell Jean's demise. Firstly, it presages the return of the past as internecine conflict. The reference to blood, hair, and violence all evoke the head-shavings of women at the liberation, here perverted into an act of decapitation. Second, these largely repressed memories are interwoven with gender-inflected anxiety about the drive for modernization. The shop dolls and glass coffins gesture towards the commodification of culture and the objectification of women, while simultaneously warning of the loss of male autonomy and the 'unmanning' of the main protagonist. The past, the narrative suggests, is unfinished business and will resurface sporadically to challenge official representations of progress and technological advance in the post-war period. Meanwhile, the social grouping most clearly identified as the losers are working-class men, dispossessed of their culture, identities, and status in the new France.

Ultimately, *La Vie est dégueulasse* projects images of male impotency, humiliation, and exclusion onto the social and political landscape of post-war France. The dream worlds of the narrating consciousness of the text throw into relief the unresolved traumas of the war years and the loss of real and symbolic power of a sizable proportion of the working-class male population. Working-class men are represented mainly as 'criminal' characters whose only form of protest is the inarticulacy of violence. Whilst prosperity and success were promised for all, the novel suggests that only a select few would be able to live the dream, leaving behind those who relied upon now outdated wartime or pre-war identities.

If Malet received critical acclaim during his lifetime, André Héléna represents one of the great forgotten authors of the early French *roman noir*. Héléna began his writing career in 1949, producing over a hundred novels of uneven quality until he died in 1972, destitute and largely unacknowledged by his peers. However, in recent years, his reputation has undergone something of a rehabilitation. A selection of his writings has been republished and reviews have paid tribute to his work, particularly of the 1950s, seeing him as 'un chaînon essentiel de cette histoire du polar français' [an essential link in this history of French crime fiction].[27] Critics have pointed to his incisive social critique and his readiness to take on some of the sacred cows of his era with novels like *Les Salauds ont la vie dure* (1949). A fictional *exposé* of political corruption and expediency during the occupation, the novel was banned four years after its publication as an affront to public decency.[28] Indeed, for some, he incarnates the mission of the French *roman noir* to act as an unsettling literary genre cursed to speak out on issues that others would prefer to pass over.

Le Bon Dieu s'en fout (1949), Héléna's second published novel has been described as 'une oeuvre fondatrice du Noir' [a founding work of the *noir* genre].[29] The text is narrated from the viewpoint of an escaped convict whom the reader first encounters trudging across a dark, rain-soaked urban landscape. Eventually arriving in a small town, the narrator, Felix Froment, searches out criminal contacts from whom he acquires counterfeit identity papers. These symbolize his hopes of starting afresh and erasing the memory of his recent past as a convicted double murderer. However, his decision to return to the unnamed town of his birth proves to be disastrous. The haven he seeks at the café *L'Étoile de mer*, where he rooms and passes his days under an assumed identity, is disrupted by the intrusion of vivid flashbacks to his convict days in French Guyana. While he searches for an illusory respite from the fear of capture and reimprisonment, all that surrounds him reminds him of a life of working-class exclusion and deprivation. Almost solely confined to the café and his rooms above it, the narrator seems destined to relive the same fear, flight, and persecution that preceded his incarceration.

This self-imposed retreat from the world is gradually eroded as events in the present bring the past sharply into focus. The graphically enacted murder of Mme Plombe in rooms adjoining the café recalls the narrator's own brutal murders of his girlfriend and former crime associate, triggering repressed feelings of guilt and remorse. In addition, his burgeoning love for Edith, the young servant from the café, offers the narrator the possibility of companionship and understanding, but at a price. For Edith, the idealistic convert, couches their hopes for a future life in the discourse of divine redemption, notions that are inimical to the narrator as one who refuses to accept that a higher being presides over the horrors he has witnessed and experienced. With the local police forces set to recapture him, the narrator sets out once more on a futile quest to escape what the reader is increasingly coming to interpret as his fate or destiny. Drawn ineluctably back to *L'Etoile de mer* and a shoot-out with the authorities, the narrator succumbs to his wounds. As Edith cradles her dying lover in her arms in the final pages of the novel, he recites after her the Lord's Prayer before an unidentified third-person narrator ends with a muted appreciation of his life.

As with *La Vie est dégueulasse, Le Bon Dieu s'en fout* ends with the elimination of the main male protagonist and the challenge he poses to the social order. Like Malet, Héléna chooses to enact a second textual 'death' that denies the narrator his rebellious stance. For the convicted convict who raged against organized religion is described in death as finally at peace, with his eyes 'tournés vers un monde meilleur' [turned towards a better world].[30] This religious discourse of salvation and forgiveness prompts the reader to consider a number of questions. To what extent has the narrator accepted the benediction of his lover, Edith, and undergone a last-minute conversion? How far has he finally capitulated to the bourgeois ideology and institutions he has so long decried? Indeed, have we witnessed a 'miracle' as the disembodied third-person narrator affirms in the last line of the book? The rich metaphorical layering of the novel suggests that there can be no resolution to such textual ambiguities, and that such normalizing explanations are at best a simplification of the gender and class inequalities of the immediate post-war period. In *Le Bon Dieu s'en fout*, Héléna's targets shift from Malet's assault on the onward march of modernization to aim at the continuing corruption and injustices of French colonialism.

Le Bon Dieu s'en fout is a damning indictment of the impact of war and occupation on a generation of men and women. The two main protagonists, Felix and Edith, are the products of war and live with the consequences of their origins. Felix is the son of a soldier who returns traumatized from the trenches and Edith is the orphaned daughter of French workers stationed in the Rhineland with the French army of occupation immediately following the First World War. The parental legacy of war is one of loss, hardship, and deprivation. Yet, if the First World War is represented as a landmark event in the text, the occupation and liberation are referred to far more obliquely. They function as collective experiences that enter the narrative as a *noir* sensibility and provide the critical frame for the author's rejection of French colonial ambitions.

Le Bon Dieu s'en fout begins by alluding to one of the most common sequence of experiences for French men during the Second World War: capture, exile, and return. The narrator, like the returning prisoner of war, has undergone exile abroad and is coming home to start afresh. However, the long anticipated homecoming does not result in resettlement and reintegration but rather isolation and violent death. This imagery of exile and return is made more powerful in the novel by Héléna's decision to harness such a shared experience of dislocation and repatriation to an *exposé* of French colonialism. The narrator's exile from metropolitan France to its colonies is not triggered by external war but internal repression. The labor camps in Germany are replaced by the penal colony of St Laurent de Maroni in French Guyana, presided over by the French authorities. Indeed, this 'grand tour' of France's colonial possessions takes in other shameful locations, such as the military camps of Foum-Tataouine in Tunisia, closed in the immediate aftermath of war, where the narrator is forcibly conscripted into an African battalion. France's colonial empire is presented as one vast penal colony, used by the post-war governing elites, like their predecessors, as places of exclusion for those who were deemed to have forfeited their right to be part of the national community.

This image of the 'criminal' project of colonialism also calls into question the legitimacy of the ruling republican elites. Héléna's text juxtaposes the myth of national resistance to occupation with France's role as a colonial oppressor. At a time when France was seeking to enhance its standing as a global power and to maintain its hold on colonial territories, *Le Bon Dieu s'en fout* highlights the human rights abuses practised in the name of the Fourth Republic. For, as the narrator comments, his periods abroad reveal to him the shared fate of French prisoners and the indigenous populations as persecuted peoples: 'Or le détenu, comme l'indigène, il a toujours tort' [now the detainee, like the native, is always wrong].[31] Treated alike by the colonial authorities, their lives are little more than a form of enslavement at the hands of brutal masters who refuse them the most basic concessions of human existence. Indeed, what the text suggests most provocatively is the extent to which, to use Kristin Ross's formulation, the 'clean' process of modernization would be twinned with a 'dirty' history of colonial exploitation, as the largely invisible labor of immigrants from far away lands would power France's post-war economic miracle.

As in *La Vie est dégueulasse*, working-class masculinities come to function as the key vector for such a critique of the modernizing trends played out in immediate post-war French society and culture. Felix Froment, the escaped convict, represents the brutalizing effects of the colonial experience on the individual. Froment's experiences of social exclusion and incarceration are writ large upon the urban landscapes he traverses, presented as places of death and disease. The dark city spaces he traverses are devoid of human figures, as if they had been expelled from the public domain. Buildings exude an aura of decay, while the city itself is depicted as a long-dead corpse whose life blood has been drained away: 'J'avais l'impression de courir les artères vidées de sang d'une ville morte depuis des années' [I felt that I was running through the bloodless arteries of a city that had been dead for years].[32] The effect of such a pervasive landscape of death on social relations is dramatic. Characters, both male and female, are presented as subject to perverse impulses and desires that rob them of their humanity and reduce them to savages, capable of cold-blooded murder. Here, sexual and social identities are subservient to an all encompassing 'law of the jungle' that reflects back the incarceration of the narrator in an unsettling image of civil society as but 'la prolongation du bagne' [the continuation of the penal colony].[33]

Violence, dehumanization, and isolation become the defining features of such a *univers pénitentiaire*, with Froment as the male narrator exemplifying the exclusions and dispossessions of the text. Yet, Héléna also prompts the reader to consider the relationship of the individual criminal to society. To what extent is Froment himself the explanatory principle of crime or is he merely representative of a generalized disorder that surrounds him? The narrative posits the troubling notion that crime has, and always will, circulate like a contagion. Froment, already infected, cannot but help spread the seeds of unrest to others: 'l'assassinat me suivait comme une ombre, à croire que j'en portais le germe dans le sinus et que je le soufflais en respirant' [Murder followed me like a shadow as if I carried the seed in my system and spread it by breathing].[34] Crime, as disease, cannot be expelled from the community and safely cordoned off in distant colonial lands. It operates as a force that crosses geopolitical boundaries; affects all strata of society and, even dormant, cannot be purged or cleansed from the body politic. In *Le Bon Dieu s'en fout*, it is an integral part of the human condition.

The last page of the novel calls upon the reader to interpret Froment's dying words of prayer as a road to Damascus conversion. However, competing discourses point to the unrepentant narrator's rejection of divine authority and judgment. The recurrent image of the narrator as cursed figure, doomed to wander the earth in penitence for his sins, reflects his outcast status and his firm location in a deeply flawed but human reality. For, as the title of the novel makes clear, *Le Bon Dieu s'en fout*, Héléna denounces the indifference and complacency of the ruling elites, whether political or spiritual. The images of diseased working-class masculinities, rootless and adrift, reflect collective feelings of alienation and a loss of cultural reference points. The working-class narrator is envisaged as a hunted beast, encaged abroad, eventually released in France and finally tracked to death. Intertwined with a history of colonialism and dark echoes of the occupation, Héléna's text, like Malet's, signals the human costs of post-war reconstruction.

In conclusion, both *La Vie est dégueulasse* and *Le Bon Dieu s'en fout* deal with outcast male protagonists whose violent opposition to the established order is effectively quashed in the final pages. Their deaths are placed in explanatory frames that deny their individual voice of revolt and neatly sidestep the need to question prevailing norms; from the medicalized discourse of individual psychosis to the religious narrative of redemption. Yet, the reader of both novels is minded to mistrust such facile recuperations. These depictions of damaged and diseased masculinities are presented as telling tales from the margins that jar with the dominant representations of a virile and resurgent France in the late 1940s. Indeed, these 'antagonistic' masculinities countered the prevailing hegemonic models of heroism and erected in their place images of the marginalized and the excluded. Such novels represent an alternate history of post-war reconstruction. They hint at the dark secrets of the occupation, the bloody memories of fratricidal conflict that would be repressed at a time of consensus-building. They accentuate the gender and class inequalities suffered in order to fashion the new nation. As two of the founding fathers of the French *roman noir* in the late 1940s, Malet and Héléna set in place the template for committed *noir* writing that would find its fullest expression in a later generation of authors inspired by the events of May 1968, writers such as Jean-Patrick Manchette and Thierry Jonquet. For if the working-class masculinities of these texts do not survive their encounter with a conservative and inflexible social order, their spirit lives on in countless French *romans noirs* that testify to the enduring appeal of such a *contestataire* tradition into the twenty-first century.

Notes

1. See Kristin Ross, *Fast Cars, Clean Bodies: Decolonization and the Reordering of French Culture* (Cambridge, MA: MIT Press, 1995), p. 4.
2. Luc Capdevila, 'The Quest for Masculinity in a Defeated France, 1940–1945,' *Contemporary European History*, 10 (3) (2001): 423–45.
3. See, among others, Fabrice Virgili, *La France 'virile': des femmes tondues à la Libération* (Paris: Payot et Rivages, 2000) for an influential analysis of what was, for much of the post-war period, a taboo topic.
4. Capdevila, 'Quest for Masculinity,' p. 445.
5. See Michael Kelly, 'The Reconstruction of Masculinity at the Liberation,' in *The Liberation of France: Image and Event*, eds H.R. Kedward and N. Wood (Oxford: Berg, 1995), pp. 117–28.
6. See Luc Capdevila, 'Le Mythe du guerrier et la construction sociale d'un "éternal masculin" après la guerre,' *Revue française de psychanalyse*, 62 (2) (1998): 607–23, for an excellent disscussion of French masculinities and the culture of reconstruction.
7. See Hilary Foottit, 'The First Women Députés: "les 33 Glorieuses"?,' in Kedward and Wood, *The Liberation of France*, pp. 129–141 (132–3).
8. R.W. Connell, *Masculinities* (Cambridge: Polity Press, 1995), p. 77.
9. See Claude-Edmonde Magny, *L'Age du roman américain* (Paris: Seuil, 1948).
10. Thomas Narcejac, *La Fin d'un bluff: essai sur le roman noir américain* (Paris: Le Portulan, 1949).
11. See Chandler's now seminal essay, originally published as 'The Simple Art of Murder' in the *Atlantic Monthly* of December 1944.
12. Lee Horsley, *The Noir Thriller* (London: Palgrave, 2001), p. 93.
13. See my article on the early work of two such writers, John Amila (Jean Meckert) and Terry Stewart (Serge Arcouët), 'Cultural Intersections: the American Hard-boiled Novel and Early French Romans Noirs,' *Modern Language Review*, 98 (3) (July 2003): 590–601.
14. Léo Malet, *La Vie est dégueulasse* (Paris: Christian Bourgeois Éditeur, 1990), p. 17.
15. Reproduced as a preface to André Héléna, *Le Bon Dieu s'en fout* (Paris: Editions Florent Massot, 1994), p. 9.
16. Héléna, *Le Bon Dieu s'en fout*, p. 11.
17. Ross, *Fast Cars, Clean Bodies*, p. 11.
18. For an overview of Malet's life and work, see Alfu, *Léo Malet: Parcours d'une oeuvre* (Amiens: Encrage, 1998).
19. For a detailed analysis of the novel and its relationship to its historical context, see my 'Malheurs et ténèbres: Narratives of Social Disorder in Léo Malet's *120, rue de la gare*,' *French Cultural Studies*, 12 (3) (October 2001): 271–83.
20. Malet was awarded the Grand Prix de littérature policière in 1948 for a Burma-inspired mystery, *Le Cinquième procédé*.
21. Malet, *La Vie est dégueulasse*, p. 190.
22. Ibid., p. 89.
23. Ibid., p. 141.
24. Ross, *Fast Cars, Clean Bodies*, p. 175.
25. Malet, *La Vie est dégueulasse*, p. 79.
26. '. . . une chevelure rousse qui serpentait à nos pieds' [red hair that snaked to our feet]. Ibid., p. 80.
27. Michel Guerguieff, 'André Héléna, noir désespéré,' *Quinzaine littéraire*, 859 (April 2003): 19.

28. See Robert Deleuse, 'Petite histoire du roman noir français,' *Les Temps modernes*, 595 (August-October 1997): 53–87 (63).
29. Jean-Pierre Deloux, 'Je suis un roman noir,' *Polar*, 23 (2000): 19–26 (24).
30. Héléna, *Le Bon Dieu s'en fout*, p. 217.
31. Ibid., p. 113.
32. Ibid., p. 16.
33. Ibid., p. 62.
34. Ibid., p. 156.

10
High-heels or Hiking Boots? Masculinity, Effeminacy and Male Homosexuals in Modern France

Michael Sibalis

In 1997, SOS-Homophobie, a French association that fights homophobia, issued a protest against one of the country's leading dictionaries, *Le Robert*, for implying that a homosexual was an effeminate man and declared it time to 'dust off' a dictionary that perpetuated 'a series of untruths and antiquated clichés' about homosexuality.[1] Of course, people consult dictionaries to learn how words are used in practice, and the effeminacy of male homosexuals – that is their reputed display of the physical and mental characteristics, mannerisms, and comportment socially defined as womanly – is an *idée reçue* that once had wide currency in France and that to some extent lingers on today.[2] Indeed, many heterosexual men construct, affirm, and defend their masculinity by rejecting both femininity and homosexuality. According to Elisabeth Badinter: 'Being a man signifies not being feminine, not being homosexual; not being docile, dependent, submissive; not being effeminate in physical appearance or behavior.'[3] Or, as Daniel Borillo has put it: '[B]eing a man implies looking down on women and detesting homosexuals.'[4]

Michel Foucault once pointed out that although denunciations of effeminate males date back to Antiquity, only in the nineteenth century did texts begin to explicitly link perceived effeminacy in men to 'the homosexual' as a new social type characterized by 'his gestures, his posture, the way he dresses, his affectation, but also the form and expression of his face, his anatomy, [and] the feminine morphology of his entire body.'[5] Prior to the mid-1800s, a man's effeminacy did not automatically raise questions about his sexual orientation (to use a modern term). When eighteenth-century French thinkers censured male effeminacy, they meant only that certain men (most especially court aristocrats) had fallen under the influence of women and taken on their characteristics, becoming frivolous, sensual, sybaritic, too refined and overly concerned with appearance.[6] As late as the mid-1870s, a book about the moral degeneracy of Paris clung to this (by then) out-of-date definition of effeminacy: effeminate young men had lost their virility through (heterosexual) debauchery with women of ill-repute, but there was no implication that they felt desire for their own sex.[7]

How and when, then, did the stereotype of the effeminate homosexual first emerge and become a commonplace in both scientific literature and popular culture? In other words, how did it come about that, in 1982, a French psychiatrist and university professor could state authoritatively, in a book intended for the general public, that '[h]omosexuals as a group present more feminine traits than heterosexuals ... In short ... the homosexual, in many cases, does not stand out only by his choice of [sexual] object but also by certain aspects of his personality'?[8] Of course there can be no doubt that effeminacy has long been – and still occasionally is – a characteristic of *some* homosexually-inclined men. The most extreme example is the *folle* (literally 'crazy woman'), the French equivalent to the American 'pansy,' 'fairy,' or 'queen' or the British 'quean,' 'poof,' or 'Nancy.' Such men were ubiquitous in the homosexual subculture of cities like New York, London, and Paris during the first five or six decades of the twentieth century. They interpreted their sexual desire as the expression of an essentially female nature, which they then exteriorized in their comportment, attire, voice inflections, and speech (for example, by taking female nicknames and referring to each other in the feminine). Their theatricalized effeminacy distinguished them from the more discreet (and therefore largely invisible) homosexual majority, making them, in the public imagination, the archetype of what it meant to be homosexual. As Jean-Louis Bory remarked, 'The *"folles"* are the most conspicuous for the very good reason that they flaunt themselves. Because one notices them above all, one no longer notices anyone but them.'[9]

The *folle*, like the English quean, can be traced at least to the eighteenth century. For example, a police informant in 1748 described the scenes he had witnessed at several gatherings of sodomites in certain Parisian taverns: 'There were some [men] who put handkerchiefs on their heads, imitating women, mincing like them.'[10] Some 150 years later, a short story published in a Paris newspaper described *les copailles*[11] as 'those little young men in their tight-fitting trousers and short jackets who go about wriggling and mincing like girls.' Conspicuously using feminine pronouns – 'it's another of their peculiarities, one says *elles* in speaking of them' – the author provided the following collective portrait:

You see them going about two by two, in little couples, simpering, putting on airs, wearing makeup ... And when they speak to one another about one of their number, they say: 'She's a sister.' But you've got to hear the titles and nicknames by which they distinguish each other. There is la Pompadour, the countess Dubarry, the duchess de Mayenne ... the Queen of Spain, the Queen of England, the Archduchess of Austria [and so on].[12]

Similar descriptions by amused or appalled observers turn up in newspapers, memoirs, and novels down to the present day; they are by no means fantasy.

The French sociologist Michaël Pollack (1948–92) has argued that, in such instances, 'the homosexual takes on, in exaggerated form, the dominant collective image of homosexuality . . . While showing . . . a certain humor that combines irony with cynicism, these "screaming queens" are in a way the living and surviving species from an oppressive social situation in which the homosexual does everything he can to correspond to the caricature that his oppressors make of him.'[13] On the other hand, the philosopher Didier Éribon remains skeptical of Pollack's explanation: 'this cultural trait is sufficiently omnipresent that it cannot simply be the fruit of the interiorization of homophobic representations . . . Why should it not be seen as one . . . of the characteristic traits of male homosexuality, of the ways in which a certain number of gay men like to think of themselves?'[14] But whatever the reason for effeminate homosexuals in general and for *folles* in particular, their existence is not in itself sufficient to explain why effeminacy and male homosexuality have come to be so consistently conjoined in the social imagination. This link may have come about in part from empirical observation of a specific subculture, but it also developed out of theoretical reflection about sexuality. In the course of the eighteenth century, the process of sorting out the 'natural' differences that supposedly made male and female distinct but complementary beings left no space for intermediate categories.[15] This ultimately gave rise to the idea that female characteristics (effeminacy) in a man were a likely marker of his sexual interest in other men. By the 1820s, for instance, one French expert could write that 'the most perfect' love between the sexes exists 'when the woman is the most feminine, and the man the most virile . . . when a brown-haired, hairy, dry, hot and impetuous male finds the other sex [to be] delicate, humid, smooth, pale, timid and modest.' And, most significantly, he added that 'the overly effeminate man has always appeared susceptible to a vice that seems to demonstrate his need to take from his own sex the creative element that he himself lacks.'[16]

Forensic medicine played a key role in defining marginal groups in nineteenth-century France.[17] One of these 'marginals' was the 'pederast' (a term that gradually supplanted 'sodomite'). The novelist Dominique Fernandez (1929–) has blamed *A Forensic Study of Offenses against Morals* (1857) by Dr August Ambroise Tardieu (1818–79) for 'the belief, so widely prevalent, that any man who refuses the virile role to which society seeks to confine him is a *folle*.'[18] Tardieu not only claimed to discern traces of same-sex activity on the pederast's body (the funnel-shaped anus or misshapen penis produced by anal sex; the crooked teeth and thick lips resulting from fellatio), he also contended that the typical pederast was feminine in both appearance and behavior: 'Curled hair, face covered with makeup, open collar, tightly cinched waist to accentuate the figure, fingers, ears and chest loaded with jewelry, the entire body reeking of the most pungent perfumes and, in his hands, a handkerchief, flowers or some needlework, such is the strange, repulsive and rightly suspect physiognomy that gives away pederasts.'[19] Tardieu based his conclusions mainly on the male prostitutes that the police brought to him for examination. For the most part, he and his contemporaries directed their charge of effeminacy against working-class male prostitutes – with long hair and clean-shaven faces, soft, high-pitched voices, and feminine mannerisms and gait – rather than against their older and presumably middle-class clients.[20] (The beardless face in particular seemed suspicious because facial hair had become a sign of manliness in nineteenth-century France.[21])

Beginning in the 1860s–70s, European psychologists went further than the forensic doctors by inventing the concept of (sexual) 'inversion.' An 'invert' had the physical appearance of one sex, but the subjective gender identity of the other; male inverts had a female nature ('a male soul in a female body'); conversely, lesbians were masculine. This shifted the emphasis from external features to the psychological makeup of the sexual deviant.[22] Male inverts were not necessarily physiologically feminine – 'Subjects of this kind,' wrote one expert in 1887, 'are often . . . tall, strong, brown-haired; their [body and facial] hair is well-developed, their muscular strength considerable, their genitals well-shaped'[23] – but they were so psychologically. As another expert remarked of male inverts: 'The outward characteristics of femininity are their principal traits. They are most often found among young men . . . who have a weak and delicate constitution, a weak, lymphatic and often highly nervous temperament . . . They often have women's tastes and occupations, becoming domestic servants, valets, clerks, dressmakers.'[24]

This pseudo-scientific concept of the effeminate male invert or 'homosexual' (the latter word came into use in France from the 1890s[25]) diffused through society within the context of a 'crisis of male identity' in the decades prior to the First World War. Between 1871 and 1914, French men constituted 'a group unsure of itself, anguished and demoralized'[26] and society reacted by reaffirming 'the ideal of masculinity,' devaluing those qualities coded as feminine and vilifying men whose sexual practices violated gender norms.[27] In this period and throughout Western Europe, the male homosexual, as John Fout has demonstrated for Wilhelmine Germany, was portrayed as 'sickly, effeminate, perverse, and out of control, just the opposite of the "normal" male' and personifying 'female characteristics, such as passivity and physical and emotional weakness.'[28] The new mass-circulation press provided the general public with coverage of a series of sensational homosexual scandals, including the Cleveland Street Scandal (1889–90) and the Oscar Wilde trials (1895) in Britain and the Harden-Eulenburg Affair (1907–08) in Germany. Indeed, Alan Sinfield has argued that the Wilde trials were pivotal to 'the emergence of a queer identity' by transforming 'the entire, vaguely disconcerting nexus of effeminacy, leisure, idleness, immorality, luxury, insouciance, decadence and aestheticism . . . into a brilliantly precise image,' such that 'the principal twentieth-century stereotype . . . of the homosexual entered our cultures.'[29] This may have been true for the English-speaking world, but in France a precisely similar 'queer identity' developed quite independently of (and even prior to) the Wilde case. Although the French press did carry reports on Wilde's troubles,[30] it devoted far more space to a number of home-grown scandals, including the trial of the Comte de Germiny (1876) for committing indecencies with an eighteen-year-old working-class youth in a public street urinal; the Affair of the Rue de Penthièvre (1891), involving the arrest and trial of eighteen men for sexual acts in a bathhouse; and the 'Affair of the Black Masses' (1903), which ended with the conviction of Baron Jacques Adelsward-Fersen for staging homoerotic *tableaux vivants* with half-naked teenage boys whom he then masturbated.[31] In all these cases (and in many others), the press tailored the information presented in such a way as to stress the alleged effeminacy and/or degeneracy of the homosexual protagonists.

The press undoubtedly also affected the way in which many homosexuals came to think. The narrator in Alain Rox's autobiographical novel, *Tu seras seul* (1936), for instance, was an impressionable teenager of fourteen when 'I used to read feverishly' newspaper reports on the Adelsward-Fersen trial. As a result of the Harden-Eulenburg Affair a few years later, once again 'sexual inversion, at this period in my life, often came to my attention.' First-hand observation reinforced what he read in the newspapers: 'how could I not notice in the street or in public places certain young men a little too obviously effeminate? . . . Once I began to frequent Montmartre, it did not take me long . . . to become aware of the existence of certain bars . . . that all the young men knew as dens of fags [*tapettes*].'[32] Paris in fact had a vibrant homosexual subculture by the early decades of the twentieth century, evident to any attentive observer well before the First World War and hard to avoid noticing in the 1920s and 1930s.[33] And while most homosexuals probably did their best to blend in with the heterosexual majority, a significant number who took part in this subculture adopted the flamboyant dress, affected air and mannered speech of the *folles*.[34]

Throughout most of the twentieth century, popular culture perpetuated the image of the homosexual as a silly and effeminate creature fit only to be ridiculed and despised. Cartoons began familiarizing the public with this stereotypical homosexual even before the First World War. For instance, *Le Rire*, a widely-read humorous magazine, published 'On the Beach' (1907), which showed a nattily-dressed young male 'of the feminine gender' (sic!) strolling beside the sea (Figure 10.1), and 'The Man Who Doesn't Understand Women' (1912), which featured an elegant dandy with long hair, plucked eyebrows and bejewelled fingers (Figure 10.2). *L'Assiette au Beurre*, a monthly satirical review, lampooned homosexuals in several special issues, including 'Aesthetes!' (1903), 'Harden-Party' (1908), which dealt with the Harden-Eulenburg Affair, and 'The Little Young Men' (1909) (Figure 10.3).[35] The lyrics of numerous songs jibed at the homosexual's effeminacy. One of the earliest was 'Those Whom People Defame,' which dates from about 1910: 'There are young men whom one sees / Pass by with a feminine appearance. / They carry a handkerchief in their hands / And put makeup on their little round

Figure 10.1 Abel Faivre, 'Sur le sable,' *Le Rire*, 242 (21 September 1907): cover

faces. / People give them a reputation / For having strange morals.' Songs of this sort were written and performed well into the 1960s, when they finally fell out of fashion.[36] Countless novels dealt with the social and personal problems posed by homosexuality. In almost all of them, the homosexual appeared as a pathetically effeminate misfit who deserved the reader's pity or

Figure 10.2   Abel Faivre, 'L'Homme qui ne comprend pas les Femmes,' *Le Rire*, 502 (14 September 1912): cover

disdain. Take this passage from Binet-Valmer's *Lucien* (1921), in which Dr Vigier distinguishes for the first time the tell-tale traits of homosexuality in his son:

There was the asymmetry in his face, the degeneracy in the shape of his ears and in the softness of his lips. And why did that haircut give him an

Figure 10.3   M. Vouvain, 'Les p'tits jeun' hommes,' *L'Assiette au beurre*, 422 (1 May 1909): cover

equivocal air? And that skin that was too transparent, too pretty, too thin, as if epilated . . . And there, on his cheeks, that trace of powder. And that precious elegance in his dress, that puffed out chest, and those timid and affected gestures, that feminine way of sitting sideways on his chair . . . and above all that shifty gaze, that guilty gaze![37]

The film industry, too, in France as elsewhere, has frequently used 'classic caricatures of the *folles*' as a seemingly inexhaustible source of humor. The best-known example is *La Cage aux Folles* (1978), later adapted by Hollywood as *The Bird Cage* (1996). This brand of humor still pays off at the box-office, as proved by such recent French comedies as *Pédale Douce* (1996) and *Pédale Dure* (2004), both directed by the openly gay Gabriel Aghion.[38]

Homosexuals are no more immune than anybody else to popular prejudice. As a result, as Didier Eribon has observed, 'The scorn, the hatred, of those [homosexuals] who prefer to think of themselves as masculine or virile for those they deem "effeminate" has been one of the major dividing lines in the self-representation of gay men.'[39] This was undoubtedly true from the earliest days, when the mimicking of women by some eighteenth-century sodomites earned them contemptuous remarks: 'Can't you behave like men rather than women?' or 'What! You're men and you give yourselves women's names?'[40] However a systematic intellectual defense of homosexual masculinity, generally accompanied by vilification of any effeminacy in men, dates only from the late nineteenth century. Marc-André Raffalovich (1864–1934), himself homosexually inclined, was considered the leading expert on French homosexuality at the turn of the century. A wealthy, Paris-born Jew of Russian descent, he spent most of his life in Britain, where he frequented Oscar Wilde's circle before converting to Roman Catholicism and embracing chastity.[41] Writing in the mid-1890s, Raffalovich stressed 'the need not to confuse [sexual] inversion and effeminacy' and called for more scientific studies of virile 'unisexuals' who were 'more numerous than effeminate inverts, more interesting, and less known.'[42] Unisexuals, he added, 'are not at all satisfied with the old explanation of a feminine soul in a masculine body. Some are more masculine than ordinary men, and are attracted to their own sex because of the similarity. They say that they hold women in too much contempt to be effeminate themselves.' Indeed, '[as] a general rule . . . the greater the moral worth of a unisexual, the less he is effeminate.'[43]

Corydon (1924) by André Gide (1869–1951), is the most famous defense of homosexual masculinity in the French language, if only because of the author's place in the literary pantheon. In Gide's pamphlet, Dr Corydon, who speaks for the author, cautions against confusing 'normal' homosexuals, who are 'healthy and virile,' with degenerate and effeminate 'inverts.' Dr Corydon also advances the claim that throughout history, those societies most accepting of homosexual behavior were also those in which martial valor, high culture, and respect for women most flourished. Gide's arguments are problematic, however. Gide defended 'pederasty' in its ancient Greek form (sex between an adult male and an adolescent boy) rather than homosexual relations between adults. And even more than Raffalovich, he accepted as a given the most conservative social values of his day, which prescribed moral purity and motherhood for women and military service and fatherhood for men.[44]

Homosexual hostility to effeminacy became almost virulent in the 1950s, most likely because of the generalized post-war craving for normalcy and undoubtedly also in reaction against the brazen homosexual subculture (and street hustling by male prostitutes) that thrived in Paris's Saint-Germain-des-Prés district.[45] For example, *Juventus*, a short-lived homosexual magazine with 'health, virility, youth' as its motto, editorialized in 1961:

> You say that people reject you? Then go one evening to Saint-Germain-des-Prés and open your eye, the good one, and look at your fellow creatures. Look at their appearance and their gestures, listen to their shrieks and think about their habits. If you are disgusted, it is because you have understood . . . that a man, a real one, cannot stand for another man to caricature a woman . . . Try to be dignified and to behave like a man . . . and you will find that everywhere people will accept you![46]

André Baudry (1922–) in particular, who founded Arcadie, France's conservative 'homophile' association, and who directed its monthly review from 1954 to 1982, waged a sustained campaign against effeminacy for almost thirty years.[47] For Baudry and his fellow Arcadians, the 'homophile' (their preferred term) might love other men, but he was otherwise just like anybody else. Baudry wanted the homophile 'to blend in with others, without singularities, without eccentricities' so that 'nothing makes him stand out.' Singularities and eccentricities were code for effeminacy.[48] Consequently, as one Arcadian explained, 'Arcadie . . . fights against this extreme and provocative public effeminacy (without necessarily expecting to change anybody's *true* nature).'[49]

Much to Baudry's dismay, radical gay liberation erupted onto the French scene in April 1971 with the founding of FHAR (Homosexual Front for Revolutionary Action).[50] FHAR, in contrast to Arcadie, rejected traditional virility and aimed to subvert existing sex and gender norms as 'patriarchal' and 'bourgeois,' which meant advocating feminist politics and accepting 'femininity' among men. One of FHAR's early manifestos, arguing that 'fascism is necessarily virile and virility fascist,' defended *folles*, whom both heterosexuals and conservative homosexuals (meaning Arcadians) 'reproach for being effeminate and mannered and for flaunting themselves,' and called them 'our brothers.'[51] In fact, FHAR's most exuberant activists were the Gazolines, a coterie of transvestite males who shocked people at political demonstrations with slogans like 'Proletarians of all countries, caress each other!' and 'Ah, it's nice to be buggered!'[52] And yet, in reality, most radical gay liberationists were uneasy with effeminacy. In 1973, for instance, one of FHAR's newspapers published (in translation) an American tract that declared: 'Revolutionary Effeminacy is a new political movement that is in the process of forming thanks to fags in every country who want to fight against their own masculine sexism and against their oppression . . . We are therefore fighting to rid ourselves of all the privileges that we have as men and to devirilize ourselves *without in any way parodying women*' (emphasis mine).

In other words, acceptance of so-called feminine values (the tract urged men 'to learn to cry,' 'to become sensitive to other people's feelings' and 'to learn to share') did not translate into approval of effeminate behaviour.[53] Similarly, in 1977 (FHAR was by then only a memory), a gay militant stressed that 'the homosexual liberation movements must play a role in challenging the virile ideal – fascist and Stalinist – and demolishing contemporary notions of masculinity.' He condemned both the theatricalized masculinity of the gay leather scene and the 'super-males' glorified in gay pornography, but he also criticized public displays of effeminacy: '[T]o show feminine behaviour during a demonstration is not provocative but, on the contrary, reinforces the racist attitude of public opinion.' Homosexuality, he argued, was most subversive when undetectable by an outside observer, 'because "the homosexual" may be . . . your neighbour, your son or your father, or you yourself!'[54]

Since the mid-1970s, only fringe elements in the gay movement have continued to embrace effeminacy. In Aix-en-Provence, for instance, Patrick Cardon led a small group of gays and lesbians who presented a list of candidates in the city's municipal elections in March 1977 and then established an ephemeral *Mouvance folle lesbienne* (Lesbian Queen Faction). A former member later recalled: 'We all had a feminine identity. We used female pseudonyms, we said "my girl," we said "sorority" and not "fraternity." We were revolutionary and subversive, therefore *folle*.'[55] This spirit survives today among the Sisters of Perpetual Indulgence (an American import), an organization of men who rig themselves out as nuns (in the most outrageous habits imaginable) and propagandize for safer sex to prevent the spread of AIDS. According to 'Sister Cunégonde,' when criticized by others for presenting a 'negative image of homosexuality,' the nuns in response 'double our makeup and high-heels in order to say that yes, we accept our share of femininity.'[56] Every year in June, a few men turn up in female attire for Paris's Gay Pride parade (an annual event since 1977). Perhaps a hundred at most among tens of thousands of participants, they are precisely the participants whom television and newspapers tend to feature in their news stories. Colourful drag-queens are undoubtedly more eye-catching and 'newsworthy' than run-of-the-mill marchers, but by focusing their cameras on them, reporters, consciously or not, cater to a public opinion that still holds homosexuals to be ersatz women.[57]

In its rejection of effeminacy, the mainstream of the gay movement has often gone to the other extreme. The 'gay clone' appeared in American 'gay ghettos' in the 1970s as homosexual men adopted a 'hypermasculine sexual code,' pumped up their bodies at the gym, donned blue-collar garb (T-shirt and Levi jeans), cut their hair short and grew a beard and/or moustache. The ideal gay man was now 'hot and masculine.'[58] French gays were quick to follow America's lead. By 1976, one Parisian gay journalist could joke: 'A ridiculous fashion, imported from the New York "Village," has prompted a good number of charming young men to deck themselves out with a thick moustache which gives these "viriles" the appearance of transvestite lesbians.'[59] According to another journalist in 1980: 'In search of his identity, the homosexual has inadvertently assumed a role that turns on its head the classical image [of effeminate homosexuality] imprinted on the collective subconscience . . . Short hair, moustache or beard, T-shirt, jeans, leather jacket. In a single season, the French fag has adopted a macho appearance.'[60] Perhaps more than anyone else, the novelist Renaud Camus (1946–) epitomized the exaggeratedly masculine gay man. In *Tricks* (1979), Camus recounted in scabrous detail his sexual encounters with forty-five different men, most, like the author himself, ostentatiously virile, with full moustaches and abundant body hair. Not surprisingly, Camus also used his column in the gay magazine *Gai Pied* to attack effeminacy and denounce *folles*.[61]

Camus's attitude was widely shared by other gays. Personal advertisements by men seeking sexual partners often invited particular types 'to refrain' (from answering). *Folles* and 'effeminates' ranked high on the 'hit-parade of outcasts,' along with men with 'small cocks' or those who were 'fat,' 'complicated,' or 'up-tight.'[62] Hard-core gay pornography (distributed legally in France only from the mid-1970s), by its choice of manly, muscled models and emphasis on 'the large cock, the traditional emblem of virility,' has reinforced this cult of hypermasculinity.[63] There have been only minor stylistic changes to the ideal gay man over the last thirty years. Facial hair is no longer fashionable, while body hair is more often than not removed above the waist and trimmed below in order to present a more youthful appearance and to show off muscles shaped by hours in the gym.[64] Taken to its extreme, the gay fascination with virility has led some to adopt the 'skin-head' look (shaved scalp, body piercings and tattoos) not from political sympathies for the right-wing views of genuine skin-heads, but for the 'image of the male, the image of virility' that it presents.[65]

This studied masculinity has come to be closely identified with the Marais district of Paris, which emerged as a 'gay ghetto' in the early 1980s.[66] A veteran gay activist complained in 1996 that the Marais 'has taken homosexuals hostage . . . A single look [prevails there]: attractive, young, muscular, white, incidentally tanned and/or smooth-bodied, with roving eye and tight clothing. Without it, one earns a scornful glance.'[67] For a gay French Arab in 2002, 'the Marais symbolises a culture that is young, white, muscled, virile to the point of being fascist.'[68] In other words, gay men who fall short of the current standards of gay beauty and manliness – the old, the overweight and most especially the effeminate – feel excluded. In 2000, a self-avowed *folle* joked that 'it doesn't matter if you're homo, bi or hetero. You've just got to be a man, like daddy' and that 'even today . . . it's more respectable [for a man] to wear hiking boots than high-heeled shoes.' On a more serious note, he added (in rhetoric that seems to echo the radicalism of the early 1970s):

> The 'gaytto' (or 'gay community') . . . has especially contributed to [homosexuality's] integration into the patriarchal and capitalist world, by

getting rid of the image of the *folles-dingues* [crazy *folles*] that stuck to it like a rash to a skin. Today, gays show themselves to be muscled, athletic, masculine and/or misogynous. Normal, in other words . . . The virility of the images in gay ads recalls Stalinist and Nazi statues, posters and other glorious monuments (without the erect cocks, of course!).[69]

In an ironic development, trendy heterosexual men in France have begun taking gays as the standard-bearers and exemplars of modern masculinity. In 2003–04, the French press began to take note of a new phenomenon: the 'metrosexual' (a term coined in Britain in 1994). French metrosexuals, like their counterparts in the Anglo-Saxon world, are young, urban male heterosexuals who, like gays, dress fashionably, work out at the gym, shave off or trim their body hair, use cosmetics, and wear jewelry. Metrosexuals 'uninhibitedly assume their share of femininity, even elevating it into a hip and refined lifestyle,' while ridiculing 'those big, homophobic boors, who think that masculinity is only a matter of strength and body hair.'[70] Sociologists, psychologists, and historians can offer multiple explanations for the rise of the French metrosexual: 'an over-emphasis on pleasure,' the decline of paternal authority over the family, a society fixated on adolescence and seeking to prolong it.[71] One might even add the desire to appeal to a generation of liberated women, who reject traditional male values (albeit perhaps not without some ambivalence): 'Today, they want lovers who are as gentle as girls but who can fuck them like truck-drivers.'[72] In reaction, the journalist Eric Zemmour, an avowed male chauvinist, has claimed that there exists an 'objective alliance' between homosexuals and feminists to emasculate the French male: 'The feminist press teaches women to love men who are groomed, depilated, gentle. Body hair is the symbol of evil.'[73] Zemmour even argues that the loss of traditional male values will have dangerous consequences for Western civilization, which is under threat from more manly cultures and yet 'prefers caution to risk, consensus to authority or law, peace to war, life to death.'[74]

But social prejudice and stereotypes have a long life. Witness a recent French poll. Asked how they recognize a homosexual in the street, an 'overwhelming majority' of the 500 respondents 'class as homosexual men who show signs of femininity (voice, clothing, *hexis corporel* [posture and body language]). Men who do not display redundant signs of virility are classed as women and/or their symbolic equivalent: homosexuals.'[75] The younger generation may be tolerant of sexual activity between men ('everybody can do what he wants'), but not of homosexual effeminacy: 'What is disapproved of is not directly related to sexual practices, but to those behaviors designated as feminine.'[76] One young gay man, whose own attitude demonstrates a degree of self-loathing, recently observed on a website that disadvantaged adolescents (often from immigrant families) living in the housing estates around Paris affirm virility as a prized virtue; for them 'a fag is a *folle* . . . We homosexuals present the image of persons who are superficial, arrogant, pretentious, misogynist, nymphomaniac and EFFEMINATE.'[77] Françoise de Panafieu, on the other hand, belongs to the elite that runs France. Chosen to be conservative candidate for mayor of Paris in the 2008 elections, she has commented that with Bertrand Delanoë – an open homosexual – as incumbent mayor, the city is at present not being governed by 'a real man.'[78] Thus, as Didier Eribon has rightly observed, 'all of the transformations that, over the course of the past thirty or forty years, have affected the image that gay men seek to provide for themselves – notably the process of bodily or gestural "masculinization," the masculinization of codes of dress, and so on – have yet to successfully challenge the traditional representation of the gay man as a "fairy," "queen," "fruit," "nelly," or "nancy-boy".'[79] Not a real man.

Notes

1. SOS Homophobie, *Rapport 1998 sur l'homophobie* (Paris: SOS Homophobie, 1998), 47.
2. Gonzague de Larocque, *Idées reçues: Les homosexuels* (Paris: Le Cavalier Bleu, 2003), pp. 23–8.
3. Elisabeth Badinter, *XY: De l'identité masculine* (Paris: Odile Jacob, 1992), p. 173.
4. Daniel Borillo, *L'homophobie* (Paris: PUF, 2000), pp. 84–7.
5. Michel Foucault, *Histoire de la sexualité*, 3 vols (Paris: Gallimard, 1976–84), 2: pp. 27–9.
6. Sylvie Steinberg, *La confusion des sexes: Le travestissement de la Renaissance à la Révolution* (Paris: Fayard, 2001), pp. 285–91.
7. Flévy d'Urville, *Les ordures de Paris* (Paris: Sartorius, 1874), pp. 15ff.
8. Jacques Corrazé, *L'homosexualité* (Paris: PUF, 1982), p. 59. This book is in the popular *Que sais-je* series. Corrazé somewhat modified his views over the course of the subsequent seven editions down to 2006.
9. George Chauncey, *Gay New York: Gender, Urban Culture and the Making of the Gay Male World 1890–1940* (New York: Basic Books, 1994), pp. 47–63; Matt Houlbrook, *Queer London: Perils and Pleasures in the Sexual Metropolis, 1918–1957* (Chicago: University of Chicago Press, 2005), pp. 139–66; Jean-Louis Bory and Guy Hocquenghem, *Comment nous appelez-vous déjà? Ces hommes que l'on dit homosexuels* (Paris: Calmann-Lévy, 1977), pp. 108–9.
10. Michael Sibalis, 'Homosexuality in Early Modern France,' in *Queer Masculinities, 1550–1800: Siting Same-sex Desire in the Early Modern World,* eds Katherine O'Donnell and Michael O'Rourke (London: Palgrave, 2006), p. 220. For England, see Rictor Norton, *Mother Clap's Molly House: the Gay Subculture in England 1700–1830* (London: GMP, 1992).
11. Napoléon Hayard, *Dictionnaire d'argot* (Paris: Veuve L. Hayard, 1907), p. 14. The feminine word *copaille* derives from *copain* ('pal') and means 'man of dubious morals' (that is, homosexual).
12. M. Talmeyr, 'L'artiste,' *Gils Blas* (26 November 1889): 1.
13. Michaël Pollack, *Les Homosexuels et le sida. Sociologie d'une épidemie* (Paris: A.M. Métailié, 1988), pp. 46–7.
14. Didier Eribon, *Insult and the Making of the Gay Self*, trans. Michael Lucey (Durham and London: Duke University Press, 2004), p. 91.

15. Thomas Laqueur, *Making Sex: Body and Gender from the Greeks to Freud* (Cambridge, MA: Harvard University Press, 1990); Steinberg, *La confusion des sexes*, pp. 175–212 (Chapter VII: 'Masculin ou féminin').

16. J.J. Virey, *De la femme sous ses rapports physiologiques, morals et littéraires*, 2nd edn (Paris: Crochard, 1825), pp. 195, 198.

17. Frédéric Chauvaud, *Les experts du crime: La médecine légale en France au XIXe siècle* (Paris: Aubier, 2000).

18. Dominique Fernandez, *Le rapt de Ganymède* (Paris: Livre de Poche, 1989), p. 56. On Tardieu, see 'Tardieu,' in *Who's Who in Gay and Lesbian History: From Antiquity to World War II*, eds Robert Aldrich and Garry Wotherspoon (London: Routledge, 2001), pp. 432–3; and Jean-Paul Aron and Roger Kempf, *Le pénis et la démoralisation de l'Occident* (Paris: Grasset, 1978), pp. 47–78.

19. A. Tardieu, *Étude médico-légale sur les attentats aux moeurs* (1857; Paris: J.-B. Baillière, 1859), p. 138 (quotation), 141ff. See Alain Corbin (ed.), *Histoire du corps*, vol. 2: *De la Révolution à la Grande Guerre* (Paris: Seuil, 2005), pp. 182–4 ('Le portrait de "l'anti-physique" ').

20. Paul-Louis-Adolphe Canler, *Mémoires de Canler, ancien chef du Service de Sûreté* (1862; Paris: Mercure de France, 1986), pp. 317–18; Félix Carlier, *Les deux prostitutions* (Paris: E. Dentu, 1887), pp. 323, 357; Gustave Macé, *Mes lundis en prison* (Paris: G. Charpentier, 1889), p. 156. See also William A. Peniston, *Pederasts and Others: Urban Culture and Sexual Identity in Nineteenth-century Paris* (New York: Harrington Park Press, 2004), pp. 102–6.

21. Gil Mihaely, 'L'Émergence du modèle militaro-viril: pratiques et représentations masculines en France au XIXe siècle' (Doctoral thesis, École des Hautes Études en Sciences Sociales, 2004).

22. Robert A. Nye, 'Sex Difference and Male Homosexuality in French Medical Discourse, 1830–1930,' *Bulletin of the History of Medicine*, 63 (1989): 32–51; Christian Bonello, 'Du médecin légiste à l'aliéniste: l'homosexualité sous le regard de la médecine au XIXe siècle,' in *Homosexualités: expression/répression*, ed. Louis-Georges Tin (Paris: Stock, 2000), pp. 65–81; Corbin, *Histoire du corps*, vol. 2: *De la Révolution à la Grande Guerre*, pp. 198–206 ('Les personnages de l'inverti et de la lesbienne').

23. Benjamin Ball, 'La folie érotique,' *L'encéphale: Journal des maladies mentales et nerveuses*, 7 (1887): 414–15.

24. P. Garnier, *Hygiène de la génération: Onanisme seul et à deux sous toutes ses formes et leurs conséquences* (Paris: Garnier frères, 1883), pp. 488–9.

25. Claude Courouve, *Vocabulaire de l'homosexualité masculine* (Paris: Payot, 1985), pp. 129–37.

26. Annelise Mauge, *L'Identité masculine en crise au tournant du siècle, 1871–1914* (Paris: Rivages/Histoire, 1987), p. 9.

27. George L. Mosse, 'Nationalism and Respectability: Normal and Abnormal Sexuality in the Nineteenth Century,' *Journal of Contemporary History*, 17 (1982): 229; idem., *Nationalism and Sexuality: Respectability and Abnormal Sexuality in Modern Europe* (Madison, WI: University of Wisconsin Press, 1985), p. 16.

28. John C. Fout, 'Sexual Politics in Wilhelmine Germany: the Male Gender Crisis, Moral Purity, and Homophobia,' in *Forbidden History: the State, Society and the Regulation of Sexuality in Modern Europe*, ed. John C. Fout (Chicago: University of Chicago Press, 1992), p. 284.

29. Alan Sinfield, *The Wilde Century: Effeminacy, Oscar Wilde and the Queer Movement* (New York: Columbia University Press, 1994), p. 3. See also Ed Cohen, *Talk on the Wilde Side: Toward a Geneology of a Discourse on Male Sexualities* (New York and London: Routledge, 1993), p. 2.

30. Nancy Erber, 'The French Trials of Oscar Wilde,' *Journal of the History of Sexuality*, 6 (1996): 549–88.

31. See Christian Gury, *L'honneur perdu d'un politicien homosexuel en 1876* (Paris: Kimé, 1999); William Peniston, 'A Public Offense against Decency: the Trial of the Count de Germiny and the "Moral Order" of the Third Republic,' in *Disorder in the Court: Trials and Sexual Conflict at the Turn of the Century*, eds George Robb and Nancy Erber (New York: New York University Press, 1999), pp. 12–32; Michael Sibalis, 'Defining Masculinity in Fin-de-siècle France: Sexual Anxiety and the Emergence of the Homosexual,' in *Proceedings of the Western Society for French Historical Studies: Selected Papers of the Annual Meeting*, 25 (University of Colorado Press, 1998), pp. 247–56 (on the rue de Penthièvre bathhouse case); and Nancy Erber, 'Queer Folies: Effeminacy and Aestheticism in *fin-de-siècle* France, the Case of Baron d'Adelsward-Fersen and Count de Warren,' in Robb and Erber, *Disorder in the Court*, pp. 186–208.

32. Alain Rox, *Tu seras seul* (Paris: Ernest Flammarion, 1936), pp. 28, 29–50.

33. Régis Revenin, *Homosexualité et prostitution masculines à Paris 1870–1918* (Paris: L'Harmattan, 2005); Gilles Barbedette and Michel Carassou, *Paris Gay 1925* (Paris: Presses de la Renaissance, 1981); Michael Sibalis, 'Paris,' in *Queer Sites: Gay Urban Histories Since 1600*, ed. David Higgs (London and New York: Routledge, 1999), pp. 10–37.

34. See Florence Tamagne, *Histoire de l'homosexualité en Europe: Berlin, Londres, Paris 1919–1939* (Paris: Seuil, 2000), pp. 51–5.

35. 'Sur le sable' and 'L'Homme qui ne comprend pas les femmes,' in *Le Rire*, 242 (21 September 1907) and 502 (14 September 1912); 'Esthètes!', 'Harden-Party,' and 'Les p'tits jeun' hommes,' thematic issues of *L'Assiette au Beurre*, 108 (28 April 1903), 377 (20 June 1908), and 422 (1 May 1909). See Florence Tamagne, *Mauvais genre? Une histoire des représentations de l'homosexualité* (Paris: EdLM, 2004).

36. 'Ceux que l'on diffame', words by Vyle and Briollet, music by P. Codini (Paris: P. Codini, n.d. [circa 1910]); the sheet music is in the private collection of Martin Pénet (Paris). For a history of these songs, see the double CD and accompanying booklet produced by Martin Pénet: *Chansons Interlopes (1906–1966)* (Paris: Labelchanson, 2006).

37. Gustave Binet-Valmer, *Lucien* (Paris: Flammarion, 1921), p. 53. Similar novels include (among many others) Francis Carco, *Jésus-la-Caille* (Paris: Mercure de France, 1914); Maurice Duplay, *Adonis Bar* (Paris: Albin Michel, 1928); Alec Scouffi, *Au Poiss' d'Or: hôtel meublé* (Paris: Éditions Montaigne, 1929); Pierre Sabatier, *Vices: Roman de moeurs* (Paris: Éditions Baudinière, 1932); André Goudin, *Terrain Vague* (Paris: Raoul Saillard, 1934); and Marcel Guersant, *Jean-Paul* (Paris: Éditions de Minuit, 1953).

38. Bertrand Philbert, *L'homosexualité à l'écran* (Paris: Henri Veyrier, 1984), pp. 14, 133 (for quotations); Fabrice Pradas, *Cinéma gay: Un siècle d'homosexualité sur grand écran* (Paris: Publibook, 2005).

39. Eribon, *Insult*, p. 2.

40. Quoted in Sibalis, 'Homosexuality in Early Modern France,' p. 220.

41. 'Raffalovich,' in Aldrich and Wotherspoon, *Who's Who in Gay and Lesbian History*, 363–4.

42. André Raffalovich, 'Unisexualité anglaise' and 'Notes et documents de psychologie normale at pathologique,' *Archives d'anthropologie criminelle*, 11 (1896): 429; 12 (1897): 88.

43. Marc-André Raffalovich, *Uranisme et unisexualité. Étude sur différentes manifestations de l'instinct sexuel* (Paris: Masson, 1896), pp. 15–16.

44. André Gide, *Corydon* (Paris: Gallimard, 1924). See Martha Hanna, 'Natalism, Homosexuality, and the Controversy over Corydon,' in *Homosexuality in Modern France*, eds. Jeffrey Merrick and Bryant T. Ragan (New York and Oxford: Oxford University Press, 1996), pp. 202–24.
45. Georges Sidéris, 'Folles, Swells, Effeminates, and Homophiles in Saint-Germain-des-Prés of the 1950s: a new "Precious" Society?,' in *Homosexuality in French History and Culture*, eds Jeffrey Merrick and Michael Sibalis (Binghamton, NY: Harrington Park Press, 2001), pp. 219–31.
46. Untitled editorial, *Juventus*, 2 (15 June 1959): 5.
47. Julian Jackson, 'Sex, Politics and Morality in France, 1954–1982,' *History Workshop Journal*, 61 (Spring 2006): 77–102.
48. André Baudry, 'La Faute' and 'Les homophiles dans la société,' *Arcadie*, 64 (April 1959): 206; 168 (December 1967): 544.
49. Jean-Pierre Maurice, 'Nouvelles de France,' *Arcadie*, 315 (March 1980): 164. For the attitudes of ordinary Arcadians, see Alain Vertadier, 'Perception des "folles" par les homosexuels,' *Arcadie*, 237 (September 1973): 403–8.
50. Michael Sibalis, 'Gay Liberation Comes to France: the *Front Homosexuel d'Action Révolutionnaire* (FHAR),' in *French History and Civilization: Papers from the George Rudé Seminar, Volume One*, eds Ian Coller, Helen Davies, and Julie Kalman (Melbourne: The George Rudé Society, 2005): pp. 267–78.
51. FHAR, *Rapport contre la normalité* (Paris: Champ Libre, 1971), p. 14.
52. Hélène Hazera, 'Rouge à lèvres et slogans: Souvenirs gazogènes,' *Gai Pied Hebdo* 460 (7 March 1991): 57–8; idem., 'Gazolines,' in *Dictionnaire des cultures gays et lesbiennes*, ed. Didier Eribon (Paris: Larousse, 2003), p. 213.
53. 'Le mouvement de l'efféminisme révolutionnaire,' *L'Antinorme*, 2 (February–March 1973): 12. I have not found the original English-language tract, distributed in New York on 26 June 1972.
54. Marc Roy, 'Homosexualités,' *Revue Sexpol*, 12 (January 1977): 11.
55. Jacques Girard, *Le mouvement homosexuel en France 1945–1980* (Paris: Syros, 1981), pp. 140–1; Frédéric Martel, *Le rose et le noir: Les homosexuels en France depuis 1968*, revised edn (Paris: Seuil, 2000), p. 163.
56. Daniel Welzer-Lang, Jean-Yves Le Talec, and Sylvie Tomdello, *Un mouvement gai dans la lutte contre le Sida: Les Soeurs de la Perpetuelle Indulgence* (Paris: L'Harmattan, 2000), p. 153.
57. Michael Sibalis, ' "La Lesbian and Gay Pride" in Paris: Community, Commerce and Carnival,' in *Gay and Lesbian Cultures in France*, ed. Lucille Cairns (Berlin: Peter Lang, 2002), pp. 51–66. The practice of demonstrating in drag can be interpreted in terms of the French tradition of carnival, which challenges the established order through transgressive behavior.
58. See Martin P. Levine, *Gay Macho: the Life and Death of the Homosexual Clone* (New York: New York University Press, 1998).
59. Yvon le Men, 'Nuits folles pour folles de nuit,' *Dialogues homophiles*, 1 (February 1976): 31.
60. Claude Lejeune, 'Le phénomène macho,' *Gai Pied*, 14 (May 1980): 12–13.
61. Renaud Camus, *Tricks* (Paris: Éditions Mazarine, 1979); Martel, *Le rose et le noir*, p. 273. Camus collected his columns in *Chroniques achriennes* (Paris: P.O.L., 1984); see especially pp. 51–8 ('Critique de la folie').
62. Gérard Bach, 'Quand les homos s'oppriment eux-mêmes,' *Homophonies*, 24 (October 1982): 24–5; Olivier Razemon, 'L'Intolérance chez les gays,' *Idol*, 22 (May 1996): 19–22.

63. René-Paul Leraton, *Gay Porn: Le film porno gay: histoire, représentations et constructions de sexualité* (Béziers: H&O, 2002): pp. 67–77, 106.
64. David Lelait, *Gay Culture* (Paris: Anne Carrière, 1998), pp. 108–9.
65. Jean-François Laforgerie, 'Skins, fachos, gays: Le mélange des sens,' *Ex Aequo*, 5 (March 1997): 97–8.
66. Michael Sibalis, 'Urban Space and Homosexuality: the Example of the Marais, Paris' "Gay Ghetto",' in *Cities of Pleasure: Sex and the Urban Socialscape*, ed. Alan Collins (London: Routledge, 2006), pp. 109–28.
67. Jean Le Bitoux, 'Marcher dans le gai Marais,' *La Revue h*, 1 (Summer 1996): 50–1.
68. Daniel Garcia, 'Dossier: Le Gay Marais, ghetto ou village?,' *Le Nouvel Observateur: Paris Île-de-France*, 1947 (28 February–March 2002): 14.
69. JeanJean, 'La cave des tantes,' in *Nouvelles approches des hommes et du masculin*, ed. D. Welzer-Lang (Toulouse: Presses Universitaires du Mirail, 2000), pp. 188–90.
70. Thibault de Montaigu, 'Métrosexuels, les hommes d'apprêt,' *Libération* (5 September 2003): 33–4 (for quotation); Jean-Michel Normand, 'L'homme prend son poil au sérieux,' and Laurence Girard, 'L'homme objets'affiche à son tour dans la publicité,' *Le Monde* (19 November 2003): 27; (22 April 2004): 30; Violaine de Montclos, 'Metrosexuel académie . . . rendez-vous aux Galéries Lafayette,' *Marianne*, 364 (12–18 April 2004): 85; Jacques Sédat, 'Hermaphrodites modernes,' *L'Express*, 2756 (26 April 2004): 84; André Rauch, *L'identité masculine à l'ombre des femmes de la Grande Guerre à la Gay Pride* (Paris: Hachette, 2004), pp. 273–80.
71. Jean-Sébastien Stehli and Natacha Czerwinski, 'Les nouveaux mâles se cherchent,' *L'Express*, 2749 (8 March 2004): 84.
72. Olivier Péretié, 'Où vont les hommes?,' *Le Nouvel Observateur*, 2067 (17 June 2004): 10, 18.
73. Éric Zemmour, *Le Premier sexe* (Paris: Denoël, 2006), pp. 22–4.
74. Jan de Kerne, 'Eric Zemmour: L'homme nouveau est féminisé et aliéné' (interview), *Baby Boy*, 21 (March 2006): 22–3. See also 'Bite génération: Eric Zemmour,' *Libération* (22–23 April 2006): 44.
75. Daniel Welzer-Lang, 'Pour une approche proféministe non homophobe des hommes et du masculin,' in Lang, *Nouvelles approches*, pp. 121–2.
76. Pascal Duret, *Les jeunes et l'identité masculine* (Paris: PUF, 1999), p. 52.
77. Théo, 'Les cités face à l'homosexualité' (June 2000), www.mag-paris.orgémagazette/magazette-31/les-cites-face-a-l-homosexualite-97.htm. (This is the site of MAG, an association of young gays and lesbians.) On the problem of homosexuality in the Paris suburbs, see Hugues Drappier and Jean-François Laforgerie, 'Dalpé: Banlieu: Comment les gays y vivent,' *Illico*, 142 (27 January 2006): 4–8.
78. Jean-François Laforgerie, 'Paris 2008: Panafieu candidate officielle, pas très friendly,' *Illico*, 145 (17 March 2006): 20.
79. Eribon, *Insult*, p. 89. For the original French terms, see Didier Eribon, *Réflexions sur la question gay* (Paris: Fayard, 1999), p. 131: 'la représentation traditionelle du pédé comme "folle," comme "tapette," "tante," "pédale," tous ces mots féminins.'

11
Cinematic Stardom, Shifting Masculinities

Martin O'Shaughnessy

Although stars have been central to French cinema for most of its history, until recently there has been little if any serious academic study of the role they play in culture and society. Overwhelmingly associated with popular cinema, they have often been considered less worthy of attention than art cinema, its 'unique' works and its culturally validated directors. At the same time, there has been, until relatively recent times, a reluctance to pay attention to the importance of gender to cinema, notably within France. Things have now changed. Since Laura Mulvey's ground-breaking 'Visual pleasure in narrative cinema' (1975), the gendered nature of the cinematic spectacle has become a common object of concern.[1] If Edgar Morin's classic *Les Stars*, first published in 1957, came too early to launch star studies, Richard Dyer's more recent and seminal *Stars* (first edition 1979) served to establish it as a routine part of cinema analysis, albeit with a decidedly slow take-up within France itself.[2] The more or less contemporary emergence of star and gender studies has meant that stars as gendered objects are now subject to relatively routine academic scrutiny. This has unsurprisingly taken a more systematic turn with respect to Hollywood, but French cinema has nonetheless seen the publication of a series of important works both on stars and gender. Ground-breaking work on the great 1930s and post-war star, Jean Gabin, was followed by articles on other figures such as Jean-Paul Belmondo and Jean Marais and, more recently, by two major and wider ranging works on French stardom.[3] Colin Crisp's important recent study of 1930s French cinema has a substantial section devoted to the discourses around stardom.[4] Burch and Sellier's *La Drôle de guerre des sexes du cinema français, 1930–1956* was the first work systematically to consider the gender dynamics of classic French cinema, not simply in individual films but across the full range of national production.[5] Although stars are not an explicit focus of that work, it productively tracks how broader shifts in representations of gender pass through and inflect individual star personae.

The availability of this burgeoning literature obviously facilitates the initial task this chapter sets itself: to note significant shifts in French masculine stardom in response to both historical events and social developments. I shall not seek to produce a single master narrative of changes in male stardom. Historically and socially-driven accounts of cinematic masculinities can only problematically be brought within one overarching frame, not least due to the interruptive temporality of the historical event and the smoother progression of social evolution. They nonetheless converge in underscoring the evolving, contingent nature of screen masculinity, particularly as embodied in stars. The roots of this contingency have traditionally been located outside cinema itself, with film in general and stardom in particular seen as either reflecting externally-driven changes or in some way compensating for them, notably through the creation of mythic star personae who could both give expression to and offer an imaginary, 'mythic' stabilization of social transformations and tensions.[6] Yet, and this will be a core contention of this chapter, if we restrict ourselves to exploring cinema's expressive and compensatory role, we run a severe risk of underestimating its own part in the production of social contradiction and, more specifically, in the destabilization of hegemonic masculinities. Cinema is not simply located neutrally in relation to social change. As the major form of popular entertainment for a substantial part of the twentieth century, cinema not only helped lay the ground for a society centered on consumption rather than production. It simultaneously announced a transformation in the nature of publicness by participating in the formation of a parallel 'public sphere' that was frivolous, mixed and eroticized alongside, and in complex interaction with, the more traditional, serious and male-dominated public domain.[7] Produced within this consumption-driven, alternative public sphere, traversed by the tension between it and more traditional enactments of masculinity, male cinematic stardom had a potential that could never fully be avowed to produce a radical destabilization of dominant versions of the masculine. It is this potential for destabilization that the final part of the chapter will examine in a way that may call upon us to modify the understanding of the evolution of male stardom derived from the earlier part of the chapter.

Male stardom and socio-historical change

If one were to seek to make an overarching statement about the evolution of male stardom from the 1930s to the 1950s one might suggest that, having helped to embody patriarchal dominance in the 1930s, male stars served to reveal a crisis of national virility in the wake of the collapse of 1940 before being enlisted in the service of a misogynistic reassertion of masculine power in the post-war years. Yet, if broadly persuasive, such an account would inevitably do scant justice to the complex and overdetermined nature of masculine stardom and its capacity to shift from star to star, film to film, and medium to medium, with stars as configured in the illustrated press, for example, clearly not simply mirroring their on-screen personae.

Crisp's work on the discourses surrounding stardom in popular cinema magazines points towards a clear shift in the face of masculine stardom as the 1930s unfolded and the threat of war grew.[8] In the earlier part of the 1930s, two discourses of stardom were particularly prominent, one around enthusiasm for sport, the other, emerging a little later, around artistic sensitivity. Significantly, neither discourse was reserved for male stars. If there was clear class distinction in the sporting preferences expressed (with golf, yachting, tennis, skiing, and aviation having clear upper-class associations, and cycling, boxing, and soccer helping to anchor the working-class credentials of such as Gabin), there was a much less sharp gender divide. Female stars could equally be associated with healthy outdoor activity and, indeed, participation in heroic activities such as fast driving or flying. Nor was artistic sensitivity reserved for female stars. Romantic leading men such as Pierre Blanchar, Jean-Louis Barrault, and Richard-Willm were all enveloped in a discourse of romantic sensitivity. As the decade progressed, these two discourses declined in importance, while others emerged. Discussion of patriotism and moral regeneration increased in magazine editorials but broadly failed to impinge on the framing of star personae, even of those like Victor Francen and Pierre Fresnay who routinely played roles such as soldiers. Cinema, it appears – and this is something to which we will return – was drawn towards the frivolous and, if it had the capacity to democratize reflexive individualism, was far better suited to producing narcissistic and consumerist role models than publicly devoted ones.[9]

However, the later 1930s saw the rise of another discourse that did adhere to specific star personae and which was more obviously gendered: this was the discourse of maturity. Attached to strong, patriarchal figures such as Jean Murat, Charles Vanel, and Harry Baur, such a language accreted to mature actors with powerful physiques. As Crisp notes, 'These figures were the antithesis of the handsome but superficial young men who had competed with them for lead roles earlier in the decade.'[10] Broadly confirming the centrality of these dominant, older men. Burch and Sellier suggest that 1930s French cinema was organized above all around the quasi-incestuous interaction between a patriarchal older male figure and a younger woman, with the former typically incarnated by one of the larger-than-life 'monstres sacrés' of the period (Raimu, Harry Baur, Jules Berry, Victor Francen, Michel Simon) and the latter by one of the more transient young female stars. This interaction routinely reaffirmed a threatened male authority, not least through the contrast between the heavy bodies of the leading males, their capacity to dominate the screen and their verbal mastery and the slighter screen presence of the women against whom they were typically cast. Occasionally, in more progressive works, it could be used to voice opposition to patriarchal power. But, when it occurred, this opposition was usually expressed in class terms as a struggle of the workers (as dominated young men) against the authority of the bourgeoisie.

Some of the legendary films of the period oppose Jean Gabin, as romantic working-class lead, to obscene bourgeois 'fathers,' reminding us, if there was any need, that representations of gender and class always overlap, with the working-class male's physical power and technical competence undermined by his social subordination. Thus, for example, the Renoir classic *La Bête humaine* (1938) opens by showing Gabin's character, Lantier, at the controls of a locomotive (an image of speed, power, and modernity) as it plunges towards Le Havre. Yet, taking us into the railway station and back into a social context governed by class inequality, the next sequence underlines the strict limits placed on male working-class power. Separated from his locomotive and the collective strength of his class, Lantier is a far less imposing figure. Gabin's classic roles from the period repeatedly show working-class or popular characters who can exert dominance over their physical surroundings and their companions but who are relatively powerless socially. Gabin's repeated on-screen deaths point to the underlying impotence of his persona as archetypal common Frenchman, a pattern obviously open to a class-driven analysis, but that one might also link more generally to the increasingly imperiled state of France in the later 1930s as well as to the more specifically cinematic determinants to which we will later come.[11]

The pre-war reign of the dominant, patriarchal males was violently disrupted by France's traumatic defeat in the war. Broadly the same individuals who had figured male authority (Jules Berry, Raimu, Baur – until his tragic death at the hands of the Gestapo) were now called upon to show a 'castrated' patriarchy thus underscoring the fragility and vulnerability of male authority.[12] But the dominant figure of the period is the 'homme doux' or 'soft' man, as enacted by a new cluster of male stars in some of the iconic films of the period (Alain Cuny in *Les Visiteurs du soir* (Carné, 1942), Jean-Louis Barrault in *Les Enfants du paradis* (Carné, 1943), and Jean Marais in *L'Éternel retour* (Delannoy, 1943)).[13] In *L'Eternel retour*, a contemporary updating of the Tristan and Isolde myth, for example, Jean Marais's romantic lead male systematically undermines dominant norms surrounding masculinity. An athletic, muscular figure with a classically handsome, sculpted face, Marais offered a performance in the film that is characterized by passivity and suffering, as shown through the objectifying display of his wounded body. His physical strength is also undercut by a voice that, if not exactly high-pitched, is in stark contrast to the deeper and more authoritative tones of a Baur or a Raimu. As Tarr notes, a generation of young wartime Frenchmen were able to recognize themselves in this passive and victimized figure.[14]

The liberation signals another shift in on-screen gender dynamics, with the idealized, virtuous women characteristic of the wartime period, giving way before a misogynistic wave.[15] A range of young male stars, including Jean Marais, Daniel Gélin, Bernard Blier, and a handsome newcomer, Gérard Philipe, incarnate weak or fragile males faced with destructively dominant women, a gendered dynamic that underlines the need to restore patriarchal control after the trauma of the occupation. At the same time, a minority of films continue to question patriarchal power. Jean Marais, for example, repeatedly plays an immature young man who achieves sensitive adulthood through the encounter with a woman. Jean Cocteau's *La Belle et la bête* (1945) might be the best known of these. The beast, as played by Marais, is an astonishing mixture of male power and a passive, sensitive vulnerability that sees him ready to die, without a blow being struck, if the beloved woman does not return his love. Cocteau's lover for a period, Marais had a particularly ambiguous screen persona. If his chiseled good looks and romantic persona made him an object of desire for young women, public knowledge of his homosexual love affair with Cocteau also opened him up for appropriation as a gay icon. This double objectification is perhaps best encapsulated in Cocteau's *Orphée* (1950) where Marais's tormented and studiously posed poet is caught between the admiring gaze of the director's camera and the love-struck look of death, as embodied by Maria Casares's princess.

If the 1950s saw a continuation of films that question patriarchal domination, the dominant tendency was far less progressive, with a range of films (detective films, police comedies, male group films), which proposed reactionary representations of women as sexual objects while celebrating male solidarity. The career of Gabin is representative in this respect. Notoriously fragile (and relatively unsuccessful) in the immediate post-war period, his career was relaunched in the 1950s when he played a series of dominant patriarchal figures, notably in crime or police films such as *Touchez-pas au grisbi* (Becker, 1953). Never notable for his mobility, the heavy-set, mature Gabin is now seemingly able to dominate the screen by his mere presence. Another heavy-set, male star, ex-wrestling champion, Lino Ventura played a similarly dominant male figure during the same period. Retreating from his role as astonishingly fragile and sexually ambiguous *jeune premier*, Jean Marais reinvents himself as a virile, dashing male in some of the swashbucklers that were so characteristic of the period. His transition is perhaps encapsulated in *Le Capitan* (Hunebelle, 1960). Wounded in an opening fight sequence, he is rescued by one young woman and tended by another, with display of his wounded, vulnerable but handsome body echoing his earlier objectified and passive screen incarnations. However, his subsequent dynamism and athleticism underline the transformation that his persona has undergone. The costume dramas that were so typical of this period allowed more generally for a 'soft' eroticization of the athletic male body configured as an object of desire and of romance yet saved for virile masculinity by its activism. Alongside Marais, the dashingly handsome and youthfully exuberant Gérard Philipe was a leading star of such films, and was routinely configured as an object of an active female desire in films such as *Fanfan la tulipe* (Christian-Jaque, 1951). Although he might be cast as a Don Juan, and thus as someone whose predatory sexuality overrode his objectification, his characters never completely shed the romantic innocence and vulnerability that were central to his star image.[16]

If Marais and Philipe could be seen to have partially updated male stardom through their bodily display and eroticized screen presences, their potential to disrupt was substantially muted by their typical framing in safely distanced costume dramas. The same cannot be said of Alain Delon and Jean-Paul Belmondo who represent a new kind of masculine stardom configured at the intersection of Nouvelle Vague *auteurism*, Franco-Italian co-productions and popular French genre films. Unlike Marais and Philipe, both are overwhelmingly associated with modernity, owing more to the world of the cosmopolitan playboy than to more traditional versions of masculinity.[17] Both have lean and muscled young bodies whose mobility lends itself admirably to the enhanced possibility of recording on-screen movement offered by widescreen.[18] Both are firmly located within the new hedonist consumer economy in terms of their frequently shown on-screen aspiration for possessions (typically the motor car) and their association with spaces and places of leisure rather than of work.

The newness of Delon's male stardom is perhaps most obvious in those films which pair him with Gabin or Ventura. *Mélodie en sous-sol* (Verneuil, 1962) allies the young Delon with the mature Gabin in one of the heist movies that flourished at the time. While Gabin embodies professionalism, solidity and experience, Delon is firmly tied to the new. The fast sports car in which we see him contrasts strikingly with Gabin's stately Rolls. His appearance by a Riviera swimming pool, clearly signaled as an object of admiring female gazes, firmly locates him within the new leisure economy in contrast to Gabin's discreet, self-effacing traditionalism, as signaled not least by his decidedly old-fashioned Paris house. René Clément's *Plein soleil* (1959) revolves around the Delon character's murderous envy of a much richer friend's conspicuous consumption in Italian holiday locations. Frequently figured in swimming costume, Delon is not only offered as a consumable object of desire, but is shown in narcissistic self-contemplation as he tries on his friend's elegant clothes.[19]

Belmondo's place as an incarnation of the new is famously figured in Godard's legendary *À bout de souffle* (1959). Associated with a holiday France (the South, the open road, a touristic Paris), he lives his life in imitation of American role models (notably Bogart), while aspiring towards (and stealing) American cars. At no stage do we see him working or behaving with the professionalism of the more traditional criminals represented in earlier films like *Du rififi chez les hommes* (Dassin, 1955) and *Bob le flambeur* (Melville, 1954). What work he does mention is firmly located within the image economy. Like Delon's young men in *Mélodie en sous-sol* and *Plein soleil*, he is also famously cool, both in his attitude of ironic detachment and in his dress.

The framing of Delon and Belmondo in films like *Plein soleil, Mélodie en sous-sol* and *A bout de souffle* might suggest a simple updating of traditional masculinities for the new era of youth, leisure, mobility, and consumption. But both personae point to deeper underlying changes. Delon is repeatedly configured as a loner, thus breaking with the male group ethos that predominates in 1950s police and heist films.[20] Whereas other males are defined by the interactions and contrasts that emerge within a group of men, Delon is marked by his detachment from the collective. Although the ostensible narrative drive behind this separation is typically a hedonistic, quasi-animalistic attraction to women that drives him to betray the group or to neglect the task in hand, it does underline the emergence of an individualistic masculinity that is no longer sustained to the same degree by the world around it. This transformation is inscribed, for example, in the spatial economy of *Mélodie en sous sol*. Whereas Delon's character's brother-in-law is associated with a garage (a site of traditional working-class masculinity), Delon's, as we noted, is tied to the casino and the swimming pool, places of consumption that sometimes seemed devirilized in comparison. Put simply, not only is male stardom taking on a new face, but the increasingly consumer-oriented world in which it moves no longer sustains traditional male identities. Of course masculinity can still be reclaimed by breaking the rules of the androgynous places of consumption, but this is a masculinity that must now increasingly be transgressive. It is not an accident that both Delon and Belmondo tend to be cast as *voyous*, as young men who have to break the rules in order to retain their masculine identity.

À bout de souffle helps us flesh out the same transformation and register its profundity. Belmondo's character in the film moves in an increasingly devirilized world.[21] When the film begins, the action seems reassuringly male-centered. Belmondo's character, Michel Poiccard, steals a large American car from a US serviceman based in a southern French port. The car contains a revolver that the hero uses to murder a policeman who has pursued him. Military and criminal masculinities, and icons of masculine power (the gun and the car) suggest a world of secure male dominance. The hero, as befits the narcissistic individualism of the world of consumption, has borrowed his masculine image from American film icon Humphrey Bogart. He imitates his idol by taking risks and by driving and living fast. But, as the film proceeds, his masculinity seems, as the film's title indicates, 'breathless.' The world of work is depicted as increasingly androgynous. His girlfriend Patricia works as a journalist, while another girlfriend is working in television. If the rising image economy can be accessed for images of maleness (Bogart), it is also a place where masculine domination is undermined. Cars and guns can be used to live dangerously, but car ownership is increasingly banal by the mid-1950s, and a heroic lifestyle sits uncomfortably alongside male identities that, derived from consumption, seem to exist only on the surface, almost as accessories that can be put on and off. This would seem to be message of the film's conclusion. Even as Poiccard lies dying in the road, Patricia steals the gesture of running the thumb over the upper lip that he had himself borrowed from Bogart. It would seem that something must give. As the world becomes less clearly gender demarcated, masculinity has to drive itself to the limit. But this quasi-existential life-and-death existence sits profoundly uneasily with the superficial and shifting identities born in the world of consumption and within the image economy. This, no doubt, is why Michel Poiccard is breathless. No matter how fast he runs, it will never be fast enough.

À bout de souffle's quasi-existential narrative would also seem to point – alongside an early elon classic like L'Insoumis (Cavalier, 1964) – to another closely related shift in the masculine. In L'Insoumis, Delon plays a former French soldier recruited by the OAS (the terrorist organization that fought to keep Algeria French) to assist in the kidnap and sequestration of a woman lawyer. Typically betraying his comrades and helping the woman, Delon is wounded and, as the film closes, dies, having traveled with the woman's help across France to Luxembourg in order to see his daughter. His doomed trip, like Belmondo/Poiccard's breathless endeavors, again suggests a heroic masculinity that has nowhere to go as the twentieth century moves into its later decades. With its roots in military values and heroic public struggle, it would seem that the character can only die once it moves away from the kind of life-or-death collective mobilizations that so marked the middle of the twentieth century.

Resolutely cast within popular, if not populist, mainstream cinema, the later Belmondo might seem to have little to do with the auteur-driven star of A bout de souffle. Yet, despite some clear differences, his persona would seem to keep some consistent traits and thus confirm the shift in the construction of screen masculinity that I have been pointing to. The Belmondo of the period from the mid-1970s to the mid-1980s was the dominant figure in the French box office, and alternated between police films, muscular adventure stories, and popular comedies. The police films that anchored his macho persona pitted him as a loner against a range of outsider figures or corrupt representatives of authority. Their titles Le Marginal (Deray, 1983), Le Professionnel (Lautner, 1981), Le Solitaire (Deray 1986), bear witness to this. No longer a vehicle of renewal, Belmondo embodies traditional masculine values – professionalism, courage, integrity, loyalty – that have become minoritarian due to women's independence and work and the corrupt, impersonal power of the state. The films routinely placed the hero in combat with some convenient villain, which required him to execute a series of spectacular and perilous stunts famously carried out by the actor himself. High-speed car chases, entry into a high building via a helicopter, a perilous run on the roof of a moving metro train: stunts such as these served to reclaim an androgynous urban landscape for heroic masculinity while the need for courageous physical combat made the necessity of traditional male qualities again apparent. Women in these films, if they were independent and sexually assertive at the start, had been placed in positions of dependence by the end, creatures in need of protection from the male hero against the deviant males to whom he was opposed.

The serious masculine hero – despite the socio-historical shifts discussed – has habitually been characterized by a complex interplay of different forms of domination: dominance of the self, of the emotions, of the body, of one's physical surroundings, of other men, of women, of the right to an active look, of the spoken word, of knowledge, and of artistic form.[22] The comic hero in contrast is typically characterized by a failure to exercise control of self or others, thus serving as a counter model whose ridiculousness confirms the rightness of the hegemonic norm. Belmondo's comic heroes, as seen in films such as *L'Animal* (Zidi, 1977), *Le Guignolo* (Lautner, 1979) or *Le Magnifique* (de Broca, 1973), partly follow this pattern but partly break with it, firstly because of our awareness that, despite apparent on-screen physical incompetence, the star is still carrying out the dangerous stunts and secondly because, it being Belmondo, there is a requirement that he win out in the end.

L'Animal is a particularly interesting film from the point of view of the argument being developed here. Belmondo plays two parts, that of a gay Italian film actor with a falsely heroic on-screen persona, and that of a stuntman who doubles for the Italian. Associated with traditional masculine attributes such as physical bravery and mechanical competence, the stuntman is a figure who has literally become invisible. All that he does seems to be done by the cowardly Italian, as appearance absorbs action, depriving masculinity of its social existence. In a similar way, when the hero earns extra cash performing stunts as part of a supermarket's advertising campaign, he is required to wear an ape-suit in a way that underlines the social invisibility of the physically competent male in the world of consumption. By the end of the film however, he will have removed his ape mask, swung down to pick up the woman he loves, and humiliated the Italian by revealing his lack of physical courage. Reflexively engaging with the production of masculinity, the film points to the devirilization of the social order and the devaluation of certain traditionally male attributes. In this it might seem purely nostalgic. But, at the same time, the struggle to reassert a virile masculinity takes place on the grounds of the new. The stuntman hero not only wins out in the end, he also destroys his rival's public image. In a similar way, in thrillers like *Le Professionnel* or *Peur sur la ville* (Verneuil, 1974), the hero not only defeats his enemies, he also stages their humiliation or his own victory, thus reasserting the claim of virile masculinity to public visibility.

The masculinity enacted by Belmondo from the mid-1970s to the mid-1980s is undoubtedly reactive. If the post-1968 period saw struggles for feminism and gay rights, and if broader social evolution witnessed the rise in female employment and the decline in the centrality and visibility of traditional, male dominated industrial labor, then the Belmondo films seemed to oppose these changes. But the films were not simply reactionary. They also recognized that the world had changed, that virile masculinity, to echo the title of one of the films, had become 'marginal.' Part of their recognition of change was the way in which hegemonic masculinity was also asserted at the level of the image. If Belmondo's newly beefed-up appearance and the theatrical nature of the humiliation of his opponents might seem to suggest that his on-screen masculinity had become parodic, they could also be seen as an updating of masculine stardom for the age of the image, an extension of domination into the area of appearances in which contemporary identities were substantially elaborated.

To sum up thus far, French male stardom would seem to respond to two kinds of exterior dynamic. On the one hand, it is open to sharp inflection by historical events such as the national collapse of 1940. On the other, as we have seen with respect to the newness of the personae of Delon and Belmondo, it also clearly responds to social evolution, although never in a mechanical way. But, returning to the central point announced in the introduction to the chapter, whether a historical or a socially-driven narrative is privileged, it is too easily assumed that cinema is somehow located neutrally with respect to change, a site where it is actively responded to but a site somehow separate from its production. This, as I have suggested, neglects the active role of cinema and stardom in the generation of tension and contradiction, the key issue to which I will now turn.

The troubling nature of male stardom

Male stardom, as Austin notes, is troubling.[23] Its troubling nature is rooted in the fact that for a substantial part of its history, cinema has been, in a series of key and interlocking ways, out of phase with its times. First, cinema is a principal location for the generation both of new forms of publicness and for a profound destabilization of the traditional public–private divide. Second, it is a place where a desiring female subjectivity habitually condemned to silence and invisibility is called upon to play a central role for the simple reason that cinema cannot survive without a female audience. Third, it plays a central role in the gradual shift from a society centered on production, the arena in which many of the foundations of modern masculinities are located, to one centered on consumption. Fourth, if the traditional, heavily masculine public sphere of civic society and political interaction is associated with seriousness and rationality, cinematic publicness is tied to the frivolity of entertainment and the irrationality of desire. If normative masculinities are traditionally constructed in a male-centered public sphere, heavily connected to the gendered world of production and reliant upon a discourse of seriousness – frivolity being a stereotypically female trait – then the kind of masculinities produced in the mixed, frivolous, consumption-driven world of film risk being decidedly problematic.

One clear symptom of cinema's structural need to appeal to a mixed audience and to inscribe a recognition of female desire within itself is its generic repertoire. Genres with a strongly masculine connotation such as the *policier* or the military drama coexist and interact with genres with a more clearly mixed appeal, such as the comedy, and the stereotypically feminine genres of the romance or melodrama. While there are certainly examples of overwhelmingly male-driven films, the broader pattern is for cinema as an institution and individual films to make mixed generic appeals, offering a range of spectatorial pleasures as a way to assemble a broad audience. This has inevitable consequences for the kind of publicness generated by film. If the need to entertain, to please the eye and the imagination, condemns cinema to a certain frivolity, its necessary location at the intersection of male and female generic appeals means that it of necessity subverts the gendered separation of spheres that characterizes the broader social order. Cinema of course takes within itself societal gender norms by routinely inscribing female domesticity within its narratives and punishing erring women and by constructing masculinities turned outwards to action in the world and associated with the range of dominations over self, others, women, spaces, and objects mentioned earlier. But, this capacity to re-inscribe a normative gender order is inevitably undermined by the enforced construction of cinematic masculinities across a generic repertoire with mixed appeals. Some examples will help bring this central point out clearly.

Let us begin by looking at two films by Marcel L'Herbier that might seem to construct masculinities tied to virile activities and public duty. The first, *Les Hommes nouveaux* (1936), is a drama set in colonial Morocco in the 1920s. It begins as French soldiers take control of a strategic position in the south of the country at the end of a hard-fought struggle. It then picks up a group of settlers as they make a road in the heart of the country. The strongest figure in the group is played by Harry Baur, one of the mature male stars that so characterized the period. Captured by rebellious tribes-people, Baur's character, along with other prisoners, dreams of exploiting the abundance of olive trees in the area. He is picked up by the narrative years later, now a major entrepreneur, one who through his work on public building projects has helped to 'civilize' and develop the land. Connecting the hero's manual labor and later entrepreneurship to the initial military effort, the film ties together different types of masculinity in a shared French project, confirming the virility of French manhood while using the national to smooth over the tensions between different masculinities.

This version of the masculine is, of course, entirely in keeping with what one would find in more official discourses around colonialism. But the film does not and cannot leave it there. After the initial condensed exposition, romance is introduced to sustain the narrative. This occurs when the hero meets a beautiful young widow on a boat returning to North Africa from France. The hero is predictably smitten. He is about to retire but is convinced by a friend that women are attracted to vigorous, active men. He returns to his work in the colony. By chance, he and his wife bump into her ex-lover, a dashing military office that she has tried to avoid seeing, but whom she still loves. The introduction of the woman shifts the film's narrative and visual economy in a range of essential ways. First, a focus on virile bodies in action is partially displaced by the consumerist pleasure of watching the range of beautiful gowns worn by the female lead. Second, a masculinity that seemed to be constructed at the intersection of military and male adventure narratives is now reconfigured within the romance where the heroine's viewpoint serves to anchor a feminine look on actions and people. The officer lover is now simultaneously framed as action hero and as dashing object of female desire, with the latter predominating. Previously located at the centre of a male action narrative and defined by his place within the male group, the hero is reframed by the romance as a suffering, jealous, emotional figure. Virile and feminine generic pleasures do not simply coexist. They reshape each other. The uniforms, active suffering bodies, and brave deeds of the male story are eroticized and made available for a desiring female look within the frame of the romance. If the film seems to locate the woman purely within the private space of relationships while allowing the men to define themselves within the public space of history, colonial territory, and entrepreneurial activity, it also radically undermines the public–private divide by eroticizing the male public sphere and offering it up within the frivolous context of the romance.

A similar analysis might be applied to L'Herbier's *L'Entente cordiale* (1939), a film made shortly before the Second World War to celebrate the Franco-British alliance. The film contains Pierre Richard-Willm as a courageous young French officer who defies the British at Fashoda, commanding the respect and admiration of his colonial rivals. His character's brother in the film meets and falls in love with a young Englishwoman, and their romance suggests the political romance between France and England. When she sees the dashing, uniformed Richard-Willm character she inevitably falls in love with him, once again providing a narrative location and visual vantage point from which to eroticize what had seemed a story of virile courage, military valor, and national devotion asserted within a context of male public inter-action and rivalry. The romance, of course, shifts the action from forts, land-scapes, and gunboats to ballrooms and other interiors associated with pleasure thus mirroring, at the level of the film's spatiality, a shift from a seri-ous, male public narrative to a more frivolous mixed story. Richard-Willm is inevitably configured as an object of erotic desire. One of the strong, mature males who marked the period, Victor Francen, plays the Prince of Wales. Worked through in restaurants, concert halls, and places of entertainment, his own love affair with France and the charm offensive he mounts to cement the union highlight how the film inextricably enmeshes a more conventionally serious and masculine publicness with an emotionally and erotically charged one. Consigning women (apart from Queen Victoria!) to the private space of the interpersonal, the film, like *Les Hommes nouveaux*, simultaneously reinforces the gendered nature of the public sphere and radically under-mines it by allowing the emotional, the erotic, and a desiring female subjec-tivity to spill out of the private and to be 'charmed.' This contradictory behavior has its roots, as we have noted, in cinema's necessary negotiation of the tension between respect for dominant social norms and its own imperative need to attract and entertain a mixed audience.

The two films help point towards two broader tendencies within French screen stardom. First, both help underline the frivolity of the grounds upon which French screen masculinity is predominantly constructed despite the fact that they can be situated towards the more serious end of the cinematic spectrum, one seeking to be an edifying tale of colonial endeavor, the other to celebrate a military alliance. They suggest an epic scope in their early stages through the staging of military encounters in vast landscapes. But neither sustains this epic dimension as both become increasingly about gendered interactions between individuals. They thus help remind us of the general absence of a truly epic French national cinema. While Hollywood has routinely produced war films and westerns which brought together star performers, large male groups, and epic action to tie heroic masculinities to a shared national project, French cinema, with rare exceptions such as Gance's *Napoléon* (1925), has preferred 'des petits récits.'[24] French male stardom has thus tended to be constructed at the uneasy interface of public and private narratives. Second, both films underline the instability of male screen stardom. It is now widely accepted that participating in the more general instability of the consumption-driven image economy, star personas shift both from film to film and from medium to medium. The construction of a star within a film, for example, is clearly not necessarily the same as the version of the same star in the popular cinematic press. But what we have seen here is that, even within individual films, star personae may shift as they are reconfigured by the need to mount different audience appeals. If dominant discourses around masculinity and masculine domination conventionally seek to give them a permanence outside of history, cinema's unstable, shifting male stars would seem problematic.

I would suggest that the same instability is also characteristic of the leading French male star of the later 1930s, Jean Gabin. Vincendeau emphasizes his persona's capacity to reconcile and stabilize a series of social tensions rooted in gender and class differences; to be an ordinary man and yet a charismatic, wealthy star, to represent solid virility but also to take on a feminine sensitivity.[25] His 1930s persona could, however, be seen as one that not so much stabilizes a series of social tensions exterior to cinema as that is in fact repeatedly destabilized by tensions which film in general and male stardom in particular help to generate. Repeatedly configured at the uneasy intersection of virile male group narratives and romantic or tragic melodramas, he is an uneasy and unstable mix of man-made and woman-made man, of solid virility and commodified surface. This becomes clear as early as his appearance in the 'Diva' movie *Paris-Béguin* (Genina, 1931) where he is presented as both a tough gangster figure and as a female fantasy object. Both his virile persona and his violent death are transfigured, emotionally saturated and eroticized by their incorporation in the central, female-dominated romance, a fact underlined when, after his death, the heroine reworks her experience with him within the lachrymose, orientalist stage fantasy over which, as diva, she has ultimate control. Something similar happens in the remarkable *Gueule d'amour* (Grémillon, 1937) where Gabin plays the part of a French colonial soldier, a *Spahi*, garrisoned in a small town. His nickname, 'gueule d'amour' ('love mug'), has been given to him by the townswomen. His photo passes from hand to hand. His public image thus literally escapes him. In the early part of the film, a male-centered military comedy, this objectifying passivity is cast back upon the women by a male narrative of multiple conquests. But, when the film shifts into melodramatic mode and Gabin falls under the spell of just one woman, he becomes an astonishingly fragile figure, someone whose personality collapses. The romantic gangster film *Pépé le Moko* (Duvivier, 1937) follows a similar trajectory. As long as Gabin's characters are man-made men defined through virile action, they seem self-assured. But when they are reconfigured within romance or melodrama, when they become objects of desire, they are marked by an astonishing vulnerability. Indeed it is this very vulnerability and the emotional response it generates that makes the persona available for articulation within female-centered narratives. It is, one might say, structurally necessary. Thus, while it is tempting, as we noted earlier, to connect the fragility of 1930s Gabin to a socio-historical context and see in his doomed heroes a reflection either of France's perilous state in the period or of the enforced subordination of working-class manhood, one should perhaps first recognize how much his persona owes to the specific contradictions of male stardom. Although differentially articulated within different star personae, this underlying tension between virility and a necessary fragility is something that runs through French male stars, from Richard-Willm, through Gabin, Marais and Gérard Philippe to Delon and, to some extent, Belmondo. In a similar way, male stars tend to be torn between dynamic action in the world and the kind of objectifying passivity required to make them available for desiring consumption.

Gabin's characters are never quite aware of what is happening to them, either when control of their image escapes them or when they are incorporated despite themselves into narratives where female characters play a forceful if not a controlling role. Part of an age where masculinity is still overwhelmingly defined within production and a male-dominated public sphere, it is as if there is no way that they can engage self-consciously with what befalls them. The still essentially patriarchal represented world is radically out of phase with what happens at the level of the construction of the male star. By the time of the young Delon and Belmondo, this will have shifted. Increasingly located in an on-screen world of leisure and consumption, narcissistically individualistic, they (or the narratives in which they are located) are more able to engage reflexively with their objectification and their insertion into the economy of the image. An increasingly consumption-oriented society has caught up with cinema that can now be of its time or oppose it but no longer runs ahead of it. At least not in general for, as I have stressed, male stardom remains deeply problematic. Despite its plural nature and historical variation, masculinity is too deeply connected to a naturalized domination to accommodate easily to the shifting, superficial, objectified forms associated with consumption.

Conclusion

A democratizing flagship of consumption before the social transformations of *les trente glorieuses*, cinema had to negotiate and internalize the tension between its own intrinsic needs to offer frivolous pleasures to a mixed audience and the conformist pressure it felt from a broader social context. Out of phase with its period in the first half of the twentieth century, it would most often mask its out-of-phaseness by internalizing dominant norms and enacting them in narratives that could rarely engage overtly with the illicit pleasures, subversive identifications, and consumable, objectified masculinities that it had to offer. Its capacity to be out of phase with the times could, in any case, cut both ways. When an increasingly androgynous world no longer seemed to sustain traditional masculinities, it could still perversely choose to reassert male dominance and embody it in regressive narratives and star personae.

Notes

1. Laura Mulvey, 'Visual Pleasure in Narrative Cinema,' *Screen*, 16 (3) (1975): 6–18.
2. Edgar Morin, *Les Stars* (1957; Paris: Seuil, 1972); Richard Dyer, *Stars* (1979; London: BFI, 1998).
3. Claude Gauteur and Ginette Vincendeau, *Jean Gabin, anatomie d'un mythe* (Paris: Nathan, 1993); Martin O'Shaughnessy, 'Jean-Paul Belmondo: Masculinity, Violence and the Outsider,' in *Violence and Conflict in Modern French Culture*, eds Renata Gunther and Jan Windebank (Sheffield: Sheffield Academic Press, 1994), pp. 215–30; Carrie Tarr, 'Représentation de la masculinité dans *L'Éternel retour*,' *Iris*, 26 (1998): 83–99; Ginette Vincendeau, *Stars and Stardom in French Cinema* (London: Continuum, 2000); Guy Austin, *Stars in Modern French Film* (London: Arnold, 2003).
4. Colin Crisp, *Genre, Myth and Convention in the French Cinema, 1929–1939* (Bloomington: Indiana University Press, 2002). For a discussion of discourses of stardom in the post-war period, see Patricia Caille, 'From French Stars to Frenchmen in Postwar National Culture,' *Quarterly Review of Film and Video*, 19 (1) (2002): 43–57.
5. Noël Burch and Geneviève Sellier, *La Drôle de Guerre des sexes du cinéma français, 1930–1956* (Paris: Nathan, 1996).
6. See, for example, Vincendeau, *Stars and Stardom*, and Dyer, *Stars*, pp. 20–30.
7. On cinema's role as alternative public sphere, see James Donald and Stephanie Hemelryk Donald, 'The Publicness of Cinema,' in *Reinventing Film Studies*, eds Christine Gledhill and Linda Williams (London: Arnold, 2000), pp. 114–29 and Miriam Hansen, 'The Mass Production of the Senses: Classical Cinema as Vernacular Modernism,' in Gledhill and Williams, *Reinventing Film Studies*, pp. 332–50.
8. Crisp, *Genre, Myth and Convention*, pp. 246–67.
9. On cinema and the democratization of reflexive individualism, see Morin, *Les Stars*, pp. 121–34.
10. Crisp, *Genre, Myth and Convention*, p. 261.
11. Films from the mid- and late 1930s at the end of which Gabin dies or disappears include *La Bandera* (Duvivier, 1935), *Pépé le Moko* (Duvivier, 1937), *Gueule d'amour*

(Grémillon, 1937), *Quai des Brumes* (Carné, 1938), *La Bête humaine* (Renoir, 1938), *Le Jour se lève* (Carné, 1939).

12. Burch and Sellier, *La Drôle de Guerre*, pp. 87–97.
13. Ibid.
14. See Tarr, 'Représentation de la masculinité,' p. 99.
15. Burch and Sellier, *La Drôle de Guerre*, pp. 217–32 and 245–77.
16. Philipe played an inveterate, but somehow innocent and vulnerable seducer in Clair's *Les Grandes Manoeuvres* (1955) and Vadim's *Les Liaisons dangereuses 1960* (1959).
17. See Vincendeau, *Stars and Stardom*, pp. 158–95 and Austin, *Stars in Modern French Film*, pp. 47–62. For a rich account of male Nouvelle Vague stars, see Alain Brassart, *Les Jeunes Premiers dans le cinéma français des années 60* (Paris: Éditions du Cerf/Éditions Corlet, 2004).
18. See Vincendeau, *Stars and Stardom*, pp. 167–70.
19. See Austin, *Stars in Modern French Film*, pp. 61–2.
20. Graeme Hayes, 'Framing the Wolf: the Spectacular Masculinity of Alain Delon,' in *The Trouble with Men: Masculinities in European and Hollywood Cinema*, eds Phil Powrie, Ann Davies, and Bruce Babington (London: Wallflower, 2004), pp. 42–53.
21. Martin O'Shaughnessy, 'Le Surhomme à bout de souffle: le Belmondo des années 1974–1985,' *CinémAction*, 112 (2004): 107–15.
22. An example of the potential complexity of this interplay of different forms of domination might be sought in films by some of the key Nouvelle Vague directors such as Truffaut, Godard, and Chabrol. If, on the one hand, the films show often fragile masculinities, the films' authorial self-expression, the close identification of the director with the leading males and the on-screen centering of their subjectivities means that masculinity becomes more pivotal even as it appears to be problematized or made fragile (see Geneviève Sellier, 'La Nouvelle Vague: un cinéma à la première personne du masculin singulier,' *Iris*, 24 (1998): 77–89). An earlier version of the combination of masculine off-screen authorial control and the on-screen centrality of the male persona and voice can be found in the films which Sacha Guitry directed and in which he often played the lead role (Raphaëlle Moine, 'The Star as "Great Man" in French Cinema: the Example of Sacha Guitry,' *Studies in French Cinema*, 4 (1) (2004): 77–86). If Guitry's self-consciously theatrical delivery and mannered performances may seem far removed from more obviously virile star figures, his capacity to build films around his own persona reminds us that domination can take a range of forms.
23. Austin, *Stars in Modern French Film*, pp. 48–9.
24. Jean-Michel Frodon, *La Projection nationale: cinéma et nation* (Paris: Editions Odile Jacob, 1998), p. 89
25. Vincendeau, *Stars and Stardom*, pp. 63–4, 70–3.

12
Virilité in Post-war France: Intellectual Masculinity, Jewishness and Sexual Potency

Jean-Pierre Boulé

In this chapter I investigate the theme of virility in post-war France by weaving together a biographical trajectory, that of the writer Serge Doubrovsky, with a more general discussion of masculine heroics and ethnicity, namely Jewishness.[1] Doubrovsky has had a successful career in France as a writer and a literary critic, notably creating a literary genre called *autofiction*, half-way between autobiography and fiction, where writer, narrator, and main character correspond to the same person while inhabiting a fictional space. Winner of the coveted Prix Médicis for his novel *Le Livre brisé* (1989), Doubrovsky has documented his life in six books, albeit through the prism of *autofiction*. Doubrovsky offers a useful example for thinking about contemporary masculinities in France because he lived through the Second World War as a teenager, spent time in hiding because he was a Jew, and then chose a career as an academic. Hence he struggled with a masculine identity where Jewishness and intellectuality were stigmatized as 'effeminate,' and he chose to counteract this stereotype through sexual performance. By the end of the twentieth century, he also witnessed the arrival of Viagra in France, which reignited debates about male sexuality and performance. Following a quick glance at Doubrovsky's early years and family relationships, I will concentrate on the Second World War and the young novelist's engagement with *virilité*, resistance, and Jewishness. We will see that, as a compensatory device for what he perceived as his failed masculinity, Doubrovsky would invest considerable importance in what Peter Redman calls 'muscular intellectualness,'[2] as a basis for both his sense of *virilité* and potential for sexual seduction. The final part of this chapter will examine what happens to masculine sexual potency when threatened by sexual impotence.

Doubrovsky was born on 22 May 1928 in Paris. His father was a tailor and his mother, a skilled secretary, was deemed not to have a profession. They were both Jews. His father came from Russia in 1912 and his mother was born in Paris, her family belonging to Alsatian Jews since the French Revolution. Serge was not quite a teenager when the phony war broke out, and he had just turned sixteen by the time the war was over. Made to wear the yellow star for two years from May 1942, including at school, the young Doubrovsky felt that he was a nobody. He once stated that he had always considered himself French – getting top marks for his knowledge of the language and culture – only to be suddenly told that he was no longer French.[3] In November 1943, a French policeman called at his home to warn his family he had been ordered to arrest them later that day. The Doubrovskys were hidden until August 1944 in a villa in Villiers by some relatives connected to his uncle Henri, whose sister-in-law was a Gentile. After the liberation, Doubrovsky would have a successful career as a professor of French, with his last chair held at New York University. His first wife was American, and his two daughters live in New York. He worked for most of his life in the United States, though, with his last post, he was able to spend every other year in Paris, where he is now retired.

One might say that Doubrovsky was predestined to be measured against heroic deeds. At birth he was given two first names, Julien and Serge: the first in honor of his mother's cousin, who had been killed in action at the Dardanelles and whom she loved 'like a brother' (F, 256), and the second for that time 'when he would be famous'[4] (his father wanted him to be a violinist, his mother a writer). As Jouan-Westlund suggests, Serge was conceived in order to replace a person who was idealized and died in action. Thus the narrator of Doubrovsky's novel *Fils* (1977) writes: 'I am born posthumously, I exist in the past . . . I am my mother's cousin. Her brother. I am born amongst family. I am reborn. From his ashes.'[5]

'My relationship to my mother has been fundamental.' This is almost an understatement by Doubrovsky, who has consistently identified with her rather than with his father.[6] Indeed, so enmeshed is his sense of self with his mother that her death in February 1968 would nearly bring Doubrovsky to total collapse.[7] Indeed, the psychoanalysis he began a few weeks after her death would last the better part of ten years. At one stage, his psychoanalyst told him: 'You must separate from your mother' (F, 314). In his last book, he lucidly concludes that he had 'too much mother,' and that he has asked each woman he has met to be his mother – that is his neurosis (LPC, 390). Doubrovsky's father, on the other hand, was described as having been hard but fair. As a young boy, his father taught him 'manly' things like killing rabbits, drowning kittens, learning to swim (like all good Jewish fathers), and riding a bike. However Doubrovsky's father was also harsh, and many of these activities ended in violence and tears. When the young Serge cries when clowns appear at the circus, his father, angry at having a coward for a son, beats him (F, 42). When, immediately following the war, Doubrovsky's father succumbed to tuberculosis and eventually died, his uncle Henri became an idealized surrogate father whom he visited regularly throughout his adult life. His uncle would become his 'totem-uncle' (AV, 55), a patriarchal figure (AV, 248). Thanks to his influence, Doubrovsky felt he was no longer a 'wandering Jew,' but that he had recovered his heritage.

In an exchange of correspondence with one of his doctoral students writing a thesis on his work, Professor Doubrovsky tells him that, as a critic of his books, he must familiarize himself with the Second World War, stating: ' "Doubrovsky" does not exist without "L'An Quarante".'[8] I propose to follow the professor's advice by exploring three interlinked themes: war, resistance and Jewishness. For the teenaged Doubrovsky, this was a time of maximum vulnerability, but also of critical self-formation in terms of masculine identity. As a Jew, Doubrovsky belongs to the category of subordinated masculinities, often historically defined by dominant Gentile gender codes as effeminate, weak, and therefore 'other.' In fact, throughout the modern era the Jew, whose work was seen as primarily intellectual and sedentary, was not considered a 'real' man; rather, the masculine credentials of Jewish men were typically tainted by suspicions of cowardice and effeminacy.[9] As Otto Weininger influentially argued in 1903, there is 'a psychological scale which runs from the Jewish mind on one end to the Aryan at the other. This scale is parallel to another, the "feminine" and the "masculine".'[10]

This equation of Jewishness with effeminacy and 'otherness' was particularly problematic during the occupation, where the young Serge, socially isolated and in hiding, fears for his life and that of his family. The persecution of Jews in France started in 1940 when, in the occupied zone, they were forced to register with the local authorities. They were soon excluded from any posts in the civil service, the media, and the cinema, and their identity cards were stamped with the word 'Jew.' By June 1941, Jews were excluded from most jobs, and, even in non-occupied France, they had to register or risk being sent to a camp (even if they were French citizens); by July their properties and businesses were confiscated. It was from the transit camp of Drancy (opened in August 1941) that the first convoy of Jews had left for Auschwitz in March of the following year. In May 1942, all Jews had to wear the yellow star in the occupied zone. In July 1942, the chief of the French police undertook that they would arrest Jews in both zones, but only if they were not French (however the French and French-born children of people arrested were also taken). In a spectacular operation which could well have netted Doubrovsky and his family, on 16 and 17 July 1942, French police arrested 13,152 Jews, including 4115 children, in the Paris area. Most were sent to Auschwitz, and by the time of the last convoy on 31 July 1944, 76,000 Jews had been deported from France.

During this period, the young Doubrovsky absorbed the anti-Semitic propaganda disseminated by German and Vichy authorities. Not only did the former describe Jews as 'Untermensch' (subhumans), but every day newspapers spread lies about the smell of Jews[11] and talked about purging them from the nation. Judging from how he writes about this period of his life, mainly in *La Dispersion* (1969) but also sporadically in his other *autofictions*, it is clear that Doubrovsky considers his period in hiding as a cowardly time (see, for instance, LB, 19–21).[12] He has not fired a single shot at a German or at a French policeman; he has not 'proven' himself as a fighting man. In a telling passage from *La Dispersion*, he juxtaposes the fact that he may be a brilliant student with the fact that he had missed the war. Chastising himself as a 'weakling, a chick, a faggot,' Doubrovsky claimed that he had been passive and figuratively 'fucked' (D, 310–11), whereas a 'real' man should be the 'active' one, the one who did the fucking. Elsewhere he writes that 'the rules of virile life' demand that a man be the one who fucks, never the one who is fucked (LPC, 306). The sexual imagery of these complaints is striking. By erecting rigid boundaries between masculine and feminine, Doubrovsky wields the gendered discourse of anti-Semitism against what he sees as his own failed manhood. Yet Doubrovsky's failure is personal rather than related to his 'Jewishness.' He was nothing like his father, a World War I veteran who boldly went to Gestapo headquarters to ask for a work permit (an *Ausweis*) to pursue trading, all the while wearing his yellow star and thus risking immediate arrest and deportation. Other heroic examples abound within his family history: his uncle Mordk (a colonel in the Red Army), his uncle Henri (a member of the resistance deported to Drancy, who miraculously returned), and his two cousins, who joined the *maquis* and used guns.[13] All these examples combine to tell him one thing; *he* failed to prove that he was a man: 'no balls a real girl CASTRATED FROM MY WAR' (F, 203). For the rest of his life, Doubrovsky puts a question mark next to his status as a 'man.'

In the historical context of the war, the Nazis were perceived as hypermasculine and in order to counteract this powerful image, both the Free French and the resistance promoted the old stereotype of the virile citizen-at-arms, often a volunteer, which had been the ideal masculine image since the revolution; maleness reverted to an image of aggressive virility.[14] After the humiliation of the occupation, how did France reconstruct its image? A long period of national re-masculinization started after the liberation; indeed, the very act of freeing France was associated with virility. Special emphasis was placed on work, discipline and duty (the latter replacing rights, which were now made partly accountable for France's downfall, especially by the right)[15] in a move destined to rebuild the nation but also to enable endurance of further sacrifices, such as food rationing, in the name of the greater good. Collaborators and the Vichy regime were constructed as feminine, having given in to the enemy (passive = feminine); collaborating artists were often presented as homosexuals. On the other hand, the resistants were the only ones worthy of being men (always heterosexual), and standing up to the enemy (active = masculine). This created a gender polarity. As in the 1920s, the liberation saw the marginalization of women who had come to occupy a more central place in society and the severe punishment of those thought to have betrayed France by sleeping with the enemy. These were hounded much more systematically than, for instance, black-marketeers. On a psychological level, Victor Seidler shows how masculinity is constantly reasserted by denying what are seen as 'feminine qualities.'[16] This gender polarity echoed Doubrovsky's earlier upbringing with his father teaching him to ride a bike

('I don't like wimps,' he told the young writer). He knew he had to eradicate what his mother had called his 'feminine' side, especially as he did not fight in the war and thus himself felt less like a man than a woman. In addition, as a Jew, he was up against representations of the Jew as feminine. Doubrovsky grew to biological manhood in an atmosphere where virility itself was being reconstructed, almost as a national project, with the iconography of the time even promoting 'hyper-virility' through the figures of the soldier and subsequently, after the war, of the worker.[17] Yet Doubrovsky himself did not participate in this 'manly' effort. Rather he spent almost two years in a sanatorium with the beginnings of tuberculosis, from 1951 until 1953. What options were available for Doubrovsky to shore up his masculine identity? Redman's 'muscular intellectualness' provided one solution.

While in hiding during the war, Doubrovsky's life resembled imprisonment, where survival meant following the same routine every day. Trapped and unable to act, this may have been the exact moment when Doubrovsky decided to define his masculinity in intellectual terms: 'Only one way to escape,' he wrote, 'towards the sky of Ideas' (LPC, 421). As part of his escape plan, he even wrote a book entitled 'Julien Doubrovsky, youthful reflections.' In his preface, he writes that his reflections are not outpourings of sensitivity motivated by *emotions* felt at the time, but 'reflections' (no doubt governed by *reason*), and that if he survives the war, he will write about his survival (LPC, 429).[18] Doubrovsky's decision to craft a 'muscular intellectualness' was also connected to his fractured sense of identity. We saw that, with the experience of the war, the young man who always considered himself French was now told that he was a stranger. This sense of marginality was to some extent vindicated in July 1945, when Doubrovsky won first prize for a national competition in philosophy, awarded at the Sorbonne by none other than the savior of France himself, General Charles de Gaulle. Serge writes that de Gaulle made him forget about the horror of Pétain, Laval, Doriot, Darnand, the policemen doing the round-ups, the Drancy gendarmes. Whereas his body had betrayed him as a Jew (that is, as foreign and unmanly), his intellectual prowess allowed him to symbolically recover his French manhood and to view France as a surrogate father: 'Now the Untermensch is climbing the stairs leading to the podium towards the great man . . . I return to the human species and my fatherland' (LPC, 164). When he then succeeds in the competition to enter the elite *École normale supérieure*, his future as a teacher is secured.

Despite this professional ascent, Doubrovsky's construction of muscular intellectualness did not constitute an impregnable armor against allegations of femininity, not least due to the continuing image of intellectuals and Jewish men as effete and cowardly weaklings. One of the stereotypes of Jewish men is that they are bookish, and have little interest in sport; Doubrovsky confides that he was no good at sport.[19] If we add to this the fact that Serge's health remained precarious, it all adds up to a brittle sense of *virilité*. This reflects a recurring stereotype in modern France, where 'excessive mental activity was often associated with neurasthenia, impotence and a host of other ailments.'[20]

In order to examine the concept of virilité in Doubrovsky, we need to look back at his relationship with his father. When the latter had taught him to kill a rabbit, he ordered him to gaze upon the animal during the slaughter; he had no right to avert his eyes during this apprenticeship in virility (F, 33). The same went for the other skills his father tried to impart. Drowning kittens held no appeal for the youth, but his father forced him to watch (F, 12). Frightened of learning to ride a bike, his father's slap forced him to mount the vehicle (F, 188). The same thing happened when learning to swim: the reluctant six-year-old only entered the small pool when his father hit him (F, 187–8). Like many men, Doubrovsky's father sets him 'masculinity challenges'[21] which he cannot meet. Serge seems to be forever measuring himself against his father and failing in his quest. This is then compounded by his experience of the war, where he cannot 'redeem' himself through action. These failed masculinity challenges haunt Doubrovsky throughout his adulthood. Hence, when his lover Elisabeth swims in the channel and he does not follow her, the narrator of *Fils* rails against a world turned upside down: in this scenario he is a wimp, a chick, while it is she who is hard, a real man (F, 159). We read: 'not a man balls cut off she castrates me phallic woman took my sting she is the one with an erection . . . the woman-man *Elisabeth* nothing left for the man-woman *Serge* in a mirror my anti-self' (F, 160–1).[22] When his father forced him into the water, he told him he would teach him to be a man before warning him: 'Me, my boy, I don't like wimps' (F, 275).[23] When Doubrovsky is not measuring himself against his father, his mother does it for him. Hence, when he writes to her in July 1945 that he was upset to leave his father for the summer, she asks him to compare his situation to that of his father, who left Russia in 1912 in order to come to France, all on his own. This was meant to encourage her son, but it does not help. Rather it all comes flooding back. His father! How can he compare himself to his father? He was a 'MAN, a real one, a MENSCH' (LPC, 328).

The passages in *Fils* where Doubrovsky talks about his uncle are very moving, but this relationship is a double-edged sword for 'Doubrovsky.' He hails his uncle as a fine example of virility acquired during the 'belle époque' between 1901 and 1914.[24] He further explains that what he liked about his father and what he likes about his uncle is the fact that they are men (using a capital 'M'), real ones, whereas he himself leans towards an indistinct zone between male and female. Doubrovsky's mother used to tell him that he had a feminine side, that he was tender, whereas his father and uncle were hard. Even if deep down these men feel some tenderness, there is no ambiguity in them (AV, 54–5). His uncle was national champion for the 100 meters in the French Army, and, at eighty-seven, he still displays a lot of courage in insisting on walking unaided, while the narrator can hardly climb stairs without being winded. As Doubrovsky leaves after a visit, he reflects that he has had his ration of war, his baptism of fire; one hour with this stooped and beaming old man re-masculinizes him. When he goes back down the stairs, he is a man once more (AV, 246). There is a strange double-bind at stake here. He idealizes his uncle ('The most prodigious character I have ever known, he incarnates all male roles' (AV, 53)), and to a lesser extent his father, and sets himself up as never measuring up to their standard. Yet he also derives some strength from his uncle, who is described as the only fixed point in his chaotic life. He relives his childhood, he exists as a whole and his dispersed fragments once again knit together. It is the only place in the world where he regenerates himself (AV, 142). Doubrovsky becomes an atheist as an adult, describing himself in an interview as a 'jew' (sic) without God but a 'jew' nevertheless who nearly died because he was a Jew.[25] As we will see, however, Doubrovsky was able to compensate for his sense of inferiority through muscular intellectualness and the world of sexual seduction.

For the intellectual Doubrovsky, masculinity is found in the power of words. As most of his readers are women, writing becomes a form of seduction.[26] He plays on his 'feminine side' and knows that women who don't like hard men find him attractive (AV 169). Ironically, the very sensitivity that often made Doubrovsky feel like a failure (that is, of not being a 'real' man) proves to be his most powerful weapon. Speaking of his many seductions of female students and colleagues in the United States, Doubrovsky confides that 'For the last twenty years, the university has been my natural breeding ground' (AV, 108). His muscular intellectualness is much in evidence when, during a conference in Sweden, he used his conference paper as way of seducing a woman half his age (AV, 123). He then bought her a plane ticket to visit Paris, quoting a phrase from Sacha Guitry: 'With women, twenty-year-old men have what it takes, forty-year-old men have the know-how [*chic*], sixty-year-old men have their check book' (AV, 124). As Doubrovsky grew older his choice of women would grow increasingly younger. A passage in *L'Après-Vivre* (1994) reveals Doubrovsky's awareness of this development as well as his inability to change (by then he is over sixty). Even his daughters tell him that he should look for a woman his own age; he knows it but does not, concluding that his intellect is feminist but that his body is macho. Inside he has the desires of a teenager, intact, ageless (104–5), outside he has the body of an aging man. We should recall that Doubrovsky had been more or less robbed of his adolescence during the war years.[27] It is almost as if his desires are frozen in time, and he is perpetually trying to relive what had been stolen from him. As his seduction inevitably leads to sexual intercourse, strangely it is his *father* that Doubrovsky evokes when he has an erection. In *Fils*, for instance, the free-associating narrator declares that his feminine side is suspended when he has an erection. He then becomes all male and talks about being virile. His blood vessels are linked by a rubber hose to another person, who is his father, and when he dreams of being a man, it is in symbiosis with this paternal figure: 'Being born masculine. From my father. I want virility. Female' (280). In Doubrovsky's typically harsh self-judgment, sexual potency is just about the only time when he really feels like a man and passes the masculinity test(s) of his childhood.

Here too the specter of Jewishness haunts Doubrovsky's masculine performance, not least because his circumcised penis bears the mark of his ethnic background. There has been a 'constant and purposeful confusion through the late nineteenth and early twentieth centuries of circumcision and castration,' associating the Jew and the prostitute;[28] another dent in Doubrovsky's virility shield. Sander Gilman further elaborates that the ' "damaged" Jewish phallus bec[a]me the Jew.'[29] In a passage in *Fils*, the narrator talks about his circumcised penis as *his* sign: 'Yellow. Jewish. Death on my chest. Between my legs. I wore it . . . It has made me. Exhibi-zionist. I had to hide it. I brandish it' (280, see also 31). So for the young Doubrovsky, as well as the yellow star, his circumcised penis is a signifier for being Jewish, and he can get arrested and deported with this physical manifestation of his Jewishness ('Vichy police in the public toilets, come on now, show us your pricks . . . knobs without hats on, we pick you up . . . police van, and then Drancy' (LPC, 328–29)). Likewise, the narrator of *Le Livre brisé* tells us he has learnt that Jews should be self-effacing, molded into the Republic rather than standing out; even his mother tells him that she detests show-offs (270). Having to hide this sign of his Jewishness, and therefore his penis, the narrator of *Fils* talks about subsequently brandishing it (as an adult). As the final part of this chapter will show, sexual potency is a fragile foundation for manhood, not least when impotence remains a possibility.

Anyone familiar with Doubrovsky's work would undoubtedly agree that his books denote an obsession with younger women and sex. Furthermore, he displays the penis-centered model of sex, a type of hegemonic sexuality. The narrator of *Fils* describes himself as 'dirty' in bed, as 'polymorphously perverse' (164). This is hardly unique in a largely phallocentric Western culture. If the erect penis is a sign of potency, the flaccid penis is a sign of failure and weakness; as Paul Hoch remarked, 'Absolutely the worst thing a man can be is impotent.'[30] Sexual performance is especially central to French masculinities (at least the heterosexual model which is the hegemonic model for both homosexuals and heterosexuals growing up), and possibly more so to the generation that was brought up after the war, following the humiliation of the French defeat and subsequent occupation. In this context, what does sexual potency exactly mean? Does it mean being able to have and sustain an erection for a prolonged sexual intercourse, or does it mean being able to satisfy a sexual partner, in Doubrovsky's case, a woman? It appears that it is the former.

Most of the sex scenes described in Doubrovsky's *autofiction* are rather brutal and vigorous, with a clear focus on penetration. Everything hinges on performance, which makes it so catastrophic when the body no longer responds.

Since penetrative sexuality has been defined as the mainstay of male identity, 'men let it – or make it – define their masculinity,'[31] even when it does not need to be overdetermined. Sexuality is, in fact, socially constructed in a number of ways. Recent research has shown that gender plays an important role in individual sexual identity and that sexual performance is more important to aging men than to aging women. Erectile dysfunction is seen as a challenge to inherent masculinity,[32] whilst performance for males is a means to express 'both "maleness" and "youthfulness".'[33] Having been robbed of his teenage years, 'Doubrovsky' says that he is recovering his youth by running after young women (LPC, 356). We saw that for him, during the war, being a coward was equated with being feminized and 'fucked.' Being impotent and unable to fuck yet again feminizes him.

Doubrovsky is not unique in this approach to sex, which is important to French culture, both historically and in the contemporary context. Robert Nye writes that, because of the profound connections between sexuality and identity, a man's sexual identity is a key element in his social identity. In nineteenth-century France, male sexual potency became a way of thinking about power, and *fin-de-siècle* observers conflated problems of population and heredity with problems of masculinity.[34] To some extent these issues continue to haunt masculinity in the present. As the millennium was approaching, a flurry of articles reported the arrival of Viagra in France. *Libération* declared that French men were finally going to be enabled to talk about sexual problems. However, the arrival of Viagra in France did not please everyone. Jean Dutourd of the *Académie Française* was reported as saying: 'Once upon a time, the reputation of the French was such that we did not need this kind of thing. We were always ready, whenever necessary and as soon as necessary. The arrival of this pill marks a major blow for France.'[35] As evidence, Dutourd went on to cite Victor Hugo, whose sexual appetite was such that at the age of eighty he was still 'doing the deed' twice a day.[36]

The link between sexual performance (more specifically, penetrative sex) and national pride was also in evidence when, in 1999, Catherine Breillat made the film *Romance*, which was controversial for its explicit portrayal of male sexual arousal. She chose as one of the main actors the Italian porn star Rocco Siffredi. Nicknamed the 'Italian stallion,' Siffredi is reputed in the profession for being extremely well-endowed, and claims to have bedded over 4000 women. In the film this legend is put to the test in a sequence of explicit penetrative sex lasting eight minutes. In his review of the film, Paul Webster writes that the real star of the show is Siffredi's penis, while the French press wondered aloud why a French actor could not have been cast in that role: 'Siffredi's organ has become the subject of television and radio debates, while the techniques needed to achieve erections of up to six hours' duration are explained with as much passion as gardening hints.'[37] Leaving aside the debate about whether *Romance* is a work of porn or art, Romney sums up the meaning of the film as follows: 'declarations from the heart mean nothing if the body won't back it up – for male viewers, a highly worrying proposition, which makes this the first real film of the Viagra era.'[38] This message strikes at the heart of French male insecurities. The Italian lover is better than the French lover, and penis size and endurance are what really matter.

Following the death of his second wife, Ilse, an alcoholic, Doubrovsky enters into a long period of depression with some panic attacks when, unsurprisingly, he suffers from erectile dysfunction. Though he is aware that he is probably more in need of a psychoanalyst than a urologist, he starts to take medication and, when the pills become less efficient, injecting his penis is suggested. He is shocked, and writes that, for him, his penis is his dignity, virility is a point of honor, and that the doctor in front of him cannot comprehend this: 'I feel disgraced. Like in 1940, it is all coming back, the heaving from the debacle, the whole of France changed into fugitive females . . . Being male is a form of ethics' (AV, 364). This passage really shows the historical background of French masculinized shame and humiliation over its collusion with the occupation and Vichy. Inevitably, he reminisces about his uncle in the resistance, and his father locked in his workshop for four years, tailoring, while he submitted, like a child, like an old man.

Victor Hugo is most definitely in the unconscious of some French men. During one of his first visits to an urologist, 'Doubrovsky' is told about male sexuality declining, starting in the late forties, but he retorts with the example of Hugo, aged eighty, who had intercourse with all the maids he could lay his hands on. When his doctor warned him that he should stop, Hugo replied that nature should have warned him. Dr Z. tells 'Doubrovsky' that there are exceptions but that statistically this is not the case (AV, 363). In evoking Hugo, 'Doubrovsky' measures himself against an idealized version of one of the most venerated French writers, setting himself up as a failure against a mythically potent man of letters.

Doubrovsky has a lot to lose in terms of his masculine status in charting, in a book thinly veiled by the label *autofiction*, his erection problems and his subsequent treatments. Despite the recent concerns about erectile dysfunction, sexual impotence remains a largely taboo subject in a culture that glorifies youth and performance; 'old age remains outside this "sexualized world".'[39] 'Doubrovsky' does not give us the story of a heroic penis, but tales of vulnerability and humiliation, insecurity and fear; to some extent he refutes the myth of the French 'stallion.' His lover in *L'Après-Vivre*, who is twenty-seven years younger than him, asks him how he thinks she feels making love for the last three years with an impotent man. She tells him that she would have preferred 'A MAN' who could make love to her in the morning, at night, spontaneously, naturally, and instead she has an old man. He becomes speechless and internalizes her discourse, feeling that he is rubbish; when one has nothing left between one's legs, one is no longer a man. He then explains: 'For me, the most beautiful word in the French language has always been VIRILE,' evoking again his father, his uncle, and the war (AV, 385).

When he is struck by impotence ('Shame is gripping me, I am submerged by self-loathing' (AV, 103)),[40] one can appreciate that it is his identity and his roots that are disappearing with his flaccid penis, not simply his pride.[41] Doubrovsky's manhood is connected to his penis in a very intricate and intimate way. When his penis goes into 'hiding' he recalls the time when he, along with his entire family, was hiding from the French police and the Germans. Becoming a man when he survived the war was partly associated with metaphorically brandishing his penis, with no longer being ashamed. When he sleeps with 'Agathe,' we read: 'WILL I BE ABLE TO . . . BEING A MAN OR NOT, virility is not in the brain, the qualifications, the accomplishments, money, it is in the heart . . . and the heart for a man is between his legs, nowhere else' (AV, 352). The narrator raises the stakes in the ultimate masculinity challenge. In the process, he totally denies his own masculinity path (muscular intellectualness), and strips himself bare – notwithstanding the fact that his own path is linked to his recovered identity as a French person with de Gaulle giving him his prize and his fatherland back. In the past, between his legs was his Jewishness, associated with being an 'Untermensch,' now it is his failure as a man. He himself makes the connection explicit and talks about having death between his legs (LPC, 323). To make matters worse, throughout this period of sexual breakdowns, he invokes an old standard against which he used to measure himself: his uncle in the camp in Drancy. When he was liberated, through amazing circumstances, his wife joined him. Though his uncle weighed a mere ninety-two pounds, he and his wife made love there and then; in contrast, the artist Doubrovsky, with his fatty lard, cannot make love to a woman and is stricken with self-disgust (AV, 386).[42] Once more, the male intellectual gets a pummeling and he recalls his status as an 'Untermensch' for the Germans, as he is one now.

War, resistance and Jewishness; these three interlinked themes have proved the defining moments of Doubrovsky's entire life since he has been haunted by the war, and his masculine identity has been defined by trying to bolster his fragile sense of manhood. It will be no surprise to learn that he returns to these in the last chapter of his latest book, *Laissé pour conte* (1999). The book ends with a section on May 1944, where the narrator recalls feeling frightened and ashamed about hiding. Harry Brod has argued that a moral ambiguity was at stake for Jewish people during the war, where making their own and their community's survival a priority was *the* act of supreme courage, 'even at the risk of the charge of non-resistance.'[43] Doubrovsky proved his *virilité* in accepting to hide and in surviving when the Nazis were bent on exterminating Jews. But 'Doubrovsky' reiterates his frustration at not having fought, or killed a German, or a French policeman, which would have meant 'BEING A MAN' (419); it is his burden and his song. ' "Doubrovsky" does not exist without "L'An Quarante".' Indeed. But in a way 'Doubrovsky,' and with him thousands of others, cannot exist *because of* 'L'An Quarante' and its overdetermined representation of *virilité*.

Notes

My thanks go to Richard Johnson, Larry Schehr, and especially Chris Forth for their help with this chapter.

1. I shall seldom quote from Doubrovsky's books for the very good reason that they are practically untranslatable. His writing is based on a play on sound and word (homophony, assonance/dissonance, alliteration, and so on). The syntax is unconventional, as is the punctuation and the use of spaces and typography. For instance *Fils*, can be translated both as 'Son' and as 'Threads' (the latter also evokes descendants since Doubrovsky's father was a tailor); one suggested translation has been 'Alliances.' References to Doubrovsky's work will be inserted in the text using the following abbreviations: *La Dispersion*, (Paris: Mercure de France, 1969) (D); *Fils* (Paris: Galilée, 1977) (F); *Le Livre brisé* (Paris: Grasset, 1989) (LB); *L'Après-vivre* (Paris: Grasset, 1994) (AV); *Laissé pour conte* (Paris: Grasset, 1999) (LPC).
2. This expression was coined by Peter Redman when exploring the making of his academic self. Not very successful with other forms of masculinities, he discovered that an alternative form was discourse: 'muscular intellectualness (. . .) it added muscle to what was otherwise "other".' Peter Redman and M. Mac an Ghaill, 'Educating Peter: The Making of a History Man,' in *Border Patrols*, eds Deborah Lynn Steinberg, Debbie Epstein, and Richard Johnson (London: Cassell, 1997), pp. 162–82 (169).
3. Serge Doubrovsky, 'Introduction à la lecture,' in Alfred Hornung/Ernstpeter Ruhe, *Autobiographie & Avant-garde* (Tübingen: Gunter Narr Verlag, 1992), pp. 133–4 (133).
4. 'L'autofiction selon Doubrovsky,' interview with Philippe Vilain, in Philippe Vilain, *Défense de Narcisse* (Paris: Grasset, 2005), pp. 180–235 (199).
5. Annie Jouan-Westlund, 'Doubrovs – Qui?: le moi, le même et l'autre,' in *Origins and Identities in French Literature*, ed. Norman Buford (Amsterdam: Rodopi, 1999), pp. 153–66 (155).
6. 'L'autofiction selon Doubrovsky,' p. 225.
7. Barbara Breitman argues that for young Jewish men who lived through the war, identifying with the father is identifying with a victim and feeling emasculated and humiliated at the hand of non-Jewish men. Breitman, 'Lifting up the Shadow of Anti-Semitism: Jewish Masculinity in a New Light,' in *A Mensch among Men*, ed. Harry Brod (Freedom, CA: The Crossing Press, 1988), pp. 101–17 (105).
8. Patrick Saveau, 'La non-reconnaissance de l'autre dans la réalisation du moi Doubrovskyen,' in *Perceptions et réalisations du moi*, ed. Mounir Laouyen (Clermont-Ferrand: Presses Universitaires de Blaise Pascal, 2000), pp. 241–66 (249). By using inverted commas, I am following a strategy generally adopted by Doubrovskian critics when referring to the narrativized character within his *autofictions*. See Alex Hughes, 'Recycling and Repetition in Recent French *Autofiction*: Marc Weitzmann's Doubrovskian Borrowings,' *Modern Languages Review*, 97 (3) (July 2002): 566–76 (569, n. 16).
9. Christopher E. Forth, *The Dreyfus Affair and the Crisis of French Manhood* (Baltimore: Johns Hopkins University Press, 2004), pp. 13–14. See also Pierre Birnbaum, *Les Fous de la République* (Paris: Fayard, 1992), p. 211.
10. Sander Gilman, *The Jew's Body* (London: Routledge, 1991), pp. 133–4.
11. Gillman reminds us that Hitler associated plague and pestilence with the Jew. Ibid., p. 101. For a detailed account of the persecution of Jews under Vichy, see Birnbaum, *Les Fous de la République*, pp. 442–85.
12. The notion of 'coward' can be traced right back to the Dreyfus affair – see Forth, *Dreyfus Affair*. For the importance of the concept of 'courage' as shoring up traditional

masculinities and rearticulating the boundaries of traditional sexual difference in the period 1890–1914, see Robert A. Nye, *Masculinity and Male Codes of Honor in Modern France* (New York: Oxford University Press, 1993), p. 226.

13. For Jewish men, fighting for France has always been a way of showing their attachment to their country. In Birnbaum, *Les Fous de la République*, p. 59 (see also pp. 237–59).

14. Luc Capdevila, 'The Quest for Masculinity in a Defeated France, 1994–1945,' *Contemporary European History*, 10 (3) (2001): 423–45 (433, 435).

15. See Luc Capdevila, 'Le mythe du guerrier et la construction sociale d'un "éternel masculin" après la guerre,' *Revue française de psychanalyse*, 2 (1998): 607–23 (607). And in the present volume, see the chapters by Judith Surkis and Miranda Pollard.

16. Victor J. Seidler, 'Reason, Desire, and Male Sexuality,' in *The Cultural Construction of Sexuality*, ed. Pat Caplan (London: Routledge, 1991), p. 99.

17. Capdevila, 'Le mythe du guerrier,' p. 617.

18. Within a Jewish context – in psychological terms – Breitman argues that feeling totally debased and helpless to change the condition of external oppression, the self compensates for the pain and humiliation suffered on the outside 'by elevating itself to almost God-like status in the inner world.' Breitman, 'Lifting up the Shadow,' p. 106. For the writer, words will become *guns* and writing will also become an act to write his survival: 'Je ne cherche aucune absolution, mais un partage,' interview with Jean-François Louette, *Les Temps Modernes*, 611–12 (2000–01): 210–18 (212, 214). But 'Doubrovsky' is also conscious that words will not free him or deliver him from his torment (LB, 20). And when there is nothing to write, there is nothing to live for (AV, 108).

19. 'Je ne cherche aucune absolution,' p. 212.

20. Forth, *Dreyfus Affair*, p. 63.

21. James W. Messerschmidt defines this notion as follows: 'Masculinity challenges arise from interactional threats and insults from peers, teachers, parents, and from situationally defined masculine expectations that are not achievable.' Messerschmidt, *Nine Lives: Adolescent Masculinities, the Body, and Violence* (Boulder: Westview Press, 2000), p. 13.

22. In my translation, I have not rendered all the extra spaces which are inserted in the text in lieu of punctuation.

23. Some of this could have sprung from the Jewish father's attempt to shrug off accusations of effeminacy by hardening himself and his son. As a Russian émigré his father might have been made even more aware of gender (I owe this comment to Chris Forth). At the turn of the century, Nordau had called for the 'new Muscle Jew' in response to accusations about the Jew's inability to serve as a citizen and the form of the Jew's body. Auerbach saw sport as the social force to reshape the Jewish body. Gilman, *The Jew's Body*, p. 53.

24. Le Naour talks about the virile fever of 1914 when being a soldier was seen as being sexually potent. In Jean-Yves Le Naour, 'Le héros, la femme honnête et la putain: la Première Guerre mondiale et les mutations de la guerre,' in *Le Genre face aux mutations*, eds Luc Capdevila et al. (Rennes: Presses universitaires de Rennes, 2003), pp. 307–16 (309). For Nye, 'It would appear that on the eve of the Great War courage was absurdly overdetermined.' Nye, *Masculinity*, p. 226.

25. 'L'autofiction selon Doubrovsky,' pp. 195, 197.

26. 'Je ne cherche aucune absolution,' p. 216.

27. 'Doubrovsky' makes the same comment (LPC, 356).

28. Gilman, *The Jew's Body*, pp. 119–20. See also pp. 124–5.

29. Ibid., p. 165.
30. Paul Hoch, *White Hero Black Beast: Racism, Sexism and the Mask of Masculinity* (London: Pluto Press, 1979), p. 102.
31. Ken Plummer, 'Male Sexualities,' in *Handbook Studies on Men and Masculinities*, eds R.W. Connell, Jeff Hearn, and Michael S. Kimmel (London: Sage, 2004), pp. 178–195 (180).
32. E.S. Person, 'Sexuality as the Mainstay of Identity: Psychoanalytic Perspectives,' *Signs*, 5 (1980): pp. 605–30 (619).
33. Merryn Gott and Sharron Hinchliff, 'Sex and Ageing: a Gendered Issue,' in *Gender and Ageing. Changing Roles and Relationships*, eds Sara Arber, Kate Davidson, and Jay Ginn (Maidenhead: The Open University Press, 2003), pp. 63–78 (72).
34. Nye, *Masculinity*, pp. 10, 67, 83.
35. John Henley, 'Viagra Demand Deals a Wallop to French Pride,' *Guardian* (18 September 1998): 17.
36. I used this remark as the basis for an article where I went on to explore the notion of heroic masculinities in France. Jean-Pierre Boulé, 'Viagra, Heroic Masculinity and France,' *French Cultural Studies*, 12 (35) (2001): 207–26.
37. Paul Webster, 'Porn Seduces French Cinema,' *Guardian* (13 April 1999).
38. Jonathan Romney, 'French Kisses,' *Guardian* (5 February 1999).
39. Gott and Hinchliff, 'Sex and Ageing,' p. 64.
40. For the link between sexual dishonor, shame and impotence in France at the beginning of the twentieth century, see Nye, *Masculinity*, p. 69.
41. For an article exploring Doubrovsky's work and Jewishness, see Régine Robin, 'Trou de mémoire: le travail de la judéité,' *Les Temps Modernes*, 611–12 (2000–01): 192–218.
42. Doubrovsky's search for virility through muscular intellectualness is thus caught in a discourse that appeared again in the 1970s, linking cerebral life with a lack of *virilité*: 'Deprived of its *élan vital* by debilitating conditions of life, comfortable habits, the slackening of bodily functions, and an excess of often adulterated food, the body gives precedence to a cerebrality that is pushed beyond its breaking point . . . Among men this ceaseless, overexcited use of intellect leads to the exhaustion of the vital forces.' Marcel Rouet, *Virilité et puissance sexuelle* (Paris: Productions de Paris, 1971), pp. 9–10.
43. Harry Brod, 'Towards a Male Jewish Feminism,' in *A Mensch among Men*, pp. 181–8 (186).

13
Threatening Virility in the French *Banlieues*, 1989–2005

André Rauch

This chapter presents a gendered analysis of a 'challenge to republican values' which, since 1989, has troubled French politics and society. Urban developments in the last third of the twentieth century created a specific new social space, the *banlieue*, as a liminal urban zone around the city. Mass immigration in its diversity and conflicts introduced new contradictions specific to post-colonial France, creating a critical social situation aggravated by mass unemployment and long-term job insecurity. This chapter examines the changes in male behavior in the *banlieues* during the last twenty years, and explores the gendered culture of violence that has developed in these neglected and largely immigrant neighborhoods. Taking in chronological turn the various episodes of this 'crisis,' this chapter begins with its premises in the 'Islamic veil' affair, to consider the *ni-putes ni-soumises* feminist response, and the more recent forms of exacerbated gang-led violence and rioting in the *banlieues*.

The 'Islamic veil'

When what the media entitled the 'Islamic veil' affair (*l'affaire du voile islamique*) emerged in 1989, French boys and girls had been co-educated for half a century in schools, colleges, *lycées* and universities. The uniformity of their attire followed fashion while their verbal exchanges more or less attested to a culture of equality. While this revolution has been largely accepted, the veil affair opened up a political debate which challenged assumptions and received very broad media coverage. Students wearing a veil (or *hijab*) around their face presented a contrast and reintroduced gender segregation among the pupils.

In partly hiding the face, the essential bodily expression of individuality, the veil seemed to forbid visual interaction between onlookers and wearers. In many ways a throwback to old fashions when women covered themselves to protect their dignity from male desires, the veil in educational spaces was thought to signal a renunciation of secular values enshrined in the 'Declaration of the Rights of Man.' For many the veil represented the opposite of these values: an expression of anti-republicanism, anti-egalitarianism and socially regressive practices, and thus the cause of discrimination and exclusion. The tale was told as if a fundamental tenet of equality and democracy had been challenged by a group imposing the veil on girls. Assuming that Muslim men were the lawmakers in these communities, few believed that the women themselves had freely chosen this garment.[1]

Controlling girls

On 4 October 1989, the national daily newspaper *Libération* covered a news item from the regional paper *Le Courrier Picard*. Three girls, two of Moroccan origin, one from a Tunisian family, had been prevented from attending school by the head teacher of their college in Creil (Oise), near Paris. This was because, when entering the classroom, they had refused to remove the veils that partly covered their faces. This sparked a crucial debate in public opinion: does this item of clothing pose a challenge to the moral values of co-education and secularism? The perceived threats posed by the veil were myriad. Will all women have to cover themselves to go through public spaces? Will this rule apply first to Muslim girls only to become more generally applied to all French women? Furthermore, will there be a multiplication of other distinctive signs that will threaten French democracy? In a crucial binary opposition, assimilation was identified as an ultimate aim of the educational system, while communitarian tendencies were portrayed as the source of all social evils.

Following the 1905 law separating churches and state, all visible markers of religious affiliation have been excluded from public schools. The veil launched a direct challenge to this secular precept. At least as disturbing was the discrimination between Muslim and non-Muslim girls that seemed to create a chasm between 'our' girls and 'your' girls in masculinist discourses. There was the suspicion that Muslim girls would be appropriated by their communities on territorial grounds. The girls were supposedly living hidden, submissive to their father and brothers. In short, the affair of the Islamic veil brought many commonplace assumptions about poorly-known immigrants to the surface. The veil was represented in the media as a repressive mechanism for the internment of women by their male prison wardens. These were variously denounced as parents, in the context of a critique of Muslim families, or as religious leaders in the context of the emergence of radical Islam on the French political scene. The political context and the rise of xenophobic extreme rightist parties led to a radicalization of attitudes leading to the banning of the veil. The veil thus shifted from a social problem to an affair of state.[2]

The passions unleashed by the affair divided families who had lived in France for years as well as immigrant groups, whether their origins were North African, Middle-Eastern, or sub-Saharan African. It also mobilized political parties, who disagreed about how to respond to this 'attack' on the republic. Those on the right who promoted repression were countered by leftist calls for more social work in the 'difficult suburbs.' But teachers' trade unions were also equally divided on what measures to take, and various anti-racist associations relent-lessly petitioned the relevant ministers (which alternated from Left to Right over the period). In public opinion the threat that the veil seemed to pose was magnified as a result of the deep economic crisis that also affected the role of the schooling system, or the role of the national state in Europe.

At the forefront of anti-veil activism were the teachers who posed as the sources and guardians of secular co-education. The feminists among them were particularly incensed by the threat of female subordination in a male-dominated world. In their eyes, the veil was a symbol of male tyranny illus-trated by examples from Taliban Afghanistan, Iran or even Arab nations in general. The story revealed a longstanding identity crisis. It relied on fears and phantasms, pre-existing ideologies and opinions. It cast the events as the conflict between a secularizing society and motley reactionary alienated groups. But the story also raised the issues of a gender crisis: on one side, the gender trans-gressions of unmarked boundaries between the sexes, on the other, the renewal of masculine hierarchical values and the territorial defense of women against exogenous seducers.

Back to normal

While the debate remained ideological, the context was far more complex. Looking at these girls in their daily reality cast a different light on the nego-tiations they entered into with their families. One could nevertheless get to the complex symbolic values of this garment for them. In their daily lives, young women from immigrant backgrounds recognize the veil as a compro-mise between the Islamic values of their families and their own desire to par-ticipate in French society. For their mothers, the veil symbolized less of an explicitly religious worldview than a sense of belonging to a set of cultural and moral values. This sense of belonging had to be expressed in public spaces for the community, for some it also served as a protection against male desires and the pornographic and publicity imagery commonly displayed around them. Samira, a 20-year-old woman living in Sarcelles near Paris, expressed this anx-iety to a journalist of the weekly *Le Nouvel Observateur*: 'On one hand, you have a society that shows stark-naked women everywhere; on other, you have families and a religion that don't allow talk about sexuality. The guys are lost. They don't know how to talk to girls.'[3] Whereas some saw only issues of sub-missive or/and provocative behavior, there was a genuine social question resulting from several cultural crises. Utterly ignored until then, the school girls of the *collège* of Creil eventually created an image for themselves that counteracted that of their brothers or cousins, who styled themselves as the young rebels or 'delinquents' of the *banlieues*. Born in a council estate of Mantes-la-Jolie, nineteen-year-old Faudel, a star of *raï* (the Algerian 'blues') who was then preparing his concerts in the largest concert hall in Paris, also recalled his life in the rotten suburbs: 'Most parents don't understand that the world has changed. They can't read or write; yet they place their kids under surveillance to the point of unsettling them. Many girls can't even have a chat with a boy after they leave school. If their dad sees them, he won't leave them in peace; he'll demand: "Why are you walking with him? What's going on with you two?"'[4]

A cultural divide between generations focused on the school system. The Islamic veil story revealed another form of oppression in schools and on the street that came to light when communities attempted to reconstitute and defend themselves. What could be more threatening to both fathers and brothers than a desire to assimilate to mainstream society? Wouldn't girls have a greater chance than boys of choosing a partner outside their original group, precisely because those partners would not share the religion or values of their families? Whereas men might endure all sorts of humiliations, many refuse to be robbed of 'their' women, and thus suffer any form of female emancipation as a personal slight. Weren't they in danger of disappearing easily in a society that rejected the males? Boys from elsewhere, flirting with 'their' women, embodied this threat. By mixing with some other Frenchmen they added to the 'daily shame' with which many men have to live. Many seemed close to regarding seduction games as literal assaults on their race or religious community (*umma*). In their local mosques, imams tend to preach defiance and repulsion for a corrupt and luxuriating society whose customs are presented as perversions. In this context women are invested with the honor of the group, and it becomes their responsibility to preserve it. Similarly, women alone can taint it by their lack of purity. In endangered traditional groups, the masculine mottos and rules become increasingly rigid and almost mythical. The myth of original purity reinforced the group and individuals by self-reinforcing 'virile' values.

Under the domination of the chiefs

Male groups became refuges precisely because public spaces escaped masculine control. To many the mechanics of this seemed simple. According to Malek Boutih, president of SOS Racisme: 'machismo is recurrent because boys are unhappy, they don't have jobs, get thrown out of nightclubs, [and] find it hard to attract girls. Suffering from social and sexual deprivation, they vent their frustration upon women. [For them] there are respectable girls, their sisters and those of their friends, who have no rights, and the other, the whores, the "*tassepé*" (*pétasses*, in slang, or slags), "ready to rip-fuck" (*bonnes à déchirer*).' This was one explanation for male support for traditional women's clothing: 'for the guys, if you dress like a woman (*meuf* or *femme* in slang) it means that you're asking for a shag.' Women who wear traditional clothing have understood that they needed to avoid the male gaze of local hard boys or their older brothers. The power of these boys, resulting from the collapse of paternal authority, and their seizure of power at the expense of women in public spaces, revealed a conflict between men in a crisis context. Yet their subjection of women contradicted the secular values of French society, in particular those of liberty and equality. Submissive either by choice or under duress, girls nevertheless manage to keep open some windows of opportunity. They put on make-up, do well at school and get some small rewards, or sometimes invent school obligations so they can meet a boyfriend. For some girls, education provides a way out. For others, the most audacious, men become the target of their rebellion: 'they use religion as they wish. They can drink, smoke, fuck and they stop us from living,' complained Sali, a girl of Malian origins.[5]

The violence of the *caïds* (chiefs) has become, in the words of sociologist Daniel Welzer-Lang, 'a hierarchical operational mode' based on strength and submission and the control over the bodies of subordinates who can be humiliated. These arrogant young men 'put pressure' on their surroundings and apply in the schools the same law that older brothers apply in the neighborhoods. Seizing bodily control, they domesticate their subordinates in gangs that are always opposed to others and in which all have to choose sides.

Virile codes

While maintaining this central bond between them, boys are not kind to one another. As one gang member explained to the journalist Anne Giudicellie: 'In a gang you're with your mates, the guys you have had a good trip with. But if you go to sleep, someone pinches your cash. They're just bastards. When you get up in the morning, you have no shoes, nothing. We play tricks on each other, but, in spite of that, we stay friends.'[6] Visible hierarchies arise and gangs have social codes, rules based on provocation and violence. Yelling as a means of communication, rough playing, swearing in order to challenge, and laughter in the face of punching matches or the throwing of objects comprise a real code of etiquette.[7]

Initiation rites serve as a means of gang induction. Outside their social reality where they have no opportunities, the worlds of reality and play become confused. Everyday life is presented as just a game played between themselves and the police: 'when we catch them after a chase in a stolen car, they think they have lost; if there is an accident or someone gets hurt, it's a riot.'[8] For these young men, transgression facilitates self-identity: belonging to a hierarchy based on strength enables them to become individuals. These structures seem to reproduce older ones that are equally under male control. But their violence demonstrates virility as much as transgressive acts against dominant social classes. The challenges and self-assertion were also mapped out on the girls' bodies. Collective rapes (*tournantes*) are commonly reported in the press, but only in the courtroom are they revealed as genuine collective rapes rather than teenage banter. 'These are like initiation rites during which boys reveal their virility by abusing a girl,' as Marie Choquet and Sylvie Ledoux, researchers at the INSERM defined them.[9] Among boys, one is a man only if he has sex with a woman, thus confirming Elisabeth Badinter's point that males often need 'to have a woman in order not to be one.'[10] The most difficult neighborhoods and dangerous housing estates of the *banlieue* have given their names to these practices. Located near Paris, Sarcelles, Les Mureaux, and La Courneuve are identified as the main sites of violence against women; yet there are many other sites outside the suburbs that have been neglected. For instance, on 23 August 1988 in Missillac, a small town of Loire-Atlantique, gendarmes of Saint-Gildas-des-Bois arrested eleven young men who were imprisoned in Saint-Nazaire.[11] These boys, from good families, had been sexually exploiting a village girl. Whether in the *banlieue* or elsewhere, such assaults represent what anthropologist Véronique Nahoum-Grappe calls the 'political use of cruelty.'[12] But in a society where gender boundaries have been relaxed, this usage of cruelty no longer exercises an acceptable central role in the definition of masculine roles but appears a regressive mode of virility. Yet one should not forget that women themselves have reacted and publicly organized their defense.

Defense groups: *Ni putes ni soumises*

Women reacted individually and then collectively. As explained by Fadela Amara, president of the Fédération nationale des Maisons des Potes (an association allied with SOS Racisme): 'In the eighties, we older sisters had started to get a bit of freedom, a first step towards equality. It all fell apart in the nineties with mass unemployment, the rise of fundamentalist Islam and communitarianism, and in the end it was the girls who took the rap.'[13] This feminist idea that the chain of social dislocation affects women most cast the situation as a reversible process for women who refuse to be the stock victims of social ailments.

With some other women, Fadela Amara published a manifesto entitled 'Ni putes, ni soumises' (Neither Whores nor Submissive) and a call to launch an organization identified by the initials of the manifesto (NPNS). Initially unsuccessful, the organization called its 'Estates General' of the neighborhood women in January 2002, demonstrated against machismo and male violence in March, organized a march in Paris against ghettos and for equality in February–March 2003 with some 30,000 people gathering on 8 March 2003. In October, during their first 'summer university' (party conference), Fadela Amara called upon the French president to launch a national debate on the state of women: 'in our country, one thing has become unbearable: it's the regressive status of women. We cannot accept it any longer.'[14] These attempts to occupy the public sphere (via the press and the internet) and to make their views part of the political debate, started to find an echo in the judicial system. Their action has shifted the points of reference for men at the end of the twentieth century, not because there might be a history of men opposed to that of women, but in the sense that history can no longer be perceived as gender neutral. These women led a resistance, often domestically, against any attempt to recompose an unequal social order where men might enjoy even illusory privileges.

Looking after the male body

On their estates, boys have adopted a number of fashion identifiers, such as shaven heads, caps worn sideways, hoodies, and labeled sportswear, in the *caillera* (*racaille*) style. The aim is to seem menacing and seductive at the same time. Some choose to adopt an American look, named '*Kainji*' (for *Ricain*, the slang for American) or a basketball player look for black boys. Adopting a certain posture and walk adds to the image. As a boy of Argenteuil puts it: 'In my 'hood, you must have the same gear as the most popular boy. It's easy to get to the same shop, special offers fall off the back of the same lorry; in the end we all get the same pair of Nike-Requin.' But one needs different gear to get out of the neighborhood. The same clothes that identify a boy in his neighborhood would make him vulnerable outside. Jeans and a T-shirt replace the uniform, and this is in order to avoid ridicule. In February 2006, *Libération* portrayed such a group:

> The NBA baseball cap on the side, large diamond in the ears, bling, chains and watch, large silver chains around the neck, Fred and William walk about, almost in slow motion in the corridors of Les Halles in Paris. They are both very tall black boys in XXL basket-ball gear, a huge sport bag on the shoulder as if they'd just come out of training but they are only shopping in Paris in Les Halles. They are slow so that girls can look them up and down, pulling girls is a high level sport on Wednesday and Saturday in les Halles for the youth of the Parisian region. 'The American look, it's the best to pull women,' argue the boys who have met in school in Bobigny. 'We've got mates who keep on dressing up like chavs (*racaille*) and wear Lacoste. They should see that it does not pull. The American look is really getting better. Even the Chinese and the Arabs try it on, but it doesn't suit everyone.

Another look calls for hairspray, baggy jeans, skateboard, earrings, and necklace which might seem to challenge some codes of virility. According to sociologist Dominique Pasquier, who studies teenagers and the power of group culture, without these codes boys named 'Abdulaye' and 'Samir' can't approach girls with names like 'Jennifer' in the metro or at school.[15]

> Aktar, 17, had to fight to get his new '*Kainry*' look in Sartrouville (Yvelines). 'In my high school, they were all chavs, I wanted to stand out.' So he chose '*17 XL*' trousers, which prevent him from walking fast because the fabric hangs between his legs. 'I'm not in a rush, ever, I'm a quiet guy.' He doesn't want to become the ghetto dandy, but he finds size 62 jeans more

comfortable. His black skin highlights his diamond earrings. 'When I chose the American look I was insulted by others who called me a "Bush dicksucker, pull up your pants or I'll sod you!"' But in the end 'that gets people talking. I like that they talk about me.' Yet the new look sticks to the skin, and recently Aktar experimented with an image change for one day at school. He borrowed his clothing from a friend and went 'dressed up in the fashion' of the local dominant look. He had borrowed narrow jeans with some holes, Diesel, low shoes, a T-shirt and a white jacket on top.

Concerns with looks and bodily appearance are not isolated from more general changes in France. Young men in general have embraced the bodily concerns of the so-called metrosexual attitude. For their parents the imaginary notion of a 'natural' man meant that any skin-care or hair-care was the realm of women. Immigrant men tended to favor more virile signs (such as a moustache, trousers, and flannel shirt), and took care never to cross conventional boundaries between masculine and feminine styles. The new playing with fashion codes does not signal a clear gender role, but is a game whose rules change according to circumstances. In that game, self-confidence and seduction relate to one another and to the visible expression of desires. Yet this expression can take spectacularly violent forms.

Celebratory fires: burning the 'hood

On Thursday 27 October 2005, in Clichy-sous-Bois near Paris in the department of Seine-Saint-Denis, the news of the accidental death of two boys, Zied Banna, 17, and Bouna Traore, 15, spread like wildfire. Around 5.20 p.m., two policemen investigating a burglary on a building site happened upon three young boys who, when spotted, ran away. When chased the boys ran into an electrical transformer to hide. Banna and Traore were electrocuted while their friend, Muttin Altun, was severely burned. As Claude Askolovitch put it 'they became the senseless martyrs of a pointless, leaderless, senseless revolt.'[16]

In the *banlieues* the news traveled fast and was quickly exaggerated. The rioting that ensued became a mode of existence. As early as Friday morning the press started enumerating instances of car arson. Rioting began in the neighboring suburb of Bois-du-Temple. The following night, in Savigny-sur-Orge, a school was set on fire. It then spread to other neighborhoods nearby: Sevran, Tremblay-en-France, Aulnay-sous-Bois, Stains, Bondy, Neuilly-sur-Marne. It reached the next department, Val d'Oise: Goussainville, Argenteuil, Villiers-le-Bel, then Mantes-la-Jolie in the Yvelines. From the entire Paris region it spread nationwide: eight trucks in Coteau (a suburb of Roanne), cars in Le Havre, Nantes, Rouen, Blois, Tour, Orléans, Toulouse, Lyon, Grenoble, Valenciennes, Lille, Belfort. Cars, buses, trucks, telephone boxes, schools, sports hall, gymnasium, police stations are set on fire. 1295 cars were destroyed on the night of 5–6 November 2005. On 7 November, the prime minister declared a state of emergency and imposed a curfew. Were these violent demonstrations an expression of frustrated virility? This requires a contextual analysis. In Clichy, the Sunday after the first riots, the riot police (CRS) took their positions in haut Clichy at the time of the prayer during Ramadan. They fired smoke grenades at the Bilal mosque. 'There was a complete panic,' according to Larbi Chouaïeb, the president of the Muslim association of Clichy. 'People were trampled. At that stage even the elders thought "there is no respect." ' The riots expressed the frustration of many years of humiliation. There were also rumors of aggressive policing techniques, even from the families of the victims. The rioters did not act in an organized manner, but all knew that sparking a large fire would put their neighborhood on the map and on television. Apart from the singer Francky Vincent, there are no 'people' in Clichy-sous-Bois. The rioters claimed the status of defenders of their neighborhoods and assumed traditional roles of manly protectors of their territorial borders.

These young men made a strange cohort, with their shared uniforms, coded deportment, identical clothing and, in their meetings, a shared discourse mixing common demands and claims to legitimacy. They emphasized their refusal to submit and their right to be respected. They claimed to be guardians of the dignity of their neighborhood, and thus projected themselves as defenders (rather than destroyers) of society. As the twenty-two-year-old student, Christophe, argued in Hauts-de-Seine: 'when I see what's going on, I always see the same thing: Nicolas Sarkozy [Home Office minister] in Argenteuil who raised his head and said "Madam, I'll clean that up." What's the result of this? By pretending to be a superhero, a super-megalomaniac, Sarko has really triggered everything. He hasn't shown respect to anyone.'[17] In this analysis, all violence originated from a minister seeking to humiliate the suburbs. Three boys in Montfermeil reiterated this analysis: 'we burn to take revenge on Sarko.'[18]

In des Bosquets, a neighborhood between Clichy-sous-Bois and Montfermeil, M'bar, 26, was educator in the local social center. Father of a little girl, he argued that these conflicts conveyed a demand for dignity. 'When Sarko claimed he wanted to pressure clean the neighborhoods as if we were all scum, he really insulted us. It's disgusting.'[19] Even the elders were shocked by the minister and allegedly backed the younger men's challenge. From this perspective, arson represented an appropriate response. Beyond saving their territory, young men spontaneously felt the need to preserve their honor. A leading policeman concurred: 'we don't think there's any concerted action between the neighborhoods, their relationships are too antagonistic. What we have is a common answer to the discourse of Nicolas Sarkozy. They emulate each other to pose as strong men because they've all been called scum.'[20] Riots and fires obeyed social mechanisms belonging to the normal life of the neighborhood, its honor codes and ways of resolving conflicts. The novelty was in the common cause around the illusion or conviction that they were fighting for justice and a moral and politically central struggle. 'The police are a symbol of the state, so we are a target for those who resent French society,'[21] argued another policeman.

Beyond collective honor there was individual honor. Policemen knew this, as Mathieu, 28, constable in a specialized anticrime unit (BAC) in Seine-Saint-Denis put it: 'some criminals will even refuse to be arrested by a cop they don't know and will demand to be arrested by such and such.'[22] Policemen were aware of complex differences: 'there is a gang issue. Each group has its territory. To do a cop in is good for the reputation of the 'hood in competition with the others.'[23] The threats did not come only from the 'strangers' in the neighborhood, but also from other gangs occupying the same sociological and geographical space. In the struggle against the police, to bring the enemy onto the home patch and defeat the cops also represented a symbolic triumph of one gang over another. According to sociologist, Amar Henni: 'To challenge Sarkozy, represents an important stake in symbolic capital. To burn a bus or a shop is to become notorious. The bigger the act of arson, the more their capital increases in value. Three months in prison is not too much for this increase of their prestige capital.'[24]

In this conflict between global and local societies, strategies of interpretation play an important role. To play on phantasms and mystify the truth enabled a group to pretend to be more dangerous and known. Any interpretation suggested to the media allowed them to create a 'version' of the events which muddled the representation and which might impact on the social representation according to relativist cultural norms. Clichés abound linking hatred to religion, Islamicizing the riots or bringing in some culturally determined views on violence that play into the hands of those whose agenda is to posit a radical rupture between local and national social values. To rename anarchic riots as a 'movement' or to link these events to the Jihad of Osama Bin Laden help to establish the very boundaries gangs seek to defend. The sense of the vulnerability of the group and its defensive stance has served the gangs of young men over the last two decades. This defensive posturing structures both their language and their vision of the world. This strategy has become central to their culture and the words and syntax of this language have been spread around nationally from north to south in neighborhoods structured around territorial notions of honor. There were two key issues at stake. The first was a call to justice and dignity, the second to that of notoriety. The challenge of another 'chief,' the minister of the interior, used the kind of language that gangs themselves use and provoked a response in gang terms. The competitive dimensions of this response found its expression on the web through which neighborhoods could compare the number of cars burnt. Various forms of the real clashed and made these events simultaneously identity clashes and games in a media world dominated by the confusion of reality shows, games, and news reporting.

Conclusion

The evolution of male behavior has to be analyzed in its changing social context in European society, which contrasts with much of the rest of the world where the gender boundaries have remained fundamental to social interactions and thus more rigid. To understand young males' self-assertion in the suburbs also means understanding broader issues, such as their double cultural affiliations, the loss of stable cultural landmarks, their social exclusion and the solidarity it creates as well as the hierarchies it reinforces. In this sense there is probably not a singular 'crisis' of masculine identity in the suburbs. These forms of self-assertion are related to several aspects of different crises. To understand these in simple binary terms does not convey the complexity of these issues: men are not simply opposed to women, the young to the elders, the suburbs to French society, the gangs to the police or other gangs, and so on. In this sense the gender question is not to be considered in isolation or reducible to one of these conflicts. It has to be contextualized in the changes of a difficult era or even several eras with complex boundaries. Nevertheless a gendered approach to this very recent history enables some forms of interpretation, neglected by most contemporary observers, which can contribute to explaining the crises of contemporary France.

Notes

This chapter translated by Bertrand Taithe and Christopher E. Forth.

1. André Rauch, *Histoire du Premier sexe de la Révolution à nos jours* (Paris: Hachette-Pluriel, 2006), p. 554.
2. Françoise Gaspard and Farhad Khosrokhavar, *Le Foulard et la République* (Paris, La Découverte, 1995); Baubérot Jean, 'L'affaire des foulards,' *L'homme et la société*, 120 (2) (1996): 9–16; Elisabeth Badinter, *Fausse route* (Paris: Odile Jacob, 2003), p. 190.
3. Sophie des Déserts, *Le Nouvel Observateur* (25 January 2001): 81. See also Catherine Simon, 'La banlieue côté filles,' *Le Monde* (9–10 March 2003): 10–11.
4. Faudel, 'L'amour au Val-Fourré,' *Le Nouvel Observateur* (22 January 1998): 17. For a sociological analysis of the *banlieue*, see Henri Rey, *La peur des banlieues* (Paris: Fondation Nationale des Sciences Politiques, 1996).
5. Sophie des Déserts, 'Ni putes ni soumises,' *Le Nouvel Observateur* (7 March 2002): 98. On young people's spatial awareness, see José Cubero, *L'Émergence des banlieues. Au cœur de la fracture sociale* (Toulouse: Privat, 2002), pp. 80–1.
6. Anne Giudicelli, 'Être beau et "bad" à la fois. Comment vivent les bandes,' *Le Nouvel Observateur* (28 May 1992): 28. On dress codes, see Michel Kokoreff, *La force des quartiers. De la délinquance à l'engagement politique* (Paris: Payot, 2003), p. 78.
7. Anne Fohr, 'Dossier: Violence scolaire,' *Le Nouvel Observateur* (14 January 1999): 20. Also see Michel Wieviorka, *Violence en France* (Paris : Seuil, 1999), pp. 118–58.
8. Caroline Beizard, 'Ca m'est arrivé de me faire canarder,' *Le Nouvel Observateur* (22 January 1998): 84; Eric Debarbieux, *La Violence en milieu scolaire. 1. État des lieux* (Paris: E.S.F., 1997 [1996]), pp. 93–99; Cubero, *L'Émergence des banlieues*; pp. 82–83. Also see Robert Castel, *L'Insécurité sociale: qu'est-ce qu'être protégé* (Paris: Seuil, 2003).

9. In 1998 Marie Choquet and Sylvie Ledoux, conducted a study of girls between 12 and 19, among whom 1 per cent claimed to have been raped while 4 per cent admitted to having been victims of sexual violence. A more recent enquiry showed that teenagers are most vulnerable. Of the 11.4 per cent of women aged 20 to 59 who have been victims of sexual violence, nearly half had endured it before they were seventeen. Eight per cent admit to having been raped or victims of attempted rape, and a third of these were under eighteen at the time. Sophie des Déserts, *Le Nouvel Observateur* (25 January 2001): 80.

10. Elisabeth Badinter, 'Le mâle-être,' *Le Nouvel Observateur* (27 August 1992): 14.

11. Sylvie Veran, 'Quand un village absout ses violeurs,' *Le Nouvel Observateur* (23 September 1988): 90.

12. Véronique Nahoum-Grappe, 'L'Usage politique de la cruauté: l'épuration ethnique (ex-Yougoslavie 1991–1995),' in *De la violence*, ed. Françoise Héritier (Paris: Odile Jacob, 1996), p. 283.

13. Des Déserts, 'Ni putes ni soumises,' p. 96. See also Fadela Amara, *Ni putes ni soumises* (Paris: La Découverte, 2003).

14. Sylvia Zappi, 'Fort de ses premiers succès, le mouvement Ni putes ni soumises interpelle le chef de l'Etat,' *Le Monde* (5–6 October 2003): 8.

15. Dominique, Pasquier, *Cultures lycéennes, la tyrannie de la majorité* (Paris: Autrement, 2005). On the conflicts between *bouffons* and *cailleras*, see David Lepoutre, *Cœur de banlieue. Codes, rites et langages* (Paris: Odile Jacob, 1997), p. 115.

16. Claude Askolovitch, 'Banlieue. Pourquoi l'incendie?' *Le Nouvel Observateur* (10 November 2005): 64; Hervé Vieillard-Baron, *Les Banlieues* (Paris: Flammarion, 1996). On the *événements* themselves, see Jean-Pierre Mignard, Emmanuel Tordjman, and Edwy Plenel, *L'Affaire Clichy* (Paris: Stock, 2006).

17. Ludovic Blecher, Jacky Durand, Karl Laske, and Gilles Wallon, 'Il faut que Sarkozy démissionne,' *Libération* (6 November 2005): 2.

18. Elisa Vigoureux, 'La guerre des mondes,' *Le Nouvel Observateur* (10 November 2005): 72; Kokoreff, *La force des quartiers*, p. 61.

19. Olivier Toscer, 'Les cités vues de la BAC,' *Le Nouvel Observateur* (17 November 2005): 98; François Dubet and Didier Lapeyronnie, *Les Quartiers d'exil* (Paris: Seuil, 1999), pp. 160–4.

20. 'Une colère qui court au-delà de Clichy,' *Libération* (3/11/2005), 6. On honor see David Lepoutre, *Cœur de banlieue: Codes, rites et langages* (Paris: Odile Jacob, 1997), pp. 293–309.

21. Toscer, 'Les cités vues de la BAC,' p. 98.

22. Ibid.

23. Ibid.; Kokoreff, *La force des quartiers*, pp. 138–44.

24. Henni Amar, quoted in Jacky Durand, 'J'aurais voulu que ces gamins soient organisés politiquement,' *Libération* (6 November 2005): 3; Henni Amar and Gilles Marinet, *Les Cités hors-la-loi* (Paris: Éditions Ramsay, 2002).

Afterword

Robert A. Nye

French masculinity has always been a little suspect. Anne Vila points out in the first pages of her chapter how self-fashioning Englishmen found French virility wanting as early as the eighteenth century. The theme then was a certain French excess in the arts of civilized comportment. In post-9/11 America, similar doubts have been raised about the 'surrender monkeys' who floated an earnest, if misinformed, Colin Powell down the river of indecisive United Nations proceduralism. The flood of anti-French invective unleashed by this purported betrayal took various forms: from the infamous 'freedom fries' to the boycotting of 'French' restaurants and wine and to bizarre interpretations of French military history by bloggers and amateur historians. American masculinity was still sufficiently affronted two and three years later that Republican politicians suggested that John Kerry 'looked French,' would permit Jacques Chirac to run American foreign policy, and would introduce 'French' socialism to Americans and turn them 'soft.'[1] The imbroglio over France's contribution to a peacekeeping force in Lebanon permitted a revisiting of the theme that America's innocent and idealistic intentions have been undermined by the cowardly and 'cynical' French. The conservative columnist Rich Lowry found the French deficient in the same way as had eighteenth-century English critics of the salon-bound *honnête homme*: 'Civilization simply lacks backbone without the United States in the lead.'[2]

As Christopher Forth points out in his chapter, the historical identification of France with 'civilization' has positioned the French for invidious comparison from several quarters, most significantly that of German 'Kultur,' as in Norbert Elias's formulation. But the critique of civilization as unmanning and unmanly has also been part of a powerful internal French dialogue in which some form of regeneration must surely follow from a loosening of the chains of civilization to liberate more 'primitive' impulses. All nations have harbored the dark suspicion that urban refinements and luxury might sap the warrior instincts of its men, but the French are confronted in this instance by a kind of identity that they have themselves embraced and made into an iconic ideal, not to mention a practical necessity, since so much of French foreign exchange and tourism trades on this ultra-civilized image.

This is just one of many ways the chapters in this volume trace the vicissitudes of manhood, at least at the level of discourse. They are remarkably suggestive about how the various materials available for the historical analysis of gender should be treated. Most of them move easily between social and cultural history and are sensitive to the complex ways that language both describes and enables gendered behavior. The chapters also demonstrate the metaphorical richness of the languages of masculinity and femininity, especially the remarkable way that gender may transmute into race, sexuality, types of corporeality, or moral or political *capacité*. Many of these essays also produce multiple examples of discourse and behavior that are meant to compensate for some perceived failure or shortcoming in particular men or male collectivities. Michael Sibalis's history of the uses of effeminacy provides an indispensable account of the most phantasmagoric of these imagined failures, and, like Sibalis, many of these authors explore the powerful historical links between masculinities and sexualities.

Though we now believe that the connections between biological 'man,' masculinity, and sexuality are discursive and historical, commentators, scientific and otherwise, from the late eighteenth century to recent times thought a man's (and a woman's) gender and sexuality were part and parcel of sexed bodies, whose different but complementary qualities were expressed naturally as gender difference and heterosexual desire, and whose biological *telos* was reproduction. Gender historians are now perfectly conversant with the requirement that we must analytically separate sex, gender, and sexuality to understand historical societies most of whose members believed them to be ineluctably conjoined. The conceptual mastery of this operation seems to have been first perfected in Anglo-American academic and feminist circles. The gradual broadening of women's history and women's studies units into gender studies, and the relative dominance in Anglo-American societies of 'equality' feminist theory (as opposed to 'difference' feminism) are certainly related to this development.

For their part, French historians and feminists have been remarkably slow to adopt gender analysis or to abandon aspects of 'difference' feminism despite their unshakable loyalty to political and civil universalism. This development in France has been analyzed from many angles – philosophical, cultural, and historical – and is often compared with Anglo-American feminisms. Writing in 1999, Éric Fassin warned historians that we must do more than apply gender analysis to history; we must historicize gender in cultural context. Only then will we be able to explain the 'ultimate paradox' that, in France, 'gender is now both omnipresent and unthinkable.'[3] Why unthinkable? The answer, I believe, lies with the historical allure in France of a deeply essentialized notion of sex difference that has made it difficult to think about difference as a cultural and social construction. Joan Wallach Scott has discussed the 'paradox' that French feminist claims for equal rights for women based on their sex have been rejected on universalist grounds based on a masculine model of rational *capacité*.[4] After French women obtained the vote, but before *parité* (June 2000), universalist ideals were regularly linked to a naturalized conception of sex difference. This was often presented as a case of French exceptionalism, as in Mona Ozouf's ode to the harmonious complementarity of French men and women, *Les Mots des femmes*.[5]

In the last decade, the French have debated and enacted two landmark pieces of legislation that appear to overturn their historic bias for an abstract conception of universal citizenship and exclusive heterosexual unions: the Pacte Civil de Solidarité on civil partnerships (1999) and the law on *parité* the following year requiring equal male and female representation on voting lists. But in the interrelated debates leading up to the passage of these two measures, it emerged that the *ultima ratio* for both these measures was a reconfigured model of the reproductively fertile heterosexual couple. Initially inspired by homosexual activists as a legal protection for homosexual partnerships, the PaCS also permitted civil unions between heterosexual partners and siblings; but it specifically prohibited same-sex couples from adopting children or employing 'medically-assisted procreation' to obtain a child. This aspect of the PaCS was no afterthought, as the debate on the legislation reveals, nor the result of a simple bias against homosexuality, but the result, as I have argued elsewhere, of a profound cultural idealization of 'natural' heterosexual procreation and the historical inertia of patrilineal filiation. The operative foundation for access to reproductive rights was not, therefore, either legal marriage or civil union, but procreative fertility rooted in sex difference.[6]

Joan Scott has analyzed the path taken by the *parité* movement from conception to political practice. She has shown how the initial supporters were 'aware of the traps posed by "nature" in discussions of sexed bodies.'[7] However, as Scott writes, 'As parité gained momentum and became a prominent and controversial movement, it drew followers who were less wary of the traps of essentialism and who, even while rejecting identity politics, naturalized the male/female opposition that others attributed to law or history. They conflated anatomical duality and sexual difference while the founders of the movement sought to distinguish them.'[8] It seems likely that these latter arguments helped overcome not only the doubts of some classically anti-feminist politicians, but also gathered votes from republican universalists who were accustomed to a rhetorical pairing of sex difference with citizenship rights.

In the last stages of the debate, the wives of two prominent socialist politicians went head-to-head on the need for a law on *parité*. In defending *parité*, Sylviane Agacinski, wife of the Prime Minister Lionel Jospin, introduced a concept of *mixité* in which the heterosexual couple formed the basis of a new abstract citizen which supplanted the male citizen of the Jacobin Revolution and Napoleonic Code. In elaborating on the nature of this 'universal' couple, Agacinski goes out of her way to distinguish *sexe* from *genre*: 'These two kinds [*genres*] of individuals have been named sexes, genetically complementary, together forming the entire humankind. Thus – and speaking in a deliberately crude fashion here – the sexual condition of humanity made up of males and females, like all higher animals, has no other basic definition than the one referring back to procreation, regardless of the many social forms this dichotomy can give rise to. There can be infinite variety in the social sense of this dichotomy, but no obliterating its necessity in the order of *generation*.'[9]

In other words, something like *genre* exists but is enabled and ultimately defined in its forms and practices by biology.[10]

Elisabeth Badinter, author of a pioneering book on masculinity and wife of Mitterrand's former Justice Minister, Robert Badinter, attacked the proposed law. She feared the consequences of Agacinski's biological reinforcement of sex difference, which she acknowledges, 'is a fact, but does not predestine social roles or functions.'[11] Inscribing sex difference in the constitution would be the same as giving special rights to religions or races, fragmenting universal citizenship into particular communities of interest *à l'Americaine*. Badinter's preference for social role over biological nature does not imply she thinks anything goes, genderwise. She deplores aggressive American feminists who want to sexually neuter men; she doubts the rape statistics employed to justify erecting a new 'protectionist regime;' and she is horrified at the American way of rearing children without gendered destinies. By letting men be men and women be women, the harmonious connivance of men and women will be re-established without legal interventions, naturally, as it were. As she writes, 'The struggle against a masculine *imperium* is necessary; but the deconstruction of masculinity newly aligned with a traditional femininity is an error, if not a shortcoming. To change a man one must not destroy him. L'Un *est* l'Autre à condition que persist l'Un *et* l'Autre.'[12] Badinter's gendered account of the singularity of French coupledom, seducing and flirting in an atmosphere of mutual respect, is scarcely less deterministic in its conception of difference than Agacinski's version.[13]

I have summarized some of these recent developments to draw attention to some important aspects of the history of French masculinity. When we historicize gender, as Fassin has asked us to do, we find that, despite certain changes, particular associations, representations, and qualities pertaining to men seem to have persisted over the long run of modern French history, if not longer. In their survey of the lexical evolution of the various terms that refer to males, Forth and Taithe show a weakening of the links between words denoting virility and procreative potency, but as I hoped to demonstrate by the foregoing examples, these connections clearly remain strong in the national imagination down to the present time. There also seems to have been a persistent connection to the anatomy or biology of sex, and courage, power, and vigor have remained part of men's attributes. However, the lexicons also pair virility and its synonyms with their opposites: *efféminer, féminiser, émasculer, affaiblir* and other words denoting the feminine. The inseparable discursive conjunction of masculine traits with verbs that describe a process of masculine derogation underlines the point that since Aristotle, the female sex has been characterized as the default sex, the final destination of any organism that did not fully develop or could not maintain its pre-ordained nature.

Notwithstanding the persistence of particular masculine norms, many of the chapters in this volume rightly emphasize the discursive and practical instability, compensatory, and labile quality of masculinity, especially the sensitivity of masculine norms to changes in the social, spatial, and political situations in which men find themselves. One particularly fruitful approach is that sketched out by Bertrand Taithe, who reminds us that social and spatial environments produce varying inflections of masculine styles and practices according to class, age, locale, club solidarities, and institutional affiliation. He provides several examples of the autonomous and territorial sense of collective honor that prevailed in local organizations, pitting them against one another and on occasion against the state and the nation itself. Sean Quinlan's essay illustrates the rapid transitions in masculine gender ideals that occurred during the tumultuous 1790s, depending on which faction was in power and the perceived needs of *La Patrie*. Robert Aldrich's 'colonial man' was obliged to display the 'higher' manhood of the metropole, but also embody the more vigorous qualities of a man on the frontiers of civilization, a clear recipe for moral confusion. Finally, André Rauch shows how young men in the contemporary outer suburbs have constituted their masculine identities and codes of honor to separate themselves from their elders, to both confirm and resist the racist stereotypes of the surrounding society, to simultaneously protect and oppress their own women, and to distinguish themselves from one another by acts of violent bravado performed within their territorial spaces.

Masculine scripts, however widely supported by the wider culture, are inherently unstable because they have to be performed. Errors inevitably occur. When it is particularly difficult or dangerous to enact these norms, compensatory mechanisms come into play and the norms may be subverted, displaced, or reconfigured. Christopher Forth shows how urban professional men in *fin-de-siècle* France found ways to assert their suspect manliness by endorsing, and in some cases practicing, military body disciplines that were alien to their ordinary routines and values. In her essay Judith Surkis asserts that anxieties about the penetrability of national borders and hygienic concerns about the quality of post-war 'native' French manhood encouraged the widespread displacement of these doubts onto the growing number of immigrant men and their families in the form of racist stereotypes. According to Robert Aldrich, the recruits to colonial service, military and otherwise, and therefore much of the drive behind the colonial endeavor was a retreat into forms of manliness not easily enacted in the feminizing consumer society of the *métropole*. Miranda Pollard suggests that Vichy was the setting for an unusually wide variety of masculinities struggling to express male prerogatives in a situation where traditional martial masculinity was both disgraced and forbidden and women were performing male tasks in unusual numbers.

We may follow this theme into the post-war domain of cultural representations, when the 're-masculinization' of the nation and its men was framed on a fraternal and exclusive model of military resistance that was impossible for most men to legitimately claim as their own. The resulting sense of masculine failure, together with the national humiliation of four years of occupation, was displaced as righteous indignation onto female collaborators and a few of the most visible male traitors, while women's role in the resistance and in keeping families intact was silently overlooked. The difficulty of sustaining a pure post-war politics of virile resistance was reflected in post-war literature and cinema, according to Claire Gorarra and Martin O'Shaughnessy. The *roman noir* exposed some of the hypocrisies of the new regime in inverted form and highlighted the sexual fragility of hyper-masculine men. Post-war cinema reconfigured the myth of masculine resistance in the form of heroic individuals living on the margins of the legal order, who partake of, but mock, modern pleasures, live lives of virile risk, but are ultimately always *à bout de souffle*, invariably ending badly.

Another theme that regularly reappears is the pattern of covariance between masculinities and sexualities. Vila's varieties of elite masculinity were linked to particular sexualities, which, perpetuated in literature and theater, probably served as models for elite men for generations thereafter. The passionate but stoic leaders of the early revolution projected their love onto women as ideal national symbols, and the men of Thermidor resuscitated the protection of property and lineage along with traditional paternity and orthodox marital sexuality. Buoyed by middle-class codes of family honor, respectable marital sexuality continued through the Napoleonic period and well into the nine-teenth century, but it was countered by a new form of exuberant, not to say predatory sexuality that flourished in the wake of the conferring of military duties and civil rights on ordinary Frenchmen. Men fighting for their father-land, as Michael Hughes shows in his essay, felt they deserved easy access to the nation's women and were also emboldened by the complementary legend that men in uniform were irresistible to women. Aldrich's colonial man also embodies this combination of a warrior masculinity and aggressive sexuality, though, as Vila's *petit-maître* and Gorarra's 'noir' hero Jean Fraiger demonstrate, hyper-masculine men are not always reliable lovers. The most spectacular sexual debâcle in these essays is represented by Serge Doubrovsky, the sub-ject of Jean-Pierre Boulé's essay, a man haunted by childhood memories of helpless impotence during the occupation. As a way of compensating for his imagined failures as a man, Doubrovsky invents an aggressive kind of intel-lectual masculinity and a hyperbolic sexuality that helps overcome the doubts he has about the rest of his masculine self. He literally becomes his erection, so when he is visited by the inevitable sexual failures of old age (the example of Victor Hugo notwithstanding), he is literally demasculinized according to his own lights. Finally, in reference to Sibalis's essay, one can only speculate whether homosexual men who have adopted an aggressively masculine habitus to avoid the onus of effeminacy have also, like heterosex-ual men who have inflated the importance of sexual performance, experi-enced bouts of impotence.

A final theme strikes an ironic note. Historians are well acquainted with French military achievements and with the reputation of the French fighting man as the embodiment of the *furia francese*. The 'Strange Defeat' of May and June 1940 and the subsequent loss of much of France's colonial empire has erased much of that reputation in the minds of historically illiterate contemporaries. Quinlan and Hughes describe in their chapters how between 1789 and 1815 a modern French military masculinity was constructed on the model of a democratic soldier-citizenry. This accomplishment rested on an ethos of honor that owed much to the military service ideologies of the French nobility and was carried over into the armies of the Republic as a fraternal defense of the honor of the fatherland (usually represented as a woman).[14] When we project regimens of warrior formation back into the Middle Ages, we find that the personal qualities of courage and resolution and a tradition of blood sacrifice are invariably present. Christian soldiers embraced this sacrifice as a vengeance for Christ's personal suffering and as a part of the chivalric pedagogy that reinforced the identity and resolve of fighting units. Allen J. Frantzen has shown how the representations and beliefs of soldiers fighting and dying for God and country were renewed and elaborated in the decades before World War I.[15]

Of course, there are different military masculinities just as there are different civilian masculinities.[16] However, courage and the willingness to risk life in personal sacrifice, qualities ideally embodied in the combat soldier, have trumped any other kind of masculinity, not only in wartime but in the run up to and in the aftermath of wars. Quinlan and Hughes show how revolutionary soldiers swore oaths to conquer or die, not for Christ, but for the Republic or the *patrie* (and one another), a sacrificial ritual perpetuated in funereal rhetoric up to the present in the memorialization of war dead.[17] Aldrich sees the same qualities in colonial soldiers, but Forth's *fin-de-siècle* civilians were equally obsessed with the sacrificial aspects of fighting for a cause, as were the post-war resistance fighters who dominated much of the political and discursive terrain throughout the 1940s and early 1950s. Finally, we must acknowledge the extent to which blood oaths sworn to brothers have been a feature of fraternal organizations from the first Masonic rituals to the present. In recent times when feminist and homosexual rights movements have threatened traditional gender identities, conservatives have trotted out the old sacrificial rhetoric in the form of jeremiads about the death of civilization (from too much civilization). Sibalis quotes Éric Zemmour as predicting doom for the culture that 'prefers caution to risk, consensus to authority or law, peace to war, life to death.'

Is there anything about these themes that distinguishes French masculinities from masculinities elsewhere in the West? Nations have had different timetables for political modernization, varying class structures, unique relationships of power with military elites, divergent colonial experiences, and many more variables that have produced quantitative and qualitative contrasts between and among the genders. However, France's long modern slide from great power status to secondary rank, and the nation's unparalleled one hundred years of demographic decline does make the French historical experience different from its European neighbors. Many historians and social scientists have considered this decline and the cultural anxieties which it has provoked, and they have addressed the material and cultural impact of pro-natalist ideologies on the welfare state, gender, sexuality, and on intellectuals' ruminations on reproduction.[18] One of the most important consequences of these developments has been the forging of a conceptual link between the sacrifice of the soldier who sheds his blood for *la patrie*, and the citizen who commits his life to generation.

Georges Bataille was one of a generation of French thinkers fascinated with sex and death. In his *L'Érotisme* (1957), Bataille discussed eroticism as an aspect of reproduction, which he linked in turn to death and a never-ending cycle of annihilation and rebirth. The 'discontinuity' of sexed beings produced the 'continuity' of a new being. He believed there was a kind of redemption in this. As he wrote, 'The discontinuousness of sexual beings gives rise to a dense and heavy world where individual separateness has terrifying foundations; the anguish of death and pain has bestowed on this wall of separation the solidity of prison walls, dismal and hostile. Yet within this unhappy world lost continuity can be found again if fertilization takes place.'[19]

This tragic-heroic characterization of heterosexual reproduction – the need to die in order to live – is still deeply embedded in the modern discourse of sex difference. Gender variation is a mere shadow-play in this perspective. As Sylviane Agacinski has written, *genre* is a product of habit: 'You cannot *habituate* a stone from falling when you throw it, nor can you habituate humans to forget that they are sexed, it seems to me, or to no longer desire each other, or to no longer wish to leave behind beings who will survive them. Even before the essential role it plays in all social organization, sexual difference is first and foremost about love, death, and procreation.'[20] In the end, she writes, 'sexual difference comes back to only one issue, the one linking birth and death. I am speaking here of death as a biological fate, the death biologists link to sexual reproduction . . . This is why we cannot separate the meaning and value of sexual difference from the question of generation.'[21] She derides the 'totalitarian fantasy' of the [American] feminist dream of a 'uniformization' (sic) of individuals, and equates it with the equally horrific dystopia of reproductive cloning, a fear often invoked in the PaCS and *parité* debates.

I am arguing that French intellectuals have largely thought about gender from inside the box of sex. This has had a particular effect on the slow emergence of gender as a concept in theoretical and historical work in France, but it also reflects a social and cultural reality that has shaped French masculinity in historical context. Masculinity has been obsessively, if unstably, linked to a particular set of martial and paternal qualities and thus to the triad 'sex, death, and reproduction' up to the very present, despite the growing number of technological refutations of this linkage and the numerous historical and contemporary resistances to it.

240   *French Masculinities*

Notes

1. See the stories reported in the *New York Times* (13 July 2003; 23 May 2004); *Los Angeles Times* (13 August 2004). See, in general, Stephen J. Ducat, *The Wimp Factor: Gender Gaps, Holy Wars, and the Politics of Anxious Masculinity* (Boston: Beacon, 2004).
2. Rich Lowry, 'Played the Fool Again by the Likes of France,' *The Oregonian*, 12 August 2006.
3. Eric Fassin, 'The Purloined Gender: American Feminism in a French Mirror,' *French Historical Studies*, 22 (1) (Winter, 1999): 138.
4. Joan Scott, *Only Paradoxes to Offers: French Feminists and the Rights of Man* (Cambridge, MA: Harvard University Press, 1996).
5. Mona Ozouf, *Les Mots des femmes: Essai sur la singularité française* (Paris: Gallimard, 1995).
6. Robert A. Nye, 'The Pacte Civil de Solidarité and the History of Sexuality,' *French Politics, Culture and Society*, 21 (1) (Spring, 2003): 87–100. See also the 'Comment' on this piece by Joan Scott, Ibid.: 101–5. See also Nye, 'Sex and Sexuality in France Since 1800,' in *Sexual Cultures in Europe: National Histories*, eds Franz X. Eder, Lesley A. Hall, and Gert Hekma (Manchester: Manchester University Press, 1999), pp. 91–113.
7. Joan W. Scott, *Parité: Sexual Equality and the Crisis of French Universalism* (Chicago: University of Chicago Press, 2005), p. 61.
8. Scott, *Parité*, p. 65.
9. Sylviane Agacinski, *Parity of the Sexes* trans. Lisa Walsh (New York: Columbia University Press, 2001), p. xv. Also see on Agacinski, Joan Scott, *Parité*, pp. 116–19.
10. One of the wholehearted French practitioners of gender analysis, Christine Delphy, points out the false logic of a gender residing on an unchanging sexual substratum. As she writes, 'The anteriority of sex over gender is not always justified; this postulate leads ineluctably to the explanation of gender by sex: one falls inevitably into the cognitivist or functionalist clichés that I expose [in this book].' Christine Delphy, *L'Ennemi principale*, vol. 2 *Penser le genre* (Paris, Editions Syllepse, 2001), p. 28.
11. Elisabeth Badinter, *Fausse Route* (Paris: Odile Jacob, 2003), p. 217. See also, idem., *XY, De l'identité masculine* (Paris: Odile Jacob, 1992).
12. Badinter, *Fausse route*, p. 175.
13. The word 'seduction' in its modern sense in French differs from anglophone usage, which is still often used in the sense of leading astray a minor or inappropriate sexual partner. See the sense seduction is employed as a *grand ronde* by Françoise Giroud and Bernard-Henry Lévy in *Les Hommes et les femmes* (Paris: Olivier Orban, 1993), pp. 218, 220–2, 236–40; in his study of seduction, Jean Baudrillard sees seduction as the constitutive strength of otherwise 'weak' women, in the absence of which (as political correctness advances), the sexes will march toward their extinction in 'general indetermination.' *Seduction*, trans. Brian Singer (New York: St Martin's Press, 1990), p. 5.
14. On this point see Joan Landes, 'Republican Citizenship and Heterosexual Desire: Concepts of Masculinity in Revolutionary France,' in *Masculinities in Politics and War: Gendering Modern History*, eds Stefan Dudink, Karen Hagemann, and John Tosh (Manchester: Manchester University Press, 2004), p. 103. Also Lynn Hunt, *The Family Romance of the French Revolution* (Berkeley: University of California Press, 1992).
15. Allen J. Frantzen, *Bloody Good: Chivalry, Sacrifice, and the Great War* (Chicago, University of Chicago Press, 2004).
16. For some modern variations see *Military Masculinities: Identity and the State*, ed. Paul R. Higate (Westport, CT: Praeger, 2003).

17. George L. Mosse, *Fallen Soldiers: Reshaping the Memory of the World Wars* (New York: Oxford, 1990); Frantzen, *Bloody Good*; for France, see Daniel Sherman, *The Construction of Memory in Interwar France* (Chicago: University of Chicago Press, 2001).
18. See Robert A. Nye, *Masculinity and Male Codes of Honor in Modern France* (Oxford: Oxford University Press, 1993); Joshua Cole, *The Power of Large Numbers: Population, Politics and Gender in Nineteenth-century France* (Ithaca, NY: Cornell University Press, 2000); Jean E. Pedersen, *Legislating the French Family: Feminism, Theater, and Republican Politics, 1870–1920* (New Brunswick, NJ: Rutgers University Press, 2003); Elinor Accampo, Rachel G. Fuchs, and Mary Lynn Stewart (eds), *Gender and the Politics of Social Reform in France, 1870–1914* (Baltimore: Johns Hopkins University Press, 1995).
19. Georges Bataille, *L'Érotisme*, trans. Mary Dalwood (San Francisco: City Lights Books, 1986), p. 98.
20. Agacinski, *Parity of the Sexes*, p. 17.
21. Ibid., p. 22.

Index

DATE DUE
